THE NAVARRE BIBLE: STANDARD

SAINT JOHN

VOLUMES IN THIS SERIES

Standard Edition

NEW TESTAMENT
St Matthew's Gospel
St Mark's Gospel
St Luke's Gospel
St John's Gospel
Acts of the Apostles
Romans and Galatians
Corinthians
Captivity Letters
Thessalonians and Pastoral Letters
Hebrews
Catholic Letters
Revelation

OLD TESTAMENT
The Pentateuch
Joshua–Kings [Historical Books 1]
Chronicles–Maccabees [Historical Books 2]
The Psalms and the Song of Solomon
Wisdom Books
Major Prophets
Minor Prophets

Reader's (Omnibus) Edition
The Gospels and Acts
The Letters of St Paul
Revelation, Hebrews and Catholic Letters

Single-volume, large-format New Testament

THE NAVARRE BIBLE

Saint John's Gospel

in the Revised Standard Version and New Vulgate
with a commentary by members of the
Faculty of Theology of the University of Navarre

FOUR COURTS PRESS • DUBLIN
SCEPTER PUBLISHERS • NEW YORK

Typeset by Carrigboy Typesetting Services for
FOUR COURTS PRESS LTD
7 Malpas Street, Dublin 8, Ireland
www.fourcourtspress.ie
Distributed in North America by
SCEPTER PUBLISHERS, INC.
P.O. Box 211, New York, NY 10018–0004
www.scepterpublishers.org

Nihil obstat: Stephen J. Greene, *censor deputatus*
Imprimi potest: Kevin, Archbishop of Dublin, 6 September 1986

The translation of introductions and commentary was made by Michael Adams.

A catalogue record for this title is available from the British Library.
First edition 1990; reprinted many times
Second edition (reset and repaged) 2005
Reprinted 2007, 2011, 2014, 2017, 2020

ISBN 978–1–85182–903–3

Library of Congress Cataloging-in-Publication Data [for first volume in this series]

Bible. O.T. English. Revised Standard. 1999.
  The Navarre Bible. – North American ed.
    p.   cm
  "The Books of Genesis, Exodus, Leviticus, Numbers, Deuteronomy in the Revised
    Standard Version and New Vulgate with a commentary by members of the
    Faculty of Theology of the University of Navarre."
  Includes bibliographical references.
  Contents: [1] The Pentateuch.
  ISBN 1–889334–21–9 (hardback: alk. paper)
I. Title.
  BS891.A1   1999.P75   99–23033
  221.7'7—dc21   CIP

The title "Navarre Bible" is © Four Courts Press 2003.

ACKNOWLEDGMENTS
Quotations from Vatican II documents are based on the translation in *Vatican Council II:
The Conciliar and Post Conciliar Documents*, ed. A. Flannery, OP (Dublin 1981).

The New Vulgate text of the Bible can be accessed via
http://www.vatican.va.archive/bible/index.htm

Printed and bound by CPI Group (UK) Ltd, Croydon, CR0 4YY.

Contents

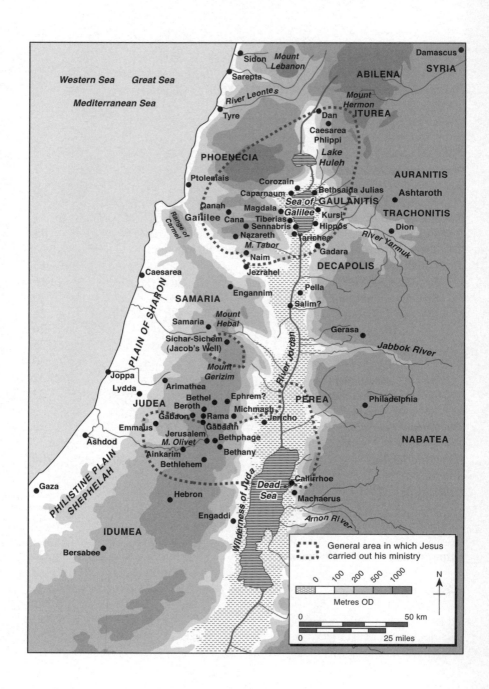

Palestine in the time of Jesus

Preface and Preliminary Notes

The Commentary

The distinguishing feature of the *Navarre Bible* is its commentary on the biblical text. Compiled by members of the Theology faculty of the University of Navarre, Pamplona, Spain, this commentary draws on writings of the Fathers, texts of the Magisterium of the Church, and works of spiritual writers, including St Josemaría Escrivá, the founder of Opus Dei; it was he who in the late 1960s entrusted the faculty at Navarre with the project of making a translation of the Bible and adding to it a commentary of the type found here.

The commentary, which is not particularly technical, is designed to explain the biblical text and to identify its main points, the message God wants to get across through the sacred writers. It also deals with doctrinal and practical matters connected with the text.

The first volume of the *Navarre Bible* (the English edition) came out in 1985 — first, twelve volumes covering the New Testament; then seven volumes covering the Old Testament. Many reprints and revised editions have appeared over the past twenty years. All the various volumes are currently in print.

The Revised Standard Version

The English translation of the Bible used in the *Navarre Bible* is the Revised Standard Version (RSV) which is, as its preface states, "an authorized revision of the American Standard Version, published in 1901, which was a revision of the King James Version [the "Authorized Version"], published in 1611".

The RSV of the entire Bible was published in 1952; its Catholic edition (RSVCE) appeared in 1966. The differences between the RSV and the RSVCE New Testament texts are listed in the "Explanatory Notes" in the end-matter of this volume. Whereas the Spanish editors of what is called in English the "Navarrre Bible" made a new translation of the Bible, for the English edition the RSV has proved to be a very appropriate choice of translation. The publishers of the *Navarre Bible* wish to thank the Division of Christian Education of the National Council of the Churches of Christ in the USA for permission to use that text.

The Latin Text

This volume also carries the official Latin version of the New Testament in the *editio typica altera* of the New Vulgate (Vatican City, 1986).

Preface

PRELIMINARY NOTES

The headings within the biblical text have been provided by the editors (they are not taken from the RSV). A full list of these headings, giving an overview of the New Testament, can be found at the back of the volume.

An asterisk *inside the biblical text* signals an RSVCE 'Explanatory Note' at the end of the volume.

References in the biblical text indicate parallel texts in other biblical books. All these marginal references come from the *Navarre Bible* editors, not the RSV.

Abbreviations

1. BOOKS OF HOLY SCRIPTURE

Acts	Acts of the Apostles	1 Kings	1 Kings
Amos	Amos	2 Kings	2 Kings
Bar	Baruch	Lam	Lamentations
1 Chron	1 Chronicles	Lev	Leviticus
2 Chron	2 Chronicles	Lk	Luke
Col	Colossians	1 Mac	1 Maccabees
1 Cor	1 Corinthians	2 Mac	2 Maccabees
2 Cor	2 Corinthians	Mal	Malachi
Dan	Daniel	Mic	Micah
Deut	Deuteronomy	Mk	Mark
Eccles	Ecclesiastes (Qoheleth)	Mt	Matthew
Esther	Esther	Nah	Nahum
Eph	Ephesians	Neh	Nehemiah
Ex	Exodus	Num	Numbers
Ezek	Ezekiel	Obad	Obadiah
Ezra	Ezra	1 Pet	1 Peter
Gal	Galatians	2 Pet	2 Peter
Gen	Genesis	Phil	Philippians
Hab	Habakkuk	Philem	Philemon
Hag	Haggai	Ps	Psalms
Heb	Hebrews	Prov	Proverbs
Hos	Hosea	Rev	Revelation (Apocalypse)
Is	Isaiah	Rom	Romans
Jas	James	Ruth	Ruth
Jer	Jeremiah	1 Sam	1 Samuel
Jn	John	2 Sam	2 Samuel
1 Jn	1 John	Sir	Sirach (Ecclesiasticus)
2 Jn	2 John	Song	Song of Solomon
3 Jn	3 John	1 Thess	1 Thessalonians
Job	Job	2 Thess	2 Thessalonians
Joel	Joel	1 Tim	1 Timothy
Jon	Jonah	2 Tim	2 Timothy
Josh	Joshua	Tit	Titus
Jud	Judith	Wis	Wisdom
Jude	Jude	Zech	Zechariah
Judg	Judges	Zeph	Zephaniah

2. OTHER ABBREVIATIONS

ad loc.	*ad locum*, commentary on this passage	f	and following (*pl*. ff)
AAS	*Acta Apostolicae Sedis*	ibid.	*ibidem*, in the same place
Apost.	Apostolic	in loc.	*in locum,* commentary on this passage
can.	canon	loc.	*locum*, place or passage
chap.	chapter	par.	parallel passages
cf.	*confer*, compare	Past.	Pastoral
Const.	Constitution	RSV	Revised Standard Version
Decl.	Declaration	RSVCE	Revised Standard Version, Catholic Edition
Dz-Sch	Denzinger-Schönmetzer, *Enchiridion Biblicum* (4th edition, Naples & Rome, 1961)	SCDF	Sacred Congregation for the Doctrine of the Faith
		sess.	session
Enc.	Encyclical	v.	verse (*pl*. vv.)
Exhort.	Exhortation		

"Sources quoted in the Commentary", which appears at the end of this book, explains other abbreviations used.

Introduction to
the Gospel according to John

THE AUTHOR

Some New Testament texts contain the writer's name, but in the case of the Gospels and the Acts of the Apostles no name is explicitly given. This might not seem to be particularly important, for what really matters is the Church's acceptance of a text as canonical, that is, inspired by God. Yet it is interesting to know who wrote a particular inspired book, especially if the human author was an eyewitness of the events he reports, and even more so if the book deals with the life of Jesus Christ, his teaching and his death and resurrection—as is the case with the Fourth Gospel, which says that "he who saw it has borne witness—his testimony is true" (Jn 19:35); and "this is the disciple who is bearing witness to these things ...; and we know that his testimony is true" (Jn 21:24).

To discover who wrote a New Testament book we must explore the very early tradition of the Church, which is contemporary with or almost contemporary with when it was written. The authenticity of these sacred writings was as much a matter of concern to the early Christians as to later generations. They were living very soon after Christ's time; they often spoke among themselves, in the way people discuss recent events, about the historical facts of the Master's life; and they believed in Jesus' divinity because these facts—the miracles, the prophecies and especially his glorious resurrection—clearly bore out that he was the Son of God. This explains why they defended Christian truth against sceptics; they were ready at any time to answer anyone who called on them to account for their hope (cf. 1 Pet 3:15), quoting for them the testimony given by those who had seen and heard Christ, for, as St Peter averred, "we did not follow cleverly devised myths when we made known to you the power and coming of our Lord Jesus Christ, but we were eyewitnesses of his majesty" (2 Pet 1:16).

The Gospel we are now discussing enjoyed great prestige from as early as the beginning of the second century, as evidenced by the fact that phrases taken from it or based on it are to be found in very early documents. Thus St Ignatius of Antioch (d. 107–115) speaks of the Spirit which knows where it comes from and where it is going to[1] and says that the Word, the Son of God,

---

1. *Letter to the Philadelphians*, 7, 1, referring to Jn 3:8.

always does what is pleasing to him who sent him (cf. Jn 1:1; 7:28; 8:29); St Polycarp in his letter to the Philippians (*c*.110) also echoes some phrases of the Fourth Gospel, as does St Justin (*c*.150) when he says it is necessary to be born again to enter the Kingdom of heaven (cf. Jn 3:5).

In addition to these references, there are explicit testimonies which clearly state that the apostle St John wrote the Fourth Gospel. The famous "Muratorian Canon" written in Rome around the year 180 contains a prologue against Marcion and his followers, in which it is said that "the Gospel of John was communicated and proclaimed to the churches by John himself, while he was still alive, according to Papias of Hierapolis." Papias lived around the year 135, and it is known that he was a disciple of John, so what he has to say is particularly valuable.

St Irenaeus, bishop of Lyons, also refers to the authenticity of this Gospel. Irenaeus was born around 130 in Smyrna (Asia Minor), where he knew St Polycarp, who according to Tertullian was made bishop of Smyrna by St John himself. St Irenaeus says that "John, the disciple of the Lord, who had even rested on his breast, himself published the Gospel, while he was living in Ephesus."[2] This testimony carries special weight, given Irenaeus' connexion with Polycarp.

Eusebius, in his *Ecclesiastical History* (6, 14, 5–7), refers to the testimony of Clement of Alexandria, who passes on a tradition which says that John wrote his Gospel after the other evangelists had written theirs. Victorinus of Pettau's witness is of a later date (*c*.305).[3] From the fourth century on there is a unanimous tradition that St John wrote the Gospel which bears his name. Internal analysis of the text confirms what tradition tells us. The developed form of doctrine we find in the Gospel indicates that, to produce it, God availed himself of a man who had for years meditated on and made his own everything which he reports to us concerning Jesus and his disciples. Besides, there are many little points in the Gospel which can be explained only if John is the author. For example, he refers to John as the Precursor of Christ, where the Synoptic Gospels call him John the Baptist: they have to call him that to avoid any possible confusion with John the apostle. But in the Fourth Gospel there is no danger of any such confusion since the name of John the evangelist is nowhere mentioned.

Also, we learn from the Gospel that its author is "the disciple whom Jesus loved" (Jn 21:20) and who was one of the twelve apostles, for he is present when the risen Lord appears among them by the Sea of Tiberias (cf. Jn 21:1). Now, the Synoptics tell us that Jesus loved three of his disciples in a special way, choosing them to see his glory on Tabor (cf. Mt 17:1–2) and his humiliation in Gethsemane (cf. Mk 14:33). These were Peter, James the Greater and John. And one of these is the "beloved disciple", who wrote the

---

2. *Against Heresies*, 3, 1, 1. **3.** Cf. *Commentary on the Apocalypse*, 11, 1.

Gospel. St Peter it cannot be, for on various occasions we see him accompanied by the beloved disciple (cf. Jn 20:2ff; 21:20). Nor can it be James the Greater, because he was martyred around the year 40 (cf. Acts 12:2) and the Fourth Gospel was written towards the end of the century—which leaves only St John the evangelist. Besides, many literary features of the Gospel confirm its authenticity. The writer is obviously Jewish, very familiar with Jewish customs and interested in Jewish feasts. He has an intimate knowledge of the geography of Palestine and gives many topographical references (cf. Jn 1:28; 3:23; 4:5–6; 10:22; 11:18). The style of writing is markedly Semitic.

The only ambiguous text in Tradition on this subject is a passage from Papias quoted by Eusebius, in which the name of John is mentioned twice. This text reads: "If someone came along who had heard the presbyters speak, I used to make a point of asking him what did the presbyters hear from the lips of Andrew or Peter or Philip or Thomas or James or John or Matthew or any other disciple of the Lord, and also what do Aristion and the presbyter John say."[4] Interpretation of this text presents two difficulties. First, was Papias referring on both occasions to the apostle St John—naming him twice simply because he lived so much longer after the death of the other disciples; or is his second reference to another John, a person of importance but not the apostle? Second, if the latter hypothesis is correct, which of the two is the author of the Gospel— "John the apostle" or "John the presbyter", both "disciples of the Lord"? Eusebius attributes the Gospel explicitly to John the apostle, and so does St Irenaeus, as we have seen.

Rationalist critics, however, on the basis of this text of Papias, argue that St Irenaeus confused this "John the presbyter" with the apostle John: they argue that it was John the presbyter who appointed St Polycarp bishop of Smyrna and who wrote the Fourth Gospel. But there is no basis for attributing this mistake to St Irenaeus, and besides, the great mass of the information that has come down to us from Christian antiquity, and the internal evidence, all argue in favour of St John the apostle as author of the Fourth Gospel. So it is not surprising that the Church has always held to the traditional attribution of the Fourth Gospel to St John.[5]

THE RELATIONSHIP BETWEEN THE GOSPEL OF ST JOHN AND THE SYNOPTIC GOSPELS

If we enter St John's Gospel after reading the Synoptics we sense that we are entering a different atmosphere. Even in the prologue the evangelist soars towards the heights of divinity. It is not surprising that St John is symbolized

---

4. *Ecclesiastical History*, 3, 39, 4. **5.** Cf. *EB*, 180–182, 200–202 and 475.

by an eagle. The evangelist "soars very high, mounts beyond the darkness of the earth and fixes his gaze on the light of truth ...".[6]

Even in the way it reports facts, the Fourth Gospel adopts an approach different from the Synoptics. For example, it centres Jesus' public ministry mainly in Judea; although the Gospel does mention his ministry in Galilee (cf. Jn 2; 6), which the Synoptics cover very well, St John concentrates mainly on Jesus' activity in Jerusalem. The first three Gospels only tell us of our Lord going up to the Holy City once during his public ministry, the occasion when he will die during the feast of the Passover, whereas John refers to at least three visits (cf. Jn 2:13, 23; 5:1; 6:4; 12:1). Of the twenty-nine miracles described in the Synoptics, St John refers to only two (cf. Jn 6:11, 19) and he tells us of five additional ones (cf. Jn 2:1–11; 4:46–54; 5:1–9; 9:1–41; 11:33–44). But he does not mention the Transfiguration; nor the institution of the Eucharist at the Last Supper—which is not to say that he is unaware of its importance, for he gives us very full and very clear accounts of Jesus' discourses about the Bread of Life (cf. Jn 6:32–58).

On the history of the passion, death and resurrection of Jesus Christ, the Fourth Gospel coincides with the Synoptics, but here also it has a perspective of its own: it describes everything very much in terms of the glorification of Christ: this is Jesus' "hour" (Jn 2:4; 7:30; 13:1; 17:1), when the Father glorifies the Son; when the Son, by dying, overcomes the devil, sin and death and is raised up above all things (cf. Jn 12:32–33). And so, when Jesus announces his passion in advance, the Synoptics focus on the appropriateness of the Son *suffering* (cf. Mt 16:21 and par.), whereas St John stresses how fitting it is that the Son of man should be "lifted up" (Jn 3:14–15; 8:28; 12:32–33).

Even Jesus' teaching contains different nuances in St John: for example, the Fourth Gospel only once mentions the "kingdom of God", whereas the Synoptics, especially St Matthew, refer to it often (Jn 3:5; cf. Mt 3:2; 4:23; 5:3; 11:12; 13:24; etc.). There are subjects not treated by St John which appear frequently in the Synoptics, such as the question of the sabbath, Pharisees' legislation, etc.; but he speaks about life, truth, light, glory—which are hardly mentioned in the first three Gospels.

Scholars have proposed various hypotheses to explain why St John wrote like this. Some say that he was not acquainted with the other Gospels and that he just wrote what he thought best fitted his purpose. This is very unlikely, given that the first three Gospels were written so much earlier: John must have known them. Besides, it does not explain why he omits important things like the Transfiguration and the institution of the Blessed Eucharist: he would only have done that if he knew they were covered in the other Gospels.

One coherent explanation is that John was mainly trying to fill out the Synoptics, focusing more light on certain episodes. His Gospel does not con-

6. St Augustine, *In Ioann. Evang.*, 15, 1.

tradict the Synoptics; what it does is give more detail. For example, he reports Jesus' triple commandment to St Peter to feed the sheep—which explains how Peter should approach the mission he has received to be the rock on which Christ will build his Church (cf. Mt 16:18).

St John himself gives us one reason why his Gospel is different. He says that it is a testimony to what he has seen and heard. Rather than speak of evangelizing or preaching, the Fourth Gospel prefers to use "testify" or "bear witness" or "teach". Thus, he presents the preaching of the Baptist as an instance of testimony to Christ (cf. Jn 1:7, 19, 32, 34; 3:26; 5:33). Our Lord is always the object of this testimony, which comes from different directions in the Fourth Gospel: first and foremost, it comes from the Father who has sent Jesus to bear witness to him (cf. Jn 5:37); then, Jesus bears witness to himself, because he knows where he has come from and where he is going to (cf. Jn 8:14) and he is attesting to what he has seen (cf. Jn 3:11); the Scriptures also bear witness to Jesus Christ (cf. Jn 5:39), as will the Holy Spirit whom he will send (cf. Jn 15:26); and, finally, our Lord says to the apostles: "You also are witnesses, because you have been with me from the beginning" (Jn 15:27).

This concept of bearing witness is also present in other inspired writers, though not as clearly as in St John—in Hebrews 12:1, for example. In the early centuries of the Church it was quite common for Christians to ratify in their blood the testimony of faith in Christ—martyrdom becoming, as it were, the climax of perfect commitment to the Lord. The word "martyr" comes from the Greek verb *martireo*, which means "bearing witness". Every Christian therefore, has to be a "martyr", a faithful witness, wherever he is, a living testimony of Christ to people around him.

Another unusual feature of St John's Gospel is that it is a "spiritual gospel", in the words of Clement of Alexandria (on account of which St John has been called "the theologian"). This refers to John's desire to explore and explain the deeper meaning of Jesus' words and actions. In St John's account our Lord usually begins his teachings with an intriguing remark or question, to awaken the curiosity of his listeners, and then moves on to explain some point of doctrine. For example, in the case of Nicodemus, when he speaks about being born again; or his conversation with the Samaritan woman about living water: what Jesus is saying obviously means much more than one would get from a first glance at the text. In fact, it is only when the Holy Spirit comes that the disciples grasp the full meaning of the Master's words (cf. Jn 14:26). And so, on a number of occasions, the Evangelist actually says that they did not understand what Jesus was trying to tell them but that after his resurrection they did understand its profound meaning (cf. Jn 2:17, 22; 12:16; 13:7; 16:4). The Master, when he sees they cannot grasp his meaning, consoles them by promising the "Spirit of truth", who will guide them into all the truth (Jn 16:13).

Also, events treated in the narrative have a deeper meaning than is at first obvious. This has led some to think that St John's narrative is not history, and that the miracles Jesus works, and even the people involved, are mere symbols, literary devices invented by the evangelist—like examples a catechist might devise to illustrate his teaching. This view means denying the inerrancy of an inspired text, and therefore, it is rejected by the Magisterium of the Church, which maintains the historicity of the text of the Fourth Gospel.[7] The Pontifical Biblical Commission teaches that it cannot be "said that the facts narrated in the Fourth Gospel were invented wholly or in part as allegories or doctrinal symbols", nor may it be affirmed that "the sermons of our Lord are not properly and truly discourses of the Lord himself, but instead theological compositions of the writer, placed on our Lord's lips."[8]

Besides, to say that St John invents facts is to fail to understand the whole character of the Fourth Gospel and the Semitic mind, which is so fond of the concrete and particular: quite often events themselves provide the starting point for explaining some matter of doctrine (cf. Hos 1:2–11; Jer 16:1–3; 18:1–5).

St John selects particular miracles of Jesus because he wants to use them to emphasize a teaching: at the wedding at Cana our Lord manifests his glory and at the same time reveals that the messianic age has begun, and light is thrown on the role of his mother, Mary, in the redemption of mankind (cf. Jn 2:1–11); the multiplication of the loaves and the fish, attested to also by the Synoptics, provides the historical prologue to Christ's words about the Bread of Life (cf. Jn 6); the curing of the man blind from birth provides the Evangelist with an opportunity to show how blind the Pharisees are to the light of the world, Christ (cf. Jn 9); by raising Lazarus, the Master shows that only he is the Resurrection and the Life (cf. Jn 11).

St John insists that he "has seen" all this; that he has "touched" it with his hands (Jn 1:14; 19:35; 1 Jn 1:2). After a lifetime of preaching and prayer, it is only logical that he should see it all from a deeper, clearer perspective. St Augustine is right when he says that St John "soared beyond the flesh, soared beyond the earth which he trod, beyond the seas which he saw, beyond the air where birds fly; soared beyond the sun, beyond the moon and the stars, beyond all spirits which are unseen, beyond his own intelligence and the very reason of his thinking soul. Soaring beyond all these, beyond his very self, where did he reach, what did he see? 'In the beginning was the Word, and the Word was with God, and the Word was God'."[9] Therefore, what he narrates, far from contradicting what we read in the Synoptics, takes it as read, and fills it out.

JOHN THE APOSTLE

Of all the Gospels, the Fourth most clearly reflects the personality of its human author. The other Gospels also tell us something about St John the

---

7. *EB*, 187. **8.** *EB*, 189. **9.** *In Ioann. Evang.*, 20, 13.

apostle, to which we can add further information—though not as much as we would like—from primitive Christian tradition. He was a native of Bethsaida, a town of Galilee on the northern shore of the Sea of Tiberias. His parents were Zebedee and Salome, and his brother James the Greater. They were fishing folk, fairly well off, a family which did not hesitate to put itself completely at Jesus' disposal. James and John, in response to Jesus' call, "left their father Zebedee in the boat with the hired servants, and followed him" (Mk 1:20 and par.). Salome, their mother, also followed Jesus, providing for him from her means, in Galilee and Jerusalem; she was with him right up to Calvary (cf. Mk 15:40–41 and par.)

Along with Andrew, Peter's brother, John had been with John the Baptist on the banks of the Jordan and had even become one of his disciples, until one day, on seeing Jesus, the Baptist exclaimed, "Behold, the Lamb of God!"; as soon as they heard him say this they followed Jesus and spent the whole day with him (Jn 1:35–39). They returned home to Bethsaida and went back to fishing; and a little later on, Jesus, who had been preparing them since that first meeting, called them, in a definitive way, to be among the Twelve. St John would not have been twenty at the time.

From then on St John follows Christ and never leaves him. The Gospels all list him among the Twelve alongside his brother James, after St Peter and, sometimes, after St Andrew (cf. Mk 3:17 and par.). The passionate love these two brothers had for the Lord led them on occasions to react energetically against people who rejected the Master. When certain Samaritans refused to receive him, the sons of Zebedee asked Jesus (Lk 9:54), "Lord, do you want us to bid fire come down from heaven and consume them?" (as happened to the messengers of King Ahaziah: 2 Kings 1:10–15). They had not yet fully understood Jesus' mission—to show men the Father's love. Gradually, taught by our Lord, they did come to understand it: so much so that it will be John who engraves on our mind the truth that "God is love" (1 Jn 4:8, 16). But, in those early days, James and John sometimes seem impatient to see the triumph of their Master and are ready to call for punishment from heaven. It is not surprising, then, that our Lord describes them as "Boanerges, that is, sons of thunder" (Mk 3:17). John's strong character and youthful spontaneity make him the disciples' mouthpiece when, on another occasion, they want to prevent someone not of their company from using Jesus' name to cast out demons (cf. Lk 9:49).

Our Lord showed the sons of Zebedee, and Peter, special signs of trust and friendship (cf. Mk 1:17; 5:37; 9:2ff; 14:32–42). St John discreetly refers to himself in the Gospel as the disciple whom Jesus loved (cf. Jn 13:23; 19:26; 20:2; 21:7, 20), meaning that our Lord had special affection for him. He puts it on record that, at that solemn point in the Last Supper when Jesus announces that one of them will betray him, he did not hesitate to ask our Lord, resting his head on his chest, who the traitor would be (cf. Jn 13:23). So much, in fact, did Jesus trust his beloved disciple that, from the cross, he gave into his charge the person he loved most in the world—his blessed Mother.

St John was very close to St Peter, whom he knew before either of them met Christ (both were fishermen from Bethsaida). They were the two to whom our Lord gave the job of preparing the paschal meal (cf. Lk 22:8), and, on the night of the Passion, it was probably John who managed to get Peter into the chief priest's house (cf. Jn 18:16). They ran together to the tomb on the morning of Easter Sunday. St John never forgot that empty sepulchre, which led him to believe in the Resurrection. In his Gospel he recalls how he ran faster than Peter and reached the tomb first but stayed outside—we must presume in deference to Peter, to whom our Lord had promised the primacy of the Church (cf. Jn 20:3–9). John was the first to recognize the risen Jesus when he appeared to a group of disciples on the lakeshore. He joyfully tells Peter, "It is the Lord!" (Jn 21:7). This was the occasion when Jesus, in reply to a question from Peter about what would happen to John, makes a reference to John's death (cf. Jn 21:20–23). The Fourth Gospel closes with this scene where the two most prominent apostles converse with Jesus.

After the Lord's ascension, St John stays close to St Peter. The Acts of the Apostles shows them going together to the temple to pray, and there, at the Beautiful Gate, through Jesus' power, they cure a man lame from birth (cf. Acts 3:1–9; 2:46). There and then, St Peter preaches the Gospel of Jesus Christ and the leading priests became "annoyed because they were teaching the people and proclaiming in Jesus the resurrection from the dead. And they arrested them and put them in custody until the morrow" (Acts 4:2–3). But this only encouraged the apostles to preach the Gospel more boldly, even to their judges (cf. Acts 4:13–22). They prayed and preached together, and they also shared the joy of being "counted worthy to suffer dishonour for the name" of Jesus (Acts 5:41). When they were set free by the Jewish authorities, they went back to their friends and all prayed the second Psalm (cf. Acts 4:25). In prayer they obtained the strength to preach boldly in the midst of adversity and persecution.

Peter and John are also seen together when they are sent by the apostolic college to administer the sacrament of Confirmation to people in Samaria already baptized by Philip (cf. Acts 8:14). Years later, around the year 50, at the first Council of the Church, held in Jerusalem, James and Peter and John appear as pillars of the Church (cf. Gal 2:9).

From this point forward, our information about St John's life comes from Church tradition. Reliable reports tell us that he left Palestine and went to Ephesus, where he looked after the churches of Asia Minor (so says St Polycarp of Smyrna, who died in 155 at the age of eighty-six and who, we are told, was a disciple of St John himself).[10] This piece of information agrees

10. Cf. *Against Heresies*, 2, 22, 5; 3, 1, 1.

with the testimony of Polycrates, bishop of Ephesus (died *c*.190)—which Eusebius of Caesarea quotes;[11] he says that John belonged to a Jewish priestly family and died in Ephesus, a tradition consistent with the fact that the Fourth Gospel mentions Jewish feasts so often and with the fact that John was known to the high priest (cf. Jn 18:16).

What is not so clear is when exactly he moved to Ephesus. We have already said that he was still in Jerusalem around the year 50. And it seems likely that he had not yet gone to Ephesus when St Paul wrote his Second Letter to Timothy, around the year 66 or 67, in which he gives him instructions on how to govern that church (cf. 2 Tim 4:1–2); all of which points to St John arriving in Ephesus after the death of St Paul, which took place in 67: for one thing, all the churches of the region would have been in need of his attention, and, also, the Jewish War, the war between Judea and Rome (which would end in the destruction of Jerusalem in the year 70), caused most Christians to flee both the Holy City and Palestine. We do not know with any certainty whether St John brought the Virgin Mary with him to Ephesus at that time or whether she had already been assumed into heaven; but we can be sure that the apostle took great care of her until the end of her life.

Tradition does not give us a clear picture of what happened to John in Ephesus. It does confirm the reports of St Irenaeus, Eusebius and other ecclesiastical writers that he was sent into exile on the island of Patmos, where he wrote the Apocalypse (cf. Rev 1:9); this took place in the fourteenth year of Domitian's reign, 95. After Domitian's death the following year, John returned to Ephesus where he had now to face not only external enemies of the Church but certain Christians who had become obstinate heretics. With fatherly solicitude the apostle tried to heal the divisions and, under the inspiration of the Holy Spirit, he wrote three letters to faithful Christians warning them of dangers. It would seem that the letter we know as 3 John was in fact the first.

This "third letter" is addressed to Gaius, a priest, who had remained loyal to John's authority and to the truth of the Gospel. The apostle's main concern at this time is to strengthen his children in the faith: "No greater joy can I have than this, to hear that my children follow the truth" (3 Jn 4); and he advises Gaius not to imitate evil people like Diotrephes who criticize the apostle out of jealousy.

The second letter is addressed to a particular church—which one, we cannot tell—whom St John calls "the elect lady", in the same way as St Peter (1 Pet 5:13) calls the church at Rome the one who is likewise "chosen". He is worried lest the truth become adulterated, and he warns the church against deceivers who deny the incarnation of our Lord Jesus Christ (cf. 2 Jn 9–11). Also, presumably because these heretics were deforming the true ideal of Christian love, he spells it out absolutely clearly: "And this is love, that we

11. *Ecclesiastical History*, 3, 31, 3; 5, 24, 3.

follow his commandments" (2 Jn 6). This and the previous letter are both very short.

St John ranges more widely in the "first letter", which is perhaps the last he wrote. It is addressed to the faithful in general, and may have been a kind of encyclical letter to the churches of Asia Minor. In it he keeps concentrating on two themes (the same as in 2 John)—Christian faith and love, which heretics are trying to undermine. He never tires of telling them, "Let what you heard from the beginning abide in you" (1 Jn 2:24; cf. 2:7, 25; 3:11). To strengthen their resolve to stand fast in faith and Christian living (cf. 5:13), he deals, one after the other, with various parallel themes—light (cf. 1:5ff), righteousness (cf. 2:29ff), love (cf. 4:7ff) and truth (cf. 5:6ff); but the same basic ideas underlie the whole letter: we are children of God, who is Love, and this means that we must live according to his commandments (cf. 3:23). St John's style and teaching in this letter are so reminiscent of the Fourth Gospel that we cannot doubt that they are written by the same hand. In fact, all the indicators are that St John wrote both these texts in the same period, but we cannot work out which came first.

We can take it therefore, that it was at Ephesus, between his exile on Patmos and his death at the start of Trajan's reign (98–117), that St John, in his solicitude for the Church, wrote the three letters and the Gospel. What little more tradition tells us about the last years of his life confirms his concern for purity of doctrine and faithfulness to the commandment of love. St Jerome tells how the disciples used to carry him to Christian meetings, his age preventing him from walking, and how he used to repeat all the time: "My little children, love one another." And when the disciples asked him why he was always saying the same thing, he replied, "It is the Lord's commandment, and if you keep it, that alone suffices."[12]

STRUCTURE AND CONTENT

The structure of St John's Gospel fits in with his aim in writing it, moved as he was by the Holy Spirit: he tells us himself that he wrote the Gospel "that you may believe that Jesus is the Christ, the Son of God, and that believing you may have life in his name" (Jn 20:31). In general, St John follows the same order as followed by the apostles in their oral preaching, and in so doing he coincides with the Synoptic Gospels: Jesus begins his public ministry after being baptized in the Jordan by John the Baptist; he preaches and works miracles in Galilee and Jerusalem; and his life on earth ends with his passion and glorious resurrection (cf. Acts 10:38–41).

Within this general framework, St John follows a plan of his own, different from that of the Synoptics. For this he uses certain basic ideas which he devel-

---

12. *Commentary on Galatians*, 3, chap. 6.

ops in the course of his Gospel—the succession of Jewish feasts which mark the different stages in his account; the treatment of certain concepts, like the New Testament taking the place of the Old; the themes of life, of the Bread of Life, of the light, truth, love, etc.; and the gradual and dramatic manifestation of Jesus as the Messiah and Son of God, contrasting with the growing blindness of those Jews who reject him, until the high point comes, the "hour" of Jesus and of the power of darkness. All these threads are woven together to form this Gospel, giving it a particular structure and thematic cohesion. Broadly, we might say that the structure of the Fourth Gospel is along these lines:

Prologue (1:1–18). This introduction is of great theological importance. Jesus Christ, the eternal word of God, with the Father, creator of the world, true Light, has become man in order to bring the world light, that is, definitive and saving revelation for all men. However, the Jews in general did not accept the Light even though John the Baptist bore witness to it; but those who do accept it and believe in him are raised to become children of God. This prologue contains, in essence, all the great themes which the Gospel will develop—Christ's revealing of himself, light, truth, life, glory, revelation of the Father, faith and unbelief.

PART ONE: JESUS IS MANIFESTED AS THE MESSIAH BY SIGNS AND WORDS
This part runs from the Baptist's testimony regarding Jesus (1:19) to the Last Supper (chap. 13). It can be divided into various sections:

1. *Introduction* and 2. *Jesus, the author of the new economy of salvation: first signs of faith in him* (1:19—4:54). Section 2 includes the Baptist's testimony (cf. 1:19–34), the calling of the first disciples (cf. 1:35–51), and our Lord's ministry in Galilee when he performed his first miracle at the wedding at Cana (cf. 2:1–12). These episodes cover the first weeks of Jesus' public life: the days are counted off, one by one. At the centre of this section we find the feast of the Passover, the first such feast in our Lord's public ministry. During his stay in Jerusalem he cleanses the temple (cf. 2:13–25) and converses with Nicodemus (cf. 3:1–21). The section ends with the Baptist's last testimony to Jesus (cf. 3:22–36) and Jesus' return from Jerusalem through Samaria, where he has the meeting with the Samaritan woman (cf. 4:1–42), and through Galilee, where he works the second miracle, curing the son of the royal official (cf. 4:46–54).

The whole section is given unity by the fact that our Lord is showing himself to be the founder of the new economy of grace, an economy superior to that of the temple and the Old Law. This is clearly reflected in the changing of the water into wine at Cana in Galilee (cf. 2:9); in St John's comment on the episode of the cleansing of the temple ("he spoke of the temple of his body": 2:21); in the revelation to Nicodemus about new birth through Baptism (cf. 3:5); and in our Lord's conversation with the Samaritan woman, where he lays down that true adoration should be "in spirit and truth" (4:24). This manifestation of the Lord causes his disciples (cf. 1:50; 2:11) and the people (cf. 2:23; 4:42–53) to begin to have faith in him, and also causes the first signs of rejection on the part of some Jews (cf. 2:24–25; 3:11, 18, etc.).

3. *Jesus reveals his divinity* (chap. 5). St John relates the curing of a paralyzed man at the pool of Bethzatha (cf. 5:1–18) and then goes on to give us one of our Lord's discourses, where he reveals that he acts in union with the Father because he is the Father's Son. All this happens on "a feast of the Jews" (5:1), which could be Passover or perhaps the feast of Pentecost, which falls fifty days after Passover. This new manifestation of our Lord, in which he clearly states his divinity, both through the miracle and through what he says in the discourse, provokes some Jews to open hatred : from then on they "sought all the more to kill him, because he not only broke the sabbath but also called God his Father, making him equal with God" (5:18).

4. *Jesus is the bread of life* (chap. 6). This has a structure very like that of the previous chapter: first, two miracles—the multiplication of the loaves and fish, and Jesus' walking on the water; and then a discourse—that of the synagogue of Capernaum, in which the Lord reveals himself as the Bread of Life, announcing the mystery of the Blessed Eucharist. St John points out that this occurred when "the Passover, the feast of the Jews, was at hand" (6:4), thereby hinting that the eucharistic banquet would in the future be the New Passover. Many of his followers were scandalized by these words of Jesus, so much so that those who chose not to believe left him, and those who believed grew more attached to him: "After this many of his disciples drew back and no longer went about with him" (6:66); whereas Simon Peter, speaking for the Twelve, confessed "we have believed, and have come to know that you are the Holy One of God" (6:69), that is, the Messiah, the Son of God.

From chapter 7 onwards it is not so easy to divide the narrative into such distinct sections. The five remaining chapters of the first part certainly have some basic cohesion in that Jerusalem or its environs provides the setting. Jesus reveals himself as Light and Life of the world, and opposition becomes more and more pronounced. However, we will divide these chapters into two sections, centering on two great miracles, in which Jesus reveals himself as Light and Life.

5. *Jesus is the light of the world* (chaps. 7–10). It opens with the observation that "Jesus went about in Galilee; he would not go about in Judea, because the Jews sought to kill him" (7:1). But, because it was the feast of Tabernacles, "about the middle of the feast Jesus went up into the temple and taught" (7:14). This visit to Jerusalem gives our Lord an opportunity to show himself more clearly to the Jewish authorities and to the people; everyone is talking

about him. Jesus teaches that he has been sent by the Father (cf. 7:28–29). The Jewish authorities want to arrest him, but they do not do so because, St John remarks, "his hour had not yet come" (7:30). On the last day of the feast Jesus reveals himself as the one the Holy Spirit is to send—which again leads to division among the people. For some he is the Messiah, "the Christ" (7:41); for others—the chief priests and Pharisees—he is not, and they want to arrest him for blasphemy, but they do not dare (cf. 7:44ff).

At dawn the next day Jesus returns to the temple to teach, and the episode of the adulterous woman occurs (cf. 8:1–11). Then Jesus reveals himself as "the light of the world" (8:12), sent by the Father (cf. 8:16), equal to God (cf. 8:19), greater than Abraham (cf. 8:58). People become so angry they want to stone him (cf. 8:59).

But Jesus also reveals he is the Light of the world by performing a miracle, a sign proving the truth of what he is saying—the miracle of curing a man born blind (cf. 9:1–38), which provides our Lord with an occasion to speak to us about God's judgment : "For judgment I came into this world, that those who do not see may see, and that those who see may become blind" (9:39). The man who has been cured, who now confesses his faith in Christ, is a model for all believers; whereas the Pharisees, who are full of pride, which they disguise with religiosity, become blind by rejecting Christ, the Light of the world.

Only through faith in Christ and by his grace can man attain salvation, for he is "the door of entry to eternal life" (10:7–10), "the Good shepherd" who guides us and has given his life for us (10:11–18). This revelation causes more arguments among the Jews, with some saying that he is possessed by a devil and others recognizing that he has worked a miracle (cf. 10:19–21).

6. *Jesus and the Father.* Then comes a further manifestation of our Lord, on the occasion of the feast of the Dedication of the Temple: it is wintertime and Jesus is walking in the portico of Solomon (cf. 10:22–23); the Jews ask him to tell them openly if he is the Christ, to which he replies that he is the Son of God, equal to the Father : "I and the Father are one" (10:30) and "the Father is in me and I am in the Father" (10:38). The Jews realize perfectly well that he is revealing himself as God; so they try once more to stone him (cf. 10:31) and arrest him (cf. 10:39); but he goes away across the Jordan, and many people follow him and believe in him (cf. 10:42).

7. *Jesus is the life of the world* (chaps. 11–12). The outstanding event here is the miracle of the raising of Lazarus. Jesus took occasion of this to reveal that he is "the resurrection and the life" for those who believe in him (11:25). Martha's reaction of faith also stands out: "I believe that you are the Christ, the Son of God, he who is coming into the world" (11:27), as does the Pharisees' reaction, which is one of hatred: they meet in council and formally decide to put him to death (cf. 11:45–53). St John observes that "the Passover

of the Jews was at hand" (11:55), which suggests that these events and those of chapter 12 are to herald Christ's redemptive death and glorious resurrection.

8. *Jesus is acclaimed as the messianic king*. Our Lord in fact links the anointing at Bethany, which takes place six days before the Passover, with the day of his burial (cf. 12:1, 7).

The triumphal entry into Jerusalem is an anticipation of Jesus' glorification in the Resurrection, which is why St John comments that "his disciples did not understand this at first; but when Jesus was glorified, then they remembered that this had been written of him and had been done to him" (12:16). Our Lord's own words, announcing that the hour has come for his glorification through death on the cross and resurrection (cf. 12:23ff, 33), are a last invitation to men to believe in him (cf. 12:35–36). Many people, even many prominent Jews, believe in him; others prefer the glory of men (12:42); but those who do not receive Jesus' words will be condemned by those very words on the last day (12:48).

This brings us to the end of the first part of the Gospel, in which Jesus progressively reveals himself as the Messiah, through his miracles (a sign of his divinity) and through his words, in which he declares that he is the Messiah, the Son of God and equal to the Father. All this moves in a dramatic crescendo to Jesus' "hour", culminating in his death and resurrection, which are the subject of the second part of the Gospel.

PART TWO: JESUS IS MANIFESTED AS THE MESSIAH, SON OF GOD, IN HIS PASSION, DEATH AND RESURRECTION
In this second part there are three sections dealing with the Last Supper, the passion and death of our Lord, and his resurrection. In each of the three we find Christ being revealed, and people reacting to him in different ways; the point of climax is imminent.

9. *The Last Supper* (chaps. 13–17). Jesus' revelation to his disciples in the intimacy of the Last Supper is given. It begins with St John informing us that it was the eve of the feast of the Passover "when Jesus knew that his hour had come to depart out of this world to the Father" (Jn 13:1). This section comprises, firstly, the account of the washing of feet and the prediction of Judas' betrayal. Christ's love contrasts with the Jews' hatred. Probably St John purposely points out that when Judas left the room "it was night" (13:30), for if one leaves the light of Christ one is submerged in the kingdom of darkness and unbelief. The Lord's discourses follow, running up to chapter 16. It is not easy to impose a pattern on them, but basically there are three main themes: first, love—*agape*—which has its root in Christ's love and becomes the commandment of the Lord (cf. 13:34–35; 15:11–17); second, the consolation Jesus gives

his disciples before he leaves them (cf. 13:33; 14:1–7), by saying he will return (cf. 14:1–3; 16:16–26) and by promising that he will send the Holy Spirit, who is called here the Paraclete (Counsellor) and who will lead them to all truth (14:15–17, 26; 16:5–15); thirdly, Christ's solidarity with his disciples, using the simile of the vine and the branches, a unity based on love and on keeping the commandments (cf. 15:1–11). Along with these subjects, there is Jesus' revelation that he is God (cf. 14:10) and also his prediction of the hatred the world will show his disciples (cf. 15:18—16:4). The section concludes with Christ's priestly prayer (chap. 17), which once again brings in the subjects of his glorification and his disciples' faith and unity, for which he prays to the Father.

10. *The passion and death of Jesus* (chaps. 18–19). It contains the account of our Lord's passion. The narrative follows the course of events of that night and of the morning of Good Friday: arrest, interrogation before Annas and Caiaphas, and Peter's denials (cf. 18:1–27); the trial before Pontius Pilate (cf. 18:28—19:26); crucifixion, death and burial (19:17–42). The sacred text gives lots of details which emphasize that the Passion is the supreme manifestation of Christ as Messiah-King and of his glory: when he says, "I am he", the people who have come to arrest him draw back and fall to the ground; to Pilate he declares that he is a king (cf. 18:33–37; 19:2–3, 19–22); and he shows that he has full knowledge and control of these events (cf. 18:4; 19:28) whereby his Father's will is being fulfilled (cf. 18:11; 19:30). Christ is the new passover lamb, by whose redemptive death the sin of the world is taken away (cf. 19:31; 1:29). From Jesus' side, water flows as well as blood, symbolizing Baptism and the promised Holy Spirit (cf. 7:37–39).

The Passion marks the climax of the Jews' and the world's hatred of Christ; it is the hour of the powers of darkness, affecting even his disciples, for they abandon him or deny him (cf. 18:25–27). But at the foot of the cross the supreme confession of faith in Jesus also takes place—the faith of the Blessed Virgin, whom our Lord makes Mother of mankind, mankind being represented by the beloved disciple, St John (cf. 19:25–27).

11. *Appearances of the risen Christ* (chaps. 20–21). This completes the glorious manifestation of Jesus as Messiah and Son of God, the story of which St John has told to strengthen our faith (cf. 20:31). This section contains the resurrection of the Lord as revealed in the empty tomb (cf. 20:1–10), and in his appearances to Mary Magdalene (cf. 20:11–18) and to the disciples (cf. 20:19–29). The resurrection, closely linked with the passion and death, is the climax of Christ's revelation. After the events of Holy Week, enlightened now by the Holy Spirit, the apostles grasp the meaning of the Old Testament prophecies about Christ, and also of what he himself said and did (cf. 20:8–9; 2:22; 12:16). The risen Christ gives the apostles the Holy Spirit and the power to forgive sins (cf. 20:22–23), and praises all those who, unlike St Thomas,

believe without having seen him (cf. 20:29). The account of the miraculous draught of fish at the Sea of Tiberias (cf. 21:1–14) prefigures the multitude of people whom the Church will bring to Christ; into this ecclesiological context fits the rest of chapter 21, which tells of St Peter being given the primacy of the Church (cf. 21:15–19). The Gospel concludes with a statement of the truthfulness of the testimony borne by the Evangelist, who has seen and heard the things he has recounted (cf. 21:24–25).

DOCTRINAL CONTENT

THE BLESSED TRINITY

St John's Gospel is the most explicit New Testament document as far as revelation of the mystery of the Blessed Trinity is concerned—as can be seen, for example, by the fact that St Augustine devotes a lot of space to the study of this mystery in his *Treatise on the Gospel of St John*.[13] The Evangelist enters deep into this unfathomable mystery, quoting the words of Christ, the Only-begotten Son who is in the bosom of the Father and who becomes man in order to tell us the secret of God's intimate inner life (cf. Jn 1:18). This is the reason why the Fourth Gospel particularly has been attacked by those who do not accept the divinity of Jesus Christ; whereas it is constantly quoted by the Magisterium of the Church when it is explaining and giving dogmatic formulation to the mystery of the Trinity or anything to do with the Incarnation of the Word.[14]

At the very beginning the Gospel asserts that the Word is God, and also that he is one in substance with the Father : when it says that "the Word was with God", the original Greek is very precise because it uses the word *Theos* with the article when it means the Person of the Father, and without the article when it refers to the divine essence. Later on, the Gospel speaks about the oneness of God and also about each of the three divine Persons. Of the One God it affirms that he has sent the Baptist (cf. 1:6), that we are born of him to the life of grace (cf. 1:12–13), that no one has ever seen him (cf. 1:18), and that in him are good deeds done (cf. 3:21); the oneness of God is proclaimed with tremendous force (cf. 5:44).[15] But also each of the three divine Persons is often referred to. The Gospel introduces the Word as the only Son of the Father (cf. 1:14), and throughout Jesus will speak again and again about his Father: for example, on the two occasions when he prays out loud he begins with the

---

13. Cf. *In Ioann. Evang.*, 15, 1. **14.** Cf. e.g., *Dz-Sch*, 178, 502, 803–806. **15.** The RSVCE gives "the glory that comes from the only God"; and the Navarre Spanish parallels that; however, the Navarre edition carries a note which reads: "in so translating we have followed the text accepted by the New Vulgate, but the oldest papyri (the Bodmer papyri) and codexes as important as the Vatican Codex do not use the word God and instead speak of the Only One—the glory that comes from the Only One—which reaffirms and emphasizes God's unicity".

word "Father" (11:41; 17:1). While making this distinction between himself and the Father, he also says that they share the same nature: "I and the Father are one" (10:30). On other occasions, he says that if they knew him, they "would know the Father also" (8:19; cf. 14:8–11), and that the Father is in him and he is in the Father (cf. 10:34–39). Jesus also teaches that God is his Father in a different way from which he is the Father of men: "I am ascending to my Father and your Father, to my God and your God ..." (20:17). This relationship of the Christian as son to his Father God, which is already taught in the prologue to the Gospel (cf. 1:12–13), is something which causes St John to exclaim: "See what love the Father has given us that we should be called children of God; and so we are" (1 Jn 3:1).

The Incarnate Word is the beginning, centre and end of the Fourth Gospel: it begins by telling us that the Word was God and was with God. We should remember that the tense used here expresses the idea of the timelessness of eternity.[16] The Word is the envoy of the Father (cf. 3:17–34; 5:36; 6:57; 7:33; etc.); the greatest possible expression of God's love for the world is the fact that God gave it his only Son (cf. 3:16). Jesus Christ, the Incarnate Word, is God's definitive rapprochement to mankind; in his most holy human nature the great God himself is made manifest (cf. Heb 1:1ff). This is why he complains when his disciples, after being with him for so long, ask him to show them the Father: when they see him they are seeing the Father also (cf. Jn 14:8–11); not only himself and his words, but his whole life, everything he does (cf. 9:4; 10:32–37; 14:12) and particularly his death and resurrection, reveal the Father. The Gospel of St John frequently tells us that Christ reveals the Father to us, and this saving revelation reaches its climax on the cross, where Christ is raised up, enthroned above the earth, which he embraces as its King. Jesus Christ crucified is thus the supreme expression of God's salvific love. Just as the bronze serpent was raised up in the wilderness to save those who had been bitten by the snakes, "so must the Son of man be lifted up, that whoever believes in him may have eternal life" (3:14–15). This is what Christ means also when he says (12:32): "I, when I am lifted up from the earth, will draw all men to myself."[17]

The Fourth Gospel also reveals the existence of the Holy Spirit as a distinct transcendent Person. In the Baptist's testimony of Jesus as "Son of God" (1:34), the unmistakable sign given is the descent of the Spirit over the Messiah in the form of a dove—the Messiah who will baptize in the Holy Spirit, whereas the Precursor's baptism is with water: "unless one is born of

---

16. This can be seen clearly in the very prologue of the Gospel when, speaking now of time past, it uses the second aorist (*egeneto*): Jesus is the Word made flesh who comes to dwell among men and who possesses the glory of the Only-begotten of the Father, full of grace and truth (1:14). **17.** And so in this way "his humanity united with the Person of the Word was the instrument of our salvation. Therefore, 'in Christ the perfect achievement of our reconciliation came forth ...'" (Vatican II, *Sacrosanctum Concilium*, 5).

water and the Spirit, he cannot enter the kingdom of God" (3:5). This relationship between water and the Spirit reappears in 7:37–39, where our Lord says that rivers of living water will flow out of him who believes in him, and the Evangelist explains that "this he said about the Spirit, which those who believed in him were to receive; for as yet the Spirit had not been given, because Jesus was not yet glorified" (7:39). This water/Spirit relationship is hinted at in the Old Testament (cf. Gen 1:2; Ezek 36:25–27), implying the power which water is given through the Spirit.

At the Last Supper, and after the Resurrection, the Evangelist gives us Jesus' words on the third Person of the Blessed Trinity and his sanctifying action: Jesus says that he will pray the Father to send them "another Counsellor", "the Spirit of truth" (14:16–17; 15:26; 16:13). The Father will listen to Christ's prayer and will send "the Holy Spirit" (14:26), who proceeds from the Father and the Son and says what the Son gives him to say (cf. 16:13–15). Thus, the Holy Spirit proceeds from the Father and the Son, who send him to their own who are still in the world.

The Holy Spirit, then, is the Counsellor who will always be with those who believe in Christ, making his home in them (cf. 14:16–17); he it is also who will remind them of all that Jesus has taught them and who will enlighten them to understand the true meaning of those words (cf. 14:26). He will bear witness to Christ for the apostles as they in their turn will do for other men (cf. 15:26–27). The Holy Spirit will also proclaim to them everything to do with the mystery of salvation (cf. 16:14–15). Under his sure guidance the disciples will reach all truth (cf. 16:13).

Then, after rising from the dead, Jesus breathes on his disciples and says: "Receive the Holy Spirit. If you forgive the sins of any, they are forgiven; if you retain the sins of any, they are retained" (20:22–23). This outpouring of the Holy Spirit for the forgiveness of sins is, as it were, a joyful anticipation of the definitive outpouring at Pentecost (cf. Acts 2:1ff), and, together with the regeneration worked by Baptism, the most moving expression of God's mercy whereby the sacrament of Penance is instituted to bring us God's forgiveness.

FAITH

St John actually says that he has written his Gospel "that you may believe that Jesus is the Christ, the Son of God, and that believing you may have life in his name" (Jn 20:31). Faith in Jesus Christ leads to eternal life, because through faith we become united to Jesus and share in his victory over sin and death: "This is the victory that overcomes the world, our faith" (1 Jn 5:4); and because by believing we fulfil *the commandment* of the Lord: "This is his commandment, that we should believe in the name of his Son Jesus Christ" (1 Jn 3:23). Faith is our loving response to God's love for us as manifested in Christ: "God so loved the world that he gave his only Son, that whoever believes in him should not perish but have eternal life" (Jn 3:16). Jesus showed us how important faith is when he worked his miracles; for example, before raising Lazarus from the dead he says to Martha: "whoever lives and believes in me shall never die" (11:26; cf. also 5:24; 6:40; 6:47; etc.).

People adopt one of two attitudes to Revelation. Some believe, and by doing so they already share in some way in eternal life: "he who believes in the Son has eternal life" (3:36; cf. 3:18; 5:24; etc.); others do not believe and therefore they are already condemned by God: "he who does not believe is condemned already, because he has not believed in the name of the only Son of God" (3:18; cf. 3:36; etc.).

The Fourth Gospel is a living testimony designed to strengthen our faith in eternal life (cf. 20:31). Faith in Jesus Christ has a reasonable basis in the witness borne by those who saw and heard Jesus (cf. Jn 21:24; Lk 1:1–4) and who faithfully pass on to us what Jesus did and taught.[18] So, believing means knowing revealed truth or, better, recognizing the authority of God revealing truth. In fact, in this Gospel we often find the verbs "to believe" and "to know" side by side in the one phrase; sometimes they seem to be interchangeable (cf. Jn 6:69; 17:8; etc.). The verb "to know" has the meaning not just of knowing intellectually, of grasping the truth; it takes on an Old Testament meaning, indicating unreserved adhesion to the Truth that is Jesus Christ. Therefore, faith includes the act of trusting commitment as well as the act of knowing. Recognizing supernatural truth through the testimony given us, we adhere to that truth and, by accepting it with our whole heart, we obtain deep knowledge of God's truth.

There are different degrees of faith. The Gospel shows us the apostles' faith growing. It tells us that our Lord was unable to trust some of those who had faith, because their faith was still weak (cf. 2:23ff). Growth in faith goes hand in hand with growth in knowledge of Jesus Christ.

Faith is at one and the same time a free gift of God and a free action on man's part: man reaches genuine freedom to believe when God gives him the grace which enables him to adhere to revealed truths; but as long as man is a wayfarer in this life, freedom means that he can ultimately reject God's gift. Jesus keeps on exhorting people to believe in him, because men, being free, can reject him (cf. 8:24; 3:36; 15:22; etc.), despite the good reasons they have for believing. But at the same time it is the Son of God himself who gives us understanding to believe (cf. 1 Jn 5:20), and no one can believe in him unless it is granted him by the Father (cf. Jn 6:65).

To sum up: faith is the result of God's action which attests to Christ by means of apostolic preaching; and it is also the result of man's freedom, whereby man recognizes the truth of the testimony God has given him and surrenders himself to Christ freely and joyfully.

---

18. Cf. Vatican II, *Dei Verbum*, 19.

CHARITY

Charity is the favourite theme of the beloved disciple of Jesus, "on whose breast he rested at the Supper, which means that he drank of the deepest secrets of (Jesus') heart."[19] He had experienced Christ's love in a special way and was therefore in a unique position to teach us how to be loved by Jesus and how to love him.[20]

It is God who takes the initiative in love (cf. Jn 1:11; 4:7; 15:16; 1 Jn 4:10), which shows that it is he who loves most. Love can be measured by the value of the gift that is given, and God gives us what he most values, what he most loves, his own Son: "God so loved the world that he gave his only Son" (Jn 3:16), him whom he most loved, who most pleased him (cf. Mt 3:17).

The supreme expression of this love occurred in the sacrifice of the cross. When Abraham was about to sacrifice his only son, God stayed his hand, but he does not prevent men from nailing his own Son to the Cross—which leads St Paul to exclaim, full of hope: "He who did not spare his own Son […], will he not also give us all things with him?" (Rom 8:32).

Seeing that God loves him so much, man feels obliged to respond, to practise the great truth that love can be repaid only with love. Man has been created "in the image of God" (Gen 1:27), and "God", St John tells us, "is love" (1 Jn 4:8). It follows that man's heart is made to love, and the more he loves, the more he becomes one with God: only when he loves can he be happy. God wants us to be happy, in this life as well as in the next. St John gives us deep insights into Jesus' teaching on charity, not only through what Jesus says, but particularly by his narrative of our Lord's life (cf. Acts 1:1).

The best proof of love is fidelity, an unswerving loyalty, total commitment to God's will: Jesus shows us his hunger to do the will of his Father and he tells us that his food is to do the will of him who sent him (cf. Jn 4:34). "I have kept my Father's commandments", our Lord says, "and abide in his love" (15:10). Jesus asserts that the world knows that he loves the Father and does what the Father has commanded him (cf. 14:31). This supreme love leads him also to love the world and man, for the lover cannot cease loving what he loves (cf. 3:16), nor can one love a father without loving his children also. All men are called to become children of God through the grace of Baptism (cf. 1:12–13; 3:3). If the Father loves the world and men, then Jesus also loves them. This love brought him even to die for them. After speaking about how right it was for the world to know that he loves the Father, he adds: "Rise, let us go hence" (14:31), showing us how eager he is to give himself, for he is on his way to Gethsemane to meet his passion and death. Jesus sacrifices himself totally, as a good shepherd who gives his life for his sheep (cf. 10:11). He

---

19. St Augustine, *In Ioann. Evang.*, 18, 1.   20. Cf. St Thomas Aquinas, *Commentary on St John*, 21, 20.

rightly says that no one has greater love than he who gives up his life for the loved one (cf. 15:13): St John explains that having loved his own who were in the world, he loved them to the end (cf. 13:1; 19:28).

St John lays special emphasis on Jesus' love, in both its divine and its human dimensions. We are shown how much he loved his friend Lazarus, and Martha and Mary (cf. 11:5); when his friend dies he makes his way to the tomb and he cannot help crying—and the people realize how deeply he loved Lazarus (cf. 11:33, 35).

Jesus has given us an example to imitate (cf. 13:15). The apostles responded to the love he showed them: "the Father himself loves you," the Master assures them, "because you have loved me and have believed that I come from the Father" (16:27). They all protest their love when Jesus tells them he is going to be betrayed (cf. Mt 26:35; Mk 14:31): "I will lay down my life for you", St Peter says (Jn 13:37). They respond in their own way to Christ's love; but the Lord points out that only he who keeps the commandments really loves him (cf. 14:21); this is a constant in his teaching: they remain in his love by keeping his commandments (cf. 15:9–10).

There is also a second commandment, which is like the first: we should imitate Christ not only in his love for his Father but also in his love for the brethren (cf. 15:9). Three times in the Last Supper our Lord gives the commandment to love: "A new commandment I give to you, that you love one another, even as I have loved you, that you also love one another" (13:34; cf. 15:12, 17). This will be the special characteristic of his true disciple, the distinguishing mark of the Christian. "Only charity distinguishes the children of God from the children of the devil. Though all may mark themselves with the sign of the cross of Christ, though all may say Amen, though all sing alleluia, though they enter the Church, though they build basilicas, nothing will distinguish the children of God from the children of the devil unless it be charity. Those who have love are born of God, those who have not, are not [...]; charity is the precious pearl (Mt 13:46); if you have it, that alone suffices."[21] Love is the source of the unity which Jesus prays for in his last prayer on this unforgettable night: "I in them and them in me, that they may become perfectly one, so that the world may know that thou hast sent me and hast loved them even as thou hast loved me" (Jn 17:23). Only through charity will people recognize the sign of the Redemption (cf. 17:21).

God wants what is best for us, what makes for our happiness and joy—which is precisely why he lays down the law of charity. In the Last Supper, also, the Master teaches the meaning of joy: seeing how sad the apostles are because they sense that he is leaving them, he tells them that if they loved him, they would be in fact rejoicing, to see him so near his moment of triumph (cf. 14:28). After speaking to them about persevering in his love and keeping faith

---

21. *In Epist. Ioann. ad Parthos*, 5, 7.

with him, he assures them that he is telling them all this so that they can share his own joy: their joy, even in the midst of the difficulties of this life, will be full (cf. 15:11). He does not hide from them the difficulties that lie ahead; yet he assures them that their sorrow will turn into joy: "You have sorrow now, but I will see you again and your hearts will rejoice, and no one will take your joy from you" (16:22). And in fact the return of the risen Jesus did fill them with hope and joy; our Lord's words, which they could not understand when they heard them first, came completely true: the Acts of the Apostles tells us how they left the Sanhedrin after being beaten, happy that they had suffered for the Lord (cf. Acts 5:40): charity had given them perfect joy (cf. Jn 16:24)

THE SACRAMENTS

St John often mentions different Jewish feasts, especially the Passover. He refers to four occasions of this great festival (2:13, 23; 5:1; 6:4; 12:1), unlike the Synoptics, which only refer to the Passover at which Jesus died. John's Gospel also refers to the deep, mysterious link between our Lord's own body and the temple of Jerusalem: the temple was the symbol of God's presence among men, a presence which was realized perfectly in Christ's human nature (cf. 2:19). In the book of Revelation it says that there will be no temple in the heavenly Jerusalem, for the Lamb of God will be the temple, Jesus Christ, forever victorious (cf. Rev 21:22).

All these festivals are a prelude to Christian celebrations, and the old Passover yields to a new one in which Christ is the perfect victim who brings about our redemption (cf. 1 Cor 5:7). St John here hints at the importance of liturgy in the sanctification of men through Christ, our Pasch.

The Evangelist goes from the sphere of the senses to that of the spirit; he discloses to us that behind our Lord's actions lie certain supernatural, saving realities, and that through Christ's human nature the splendour of his divinity is made manifest. All this is closely connected with the basic principle of the sacramental system: material, visible, natural elements are instruments which God selects to signify and produce invisible grace, the sanctification of the soul.

In a broad sense it can be said that Christ is the Sacrament of the Father, and "the Church, in Christ, is in the nature of a sacrament — a sign and instrument, that is, of communion with God and of unity among all men."[22] Here Vatican II is speaking of a "sacrament" not in the strict sense in which the essence of the sacraments of the New Alliance is dogmatically defined (for Trent categorically states that, strictly speaking, there are only seven sacraments).[23] Of these seven sacraments St John refers explicitly to Baptism, Eucharist and Penance. We can say that he also speaks of Confirmation,

22. Vatican II, *Lumen gentium*, 1.   **23.** Council of Trent, sess. VII, c. 1.

Marriage and priestly Order, though not in a direct way. As regards Confirmation he includes Jesus' promise to send the Holy Spirit to the apostles (cf. Jn 14:26; 16:13), who will confirm them in the mission entrusted to them and guide them into all truth. On Marriage there is a passage which is usually regarded as important—the wedding at Cana (cf. 2:1–11). "Our Lord, in coming to the wedding, to which he had been invited," St Augustine says, "wished to enhance it and to confirm again that he is the author of marriage."[24] It can also be said that in this event there is a clear echo of Christ's espousal of the Church, which the prophets had foretold (cf. Is 54:4–8; 62:4–5; Ezek 16; etc.) and which St Paul takes up when he speaks about marriage as *sacramentum magnum* (Eph 5:3), a great sacrament, and refers to Jesus Christ as spouse of the Church (cf. Eph 5:27). In the book of Revelation St John also speaks about the wedding between the Lamb and the new Bride, the new Jerusalem, "coming down out of heaven from God, prepared as a bride adorned for her husband" (Rev 21:2). As far as priestly Order is concerned, this sacrament is covered in what is called "the priestly prayer of Jesus" (cf. Jn 17), where our Lord intercedes as High Priest before the Eternal Father on behalf of his own and offers himself as a holy victim "that they also may be consecrated in truth" (17:19).

As regards Baptism, Jesus' conversation with Nicodemus (cf. Jn 3:1–21) can be seen as really a form of baptismal instruction: it is necessary to be born again of water and the Spirit to be able to enter the Kingdom of heaven. (In Romans 6, St Paul speaks about this new life which is infused by Baptism.) And the episode at the pool of Bethzatha (cf. Jn 5) prefigures the baptismal rite of the early Church: the neophytes, on leaving the water after the words of Baptism have been spoken over them, are cleared of all sin and reborn into the life of grace.

Chapter 6 of the Gospel deals almost entirely with the Blessed Eucharist. Our Lord uses the miracle of the multiplication of the loaves and the fish (also recounted in the Synoptics) to explain in detail his teaching about the Bread of Life, the Bread which has come down from heaven to give eternal life. His words are clear and final: "Truly, truly, I say to you, unless you eat the flesh of the Son of man and drink his blood, you have no life in you" (6:53). "My flesh," Jesus says, "is food indeed, and my blood is drink indeed. He who eats my flesh and drinks my blood abides in me, and I in him" (6:55–56). Our Lord could not have spoken in a more explicit, more realistic, way about his own sacrifice: by which, after dying in a bloody way on the cross, he gives himself to us in the Eucharist, in an unbloody way as nourishment for our soul and leads us to the closest intimacy with God.

In this chapter there is an allusion to the Old Testament: "It is written in the prophets, 'And they shall all be taught by God' " (6:45), the prophets being

---

24. *In Ioann. Evang.*, 9, 2.

Isaiah and Jeremiah (cf. Is 54:13 and Jer 31:33), who were referring to the messianic times, when the people of God would be given a New Law written on their hearts, times when God would seal a New Alliance by the sacrifice of the Messiah. By this reference to the Old Testament, our Lord is teaching that the messianic times have arrived, and that the New Alliance is ratified by the sacrifice of Christ, who brings "eternal life" through his death (6:54). The institution of the Eucharist reminds us of all this.[25]

The Gospel speaks about the sacrament of Penance when the risen Lord appears to the apostles in the Cenacle: " 'As the Father has sent me, even so I send you.' And when he had said this, he breathed on them, and said to them, 'Receive the Holy Spirit. If you forgive the sins of any, they are forgiven; if you retain the sins of any, they are retained' " (20:21–23). According to the interpretation authorized by the Magisterium of the Church,[26] this passage refers to the institution of the sacrament of Penance.

THE BLESSED VIRGIN MARY

The apostle St John also found himself in a privileged position in relation to our Lady, for Jesus entrusted his Mother to John just before he died on the cross. From then on she would always be close to him, and to him, as to none other, she could speak about everything she kept in her heart (cf. Lk 2:51).

In Mary, the Gospel says, the Word became flesh. The very Son of the Eternal Father became Son of man, to enable the sons of men to become sons of God. The Song of Consolation (cf. Is 40:1–11) had spoken of God coming to those who suffered: now God himself will personally guide his people in a new exodus to the Promised Land. Once she consents to the Word becoming flesh, the Mother of God retires into the background; this is to be her usual role in the Gospel—that of passing unnoticed, especially at Jesus' moments of glory. Later, as no other creature does, she will share in Christ's glorious triumph, and it will be John who describes her in all her splendour: "A great portent appeared in heaven, a woman clothed with the sun, with the moon under her feet, and on her head a crown of twelve stars" (Rev 12:1).

In John 2:1–11 the wedding at Cana is described, and in 19:25–27 we are told of Mary's presence on Calvary. The two accounts are quite in parallel: in both she is described as the Mother of Jesus and in both our Lord refers to her as "woman". At both Cana and Calvary Jesus' "hour" is referred to—in the first case as something which has not yet arrived, and in the second as a present fact. This "hour" of Jesus is something which marks his whole life until it culminates in the cross (cf. Jn 7:30; 8:20; 12:27; 13:1; 17:1). "When he had done everything which he judged it appropriate to do", St Augustine says, "that is when the appointed hour arrived—through his will and not of neces-

---

25. Cf. Roman Canon of the Mass (Eucharistic Prayer 1). **26.** Council of Trent, *De Paen.*, can. 3.

sity, through his power and no exigency of any kind."[27] And St Thomas Aquinas says, "the hour of the Passion is to be understood not as imposed by necessity but as determined by divine providence."[28]

The first thing one notices in the story of the wedding at Cana is Mary's exquisite charity and her absolute faith in Jesus' power. We can also see that here, as at Calvary, Mary has a role closely linked with the Messiah's role as Redeemer. When Jesus changes into wine the water set aside for Jewish ritual purification, he is implying that the messianic times have begun. For, in the prophecies wine symbolizes the times of the Messiah, when the vats will be full of good wine (cf. Amos 9:13ff; Joel 2:24; 4:18), and on Mount Zion a feast will be celebrated with succulent food and fine wines (cf. Is 25:6). Jesus himself speaks about the fruit of the vine which will be drunk in the Kingdom (cf. Mt 26:29), and contrasts the new wine with the old (Mk 2:22). The wedding feast also evokes the marriage banquet for Yahweh and the daughter of Zion, meaning the Old Alliance (cf. Is 54:4–8; 62:4–5; Ezek 16), just as Christ's espousal of the Church means the New Alliance (cf. Eph 5:25; Rev 21), which is also alluded to in certain parables (cf. Mt 22:1–14; 25:1–13). All of which implies that the figure of the Virgin Mary and the words which refer to her should be contemplated in the light of the messianic meaning of the whole passage.

The Fourth Gospel contemplates Mary's divine motherhood in all its fulness, aware that she is the Mother not only of the head but also of the members of Christ's mystical body. This is why, instead of referring to Mary by name, the Fourth Gospel uses the titles of "Mother of Jesus" and "woman", which have a special significance connected with her spiritual motherhood; this is why at Cana, Jesus calls his Mother "woman" (Jn 2:4). Similarly in 19:25–27, where the Gospel speaks of our Lady's presence on Calvary, our Lord's words have a deeper meaning than might at first appear. After entrusting his Mother to the care of John, Jesus announces that his mission is accomplished (cf. 19:28); only "now", not before. His announcement that Mary is the Mother of the beloved disciple, therefore, establishes her role in the work of salvation which has at that moment reached its climax: in addition to being a son's act of devotion it has a more transcendental meaning—Mary's spiritual maternity. This is the moment at which the Virgin Mary's co-redemption acquires its full force and meaning. Now we can indeed see how closely united Mary is to Jesus, now her divine motherhood attains its full measure, now she is made spiritual Mother of all believers. The beloved disciple stands for all those who will follow the Master and who in the apostle John receive Mary as their Mother.

The word "woman" also implies a certain solemnity and contains a special emphasis: most authors are inclined to see in this title given to Mary a clear

---

27. *In Ioann. Evang.*, 8, 12.   **28.** *Commentary on St John*, 2, 3.

allusion to the "protoevangelium" (cf. Gen 3:15), which speaks of the triumph of the woman and her seed over the serpent. In addition to being endorsed by the text itself (the use of the word "woman"), this allusion is confirmed by interpretations given by the Fathers when they speak of the parallelism between Eve and Mary, a parallelism similar to that between Adam and Christ (cf. Rom 5:12–14). In Christ's death that triumph over the serpent takes place, because by dying Jesus redeems us from slavery to the devil. *Mors per Evam, vita per Mariam*, death came upon us through Eve, Mary brings us life.[29] "The first Eve," St Irenaeus teaches, "disobeyed God; but the second obeyed him; and so the Virgin Mary can be the advocate of the virgin Eve."[30] Our Lady "in a wholly singular way cooperated by her obedience, faith, hope and burning charity in the work of the Saviour in restoring supernatural life to souls. For this reason she is a Mother to us in the order of grace"[31] and "continues in heaven her maternal role towards the members of Christ, in that she cooperates with the birth and growth of divine life in the souls of the redeemed".[32]

Origen comments: "We dare to say that the Gospels are the flower of the Scriptures, and the flower of the Gospels is that of St John. But no one can penetrate its meaning who has not rested on Jesus' breast and taken Mary as his Mother. To be like John one needs to be able, like him, to be pointed out by Jesus as another Jesus. And so, if Mary had no other children but Jesus, and Jesus says to his Mother: 'Behold, your son' and not 'Behold, another son', then it is as if he were saying, 'Behold, Jesus, to whom you have given life.' And so it is: anyone who has identified with Christ, no longer lives for himself: Christ lives in him (cf. Gal 2:20), and given that Christ lives in him, Jesus says of him to Mary: 'Behold, your son—Christ'."[33]

We have received through Baptism, by sharing in the death and resurrection of Christ (cf. Rom 6:1–14), the gift of divine sonship (cf. Jn 1:12–13), but in order to become completely one with Jesus, "we have to join him through faith, letting his life show forth in ours to such an extent that each Christian is not simply *alter Christus*, another Christ, but also *ipse Christus*, Christ himself!"[34]

---

29. St Jerome, *Letter to Eustochium*, PL 22, 408. **30.** *Against Heresies*, 5, 19, 1. **31.** Vatican II, *Lumen gentium*, 61. **32.** Paul VI, *Creed to the People of God*, 15. **33.** *Comm. in Evang. Ioann.*, on Jn 19:26–27. **34.** St Josemaría Escrivá, *Christ Is Passing By*, 104.

THE GOSPEL ACCORDING TO JOHN

The Revised Standard Version, with notes

PROLOGUE

1 ¹In the beginning was the Word, and the Word was with God, and the Word was God.* ²He was in the beginning with God;

Jn 1:1–2
Rev 19:13
Gen 1:1–5
Prov 8:22–27

1:1–18. These verses form the introduction to the Fourth Gospel; they are a poem prefacing the account of Jesus Christ's life on earth, proclaiming and praising his divinity and eternity. Jesus is the uncreated Word, God the Only-begotten, who takes on our human condition and offers us the chance to become sons and daughters of God, that is, to share in God's own life in a real and supernatural way.

Right through his Gospel St John lays special emphasis on our Lord's divinity; his existence did not begin when he became man in Mary's virginal womb: before that he existed in divine eternity as the Word, one in substance with the Father and the Holy Spirit. This luminous truth helps us understand all that Jesus says and does as reported in this Gospel.

St John's personal experience with Jesus' public ministry and his appearances after the Resurrection were the material he drew on to contemplate God's divinity and express it as "the Word of God". By placing this poem as a prologue to his Gospel, the apostle is giving us a key to understand all that follows, in the same sort of way as the first chapters of the Gospels of St Matthew and St Luke initiate us into the contemplation of the life of Christ by telling us about the virgin birth and other episodes to do with his infancy; in structure and content, however, this passage is akin to the opening passages of other New Testament books, such as Col 1:15–20, Eph 1:13–14 and 1 Jn 1–4.

The prologue is a magnificent hymn in praise of Christ. We do not know whether St John composed it when writing his Gospel, or whether he based it on some existing liturgical hymn; but there is no trace of any such text in other early Christian documents.

The prologue is very reminiscent of the first chapter of Genesis, on a number of scores: 1) the opening words are the same: "In the beginning ..."; in the Gospel they refer to absolute beginning, that is, eternity, whereas in Genesis they mean the beginning of creation and time; 2) there is a parallelism in the role of the Word: in Genesis, God creates things by his word ("And God said ... "); in the Gospel, we are told that they were made through the Word of God; 3) in Genesis, God's work of creation reaches its peak when he creates man in his own image and likeness; in the Gospel, the work of the Incarnate Word culminates when man is raised (by a new creation, as it were) to the dignity of being a son of God.

The main teachings in the prologue are: 1) the divinity and eternity of the Word; 2) his incarnation and manifestation as man; 3) the part played by him in creation and in the salvation of mankind; 4) the ways in which people react to his coming—some accepting him with faith, others rejecting him; 5) finally, John the Baptist bears witness to the presence of the Word in the world.

The Church has always given special importance to this prologue; many Fathers and ancient Christian writers wrote commentaries on it, and for centuries it was always read at the end of Mass for instruction and meditation.

The prologue is poetic in style. Its teaching is given in verses, which combine to make up stanzas (vv. 1–5; 6–8;

39

Col 1:15–20
Heb 1:1–3

³all things were made through him, and without him was not anything made that was made. ⁴In him was life,ᵃ and the life was the

9–13; 14–18). Just as a stone dropped in a pool produces ever widening ripples, so the idea expressed in each stanza tends to be expanded in later verses. This kind of exposition was much favoured in olden times because it makes it easier to get the meaning across—and God used it to help us go deeper into the central mysteries of our faith.

1:1. The sacred text calls the Son of God "the Word". The following comparison may help us understand the notion of "Word": just as a person becoming conscious of himself forms an image of himself in his mind, in the same way God the Father on knowing himself begets the eternal Word. This Word of God is singular, unique; no other can exist because in him is expressed the entire essence of God. Therefore, the Gospel does not call him simply "Word", but "the Word". Three truths are affirmed regarding the Word—that he is eternal, that he is distinct from the Father, and that he is God. "Affirming that he existed in the beginning is equivalent to saying that he existed before all things" (St Augustine, *De Trinitate*, 6, 2). Also, the text says that he was with God, that is, with the Father, which means that the person of the Word is distinct from that of the Father and yet the Word is so intimately related to the Father that he even shares his divine nature: he is one in substance with the Father (cf. *Nicene Creed*).

To mark the Year of Faith (1967–1968) Pope Paul VI summed up this truth concerning the most Holy Trinity in what is called the *Creed of the People of God* (n. 11) in these words: "We believe in our Lord Jesus Christ, who is the Son of God. He is the eternal Word, born of the Father before time began, and one in substance with the Father, *homoousios to Patri*, and through him all things were made. He was incarnate of the Virgin Mary by the power of the Holy Spirit, and was made man: equal therefore to the Father according to his divinity, and inferior to the Father according to his humanity and himself one, not by some impossible confusion of his natures, but by the unity of his person."

"In the beginning": "what this means is that he always was, and that he is eternal. [...] For if he is God, as indeed he is, there is nothing prior to him; if he is creator of all things, then he is the First; if he is Lord of all, then everything comes after him—created things and time" (St John Chrysostom, *Hom. on St John*, 2, 4).

1:3. After showing that the Word is in the bosom of the Father, the prologue goes on to deal with his relationship to created things. Already in the Old Testament the Word of God is shown as a creative power (cf. Is 55:10–11), as Wisdom present at the creation of the world (cf. Prov 8:22–26). Now Revelation is extended: we are shown that creation was caused by the Word; this does not mean that the Word is an instrument subordinate and inferior to the Father: he is an active principle along with the Father and the Holy Spirit. The work of creation is an activity common to the three divine Persons of the Blessed Trinity: "the Father generating, the Son being born, the Holy Spirit proceeding; consubstantial, co-equal, co-

ᵃ. Or *was not anything made. That which has been made was life in him*

light of men. ⁵The light shines in the darkness,* and the darkness has not overcome it.

Jn 3:19; 5:26; 12:35–36

---

omnipotent and co-eternal; one origin of all things: the creator of all things visible and invisible, spiritual and corporal" (Fourth Lateran Council, *De fide catholica, Dz-Sch*, 800). From this can be deduced, among other things, the hand of the Trinity in the work of creation and, therefore, the fact that all created things are basically good.

1:4. The prologue now goes on to expound two basic truths about the Word—that he is Life and that he is Light. The Life referred to here is divine life, the primary source of all life, natural and supernatural. And that Life is the light of men, for from God we receive the light of reason, the Light of truth and the light of glory, which are a participation in God's mind. Only a rational creature is capable of having knowledge of God in this world and of later contemplating him joyfully in heaven for all eternity. Also the Life (the Word) is the Light of men because he brings them out of the darkness of sin and error (cf. Is 9:1–2; Mt 4:15–16; Lk 1:79). Later on Jesus will say: "I am the light of the world; he who follows me will not walk in darkness, but will have the light of life" (Jn 8:12; cf. 12:46).

Verses 3 and 4 can be read with another punctuation, now generally abandoned but which had its supporters in ancient times: "All things were made through him, and without him nothing was made; in so far as anything was made in him, he was the life and the life was the light of men." This reading would suggest that everything that has been created is life in the Word, that is, that all things receive their being and activity, their life, through the Word: without him they cannot possibly exist.

1:5. "And the darkness has not overcome it": the original Greek verb, given in Latin as *comprehenderunt*, means to embrace or contain as if putting one's arms around it—an action which can be done with good dispositions (a friendly embrace) or with hostility (the action of smothering or crushing someone). So there are two possible translations: the former is that given in the Navarre Spanish, the latter that in the RSV. The RSV option would indicate that Christ and the Gospel continue to shine among men despite the world's opposition, indeed overcoming it, as Jesus later says: "Be of good cheer, I have overcome the world" (Jn 16:33; cf. 12:31; 1 Jn 5:4). Either way, the verse expresses the darkness' resistance to, repugnance for, the light. As his Gospel proceeds, St John explains further about the light and darkness: soon, in vv. 9–11, he refers to the struggle between them; later he will describe evil and the powers of the evil one, as a darkness enveloping man's mind and preventing him from knowing God (cf. Jn 12:15–46; 1 Jn 5:6).

St Augustine (*In Ioann. Evang.*, 1, 19) comments on this passage as follows: "But, it may be, the dull hearts of some cannot yet receive this light. Their sins weigh them down, and they cannot discern it. Let them not think, however, that, because they cannot discern it, therefore it is not present with them. For they themselves, because of their sins, are darkness. Just as if you place a blind person in the sunshine, although the sun is present to him, yet he is absent from the sun; in the same way, every foolish man, every unrighteous man, every ungodly man, is blind in heart. [...] What course then ought such a one to take? Let him cleanse the eyes of his

Lk 1:3–17;
1:57–60
Mt 3:1
Mk 1:4
Jn 1:19–34
Lk 3:3

⁶There was a man sent from God, whose name was John. ⁷He came for testimony, to bear witness to the light, that all might believe through him. ⁸He was not the light, but came to bear witness to the light.

---

heart, that he may be able to see God. He will see Wisdom, for God is Wisdom itself, and it is written: 'Blessed are the clean of heart, for they shall see God.'" There is no doubt that sin obscures man's spiritual vision, rendering him unable to see and enjoy the things of God.

1:6–8. After considering the divinity of the Lord, the text moves on to deal with his incarnation, and begins by speaking of John the Baptist, who makes his appearance at a precise point in history to bear direct witness before man to Jesus Christ (Jn 1:15, 19–36; 3:22ff). As St Augustine comments: "For as much as he [the Word Incarnate] was man and his Godhead was concealed, there was sent before him a great man, through whose testimony he might be found to be more than man" (*In Ioann. Evang.*, 2, 5).

All of the Old Testament was a preparation for the coming of Christ. Thus, the patriarchs and prophets announced, in different ways, the salvation the Messiah would bring. But John the Baptist, the greatest of those born of woman (cf. Mt 11:11), was actually able to point out the Messiah himself; his testimony marked the culmination of all the previous prophecies.

So important is John the Baptist's mission to bear witness to Jesus Christ that the Synoptic Gospels start their account of the public ministry with John's testimony. The discourses of St Peter and St Paul recorded in the Acts of the Apostles also refer to this testimony (Acts 1:22; 10:37; 12:24). The Fourth Gospel mentions it as many as seven times (1:6, 15, 19, 29, 36; 3:27; 5:33).

We know, of course, that St John the apostle was a disciple of the Baptist before becoming a disciple of Jesus, and that it was in fact the Baptist who showed him the way to Christ (cf. 1:37ff).

The New Testament, then, shows us the importance of the Baptist's mission, as also his own awareness that he is merely the immediate Precursor of the Messiah, whose sandals he is unworthy to untie (cf. Mk 1:7): the Baptist stresses his role as witness to Christ and his mission as preparer of the way for the Messiah (cf. Lk 1:15–17; Mt 3:3–12). John the Baptist's testimony is undiminished by time: he invites people in every generation to have faith in Jesus, the true Light.

1:9. "The true light ... ". The Spanish translation of this verse is along these lines: "It was the true light that enlightens every man who comes into the world." The Fathers, early translations and most modern commentators see "the Word" as being the subject of this sentence, which could therefore be translated as "the Word was the true light that enlightens every man who comes into the world ... ". Another interpretation favoured by many modern scholars makes "the light" the subject, in which case it would read "the true light existed, which enlightens ...". Either way, the meaning is much the same.

"Coming into the world": it is not clear in the Greek whether these words refer to "the light" or to "every man". In the first case it is the Light (the Word) that is coming into this world to enlighten all men; in the second it is the

⁹The true light that enlightens every man was coming into the world. ¹⁰He was in the world, and the world was made through him, yet the world knew him not. ¹¹He came to his own home, and

men who, on coming into this world, on being born, are enlightened by the Word; the RSV and the New Vulgate opt for the first interpretation. The Word is called "the true light" because he is the original light from which every other light or revelation of God derives. By the Word's coming, the world is fully lit up by the authentic Light. The prophets and all the other messengers of God, including John the Baptist, were not the true light but his reflection, attesting to the Light of the Word.

Apropos of the fulness of light which the Word is, St John Chrysostom asks: "If he enlightens every man who comes into the world, how is it that so many have remained unenlightened? For not all, to be sure, have recognized the high dignity of Christ. How, then, does he enlighten every man? As much as he is permitted to do so. But if some, deliberately closing the eyes of their minds, do not wish to receive the beams of this light, darkness is theirs. This is not because of the nature of the light, but is a result of the wickedness of men who deliberately deprive themselves of the gift of grace" (*Hom. on St John*, 8, 1).

1:10. The Word is in this world as the maker who controls what he has made (cf. St Augustine, *In Ioann. Evang.*, 2, 10). In St John's Gospel the term "world" means "all creation, all created things (including all mankind)"; thus, Christ came to save all mankind: "For God so loved the world that he gave his only Son, that whoever believes in him should not perish but have eternal life. For God sent the Son into the world, not to condemn the world, but that the world might

be saved through him" (Jn 3:16–17). But insofar as many people have rejected the Light, that is, rejected Christ, "world" also means everything opposed to God (cf. Jn 17:14–15). Blinded by their sins, men do not recognize in the world the hand of the Creator (cf. Rom 1:18–20; Wis 13:1–15): "they become attached to the world and relish only the things that are of the world" (St John Chrysostom, *Hom. on St John*, 7). But the Word, "the true light", comes to show us the truth about the world (cf. Jn 1:9; 18:37) and to save us.

1:11. "His own home, his own people": this means, in the first place, the Jewish people, who were chosen by God as his own personal "property", to be the people from whom Christ would be born. It can also mean all mankind, for mankind is also his: he created it and his work of redemption extends to everyone. So the reproach that they did not receive the Word made man should be understood as addressed not only to the Jews but to all those who rejected God despite his calling them to be his friends: "Christ came; but by a mysterious and terrible misfortune, not everyone accepted him. [...] It is the picture of humanity before us today, after twenty centuries of Christianity. How did this happen? What shall we say? We do not claim to fathom a reality immersed in mysteries that transcend us — the mystery of good and evil. But we can recall that the economy of Christ, for its light to spread, requires a subordinate but necessary cooperation on the part of man — the cooperation of evangelization, of the apostolic and missionary Church. If there is still work to

Gal 3:26
Jn 10:35
1 Jn 3:2; 5:13 his own people received him not. ¹²But to all who received him, who believed in his name, he gave power to become children of

---

be done, it is all the more necessary for everyone to help her" (Paul VI, General Audience, 4 December 1974).

1:12. Receiving the Word means accepting him through faith, for it is through faith that Christ dwells in our hearts (cf. Eph 3:17). Believing in his name means believing in his Person, in Jesus as the Christ, the Son of God. In other words, "those who believe in his name are those who fully hold the name of Christ, not in any way lessening his divinity or his humanity" (St Thomas Aquinas, *Comm. on St John*, in loc.).

"He gave power [to them]" is the same as saying "he gave them a free gift" — sanctifying grace — "because it is not in our power to make ourselves sons of God" (ibid.). This gift is extended through Baptism to everyone, whatever his race, age, education etc. (cf. Acts 10:45; Gal 3:28). The only condition is that we have faith.

"The Son of God became man", St Athanasius explains, "in order that the sons of men, the sons of Adam, might become sons of God. [...] He is the Son of God by nature; we, by grace" (*De incarnatione contra arrianos*). What is referred to here is birth to supernatural life: in which "Whether they be slaves or freemen, whether Greeks or barbarians or Scythians, foolish or wise, female or male, children or old men, honourable or without honour, rich or poor, rulers or private citizens, all, he meant, would merit the same honour. [...] Such is the power of faith in him; such the greatness of his grace" (St John Chrysostom, *Hom. on St John*, 10, 2).

"Christ's union with man is power and the source of power, as St John stated so incisively in the prologue of his Gospel: '(The Word) gave power to become children of God.' Man is transformed inwardly by this power as the source of a new life that does not disappear and pass away but lasts to eternal life (cf. Jn 4:14)" (John Paul II, *Redemptor hominis*, 18).

1:13. The birth spoken about here is a real, spiritual type of generation which is effected in Baptism (cf. 3:6ff). Instead of the plural adopted here, referring to the supernatural birth of men, some Fathers and early translations read it in the singular: "who was born, not of blood ... but of God", in which case the text would refer to the eternal generation of the Word and to Jesus' generation through the Holy Spirit in the pure womb of the Virgin Mary. Although the second reading is very attractive, the documents (Greek manuscripts, early translations, references in the works of ecclesiastical writers, etc.) show the plural text to be the more usual, and the one that prevailed from the fourth century forward. Besides, in St John's writings we frequently find reference to believers as being born of God (cf. Jn 3:3–6; 1 Jn 2:29; 3:9; 4:7; 5:1, 4, 18).

The contrast between man's natural birth (by blood and the will of man) and his supernatural birth (which comes from God) shows that those who believe in Jesus Christ are made children of God not only by their creation but above all by the free gift of faith and grace.

1:14. This is a text central to the mystery of Christ. It expresses in a very condensed form the unfathomable fact of the incarnation of the Son of God. "When the time had fully come, God sent forth his Son, born of woman" (Gal 4:4).

God; ¹³who were born, not of blood nor of the will of the flesh nor of the will of man, but of God.

¹⁴And the Word became flesh and dwelt among us, full of grace and truth; we have beheld his glory, glory as of the only Son from

Jn 3:3–6
Ex 25:8
Is 7:4; 60:1
1 Jn 4:2
2 Pet 1:16–17
Rev 21:3

The word "flesh" means man in his totality (cf. Jn 3:6; 17:2; Gen 6:3; Ps 56:4); so the sentence "the Word became flesh" means the same as "the Word became man." The theological term "incarnation" arose mainly out of this text. The noun "flesh" carries a great deal of force against heresies which deny that Christ is truly man. The word also accentuates that our Saviour, who dwelt among us and shared our nature, was capable of suffering and dying, and it evokes the "Book of the Consolation of Israel" (Is 40:1–11), where the fragility of the flesh is contrasted with the permanence of the Word of God: "The grass withers, the flower fades; but the word of our God will stand for ever" (Is 40:8). This does not mean that the Word's taking on human nature is something precarious and temporary.

"And dwelt among us": the Greek verb which St John uses originally means "to pitch one's tent", hence, to live in a place. The careful reader of Scripture will immediately think of the tabernacle, or tent, in the period of the exodus from Egypt, where God showed his presence before all the people of Israel through certain sights of his glory such as the cloud covering the tent (cf., for example, Ex 25:8; 40:34–35). In many passages of the Old Testament it is announced that God "will dwell in the midst of the people" (cf., for example, Jer 7:3; Ezek 43:9; Sir 24:8). These signs of God's presence, first in the pilgrim tent of the Ark in the desert and then in the temple of Jerusalem, are followed by the most wonderful form of God's presence among us — Jesus Christ, perfect God and

perfect Man, in whom the ancient promise is fulfilled in a way that far exceeded men's greatest expectations. Also the promise made through Isaiah about the "Immanuel" or "God-with-us" (Is 7:14; cf. Mt 1:23) is completely fulfilled through this dwelling of the Incarnate Son of God among us. Therefore, when we devoutly read these words of the Gospel "and dwelt among us" or pray them during the Angelus, we have a good opportunity to make an act of deep faith and gratitude and to adore our Lord's most holy human nature.

"Remembering that 'the Word became flesh', that is, that the Son of God became man, we must become conscious of *how great* each man has become through this mystery, *through the Incarnation of the Son of God!* Christ, in fact, was conceived in the womb of Mary and became man to reveal the eternal love of the Creator and Father and to make known the dignity of each one of us" (John Paul II, Angelus Address at Jasna Gora Shrine, 5 June 1979).

Although the Word's self-emptying by assuming a human nature concealed in some way his divine nature, of which he never divested himself, the Apostles did see the glory of his divinity through his human nature: it was revealed in the transfiguration (Lk 9:32–35), in his miracles (Jn 2:11; 11:40), and especially in his resurrection (cf. Jn 3:11; 1 Jn 1:1). The glory of God, which shone out in the early tabernacle in the desert and in the temple at Jerusalem, was nothing but an imperfect anticipation of the reality of God's glory revealed through the holy human nature of the Only-begotten of the

Lk 9:28–35
Jn 1:30
Col 1:19;
2:9–10
the Father. ¹⁵(John bore witness to him, and cried, "This was he of whom I said, 'He who comes after me ranks before me, for he was before me.'") ¹⁶And from his fullness have we all received, grace

---

Father. St John the Apostle speaks in a very formal way in the first person plural: "we have beheld his glory", because he counts himself among the witnesses who lived with Christ and, in particular, were present at his transfiguration and saw the glory of his resurrection.

The words "only Son" ("Only-begotten") convey very well the eternal and unique generation of the Word by the Father. The first three Gospels stressed Christ's birth in time; St John complements this by emphasizing his eternal generation.

The words "grace and truth" are synonyms of "goodness and fidelity", two attributes which, in the Old Testament, are constantly applied to Yahweh (cf., e.g., Ex 34:6; Ps 118; Ps 136; Hos 2:16–20): so, grace is the expression of God's love for men, the way he expresses his goodness and mercy. Truth implies permanence, loyalty, constancy, fidelity. Jesus, who is the Word of God made man, that is, God himself, is therefore "the only Son of the Father, full of grace and truth"; he is the "merciful and faithful high priest" (Heb 2:17). These two qualities, being good and faithful, are a kind of compendium or summary of Christ's greatness. And they also parallel, though on an infinitely lower level, the quality essential to every Christian, as stated expressly by our Lord when he praised the "good and faithful servant" (Mt 25:21).

As Chrysostom explains: "Having declared that they who received him were 'born of God' and 'become sons of God,' he then set forth the cause and reason for this ineffable honour. It is that

'the Word became flesh' and the Master took on the form of a slave. He became the Son of Man, though he was the true Son of God, in order that he might make the sons of men children of God" (*Hom. on St John*, 11,1).

The profound mystery of Christ was solemnly defined by the Church's Magisterium in the famous text of the ecumenical Council of Chalcedon (in the year 451): "Following the holy Fathers, therefore, we all with one accord teach the profession of faith in the one identical Son, our Lord Jesus Christ. We declare that he is perfect both in his divinity and in his humanity, truly God and truly man, composed of body and rational soul; that he is consubstantial with the Father in his divinity, consubstantial with us in his humanity, like us in every respect except for sin (cf. Heb 4:15). We declare that in his divinity he was begotten in this last age of Mary the Virgin, the Mother of God, for us and for our salvation" (*Dz-Sch*, 301).

1:15. Further on (Jn 1:19–36) the Gospel tells us more about John the Baptist's mission as a witness to the messiahship and divinity of Jesus. Just as God planned that the apostles should bear witness to Jesus after the resurrection, so he planned that the Baptist would be the witness chosen to proclaim Jesus at the very outset of his public ministry (cf. the note on Jn 1:6–8).

1:16. "Grace upon grace": this can be understood, as it was by Chrysostom and other Fathers, as "grace for grace", the Old Testament economy of salvation giving way to the new economy of grace

upon grace. [17]For the law was given through Moses; grace and truth came through Jesus Christ. [18]No one has ever seen God; the only Son,[b] who is in the bosom of the Father, he has made him known.

Ex 34:6
Rom 3:24; 6:14;
10:4
40:11; 85:11
Jn 6:46
Mt 11:27
Lk 10:22
1 Tim 6:16

brought by Christ. It can also mean (as the RSV suggests) that Jesus brings a superabundance of gifts, adding on, to existing graces, others—all of which pour out of the one inexhaustible source, Christ, who is for ever full of grace. "Not by sharing with us, says the Evangelist, does Christ possess the gift, but he himself is both fountain and root of all virtues. He himself is life, and light, and truth, not keeping within himself the wealth of these blessings, but pouring it forth upon all others, and even after the outpouring still remaining full. He suffers no loss by giving his wealth to others, but, while always pouring out and sharing these virtues with all men, he remains in the same state of perfection" (St John Chrysostom, *Hom. on St John*, 14, 1).

1:17. Here, for the first time in St John's Gospel, the name of Jesus Christ appears, identified with the Word of whom John has been speaking.

Whereas the Law given by Moses went no further than indicate the way man ought follow (cf. Rom 8:7–10), the grace brought by Jesus has the power to save those who receive it (cf. Rom 7:25). Through grace "we have become dear to God, no longer merely as servants, but as sons and friends" (St John Chrysostom, *Hom. on St John*, 14, 2).

On "grace and truth" see the note on Jn 1:14.

1:18. "No one has ever seen God": in this world men have never seen God other than indirectly: all that they could contemplate was God's "glory", that is, the aura of his greatness: for example, Moses saw the burning bush (Ex 3:2); Elijah felt the breeze on Mount Horeb—the "still small voice" (1 Kings 19:11–13). But in the fulness of time God comes much closer to man and reveals himself almost directly, for Jesus Christ is the visible image of the invisible God (cf. Col 1:15), the maximum revelation of God in this world, to such an extent that he assures us that "he who has seen me has seen the Father" (Jn 14:9). "The most intimate truth which this revelation gives us about God and the salvation of man shines forth in Christ, who is himself both the mediator and the sum total of Revelation" (Vatican II, *Dei Verbum*, 2).

There is no greater revelation God could make of himself than the incarnation of his eternal Word. As St John of the Cross puts it so well: "In giving to us, as he has done, his Son, who is his only Word, he has spoken to us once and for all by his own and only Word, and has nothing further to reveal" (*Ascent of Mount Carmel*, book II, chap. 22).

"The only Son": the RSV note says that "other ancient authorities read *God*" (for *Son*); the Navarre Spanish has "the Only-begotten God" and comments as follows: some Greek manuscripts and some translations give "the Only-begotten Son" or "the Only-begotten". "The Only-begotten God" is preferable because it finds best support in the codexes. Besides, although the meaning does not change substantially, this translation has a richer content because it again explicitly reveals Christ's divinity.

b. Other ancient authorities read *God*

PART ONE

Jesus is manifested as the Messiah by his signs and words

1. INTRODUCTION

The witness of John the Baptist

Jn 5:33
Lk 3:15–16
Acts 13:25
Jn 6:14; 7:40
Mt 17:10
Deut 18:15

¹⁹And this is the testimony of John, when the Jews sent priests and Levites from Jerusalem to ask him, "Who are you?" ²⁰He confessed, he did not deny, but confessed, "I am not the Christ." ²¹And they asked him, "What then? Are you Elijah?" He said, "I

1:19–34. This passage forms a unity, beginning and ending with reference to the Baptist's "testimony": it thereby emphasizes the mission given him by God to bear witness, by his life and preaching, to Jesus as the Messiah and Son of God. The Precursor exhorts people to do penance and he practises the austerity he preaches; he points Jesus out as the Lamb of God who takes away the sin of the world; and he proclaims him boldly in the face of the Jewish authorities. He is an example to us of the fortitude with which we should confess Christ: "All Christians by the example of their lives and the witness of the word, wherever they live, have an obligation to manifest the new man which they put on in Baptism" (Vatican II, *Ad gentes*, 11).

1:19–24. In this setting of intense expectation of the imminent coming of the Messiah, the Baptist is a personality with enormous prestige, as is shown by the fact that the Jewish authorities send qualified people (priests and Levites from Jerusalem) to ask him if he is the Messiah.

John's great humility should be noted: he is quick to tell his questioners:

"I am not the Christ". He sees himself as someone insignificant compared with our Lord: "I am not worthy to untie [the thong of his sandal]" (v. 27). He places all his prestige at the service of his mission as precursor of the Messiah, and, leaving himself completely to one side, he asserts that "he must increase, but I must decrease" (Jn 3:30).

1:25–26. "Baptize": this originally meant to submerge in water, to bathe. For the Jews the rite of immersion meant legal purification of those who had contracted some impurity under the Law. Baptism was also used as a rite for the incorporation of Gentile proselytes into the Jewish people. In the Dead Sea scrolls there is mention of a baptism as a rite of initiation and purification into the Jewish Qumran community, which existed in our Lord's time.

John's baptism laid marked stress on interior conversion. His words of exhortation and the person's humble recognition of his sins prepared people to receive Christ's grace: it was a very efficacious rite of penance, preparing the people for the coming of the Messiah, and it fulfilled the prophecies that spoke precisely

am not." "Are you the prophet?" And he answered, "No." ²²They said to him then, "Who are you? Let us have an answer for those who sent us. What do you say about yourself?" ²³He said, "I am the voice of one crying in the wilderness, 'Make straight the way of the Lord,' as the prophet Isaiah said."

> Is 40:3
> Mt 3:3

²⁴Now they had been sent from the Pharisees. ²⁵They asked him, "Then why are you baptizing, if you are neither the Christ, nor Elijah, nor the prophet?" ²⁶John answered them, "I baptize with water; but among you stands one whom you do not know, ²⁷even he who comes after me, the thong of whose sandal I am not worthy to untie." ²⁸This took place in Bethany beyond the Jordan, where John was baptizing.

> Mt 16:24;
> 21:25
>
> Mt 3:11
> Mk 1:7ff
>
> Jn 3:26
> Acts 3:25
>
> Jn 10:40
> Mt 3:6–13

²⁹The next day he saw Jesus coming toward him, and said, "Behold, the Lamb of God, who takes away the sin of the world!*

> Jn 1:36
> Is 53:7
> Rev 5:6

---

of a cleansing by water prior to the coming of the Kingdom of God in the messianic times (cf. Zech 13:1; Ezek 36:25; 37:23; Jer 4:14). John's baptism, however, had no power to cleanse the soul of sins, as Christian Baptism does (cf. Mt 3:11; Mk 1:4)

"One whom you do not know": Jesus had not yet publicly revealed himself as Messiah and Son of God; although some people did know him as a man, St John the Baptist could assert that really they did not know him.

1:27. The Baptist declares Christ's importance by comparing himself to a slave undoing the laces of his master's sandals. If we want to approach Christ, whom St John heralds, we need to imitate the Baptist. As St Augustine says: "He who imitates the humility of the Precursor will understand these words. [...] John's greatest merit, my brethren, is this act of humility" (*In Ioann. Evang.*, 4, 7).

1:28. This is a reference to the town of Bethany which was situated on the eastern bank of the Jordan, across from Jericho—different from the Bethany where Lazarus and his family lived, near Jerusalem (cf. Jn 11:18).

1:29. For the first time in the Gospel Christ is called the "Lamb of God". Isaiah had compared the sufferings of the Servant of Yahweh, the Messiah, with the sacrifice of a lamb (cf. Is 53:7); and the blood of the paschal lamb smeared on the doors of houses had served to protect the first-born of the Israelites in Egypt (cf. Ex 12:6–7): all this was a promise and prefiguring of the true Lamb, Christ, the victim in the sacrifice of Calvary on behalf of all mankind. This is why St Paul will say that "Christ, our paschal lamb, has been sacrificed" (1 Cor 5:7). The expression "Lamb of God" also suggests the spotless innocence of the Redeemer (cf. 1 Pet 1:18–20; 1 Jn 3:5).

The sacred text says "the sin of the world", in the singular, to make it absolutely clear that every kind of sin is taken away: Christ came to free us from original sin, which in Adam affected all men, and from all personal sins.

The book of Revelation reveals to us that Jesus is victorious and glorious in heaven as the slain lamb (cf. Rev 5:6–14), surrounded by saints, martyrs and virgins (Rev 7:9, 14; 14:1–5), who render him the praise and glory due him as God (Rev 7:10). Since Holy Communion is a

Jn 1:15–17

Mt 3:16
Mk 1:10
Lk 3:22

Mt 3:11–26

Mt 3:17

³⁰This is he of whom I said, 'After me comes a man who ranks before me, for he was before me.' ³¹I myself did not know him; but for this I came baptizing with water, that he might be revealed to Israel." ³²And John bore witness, "I saw the Spirit descend as a dove from heaven, and it remained on him. ³³I myself did not know him; but he who sent me to baptize with water said to me, 'He on whom you see the Spirit descend and remain, this is he who baptizes with the Holy Spirit.' ³⁴And I have seen and borne witness that this is the Son of God."

---

sharing in the sacrifice of Christ, priests say these words of the Baptist before administering it, to encourage the faithful to be grateful to our Lord for giving himself up to death to save us and for giving himself to us as nourishment for our souls.

1:30–31. John the Baptist here asserts Jesus' superiority by saying that he existed before him, even though he was born after him. Thereby he shows us the divinity of Christ, who was generated by the Father from all eternity and born of the Virgin Mary in time. It is as if the Baptist were saying: "Although I was born before him, he is not limited by the ties of his birth; for although he is born of his mother in time, he was generated by his Father outside of time" (St Gregory the Great, *In Evangelia homiliae*, 7).

By saying what he says in v. 31, the Precursor does not mean to deny his personal knowledge of Jesus (cf. Lk 1:36 and Mt 3:14), but to make it plain that God revealed to him the moment when he should publicly proclaim Jesus as Messiah and Son of God, and that he also understood that his own mission as precursor had no other purpose than to bear witness to Jesus Christ.

1:32–34. To emphasize the divinity of Jesus Christ, the evangelist includes here the Precursor's testimony regarding Jesus' Baptism (cf. the other Gospels, which describe in more detail what happened on this occasion: Mt 3:13–17 and par.). It is one of the key points in our Lord's life, in which the mystery of the Blessed Trinity is revealed (cf. the note on Mt 3:16).

The dove is a symbol of the Holy Spirit, of whom it is said in Genesis 1:2 that he was moving over the face of the waters. Through this sign of the dove, the Isaiah prophecies (11:2–5; 42:1–2) are fulfilled which say that the Messiah will be full of the power of the Holy Spirit. The Baptist points to the great difference between the baptism he confers and Christ's Baptism; in John 3, Jesus will speak about this new Baptism in water and in the Spirit (cf. Acts 1:5; Tit 3:5).

"The Son of God": it should be pointed out that in the original text this expression carries the definite article, which means that John the Baptist confesses before his listeners the supernatural and transcendent character of Christ's messiahship—very far removed from the politico-religious notion which Jewish leaders had forged.

1:35–39. Through these words of the Baptist, these two disciples are moved by grace to approach the Lord. John's testimony is an example of the special graces God distributes to attract people to himself. Sometimes he addresses a person

The calling of the first disciples

Jn 1:29
Is 53:7

³⁵The next day again John was standing with two of his disciples; ³⁶and he looked at Jesus as he walked, and said, "Behold, the Lamb of God!" ³⁷The two disciples heard him say this, and they followed Jesus. ³⁸Jesus turned, and saw them following, and said to them, "What do you seek?" And they said to him, "Rabbi" (which means Teacher), "where are you staying?" ³⁹He said to them, "Come and see." They came and saw where he was staying; and they stayed with him that day, for it was about the tenth hour. ⁴⁰One of the two who heard John speak, and followed him, was Andrew, Simon Peter's brother. ⁴¹He first found his brother

Mt 4:18

directly by stirring his soul and inviting him to follow him; at other times, as in the present case, he chooses to use someone close to us who knows us, to bring us to meet Christ.

The two disciples already had a keen desire to see the Messiah; John's words move them to try to become friends of our Lord: it is not merely natural curiosity but Christ's personality which attracts them. They want to get to know him, to be taught by him and to enjoy his company. "Come and see" (1:39; cf. 11:34)—a tender invitation to begin that intimate friendship they were seeking. Time and personal contact with Christ will be needed to make them more secure in their vocation. The apostle St John, one of the protagonists in this scene, notes the exact time it took place: "it was about the tenth hour", roughly four in the afternoon.

Christian faith can never be just a matter of intellectual curiosity; it affects one's whole life: a person cannot understand it unless he really lives it; therefore, our Lord does not at this point tell them in detail about his way of life; he invites them to spend the day with him. St Thomas Aquinas comments on this passage saying that our Lord speaks in a lofty, mystical way because what God is (in himself or in grace) can only be understood through experience: words cannot describe it. We grow in this understanding by doing good works (they immediately accepted Christ's invitation and as a reward "they saw"), by recollection and by applying our mind to the contemplation of divine things, by desiring to taste the sweetness of God, by assiduous prayer. Our Lord invited everyone to do all this when he said, "Come and see", and the disciples discovered it all when, in obedience to our Lord, "they went" and were able to learn by personal experience, whereas they could not understand the words alone (cf. *Comm. on St John*, in loc.).

1:40–41. The evangelist now gives us the name of one of the two disciples involved in the previous scene; he will mention Andrew again in connexion with the multiplication of the loaves (cf. 6:8) and the last Passover (cf. 12:22).

We cannot be absolutely sure who the second disciple was; but since the very earliest centuries of the Christian era he has always been taken to be the Evangelist himself. The vividness of the account, the detail of giving the exact time, and even John's tendency to remain anonymous (cf. 19:26; 20:2; 21:7, 20) seem to confirm this.

"St John the Apostle, who pours into his narrative so much that is first-hand, tells of his first unforgettable conversation

Mt 16:18
Mk 3:16
Lk 6:14

Mk 8:22
Lk 9:59; 9:9

Deut 18:18
Is 7:14; 53:2
Jer 23:5
Ezek 34:23

Jn 7:41, 52
Mt 13:54ff

Simon, and said to him, "We have found the Messiah" (which means Christ). [42]He brought him to Jesus. Jesus looked at him, and said, "So you are Simon the son of John? You shall be called Cephas" (which means Peter[c]).

[43]The next day Jesus decided to go to Galilee. And he found Philip and said to him, "Follow me." [44]Now Philip was from Bethsaida, the city of Andrew and Peter. [45]Philip found Nathanael, and said to him, "We have found him of whom Moses in the law and also the prophets wrote, Jesus of Nazareth, the son of Joseph." [46]Nathanael said to him, "Can anything good come out

---

with Christ. '"Master, where are you staying?" He said to them, "Come and see." They went and saw where he was staying; and they stayed with him that day, for it was about the tenth hour' (Jn 1:38–39).

"This divine and human dialogue completely changed the life of John and Andrew, and Peter and James and so many others. It prepared their hearts to listen to the authoritative teaching which Jesus gave them beside the Sea of Galilee" (St J. Escrivá, *Christ Is Passing By*, 108).

Those hours spent with our Lord soon produce the first results of apostolate. Andrew, unable to contain his joy, tells Simon Peter the news that he has found the Messiah, and brings him to him. Now, as then, there is a pressing need to bring others to know the Lord.

"Open your own hearts to Jesus and tell him your story. I don't want to generalize. But one day perhaps an ordinary Christian, just like you, opened your eyes to horizons both deep and new, yet as old as the Gospel. He suggested to you the prospect of following Christ earnestly, seriously, of becoming an apostle of apostles. Perhaps you lost your balance then and didn't recover it. Your complacency wasn't quite replaced by true peace until you freely said 'yes' to God, because you wanted to, which is the most supernatural of reasons. And in its wake came a

strong, constant joy, which disappears only when you abandon him" (ibid., 1).

1:42. What was it like when Jesus looked at someone? From what he says here, he seems both imperious and tender. On other occasions his glance is enough to invite a person to leave everything and follow him, as in the case of Matthew (Mt 9:9); or he seems to be full of love, as in his meeting with the rich young man (Mk 10:21); or he seems angry or sad, because of the Pharisees' unbelief (Mk 2:5), or compassionate, towards the widow of Nain (Lk 7:13). He is able to move Zacchaeus' heart to conversion (Lk 19:5); and he himself is moved by the faith and generosity of the poor widow who gave in alms everything she had (Mk 12:41–44). His penetrating look seems to lay the soul bare to God and provoke one to self-examination and contrition—as happened to the adulterous woman (Jn 8:10) and to Peter who, after denying Christ (Lk 22:61) wept bitterly (Mk 14:72).

"You shall be called Cephas": naming something is the same as taking possession of the thing named (cf. Gen 17:5; 22:28; 32:28; Is 62:2). Thus, for example, Adam when he was made lord of creation, gave names to created things (Gen 2:20). "Cephas" is the Greek transcription of an Aramaic word meaning

---

c. From the word for *rock* in Aramaic and Greek respectively

of Nazareth?" Philip said to him, "Come and see." [47]Jesus saw Nathanael coming to him, and said to him, "Behold, an Israelite indeed, in whom is no guile!" [48]Nathanael said to him, "How do you know me?" Jesus answered him, "Before Philip called you, when you were under the fig tree, I saw you." [49]Nathanael answered him, "Rabbi, you are the Son of God! You are the King of Israel!" [50]Jesus answered him, "Because I said to you, I saw you under the fig tree, do you believe? You shall see greater things than these." [51]And he said to him, "Truly, truly, I say to you, you will see heaven opened, and the angels of God ascending and descending upon the Son of man."

Jn 21:2

Jn 6:69
2 Sam 7:14
Ps 2:7
Mt 14:33;
16:16

Gen 28:12
Mt 4:11
Mk 1:13
Mt 25:31

---

stone, rock: therefore, St John, writing in Greek, has to explain the meaning of the word Jesus used. Cephas was not a proper name, but our Lord put it on Peter to indicate his role as his vicar, which he will later on reveal (Mt 16:16–18): Simon was destined to be the stone, the rock, of the Church.

The first Christians regarded this new name as so significant that they used it without translating it (cf. Gal 2:9, 11, 14); later its translation "Peter" (Petros, Petrus) became current, pushing the Apostle's old name *Simon* into the background.

"Son of John": ancient manuscripts include variants, such as "son of Jona".

1:43. "Follow me" is what Jesus usually says to all his disciples (cf. Mt 4:19; 8:22; 9:9). During Jesus' lifetime, his invitation to follow him implied being with him in his public ministry, listening to his teaching, imitating his lifestyle, etc. Once the Lord ascended into heaven, following him obviously does not mean going with him along the roads of Palestine; it means that "a Christian should live as Christ lived, making the affections of Christ his own, so that he can exclaim with St Paul: 'It is now no longer I that live, but Christ lives in me (Gal 2:20)'" (St J. Escrivá, *Christ Is Passing By*, 103). In all cases our Lord's invitation involves setting out on a jour-

ney: that is, it requires one to lead a life of striving always to do God's will even if this involves generous self-sacrifice.

1:45–51. The apostle Philip is so moved that he cannot but tell his friend Nathanael (Bartholomew) about his wonderful discovery (v. 45). "Nathanael had heard from Scripture that Jesus must come from Bethlehem, from the people of David. This belief prevailed among the Jews and also the prophet had proclaimed it of old, saying: 'But you, O Bethlehem, who are little to be among the clans of Judah, from you shall come forth for me one who is to be ruler of Israel' (Mic 5:2). Therefore, when he heard that he was from Nazareth, he was troubled and in doubt, since he found that the announcement of Philip was not in agreement with the words of the prophecy" (St John Chysostom, *Hom. on St John*, 20, 1).

A Christian may find that, in trying to communicate his faith to others, they raise difficulties. What should he do? What Philip did—not trust his own explanation, but invite them to approach Jesus personally: "Come and see" (v. 46). In other words, a Christian should bring his fellowmen, his brothers into Jesus' presence through the means of grace which he has given them and which the Church ministers—frequent reception of the sacraments, and devout Christian practices.

2. JESUS, THE AUTHOR OF THE NEW ECONOMY OF SALVATION. FIRST SIGNS OF FAITH

The wedding at Cana—the first sign worked by Jesus

2 ¹On the third day there was a marriage at Cana in Galilee, and the mother of Jesus was there; ²Jesus also was invited to the

Nathanael, a sincere person (v. 47), goes along with Philip to see Jesus; he makes personal contact with our Lord (v. 48), and the outcome is that he receives faith (the result of his ready reception of grace, which reaches him through Christ's human nature: v. 49).

As far as we can deduce from the Gospels, Nathanael is the first apostle to make an explicit confession of faith in Jesus as Messiah and as Son of God. Later on St Peter, in a more formal way, will recognize our Lord's divinity (cf. Mt 16:16). Here (v. 51) Jesus evokes a text from Daniel (7:13) to confirm and give deeper meaning to the words spoken by his new disciple.

2:1. Cana in Galilee was probably what is now Kef Kenna, seven kilometres (four miles) north-east of Nazareth. The first guest to be mentioned is Mary: St Joseph is not mentioned, which cannot be put down to St John's forgetfulness: his silence here and on other occasions in his Gospel leads us to believe that Joseph had already died. Wedding celebrations lasted quite a while in the East (Gen 29:27; Judg 14:10, 12, 17; Job 9:12; 10:1). In the course of the celebrations, relatives and friends would come to greet the newly-weds; even people passing through could join in. Wine was regarded as an indispensable element in meals and also helped to create a festive atmosphere. The women looked after the catering: here our Lady would have lent a hand, which was how she realized they were running out of wine.

2:2. "To show that all states in life are good, [...] Jesus deigned to be born in the pure womb of the Virgin Mary; soon after he was born he received praise from the prophetic lips of Anna, a widow, and, invited in his youth by the betrothed couple, he honoured the wedding with the power of his presence" (St Bede, *Hom.*, 13, for the 2nd Sunday after the Epiphany). Christ's presence at the wedding is a sign that he blesses love between man and woman joined in marriage: God instituted marriage at the beginning of creation (cf. Gen 1:27–28; 2:24); Jesus confirmed it and raised it to the dignity of a sacrament (cf. Mt 19:6).

2:3. In the Fourth Gospel the Mother of Jesus (this is the title St John gives her) appears only twice—here and on Calvary (Jn 19:25). This suggests Mary's involvement in the Redemption. A number of analogies can be drawn between Cana and Calvary. They are located at the beginning and at the end of Jesus' public life, as if to show that Mary was present in everything that Jesus did. Her title—Mother—carries very special tones: Mary acts as Jesus' true Mother at these two points in which his divinity is being revealed. Also, both episodes demonstrate Mary's special solicitude towards everyone: in one case she intercedes when "the hour" has not yet come; in the other she offers the Father the redeeming death of her Son, and accepts the mission Jesus confers on her to be the Mother of all believers, who are represented on Calvary by the beloved disciple.

marriage, with his disciples. ³When the wine failed, the mother of Jesus said to him, "They have no wine." ⁴And Jesus said to her, "O woman, what have you to do with me?* My hour has not yet come." ⁵His mother said to the servants, "Do whatever he tells

Jn 19:26
Mt 12:48
Mk 1:24
Gen 41:55

"In the public life of Jesus Mary appears prominently; at the very beginning when at the marriage feast of Cana, moved with pity, she brought about by her intercession the beginning of the miracles of Jesus the Messiah (cf. John 2:1–11). In the course of her Son's preaching she received the words whereby, in extolling a kingdom beyond the concerns and ties of flesh and blood, he declared blessed those who heard and kept the word of God (cf. Mk 3:35; Lk 11:27–28) as she was faithfully doing (cf. Lk 2:19, 51). Thus the Blessed Virgin advanced in her pilgrimage of faith, and faithfully persevered in her union with her Son unto the cross, where she stood (cf. Jn 19:25), in line with the divine plan, enduring with her only-begotten Son the intensity of his passion, with his sacrifice, associating herself in her mother's heart, and lovingly consenting to the immolation of this victim who was born of her. Finally, she was given by the same Christ Jesus dying on the cross as a mother to his disciple, with these words: 'Woman, behold, thy son' (Jn 19:26–27)" (Vatican II, *Lumen gentium*, 58).

2:4. For the meaning of the words of this verse see the section on our Lady above (pp. 34ff). It should also be said that the Gospel account of this dialogue between Jesus and his Mother does not give us his gestures, tone of voice etc.: to us, for example, his answer sounds harsh, as if he were saying, "This is no concern of ours". But that was not the case.

"Woman" is a respectful title, rather like "lady" or "madam"; it is a formal way of speaking. On the cross Jesus will use the same word with great affection and veneration (Jn 19:26).

[The sentence rendered "What have you to do with me?" is the subject of a note in RSVCE which says "while this expression always implies a divergence of view, the precise meaning is to be determined by the context, which here shows that it is not an unqualified rebuttal, still less a rebuke." The Navarre Spanish is the equivalent of "What has it to do with you and me?"] The sentence "What has it to do with you and me?" is an Eastern way of speaking which can have different nuances. Jesus' reply seems to indicate that although in principle it was not part of God's plan for him to use his power to solve the problem the wedding feast had run into, our Lady's request moves him to do precisely that. Also, one could surmise that God's plan envisaged that Jesus should work the miracle at his Mother's request. In any event, God willed that the Revelation of the New Testament should include this important teaching: so influential is our Lady's intercession that God will listen to all petitions made through her; which is why Christian piety, with theological accuracy, has called our Lady "supplicant omnipotence".

"My hour has not yet come": the term "hour" is sometimes used by Jesus to designate the moment of his coming in glory (cf. Jn 5:28), but generally it refers to the time of his passion, death and resurrection (cf. Jn 7:30; 12:23; 13:1; 17:1).

2:5. Like a good mother, the Virgin Mary knows perfectly well what her son's reply means—though to us it is ambiguous ("What has it to do with you and me?"): she is confident that Jesus will do something to come to the family's rescue.

Mk 7:3–4 you." ⁶Now six stone jars were standing there, for the Jewish rites of purification, each holding twenty or thirty gallons. ⁷Jesus said to them, "Fill the jars with water." And they filled them up to the brim. ⁸He said to them, "Now draw some out, and take it to the steward of the feast." So they took it. ⁹When the steward of the feast tasted the water now become wine, and did not know where it came from (though the servants who had drawn the water knew), the steward of the feast called the bridegroom ¹⁰and said to him, "Every man serves the good wine first; and when men have drunk freely, then the poor wine; but you have kept the good wine

This is why she tells the servants so specifically to do what Jesus tells them. These words of our Lady can be seen as a permanent invitation to each of us: "in that all Christian holiness consists: for perfect holiness is obeying Christ in all things" (St Thomas Aquinas, *Comm. on St John*, in loc.).

We find the same attitude in Pope John Paul II's prayer at our Lady's shrine at Knock, when he consecrated the Irish people to God: "At this solemn moment *we listen* with particular attention to your words: 'Do whatever my Son tells you.' And *we wish* to respond to your words with all our heart. We wish to do what your Son tells us, what he commands us, for he has the words of eternal life. We wish to carry out and fulfil all that comes from him, all that is contained in the Good News, as our forefathers did for many centuries. [...] Today, therefore, [...] we entrust and consecrate to you, Mother of Christ and Mother of the Church, our hearts, our consciences, and our works, in order that they may be in keeping with the faith we profess. We entrust and consecrate to you each and every one of those who make up both the community of the Irish people and the community of the People of God living in this land" (Homily at Knock Shrine, 30 September 1979).

2:6. We are talking about 500–700 litres (100–150 gallons) of top quality wine. St

John stresses the magnificence of the gift produced by the miracle—as he also does at the multiplication of the loaves (Jn 6:12–13). One of the signs of the arrival of the Messiah was abundance; here we have the fulfilment of the ancient prophecies: "the Lord will give what is good, and our land will yield its increase", as Psalm 85:12 proclaims; "the threshing floors shall be full of grain, the vats shall overflow with wine and oil" (Joel 2:24; cf. Amos 9:13–15). This abundance of material goods is a symbol of the supernatural gifts Christ obtains for us through the Redemption: later on St John highlights our Lord's words: "I came that they may have life, and have it abundantly" (Jn 10:10; cf. Rom 5:20).

2:7. "Up to the brim": the Evangelist gives us this further piece of information to emphasize the superabundance of the riches of Redemption and also to show how very precisely the servants did what they were told, as if hinting at the importance of docility in fulfilling the will of God, even in small details.

2:9–10. Jesus works miracles in a munificent way; for example, in the multiplication of the loaves and fish (cf. Jn 6:10–13) he feeds five thousand men—who eat as much as they want—and the left-overs fill twelve baskets. In this present miracle he does not change the water

till now." ¹¹This, the first of his signs, Jesus did at Cana in Galilee, Jn 1:14; 11:40
and manifested his glory; and his disciples believed in him.

¹²After this he went down to Capernaum, with his mother and Mt 4:13
his brethren* and his disciples; and there they stayed for a few
days.

Cleansing of the temple—Christ, God's new temple

¹³The Passover of the Jews was at hand, and Jesus went up to Jn 2:23; 6:4;
11:55; 12:1
Mt 21:12
Jerusalem. ¹⁴In the temple he found those who were selling oxen

---

into just any wine but into wine of excellent quality.

The Fathers see in this good wine, kept for the end of the celebrations, and in its abundance, a prefiguring of the crowning of the history of salvation: formerly God sent the patriarchs and prophets, but in the fullness of time he sent his own Son, whose teaching perfects the old revelation and whose grace far exceeds the expectations of the righteous in the Old Testament. They also have seen, in this good wine coming at the end, the reward and joy of eternal life which God grants to those who desire to follow Christ and who have suffered bitterness and contradiction in this life (cf. St Thomas Aquinas, *Comm. on St John*, in loc.).

2:11. Before he worked this miracle the disciples already believed that Jesus was the Messiah; but they had too earthbound a concept of his salvific mission. St John testifies here that this miracle was the beginning of a new dimension in their faith; it became much deeper. "At Cana, Mary appears once more as the Virgin in prayer: when she tactfully told her Son of a temporal need, she also obtained an effect of grace, namely, that Jesus, in working the first of his 'signs', confirmed his disciples' faith in him" (Paul VI, *Marialis cultus*, 18).

"Why are Mary's prayers so effective with God? The prayers of the saints are prayers of servants, whereas Mary's are a Mother's prayer, whence flows their efficacy and their authority; and since Jesus has immense love for his Mother, she cannot pray without being listened to. […]

"To understand Mary's great goodness, let us remember what the Gospel says. […] There was a shortage of wine, which naturally worried the married couple. No one asks the Blessed Virgin to intervene and request her Son to come to the rescue of the couple. But Mary's heart cannot but take pity on the unfortunate couple […]; it stirs her to act as intercessor and ask her Son for the miracle, even though no one asks her to. […] If our Lady acted like this without being asked, what would she not have done if they actually asked her to intervene?" (St Alphonsus, *Sunday Sermons*, 48).

2:12. Regarding the "brethren" of Jesus cf. the notes on Mt 12:46–47 and Mk 6:1–3.

2:13. "The Passover of the Jews": this is the most important religious feast for the people of the Old Testament, the prefiguring of the Christian Easter (cf. the note on Mt 26:2). The Jewish Passover was celebrated on the fourteenth day of the month of Nisan and was followed by the festival week of the Azymes (unleavened bread). According to the Law of Moses, on those days every male Israelite had to "appear before the Lord God" (Ex 34:23; Deut 16:16)—hence the pious custom of

Mk 11:15ff
Lk 19:45

and sheep and pigeons, and the money-changers at their business. [15]And making a whip of cords, he drove them all, with the sheep and oxen, out of the temple; and he poured out the coins of the

Zech 14:21
Lk 2:49

money-changers and overturned their tables. [16]And he told those who sold the pigeons, "Take these things away; you shall not

Ps 69:9

make my Father's house a house of trade." [17]His disciples remembered that it was written, "Zeal for thy house will consume me."

Mt 21:23

[18]The Jews then said to him, "What sign have you to show us for

Mt 26:61;
27:40

doing this?" [19]Jesus answered them, "Destroy this temple, and in three days I will raise it up." [20]The Jews then said, "It has taken

---

making a pilgrimage to the temple of Jerusalem for these days, hence the crowd and all the vendors to supply the needs of the pilgrims; this trading gave rise to abuses.

"Jesus went up to Jerusalem": by doing this Jesus publicly shows that he observes the Law of God. But, as we shall soon see, he goes to the temple as the Only-begotten Son who must ensure that all due decorum is observed in the House of the Father: "And from thenceforth Jesus, the Anointed of God, always begins by reforming abuses and purifying from sin; both when he visits his Church, and when he visits the Christian soul" (Origen, *Hom. on St John*, 1).

2:14–15. Every Israelite had to offer as a passover sacrifice an ox or a sheep, if he was wealthy; or two turtledoves or two pigeons if he was not (Lev 5:7). In addition he had to pay a half shekel every year, if he was twenty or over. The half shekel, which was the equivalent of a day's pay of a worker, was a special coin also called temple money (cf. Ex 30:13); other coins in circulation (denarii, drachmas etc.) were considered impure because they bore the image of pagan rulers. During the Passover, because of the extra crowd, the outer courtyard of the temple, the court of the Gentiles, was full of traders, money-changers etc., and inevit-

ably this meant noise, shouting, bellowing, manure etc. Prophets had already fulminated against these abuses, which grew up with the tacit permission of the temple authorities, who made money by permitting trading. Cf. the notes on Mt 21:12–13 and Mk 11:15–18.

2:16–17. "Zeal for thy house will consume me"—a quotation from Psalm 69:9. Jesus has just made a most significant assertion: "You shall not make my Father's house a house of trade." By calling God his Father and acting so energetically, he is proclaiming he is the Messiah, the Son of God. Jesus' zeal for his Father's glory did not escape the attention of his disciples who realized that what he did fulfilled the words of Psalm 69.

2:18–22. The temple of Jerusalem, which had replaced the previous sanctuary which the Israelites carried around in the wilderness, was the place selected by God during the Old Covenant to express his presence to the people in a special way. But this was only an imperfect anticipation or prefiguring of the full expression of his presence among men— the Word of God became man. Jesus, in whom "the whole fulness of deity dwells bodily" (Col 2:9), is the full presence of God here on earth and, therefore, the true

forty-six years to build this temple, and will you raise it up in three days?" ²¹But he spoke of the temple of his body. ²²When therefore he was raised from the dead, his disciples remembered that he had said this; and they believed the scripture and the word which Jesus had spoken.

1 Cor 3:17; 6:19

²³Now when he was in Jerusalem at the Passover feast, many believed in his name when they saw the signs which he did; ²⁴but Jesus did not trust himself to them, ²⁵because he knew all men and needed no one to bear witness of man; for he himself knew what was in man.

Lk 16:15

---

temple of God. Jesus identifies the temple of Jerusalem with his own body, and by so doing refers to one of the most profound truths about himself—the Incarnation. After the ascension of the Lord into heaven this real and very special presence of God among men is continued in the sacrament of the Blessed Eucharist.

Christ's words and actions as he expels the traders from the temple clearly show that he is the Messiah foretold by the prophets. That is why some Jews approach him and ask him to give a sign of his power (cf. Mt 16:1; Mk 8:11; Lk 11:29). Jesus' reply (v. 19), whose meaning remains obscure until his resurrection, the Jewish authorities try to turn into an attack on the temple—which merits the death penalty (Mt 26:61; Mk 14:58; cf. Jer 26:4ff); later they will taunt him with it when he is suffering on the cross (Mt 27:40; Mk 15:29) and later still in their case against St Stephen before the Sanhedrin they will claim to have heard him repeat it (Acts 6:14).

There was nothing derogatory in what Jesus said, contrary to what false witnesses made out. The miracle he offers them, which he calls "the sign of Jonah" (cf. Mt 16:4), will be his own resurrection on the third day. Jesus is using a metaphor, as if to say: Do you see this

temple? Well, imagine if it were destroyed, would it not be a great miracle to rebuild it in three days? That is what I will do for you as a sign. For you will destroy my body, which is the true temple, and I will rise again on the third day.

No one understood what he was saying. Jews and disciples alike thought he was speaking about rebuilding the temple which Herod the Great had begun to construct in 19–20 BC. Later on the disciples grasped what he really meant.

2:23–25. Jesus' miracles moved many to recognize that he had extraordinary, divine powers. But that falls short of perfect theological faith. Jesus knew their faith was limited, and that they were not very deeply attached to him: they were interested in him as a miracle-worker. This explains why he did not trust them (cf. Jn 6:15, 26). "Many people today are like that. They carry the name of faithful, but they are fickle and inconstant", comments Chrysostom (*Hom. on St John*, 23, 1).

Jesus' knowledge of men's hearts is another sign of his divinity; for example, Nathanael and the Samaritan woman recognized him as the Messiah because they were convinced by the evidence of supernatural power he showed by reading their hearts (cf. Jn 1:49; 4:29).

Nicodemus visits Jesus

Jn 7:50; 9:39
Mt 22:16

3 ¹Now there was a man of the Pharisees, named Nicodemus, a ruler of the Jews. ²This man came to Jesus^d by night and said to him, "Rabbi, we know that you are a teacher come from God; for no one can do these signs that you do, unless God is with him."

Mt 18:3
Lk 17:21
1 Pet 1:23

³Jesus answered him, "Truly, truly, I say to you, unless one is born anew,^e he cannot see the kingdom of God." ⁴Nicodemus said to him, "How can a man be born when he is old? Can he enter a

---

3:1–21. Nicodemus was a member of the Sanhedrin of Jerusalem (cf. Jn 7:50). He must also have been an educated man, probably a scribe or teacher of the Law: Jesus addresses him as a "teacher of Israel". He would have been what is called an intellectual—a person who reasons things out, for whom the search for truth is a basic part of life. He was, naturally, much influenced by the Jewish intellectual climate of his time. However, if divine things are to be understood, reason is not enough: a person must be humble. The first thing Christ is going to do in his conversation with Nicodemus is to highlight the need for this virtue; that is why he does not immediately answer his questions: instead, he shows him how far he is from true wisdom: "Are you a teacher of Israel, and yet you do not understand this?" Nicodemus needs to recognize that, despite all his studies, he is still ignorant of the things of God. As St Thomas Aquinas comments: "The Lord does not reprove him to offend him but rather because Nicodemus still relies on his own learning; therefore he desired, by having him experience this humiliation, to make him a fit dwelling-place for the Holy Spirit" (*Comm. on St John*, in loc.). From the way the conversation develops Nicodemus obviously takes this step of humility and he sits before Jesus as a disciple before his master. Then our Lord reveals to him the mysteries of

faith. From this moment onwards Nicodemus will be much wiser than all those colleagues of his who have not taken this step.

Human knowledge, on any scale, is something minute compared with the truths—simple to state but extremely profound—of the articles of faith (cf. Eph 3:15–19; 1 Cor 2:9). Divine truths need to be received with the simplicity of a child (without which we cannot enter the Kingdom of heaven); then they can be meditated on right through one's life and studied with a sense of awe, aware that divine things are always far above our heads.

3:1–2. Throughout this intimate dialogue, Nicodemus behaves with great refinement: he addresses Jesus with respect and calls him Rabbi, Master. He had probably been impressed by Christ's miracles and preaching and wanted to know more. The way he reacts to our Lord's teaching is not as yet very supernatural, but he is noble and upright. His visiting Jesus by night, for fear of the Jews (cf. Jn 19:39), is very understandable, given his position as a member of the Sanhedrin: but he takes the risk and goes to see Jesus.

When the Pharisees tried to arrest Jesus (Jn 7:32), failing to do so because he had such support among the people, Nicodemus energetically opposed the

---

d. Greek *him*

second time into his mother's womb and be born?" ⁵Jesus answered, "Truly, truly, I say to you, unless one is born of water and the Spirit, he cannot enter the kingdom of God. ⁶That which is born of the flesh is flesh, and that which is born of the Spirit is spirit.ᶠ ⁷Do not marvel that I said to you, 'You must be born anew.'ᵉ ⁸The windᶠ blows where it wills, and you hear the sound of it, but you do not know whence it comes or whither it goes; so it is with every one who is born of the Spirit." ⁹Nicodemus said to him,

Ezek 36:25–27
Eph 5:26
Tit 3:5
1 Jn 3:9; 5:1
Jn 1:13
Gen 6:3

Eccles 11:5

Lk 1:34

injustice of condemning a man without giving him a hearing; he also showed no fear, at the most difficult time of all, by honouring the dead body of the Lord (Jn 19:40).

3:3–8. Nicodemus' first question shows that he still has doubts about Jesus (Is he a prophet? Is he the Messiah?); and our Lord replies to him in a completely unexpected way: Nicodemus presumed he would say something about his mission and, instead, he reveals to him an astonishing truth: one must be born again, in a spiritual birth, by water and the spirit; a whole new world opens up before Nicodemus.

Our Lord's words also paint a limitless horizon for the spiritual advancement of any Christian who willingly lets himself or herself be led by divine grace and the gifts of the Holy Spirit, which are infused at Baptism and enhanced by the sacraments. As well as opening his soul to God, the Christian also needs to keep at bay his selfish appetites and the inclinations of pride, if he is to understand what God is teaching him in his soul: "Therefore must the soul be stripped of all things created, and of its own actions and abilities—namely, of its understanding, perception and feelings—so that, when all that is unlike God and unconformed to him is cast out, the soul may receive the likeness of God; and nothing

will then remain in it that is not the will of God and it will thus be transformed in God. Wherefore, although it is true that, as we have said, God is ever in the soul, giving it, and through his presence conserving within it, its natural being, yet he does not always communicate supernatural being to it. For this is communicated only by love and grace, which not all souls possess; and all those that possess it have it not in the same degree; for some have attained more degrees of love and others fewer. Wherefore God communicates himself most to that soul that has progressed farthest in love; namely, that has its will in closest conformity with the will of God. And the soul that has attained complete conformity and likeness of will is totally united and transformed in God supernaturally" (St John of the Cross, *Ascent of Mount Carmel*, book 2, chap. 5).

Jesus speaks very forcefully about man's new condition: it is no longer a question of being born of the flesh, of the line of Abraham (cf. Jn 1:13), but of being reborn through the action of the Holy Spirit, by means of water. This is our Lord's first reference to Christian Baptism, confirming John the Baptist's prophecy (cf. Mt 3:11; Jn 1:33) that he had come to institute a baptism with the Holy Spirit.

"Nicodemus had not yet savoured this spirit and this life. [...] He knew but

e. Or *from above* **f.** The same Greek word means both *wind* and spirit

"How can this be?" [10]Jesus answered him, "Are you a teacher of Israel, and yet you do not understand this? [11]Truly, truly, I say to you, we speak of what we know, and bear witness to what we have seen; but you do not receive our testimony. [12]If I have told you earthly things and you do not believe, how can you believe if I tell you heavenly things? [13]No one has ascended into heaven but he who descended from heaven, the Son of man.[g] [14]And as Moses lifted up the serpent in the wilderness, so must the Son of man be lifted up, [15]that whoever believes in him may have eternal life."[h]

[16]For God so loved the world that he gave his only Son, that whoever believes in him should not perish but have eternal life.

Jn 7:16; 8:26ff; 12:49

Lk 22:67
Wis 9:16

Prov 30:4
Eph 4:9

Jn 8:28; 12:32; 18:32
Num 21:8–9

Rom 5:8; 8:32
1 Jn 4:9

---

one birth, which is from Adam and Eve; that which is from God and the Church, he did not yet know; he knew only the paternity which engenders to death; he did not yet know the paternity which engenders to life. [...] Whereas there are two births, he knew only of one. One is of earth, the other of heaven; one of the flesh, the other of the Spirit; one of mortality, the other of eternity; one of male and female, the other of God and the Church. But the two are each unique; neither one nor the other can be repeated" (St Augustine, *In Ioann. Evang.*, 11, 6).

Our Lord speaks of the wonderful effects the Holy Spirit produces in the soul of the baptized. Just as with the wind — when it blows we realize its presence, we hear it whistling, but we do not know where it came from, or where it will end up — so with the Holy Spirit, the divine "breath" (*pneuma*) given us in Baptism: we do not know how he comes to penetrate our heart but he makes his presence felt by the change in the conduct of whoever receives him.

3:10–12. Even though Nicodemus finds them puzzling, Jesus confirms that his words still stand, and he explains that he

speaks about the things of heaven because that is where he comes from, and to make himself understood he uses earthly comparisons and images. Even so, this language will fail to convince those who adopt an attitude of disbelief.

Chrysostom comments: "It was with reason that he said not: 'You do not understand,' but: 'You do not believe.' When a person baulks and does not readily accept things which it is possible for the mind to receive, he may with reason be accused of stupidity; when he does not accept things which it is not possible to grasp by reason but only by faith, the charge is no longer that of stupidity, but of incredulity" (*Hom. on St John*, 27, 1).

3:13. This is a formal declaration of the divinity of Jesus. No one has gone up into heaven and, therefore, no one can have perfect knowledge of God's secrets, except God himself who became man and came down from heaven — Jesus, the second Person of the Blessed Trinity, the Son of man foretold in the Old Testament (cf. Dan 7:13), to whom has been given eternal lordship over all peoples.

The Word does not stop being God on becoming man: even when he is on earth as man, he is in heaven as God. It is

---

g. Other ancient authorities add *who is in heaven*   **h.** Some interpreters hold that the quotation continues through verse 21

[17]For God sent the Son into the world, not to condemn the world, but that the world might be saved through him. [18]He who believes in him is not condemned; he who does not believe is condemned already, because he has not believed in the name of the only Son of God. [19]And this is the judgment, that the light has come into the world, and men loved darkness rather than light, because their deeds were evil. [20]For every one who does evil hates the light, and does not come to the light, lest his deeds should be exposed. [21]But he who does what is true comes to the light, that it may be clearly seen that his deeds have been wrought in God.

Jn 5:22; 12:47
Lk 19:10
Acts 17:31

Jn 3:36; 5:24

Jn 1:5, 9–11;
12:48

Eph 5:13

---

only after the Resurrection and the Ascension that Jesus is in heaven as man also.

3:14–15. The bronze serpent which Moses set up on a pole was established by God to cure those who had been bitten by the poisonous serpents in the desert (cf. Num 21:8–9). Jesus compares this with his crucifixion, to show the value of his being raised up on the cross: those who look on him with faith can obtain salvation. We could say that the good thief was the first to experience the saving power of Christ on the cross: he saw the crucified Jesus, the King of Israel, the Messiah, and was immediately promised that he would be in Paradise that very day (cf. Lk 23:39–43).

The Son of God took on our human nature to make known the hidden mystery of God's own life (cf. Mk 4:11; Jn 1:18; 3:1–13; Eph 3:9) and to free from sin and death those who look at him with faith and love and who accept the cross of every day.

The faith of which our Lord speaks is not just intellectual acceptance of the truths he has taught: it involves recognizing him as Son of God (cf. 1 Jn 5:1), sharing his very life (cf. Jn 1:12) and surrendering ourselves out of love and therefore becoming like him (cf. Jn 10:27; 1 Jn 3:2). But this faith is a gift of God (cf. Jn 3:3, 5–8), and we should ask

him to strengthen it and increase it as the Apostles did: Lord "increase our faith!" (Lk 17:5). While faith is a supernatural, free gift, it is also a virtue, a good habit, which a person can practise and thereby develop: so the Christian, who already has the divine gift of faith, needs with the help of grace to make explicit acts of faith in order to make this virtue grow.

3:16–21. These words, so charged with meaning, summarize how Christ's death is the supreme sign of God's love for men (cf. the section on charity, pp. 30ff above). "'For God so loved the world that he gave his only Son' for its salvation. All our religion is a revelation of God's kindness, mercy and love for us. 'God is love' (1 Jn 4:16), that is, love poured forth unsparingly. All is summed up in this supreme truth, which explains and illuminates everything. The story of Jesus must be seen in this light. '(He) loved me', St Paul writes. Each of us can and must repeat it for himself—'He loved me, and gave himself for me' (Gal 2:20)" (Paul VI, Homily on Corpus Christi, 13 June 1976).

Christ's self-surrender is a pressing call to respond to his great love for us: "If it is true that God has created us, that he has redeemed us, that he loves us so much that he has given up his only-begotten Son for us (cf. Jn 3:16), that he waits for us—every day!—as eagerly as

The Baptist again bears witness

Jn 2:12; 4:2; 5:1; 6:1; 7:1
²²After this Jesus and his disciples went into the land of Judea; there he remained with them and baptized.* ²³John also was bap-

Mt 4:12
tizing at Aenon near Salim, because there was much water there;

Lk 3:20
and people came and were baptized. ²⁴For John had not yet been put in prison.*

Jn 1:26–34
²⁵Now a discussion arose between John's disciples and a Jew over purifying. ²⁶And they came to John, and said to him, "Rabbi,

---

the father of the prodigal son did (cf. Lk 15:11–32), how can we doubt that he wants us to respond to him with all our love? The strange thing would be not to talk to God, to draw away and forget him, and busy ourselves in activities which are closed to the constant prompt-ings of his grace" (St Josemaría Escrivá, *Friends of God*, 251).

"Man cannot live without love. He remains a being that is incomprehensible for himself, his life is senseless, if love is not revealed to him, if he does not encounter love, if he does not experience it and make it his own, if he does not par-ticipate intimately in it. This […] is why Christ the Redeemer 'fully reveals man to himself'. If we may use the expres-sion, this is the human dimension of the mystery of the Redemption. In this dimension man finds again the greatness, dignity and value that belong to his humanity. […] The one who wishes to understand himself thoroughly […] must, with his unrest and uncertainty and even his weakness and sinfulness, with his life and death, draw near to Christ. He must, so to speak, enter into him with all his own self, he must 'appropriate' and assimilate the whole of the reality of the Incarnation and Redemption in order to find himself. If this profound process takes place within him, he then bears fruit not only of adoration of God but also of deep wonder at himself. How pre-cious must man be in the eyes of the Creator, if he 'gained so great a Redeem-

er' (*Roman Missal, Exultet* at Easter Vigil), and if God 'gave his only Son' in order that man 'should not perish but have eternal life'. […]

"Increasingly contemplating the whole of Christ's mystery, the Church knows with all the certainty of faith that the Redemption that took place through the Cross has definitively restored his dignity to man and given back meaning to his life in the world, a meaning that was lost to a considerable extent because of sin. And for that reason, the Redemption was accomplished in the paschal mystery, leading through the Cross and death to Resurrection" (John Paul II, *Redemptor hominis*, 10).

Jesus demands that we have faith in him as a first prerequisite to sharing in his love. Faith brings us out of darkness into the light, and sets us on the road to salvation. "He who does not believe is condemned already" (v. 18). "The words of Christ are at once words of judgment and grace, of life and death. For it is only by putting to death that which is old that we can come to newness of life. Now, although this refers primarily to people, it is also true of various worldly goods which bear the mark both of man's sin and the blessing of God. […] No one is freed from sin by himself or by his own efforts, no one is raised above himself or completely delivered from his own weakness, solitude or slavery; all have need of Christ, who is the model, master, liberator, saviour, and giver of life. Even

he who was with you beyond the Jordan, to whom you bore witness, here he is, baptizing, and all are going to him." [27]John answered, "No one can receive anything except what is given him from heaven. [28]You yourselves bear me witness, that I said, I am not the Christ, but I have been sent before him. [29]He who has the bride is the bridegroom; the friend of the bridegroom, who stands and hears him, rejoices greatly at the bridegroom's voice; therefore this joy of mine is now full. [30]He must increase, but I must decrease."[i]

Heb 5:4
1 Cor 4:7

Jn 1:20, 23, 27
Mt 11:10
Mk 1:2

Mt 9:15; 22:2

2 Sam 3:1

in the secular history of mankind the Gospel has acted as a leaven in the interests of liberty and progress, and it always offers itself as a leaven with regard to brotherhood, unity and peace" (Vatican II, *Ad gentes*, 8).

3:22–24. A little later on (Jn 4:2) the Evangelist makes it clear that it was not Jesus himself who baptized, but his disciples. Our Lord probably wanted them from the very beginning to get practice in exhorting people to conversion. The rite referred to here was not yet Christian Baptism—which only began after the resurrection of Christ (cf. Jn 7:39; 16:7; Mt 28:19)—but "both baptisms, that of St John the Baptist and that of our Lord's disciples [...], had a single purpose—to bring the baptized to Christ [...] and prepare the way for future faith" (St John Chrysostom, *Hom. on St John*, 29, 1).

The Gospel gives the exact time and place of this episode. Aenon is an Aramaic word meaning "wells". Salim was situated to the northeast of Samaria, south of the town of Scythopolis or Beisan, near the western bank of the Jordan, about twenty kilometres (thirteen miles) to the south of the Lake of Gennesaret.

The Gospel notes that "John had not yet been put in prison" (v. 24), thus rounding out the information given by the Synoptics (cf. Mt 4:12; Mk 1:14). We

know, therefore, that Jesus' public ministry began when John the Baptist's mission was still going on, and, particularly, that there was no competition of any kind between them; on the contrary, the Baptist, who was preparing the way of the Lord, had the joy of actually seeing his own disciples follow Jesus (cf. Jn 1:37).

3:27–29. John the Baptist is speaking in a symbolic way here, after the style of the prophets; our Lord himself does the same thing. The bridegroom is Jesus Christ. From other passages in the New Testament we know that the Church is described as the Bride (cf. Eph 5:24–32; Rev 19:7–9). This symbol of the wedding expresses the way Christ unites the Church to himself, and the way the Church is hallowed and shaped in God's own life. The Baptist rejoices to see that the Messiah has already begun his public ministry, and he recognizes the infinite distance between his position and that of Christ: his joy is full because he sees Jesus calling people and them following him.

"The friend of the bridegroom", according to Jewish custom, refers to the man who used to accompany the bridegroom at the start of the wedding and play a formal part in the wedding celebration—the best man. Obviously,

i. Some interpreters hold that the quotation continues through verse 36

Jn 8:23

Jn 3:11

Jn 1:33–34
Jn 5:20; 17:2

Mt 11:27

Jn 1:18; 20:31

³¹He who comes from above is above all; he who is of the earth belongs to the earth, and of the earth he speaks; he who comes from heaven is above all. ³²He bears witness to what he has seen and heard, yet no one receives his testimony; ³³he who receives his testimony sets his seal to this, that God is true. ³⁴For he whom God has sent utters the words of God, for it is not by measure that he gives the Spirit; ³⁵the Father loves the Son, and has given all things into his hand. ³⁶He who believes in the Son has eternal life; he who does not obey the Son shall not see life, but the wrath of God rests upon him.

---

as the Baptist says, there is a great difference between him and the bridegroom, who occupies the centre of the stage.

3:30. The Baptist knew his mission was one of preparing the way of the Lord; he was to fade into the background once the Messiah arrived, which he did faithfully and humbly. In the same way, a Christian, when engaged in apostolate, should try to keep out of the limelight and allow Christ to seek men out; he should be always emptying himself, to allow Christ to fill his life. "It is necessary for Christ to grow in you, for you to progress in your knowledge and love of him: for, the more you know him and love him, the more he grows in you. [...] Therefore, people who advance in this way need to have less self-esteem, because the more a person discovers God's greatness the less importance he gives to his own human condition" (St Thomas Aquinas, *Comm. on St John*, in loc.).

3:31–36. This paragraph shows us Christ's divinity, his relationship with the Father and the Holy Spirit, and the share those have in God's eternal life who believe in Jesus Christ. Outside of faith there is no life nor any room for hope.

4:3. This point marks the beginning of the Pharisees' hostility towards Jesus.

Because it was not yet time for him to suffer, the Lord retired to the north of Palestine, to Galilee, where the Pharisees had less influence, thereby avoiding their killing him before the time appointed by God the Father.

Divine providence does not exempt the believer from using his reason and will—as Christ did—to prudently discover what God wants him to do: "Such wisdom of the heart, such prudence will never become the prudence of the flesh that St Paul speaks of (cf. Rom 8:6), the prudence of those who are intelligent but try not to use their intelligence to seek and love our Lord. A truly prudent person is ever attentive to God's promptings and, through this vigilant listening, he receives in his soul the promise and reality of salvation. [...] Wisdom of the heart guides and governs many other virtues. Through prudence, a man learns to be daring without being rash. He will not make excuses (based on hidden motives of indolence) to avoid the effort involved in living wholeheartedly according to God's plans" (St Josemaría Escrivá, *Friends of God*, 87).

4:4–5. There were two normal routes for going from Judea to Galilee. The shorter one went through the city of Samaria; the other, which followed the Jordan, was longer. Jesus took the Samaria route, per-

Jesus and the Samaritan woman

4 ¹Now when the Lord knew that the Pharisees had heard that Jesus was making and baptizing more disciples than John ²(although Jesus himself did not baptize, but only his disciples), ³he left Judea and departed again to Galilee. ⁴He had to pass through Samaria. ⁵So he came to a city of Samaria, called Sychar, near the field that Jacob gave to his son Joseph. ⁶Jacob's well was there, and so Jesus, wearied as he was with his journey, sat down beside the well. It was about the sixth hour.

⁷There came a woman of Samaria to draw water. Jesus said to her, "Give me a drink." ⁸For his disciples had gone away into the

Jn 3:22–26

1 Cor 1:17
Lk 9:52
Gen 48:22
Josh 24:32

---

haps not just because it was shorter and busier but also to have a chance of preaching to the Samaritans. When he was approaching Samaria, near Sychar, the present-day El 'Askar, at the foot of Mount Ebal, he met this Samaritan woman.

4:6. The Gospels, particularly St John's, sometimes give us little bits of information which seem irrelevant but really are not. Like us, Jesus did get tired, he needed to take regular rest, he felt hunger and thirst; but despite his tiredness he does not waste an opportunity to do good to souls.

"Recollect yourselves and go over the scene again slowly in your minds. Jesus Christ, *perfectus Deus, perfectus homo*, is tired out from his travels and his apostolic work. Perhaps there have been times when the same thing has happened to you and you have ended up worn out, because you have reached the limit of your resources. It is a touching sight to see our Master so exhausted. He is hungry too—his disciples have gone to a neighbouring village to look for food. And he is thirsty [...].

"Whenever we get tired—in our work, in our studies, in our apostolic endeavours—when our horizon is darkened by lowering clouds, then let us turn our eyes to Jesus, to Jesus who is so

good, and who also gets tired; to Jesus who is hungry and suffers thirst. Lord, how well you make yourself understood! How lovable you are! You show us that you are just like us, in everything but sin, so that we can feel utterly sure that, together with you, we can conquer all our evil inclinations, all our faults. For neither weariness nor hunger matters, nor thirst, nor tears ... since Christ also grew weary, knew hunger, was thirsty, and wept. What is important is that we struggle to fulfil the will of our heavenly Father (cf. Jn 4:34), battling away good-heartedly, for our Lord is always at our side" (St Josemaría Escrivá, *Friends of God*, 176 and 201).

4:7. Jesus has come to save what was lost. He spares no effort in this mission. The hostility between Jews and Samaritans was proverbial; but Jesus embraced everyone, he loved all souls and he shed his blood for each and every person. He begins his conversation with this woman, by asking a favour of her—which indicates God's great respect for us: here we have Almighty God asking a mere creature to do him a favour. "Give me a drink": Jesus makes this request not just to slake his physical thirst but because his love made him thirst for the salvation of all men. When nailed to the cross he again said: "I thirst" (Jn 19:28).

67

Lk 9:53

Jn 7:38–39

Jn 8:53

Jn 6:58

Jn 6:27, 35;
7:37–39
Is 58:11

city to buy food. ⁹The Samaritan woman said to him, "How is it that you, a Jew, ask a drink of me, a woman of Samaria?" For Jews have no dealings with Samaritans. ¹⁰Jesus answered her, "If you knew the gift of God, and who it is that is saying to you, 'Give me a drink,' you would have asked him, and he would have given you living water." ¹¹The woman said to him, "Sir, you have nothing to draw with, and the well is deep; where do you get that living water? ¹²Are you greater than our father Jacob, who gave us the well, and drank from it himself, and his sons, and his cattle?" ¹³Jesus said to her, "Every one who drinks of this water will thirst again, ¹⁴but whoever drinks of the water that I shall give him will never thirst; the water that I shall give him will become in him a

---

4:9. The Samaritan woman's reply starts the dialogue and shows how well she is responding to the action of grace in her soul: her readiness to talk to Christ, who was a Jew, is the first stage in her change of heart. Later (v. 11), by taking a real interest in what Christ is saying, she opens up further to God's influence. Her religious feelings begin to revive ("our father Jacob": v. 12). Jesus rewards her and she replies truthfully: "I have no husband" (v. 17); and, seeing that Jesus has penetrated the intimacy of her conscience, she makes an act of faith: "I perceive that you are a prophet" (v. 19).

4:10. As in his dialogue with Nicodemus, Jesus makes use of common expressions to get across teachings of a much deeper nature. Everyone knows from experience that water is absolutely necessary for human life; similarly, the grace of Christ is absolutely necessary for supernatural life. The water which can truly quench man's thirst does not come from this or any other well: it is Christ's grace, the "living water" which provides eternal life.

Once again, taking occasion of human interests and preoccupations, Jesus awakens a desire for things supernatural; in the same way as he led St Peter and others away from their work as fishermen to involve them in the apostolic

work of being fishers of men, he leads the Samaritan woman away from her chore of drawing water from the well to the point where she desires to find this better water which wells up to eternal life (v. 14).

4:13–14. Our Lord's reply is surprising and really captures the woman's attention. Here is someone greater than Jacob, someone offering her water that will quench her thirst once and for all. Christ is referring to the change worked in every person by sanctifying grace, a share in God's own life, the presence of the Holy Spirit in the soul, the great gift which those who believe in him will receive.

We worry about the future, we are full of desires to be happy and at peace; a person who receives our Lord and remains united to him as a branch to the vine (cf. Jn 15:4–5) will not only slake his thirst but become a well of living water (cf. Jn 7:37–39).

4:16–19. Although the woman cannot yet realize the deep meaning of what he is saying, Jesus uses her growing interest to reveal to her his divinity, little by little: he shows that he knows about her life, the secrets of her heart; he can read her conscience. In this way he gives her enough to motivate her to make her first

spring of water welling up to eternal life." [15]The woman said to him, "Sir, give me this water, that I may not thirst, nor come here to draw."

[16]Jesus said to her, "Go, call your husband, and come here." [17]The woman answered him, "I have no husband." Jesus said to her, "You are right in saying, 'I have no husband'; [18]for you have had five husbands, and he whom you now have is not your husband; this you said truly." [19]The woman said to him, "Sir, I perceive that you are a prophet. [20]Our fathers worshipped on this mountain;* and you say that in Jerusalem is the place where men ought to worship." [21]Jesus said to her, "Woman, believe me, the hour is coming when neither on this mountain nor in Jerusalem

1 Cor 14:24–25

Deut 12:5
Ps 122

---

act of faith: "I perceive that you are a prophet." Her conversion has begun.

4:20. The origin of the Samaritan people goes back to the period of the conquest of Samaria by the Assyrians in the eighth century before Christ (cf. 2 Kings 13:24–31). They were foreigners who very quickly integrated with the Israelites in the region. After the Babylonian captivity they tried to ally themselves with the Jews for political reasons and to contribute to the rebuilding of the temple, but the Jews would have none of them. From that time onwards the Jews and the Samaritans were always hostile to each other (cf. Ezra 4:1ff; Jn 4:9).

On this occasion, the Samaritan woman, now fully aware that she is speaking to someone of authority, asks our Lord one of the key questions affecting the religious life of the two peoples: where was the right place to offer worship to God; the Jews held that only Jerusalem would do; whereas the Samaritans claimed that the shrine erected on Mount Gerizim was also legitimate (they based their claim on some passages in the Pentateuch: cf. Gen 12:7; 22:2; 33:20).

4:21–24. Jesus not only answers the question but takes advantage of it to confirm the value of the teachings of the prophets and thereby reaffirm revealed truth: the Samaritans are in the dark about many of God's plans because they do not accept any revelation not found in the first five books of Holy Scripture, that is, in the Law of Moses; the Jews, on the other hand, are much nearer the truth because they accept the whole of the Old Testament. But both Samaritans and Jews need to open themselves to the new revelation of Jesus Christ. With the coming of the Messiah, whom both peoples are awaiting, and who is the true dwelling-place of God among men (cf. Jn 2:19), the new, definitive Alliance has begun; and neither Gerizim nor Jerusalem count any more; what the Father wishes is for all to accept the Messiah, his Son, the new temple of God, by offering him a form of worship which comes right from the heart (cf. Jn 1:12; 2 Tim 2:22) and which the Spirit of God himself stirs people to render (cf. Rom 8:15).

This is why the Church's solemn Magisterium teaches that through Baptism we become true worshippers of God: "By Baptism men are grafted into the paschal mystery of Christ; they die with him, are buried with him, and rise with him. They receive the spirit of adoption as sons 'in which we cry, Abba, Father' (Rom 8:15) and thus become true adorers

2 Kings
17:29–41
Is 2:3

Rom 12:1
2 Cor 3:17

Jn 1:14

Jn 9:37; 10:25

will you worship the Father. ²²You worship what you do not know; we worship what we know, for salvation is from the Jews. ²³But the hour is coming, and now is, when the true worshippers will worship the Father in spirit and truth, for such the Father seeks to worship him. ²⁴God is spirit, and those who worship him must worship in spirit and truth." ²⁵The woman said to him, "I know that Messiah is coming (he who is called Christ); when he comes, he will show us all things." ²⁶Jesus said to her, "I who speak to you am he."

²⁷Just then the disciples came. They marvelled that he was talking with a woman, but none said, "What do you wish?" or, "Why are you talking with her?" ²⁸So the woman left her water jar, and went away into the city, and said to the people, ²⁹"Come, see a man who told me all that I ever did. Can this be the Christ?" ³⁰They went out of the city and were coming to him.

---

such as the Father seeks" (Vatican II, *Sacrosanctum Concilium*, 6).

4:25–26. This is the last stage in the Samaritan woman's conversion: she has come from acknowledging her sins to accepting the true teaching about worshipping the Father in spirit and truth. But she still has to recognize Jesus as the Messiah; on this subject she simply confesses her ignorance. Seeing that she is favourably disposed, Jesus explictly reveals that he is the Messiah: "I who speak to you am he".

These words of our Lord are especially significant: he declares that he is the Messiah, and he uses words—"I ... am he"—which evoke the words Yahweh used to reveal himself to Moses (cf. Ex 3:14) and which on Jesus' lips indicate a revelation not only of his messiahship but also of his divinity (cf. Jn 8:24, 28, 58; 18:6).

4:27. "During the course of his life on earth, Jesus our Lord had all manner of insults heaped upon him and was mistreated in every way possible. Remember the way it was rumoured that he was a trouble-maker and how he was said to be

possessed (cf. Mt 11:18)? At other times, demonstrations of his infinite Love were deliberately misinterpreted, and he was accused of being a friend of sinners (cf. Mt 9:11).

"Later on he, who personified penance and moderation, was accused of haunting the tables of the rich (cf. Lk 19:7). He was also contemptuously referred to as *fabri filius* (Mt 13:55), the carpenter's son, the worker's son, as if this were an insult. He allowed himself to be denounced as a glutton and a drunkard ... He let his enemies accuse him of everything, except that he was not chaste. On this point he sealed their lips, because he wanted us to keep a vivid memory of his immaculate example—a wonderful example of purity, of cleanliness, of light, of a love that can set the whole world on fire in order to purify it.

"For myself, I always like to consider holy purity in the light of our Lord's own behaviour. In practising this virtue, what refinement he showed! See what St John says about Jesus when *fatigatus ex itinere, sedebat sic super fontem* (Jn 4:6), wearied as he was from the journey, he was sitting by the well. [...]

³¹Meanwhile the disciples besought him, saying, "Rabbi, eat." ³²But he said to them, "I have food to eat of which you do not know." ³³So the disciples said to one another, "Has any one brought him food?" ³⁴Jesus said to them, "My food is to do the will of him who sent me, and to accomplish his work. ³⁵Do you not say, 'There are yet four months, then comes the harvest'? I tell you, lift up your eyes, and see how the fields are already white for harvest. ³⁶He who reaps receives wages, and gathers fruit for eternal life, so that sower and reaper may rejoice together. ³⁷For here the saying holds true, 'One sows and another reaps.' ³⁸I sent you to reap that for which you did not labour; others have laboured, and you have entered into their labour."

Jn 5:36; 17:4

Mt 9:37
Lk 10:2

Mic 6:15

"But tired though his body is, his thirst for souls is even greater. So when the Samaritan woman, the sinner, arrives, Christ with his priestly heart turns eagerly to save the lost sheep, and he forgets his tiredness, his hunger and his thirst.

"Our Lord was busy with this great work of charity when the Apostles came back from the village, and they *mirabantur quia cum muliere loquebatur* (Jn 4:27), they were astonished to find him talking to a woman, alone. How careful he was! What love he had for the beautiful virtue of holy purity, that virtue which helps us to be stronger, more manly, more fruitful, better able to work for God, and more capable of undertaking great things!" (St Josemaría Escrivá, *Friends of God*, 176).

4:28–30. Grace brings about an amazing change in this woman. Now her whole thinking centres around Jesus; she forgets what brought her to the well; she leaves her pitcher behind her and goes off to the town to tell people about her discovery. "The Apostles, when they were called, left their nets; this woman leaves her water jar and proclaims the Gospel, calling not just one person but influencing the whole city" (St John Chrysostom,

Hom. on St John, 33). Every genuine conversion is necessarily projected towards others, in a desire to have them share in the joy of encountering Jesus.

4:32–38. Our Lord uses the occasion to speak about a spiritual form of food — doing the will of God. He has just brought about the conversion of a sinful woman and his spirit feels replete. The conversion of souls must be the apostles' food also, and the food of all those who through priestly ordination are sacramentally associated with Christ's ministry (cf. 1 Cor 4:9–15; 2 Cor 4:7–12; 11:27–29). Apostolic work sometimes means sowing, with no apparent results, and sometimes reaping where others sowed. The apostles will reap what was generously sown by the patriarchs and prophets and especially by Christ. And they in their turn must prepare the ground, with the same generosity, so that others can later reap the harvest.

But it is not only ministers who have this apostolic role: all the faithful are called to take part in the work of apostolate: "Since Christians have different gifts they should collaborate in the work of the Gospel, each according to his opportunity, ability, charism and ministry; all who sow and reap, plant and water, should be one so that 'working

1 Jn 4:14
1 Tim 4:10

Mt 4:12
Mt 13:57
Mk 6:4
Lk 4:24
Jn 2:23

Jn 2:1–9
Mt 8:5ff

³⁹Many Samaritans from that city believed in him because of the woman's testimony, "He told me all that I ever did." ⁴⁰So when the Samaritans came to him, they asked him to stay with them; and he stayed there two days. ⁴¹And many more believed because of his word. ⁴²They said to the woman, "It is no longer because of your words that we believe, for we have heard for ourselves, and we know that this is indeed the Saviour of the world."

⁴³After the two days he departed to Galilee. ⁴⁴For Jesus himself testified that a prophet has no honour in his own country. ⁴⁵So when he came to Galilee, the Galileans welcomed him, having seen all that he had done in Jerusalem at the feast, for they too had gone to the feast.

Curing of a royal official's son—the second sign worked by Jesus

⁴⁶So he came again to Cana in Galilee, where he had made the water wine. And at Capernaum there was an official whose son

together for the same end in a free and orderly manner' they might together devote their powers to the building up of the Church" (Vatican II, *Ad gentes*, 28).

4:39–42. This episode shows a whole evangelization process at work, beginning with the Samaritan woman's enthusiasm. "The same thing happens today with those who are outside, who are not Christians: they receive tidings of Christ through Christian friends; like that woman, they learn of Christ through the Church; then they come to Christ, that is, they believe in Christ through this report, and then Jesus stays two days among them and many more believe, and believe more firmly, that he indeed is the Saviour of the world" (St Augustine, *In Ioann. Evang.*, 15, 33).

4:46. St John is speaking about a royal official, probably in the service of Herod Antipas who, although he was only tetrarch or governor of Galilee (cf. Lk 3:1), was also referred to as king (cf. Mk 6:14). The official, therefore, would have been someone of high rank (v. 51), who

lived in Capernaum, a town with a customs post. This is why St Jerome thought he must have been a *palatinus*, a palace courtier, as the corresponding Greek word implies.

4:48. Jesus seems to be addressing not so much the official as the people of Galilee who flock to him to get him to perform miracles and work wonders. On another occasion our Lord reproaches the towns of Chorazin, Bethsaida and Capernaum for their disbelief (Mt 11:21–23), because the miracles he worked there would have been enough to move the Phoenician cities of Tyre and Sidon, and even Sodom itself, to do penance. The Galileans in general were more inclined to watch him perform miracles than listen to his preaching. Later on, after the miracle of the multiplication of the loaves, they will look for Jesus to make him king—but they are slower to believe when he tells them about the Eucharist (Jn 6:15, 53, 62). Jesus asks people to have a strong, committed faith which, though it may draw support from miracles, does not require them. Be that as it

was ill. [47]When he heard that Jesus had come from Judea to Galilee, he went and begged him to come down and heal his son, for he was at the point of death. [48]Jesus therefore said to him, "Unless you see signs and wonders you will not believe." [49]The official said to him, "Sir, come down before my child dies." [50]Jesus said to him, "Go, your son will live." The man believed the word that Jesus spoke to him and went his way. [51]As he was going down, his servants met him and told him that his son was living. [52]So he asked them the hour when he began to mend, and they said to him, "Yesterday at the seventh hour the fever left him." [53]The father knew that was the hour when Jesus had said to him, "Your son will live"; and he himself believed, and all his household. [54]This was now the second sign that Jesus did when he had come from Judea to Galilee.

Lk 7:2

Jn 2:18
1 Cor 1:22

Acts 16:15–31

Jn 2:11–23

---

may, in all ages God continues to work miracles, which help bolster our faith.

"I'm not one for miracles. I have told you that in the Holy Gospel I can find more than enough miracles to confirm my faith. But I can't help pitying those Christians—pious people, 'apostles' many of them—who smile at the idea of extraordinary ways, of supernatural events. I feel the urge to tell them: Yes, this is still the age of miracles. We too would work them if we had faith!" (St Josemaría Escrivá, *The Way*, 583).

4:49–50. In spite of Jesus' apparent coldness, the official keeps trying: "Sir, come down before my child dies". Although his faith is imperfect, it did bring him to travel the 33 kilometres (20 miles) between Capernaum and Cana, and despite his important position here he was, begging our Lord for help. Jesus likes the man's perseverance and humility; he rewards his faith: "'*Si habueritis fidem, sicut granum sinapis!* If your faith were the size of a mustard seed ... !' What promises are contained in this exclamation of the Master!" (*The Way*, 585).

The Fathers compare this miracle with that of the centurion's servant, contrasting the amazing faith of the centurion—from the start—with the initially imperfect faith of this official from Capernaum. St John Chrysostom comments: "Here was a robust faith [in the case of this official]; therefore, Jesus made him the promise, so that we might learn from this man's devotion; his faith was as yet imperfect, and he did not clearly realize that Jesus could effect the cure at a distance; thus, the Lord, by not agreeing to go down to the man's house, wished us to learn the need to have faith" (*Hom. on St John*, 35).

4:53. The miracle is so convincing that this man and all his family become believers. All parents should do what they can to bring their household to the faith. As St Paul says, "If anyone does not provide for his relatives, and especially for his own family, he has disowned the faith, and is worse than an unbeliever" (1 Tim 5:8). In Acts 16:14, we are told that Lydia brought her whole household along with her to be baptized; Acts 18:8 mentions Crispus, the ruler of the synagogue, doing the same thing, as does the prison warden (Acts 16:33).

3. JESUS REVEALS HIS DIVINITY

Curing of a paralyzed man

5 ¹After this there was a feast of the Jews, and Jesus went up to Jerusalem. ²Now there is in Jerusalem by the Sheep Gate a pool, in Hebrew called Bethzatha,ʲ which has five porticoes. ³In these lay a multitude of invalids, blind, lame, paralyzed.ᵏ ⁵One man was there, who had been ill for thirty-eight years. ⁶When Jesus saw him and knew that he had been lying there a long time, he said to him, "Do you want to be healed?" ⁷The sick man answered him, "Sir, I have no man to put me into the pool when the water is troubled, and while I am going another steps down before me." ⁸Jesus said to him, "Rise, take up your pallet, and

Mt 9:6

5:1. We cannot be certain what festival this was; it probably refers to the Passover, known the world over at the time as the national festival of the Jewish people. But it could refer to another festival, Pentecost perhaps.

5:2. This pool was also called the "Probatic" pool because it was located on the outskirts of Jerusalem, beside the Probatic Gate or Sheep Gate (cf. Neh 3:1–32; 12:39) through which came the livestock to be sacrificed in the temple. Around the end of the nineteenth century the remains of a pool were discovered: excavated out of rock, it was rectangular in shape and was surrounded by four galleries or porches, with a fifth porch dividing the pool into two.

5:3–4. The Fathers teach that this pool is a symbol of Christian Baptism; but that whereas the pool of Bethzatha cured physical ailments, Baptism cures those of the soul; in Bethzatha's case only one person was cured, now and again; Baptism is available to everyone, at all

times; in both cases God's power is shown through the medium of water (cf. Chrysostom, *Hom. on St John*, 36, 1).

The Sixto-Clementine edition of the Vulgate includes here, as a second part of v. 3 and all v. 4: "*Exspectantium aquae motum. ⁴Angelus autem Domini descendebat secundum tempus in piscinam et movebatur aqua. Et qui prior descendisset in piscinam post motionem aquae sanus fiebat a quacumque detinebatur infirmitate*" [which translates as the RSV note k below]. The New Vulgate, however, omits this passage, assigning it to a footnote, because it does not appear in important Greek codexes and papyri, nor in many ancient translations.

5:14. The man may have come to the temple to thank God for his cure. Jesus goes over to him and reminds him that the health of the soul is more important than physical health.

Our Lord uses holy fear of God as motivation in the struggle against sin: "Sin no more, that nothing worse befall you". This holy fear is born out of

---

j. Other ancient authorities read *Bethesda*, others *Bethsaida* **k.** Other ancient authorities insert, wholly or in part, *waiting for the moving of the water;* ⁴*for an angel of the Lord went down at certain seasons into the pool, and troubled the water: whoever stepped in first after the troubling of the water was healed of whatever disease he had*

walk." ⁹And at once the man was healed, and he took up his pallet and walked.

Now that day was the sabbath. ¹⁰So the Jews said to the man who was cured, "It is the sabbath, it is not lawful for you to carry your pallet." ¹¹But he answered them, "The man who healed me said to me, 'Take up your pallet, and walk.'" ¹²They asked him, "Who is the man who said to you, 'Take up your pallet, and walk'?" ¹³Now the man who had been healed did not know who it was, for Jesus had withdrawn, as there was a crowd in the place. ¹⁴Afterward, Jesus found him in the temple, and said to him, "See, you are well! Sin no more, that nothing worse befall you." ¹⁵The man went away and told the Jews that it was Jesus who had healed him. ¹⁶And this was why the Jews persecuted Jesus,

Jn 9:14

Jer 17:21
Lk 6:2

Lk 5:24

Jn 8:11

Mt 12:14

---

respect for God our Father; it is perfectly compatible with love. Just as children love and respect their parents and try to avoid annoying them partly because they are afraid of being punished, so we should fight against sin firstly because it is an offence against God, but also because we can be punished in this life and, above all, in the next.

5:16–18. The Law of Moses established the sabbath as a weekly day of rest. Through keeping the sabbath the Jews felt they were imitating God, who rested from the work of creation on the seventh day. St Thomas Aquinas observes that Jesus rejects this strict interpretation: "(The Jews), in their desire to imitate God, did nothing on the sabbath, as if God on that day had ceased absolutely to act. It is true that he rested on the sabbath from his work of creating new creatures, but he is always continually at work, maintaining them in existence. [...] God is the cause of all things in the sense that he also maintains them in existence; for if for one moment he were to stop exercising his power, at that very moment everything that nature contains would cease to exist" (*Comm. on St John*, in loc.).

"My Father is working still, and I am working": we have already said that God is continually acting. Since the Son acts together with the Father, who with the Holy Spirit are the one and only God, our Lord Jesus Christ, the Son of God, can say that he is always working. These words of Jesus contain an implicit reference to his divinity: the Jews realize this and they want to kill him because they consider it blasphemous. "We all call God our Father, who is in heaven (Is 63:16; 64:8). Therefore, they were angry, not at this, that he said God was his Father, but that he said it in quite another way than men. Notice: the Jews understand what Arians do not understand. Arians affirm the Son to be not equal to the Father, and that was why their heresy was driven from the Church. Here, even the blind, even the slayers of Christ, understand the words of Christ" (St Augustine, *In Ioann. Evang.*, 17, 16). We call God our Father because through grace we are his adopted children; Jesus calls him his Father because he is his Son by nature. This is why he says after the Resurrection: "I am ascending to my Father and your Father" (Jn 20:17), making a clear distinction between the two ways of being a son of God.

Jn 9:4

Jn 7:1, 19, 30;
10:33–36

because he did this on the sabbath. [17]But Jesus answered them, "My Father is working still, and I am working." [18]This was why the Jews sought all the more to kill him, because he not only broke the sabbath* but also called God his Father, making himself equal with God.

The authority of the Son of God

Jn 3:11, 32;
5:30

Jn 3:35

[19]Jesus said to them, "Truly, truly, I say to you, the Son can do nothing of his own accord, but only what he sees the Father doing; for whatever he does, that the Son does likewise. [20]For the

---

5:19. Jesus speaks of the equality and also the distinction between Father and Son. The two are equal: all the Son's power is the Father's, all the Son does the Father does; but they are two distinct persons: which is why the Son does what he has seen the Father do.

These words of our Lord should not be taken to mean that the Son sees what the Father does and then does it himself, like a disciple imitating his master; he says what he says to show that the Father's powers are communicated to the Son through generation. The word "see" is used because men come to know things through the senses, particularly through sight; to say that the Son sees what the Father does is a way of referring to all the powers which he receives from him for all eternity (cf. St Thomas Aquinas, *Comm. on St John,* in loc.).

5:20–21. When he says that the Father shows the Son "all that he himself is doing", this means that Christ can do the same as the Father. Thus, when Jesus does things which are proper to God, he is testifying to his divinity through them (cf. v. 36).

"Greater works": this may be a reference to the miracles Jesus will work during his lifetime and to his authority to execute judgment. But *the* miracle of Jesus was his own resurrection, the cause and pledge of our own (cf. 1 Cor

15:20ff), and our passport to supernatural life. Christ, like his Father, has unlimited power to communicate life. This teaching is developed in verses 22–29.

5:22–30. Authority to judge has also been given by the Father to the Incarnate Word. Whoever does not believe in Christ and in his word will be condemned (cf. 3:18). We must accept Jesus Christ's lordship; by doing so we honour the Father; if we do not know the Son we do not know the Father who sent him (v. 23). Through accepting Christ, through accepting his word, we gain eternal life and are freed from condemnation. He, who has taken on human nature which he will retain for ever, has been established as our judge, and his judgment is just, because he seeks to fulfil the will of the Father who sent him, and he does nothing on his own account: in other words, his human will is perfectly at one with his divine will; which is why Jesus can say that he does not do his own will but the will of him who sent him.

5:22. God, being Creator of the world, is the supreme Judge of all creation. He alone can know with absolute certainty whether the people and things he has created achieve the end he has envisaged for them. Jesus Christ, the Incarnate Word, has received divine authority (cf.

Father loves the Son, and shows him all that he himself is doing; and greater works than these will he show him, that you may marvel. [21]For as the Father raises the dead and gives them life, so also the Son gives life to whom he will. [22]The Father judges no one, but has given all judgment to the Son, [23]that all may honour the Son, even as they honour the Father. He who does not honour the Son does not honour the Father who sent him. [24]Truly, truly, I say to you, he who hears my word and believes him who sent me, has eternal life; he does not come into judgment, but has passed from death to life.

Deut 32:39
1 Sam 2:6
2 Kings 5:7
Dan 7, 10, 13, 14
Acts 10:42
Lk 10:16
Phil 2:10, 11
1 Jn 2:23
Jn 3:16, 18; 8:51
1 Jn 3:14

Mt 11:27; 28:18; Dan 7:14), including authority to judge mankind. Now, it is God's will that everyone should be saved: Christ did not come to condemn the world but to save it (cf. Jn 12:47). Only someone who refuses to accept the divine mission of the Son puts himself outside the pale of salvation. As the Church's Magisterium teaches: "He claimed judicial power as received from his Father, when the Jews accused him of breaking the sabbath by the miraculous cure of a sick man. [...] In this power is included the right of rewarding and punishing all men, even in this life" (Pius XI, *Quas primas, Dz-Sch* 3677). Jesus Christ, therefore, is the Judge of the living and the dead, and will reward everyone according to his works (cf. 1 Pet 1:17).

"We have, I admit, a rigorous account to give of our sins; but who will be our judge? The Father [...] has given all judgment to the Son. Let us be comforted: the eternal Father has placed our cause in the hands of our Redeemer himself. St Paul encourages us, saying, Who is [the judge] who is to condemn us? It is Jesus Christ, who died [...] who indeed intercedes for us (Rom 8:34). It is the Saviour himself, who, in order that he should not condemn us to eternal death, has condemned himself to death for our sake, and who, not content with this, still continues to intercede for us in heaven

with God his Father" (St Alphonsus Liguori, *The Love of Our Lord Jesus Christ*, chap. 3).

5:24. There is also a close connexion between hearing the word of Christ and believing in him who has sent him, that is, in the Father. Whatever Jesus Christ says is divine revelation; therefore, accepting Jesus' words is equivalent to believing in God the Father: "He who believes in me, believes not in me, but in him who sent me. [...] For I have not spoken on my own authority; the Father who sent me has himself given me commandment what to say and what to speak" (Jn 12:44, 49).

A person with faith is on the way to eternal life, because even in this earthly life he is sharing in divine life, which is eternal; but he has not yet attained eternal life in a definitive way (for he can lose it), nor in a full way: "Beloved, we are God's children now; it does not yet appear what we shall be, but we know that when he appears we shall be like him" (1 Jn 3:2). If a person stays firm in the faith and lives up to its demands, God's judgment will not condemn him but save him.

Therefore, it makes sense to strive, with the help of grace, to live a life consistent with the faith: "If men go to so much trouble and effort to live here a little longer, ought they not strive so much

Mt 8:22
Eph 2:5f; 5:14
Jn 1:1–4; 6:53,
57

Dan 7:13, 14,
22

Jn 6:40
Dan12:2
Mt 16:27

Jn 5:19; 6:38

Jn 8:14

Jn 5:36–37
1 Jn 5:9

²⁵"Truly, truly, I say to you, the hour is coming, and now is, when the dead will hear the voice of the Son of God, and those who hear will live. ²⁶For as the Father has life in himself, so he has granted the Son also to have life in himself, ²⁷and has given him authority to execute judgment, because he is the Son of man. ²⁸Do not marvel at this; for the hour is coming when all who are in the tombs will hear his voice ²⁹and come forth, those who have done good, to the resurrection of life, and those who have done evil, to the resurrection of judgment.

³⁰"I can do nothing on my own authority; as I hear, I judge; and my judgment is just, because I seek not my own will but the will of him who sent me. ³¹If I bear witness to myself, my testimony is not true; ³²there is another who bears witness to me, and I know that the testimony which he bears to me is true. ³³You sent to John,

harder to live eternally?" (St Augustine, *De verb. Dom. serm.*, 64).

5:25–30. These verses bring the first part of our Lord's discourse to a close (it runs from 5:19 to 5:47); its core is a revelation about his relationship with his Father. To understand the statement our Lord makes here we need to remember that, because he is a single (divine) person, a single subject of operations, a single I, he is expressing in human words not only his sentiments as a man but also the deepest dimension of his being: he is the Son of God, both in his generation in eternity by the Father, and in his generation in time through taking up human nature. Hence Jesus Christ has a profound awareness (so profound that we cannot even imagine it) of his Sonship, which leads him to treat his Father with a very special intimacy, with love and also with respect; he is aware also of his equality with the Father; therefore when he speaks about the Father having given him life (v. 26) or authority (v. 27), it is not that he has received part of the Father's life or authority: he has received absolutely all of it, without the Father losing any.

"Do you perceive how their equality is shown and that they differ in one respect only, namely, that one is the Father, while the other is the Son? The expression 'he has given' implies this distinction only, and shows that all the other attributes are equal and without difference. From this it is clear that he does everything with as much authority and power as the Father and is not endowed with power from some outside source, for he has life as the Father has" (St John Chrysostom, *Hom. on St John*, 39, 3).

One of the amazing things about these passages of the Gospel is how Jesus manages to express the sentiments of God-Man despite the limitations of human language. Christ, true God, true man, is a mystery which the Christian should contemplate even though he cannot understand it: he feels bathed in a light so strong that it is beyond understanding, yet fills his soul with faith and with a desire to worship his Lord.

5:31–40. Because Jesus is Son of God, his own word is self-sufficient, it needs no corroboration (cf. 8:18); but, as on other occasions, he accommodates himself to human customs and to the mental outlook of his hearers: he anticipates a possible objection from the Jews to the effect that it is not enough for a person to

and he has borne witness to the truth. ³⁴Not that the testimony which I receive is from man; but I say this that you may be saved. ³⁵He was a burning and shining lamp, and you were willing to rejoice for a while in his light. ³⁶But the testimony which I have is greater than that of John; for the works which the Father has granted me to accomplish, these very works which I am doing, bear me witness that the Father has sent me. ³⁷And the Father who sent me has himself borne witness to me. His voice you have never heard, his form you have never seen; ³⁸and you do not have his word abiding in you, for you do not believe him whom he has sent. ³⁹You search the scriptures, because you think that in them you have eternal life; and it is they that bear witness to me; ⁴⁰yet you refuse to come to me that you may have life. ⁴¹I do not receive glory from men. ⁴²But I know that you have not the love of God

Jn 1:19–34

Jn 1:8
Lk 1:17

Jn 1:33; 3:2
1 Jn 5:9

Deut 4:12
Mt 3:17

Lk 24:27, 44
2 Tim 3:15–17
1 Pet 1:11

---

testify in his own cause (cf. Deut 19:15) and he explains that what he is saying is endorsed by four witnesses—John the Baptist, his own miracles, the Father, and the Sacred Scriptures of the Old Testament.

John the Baptist bore witness that Jesus was the Son of God (1:34). Although Jesus had no need to have recourse to any man's testimony, not even that of a great prophet, John's testimony was given for the sake of the Jews, that they might recognize the Messiah. Jesus can also point to another testimony, better than that of the Baptist—the miracles he has worked, which are, for anyone who examines them honestly, unmistakable signs of his divine power, which comes from the Father; Jesus' miracles, then, are a form of witness the Father bears concerning his Son, whom he has sent into the world. The Father manifests the divinity of Jesus on other occasions—at his Baptism (cf. 1:31–34); at the Transfiguration (cf. Mt 17:1–8), and later, in the presence of the whole crowd (cf. Jn 12:28–30).

Jesus appeals to another divine testimony—that of the Sacred Scriptures. These speak of him, but the Jews fail to grasp the Scriptures' true meaning, because they read them without letting themselves be enlightened by him whom God has sent and in whom all the prophecies are fulfilled: "The economy of the Old Testament was deliberately so orientated that it should prepare for and declare in prophecy the coming of Christ, redeemer of all men, and of the messianic kingdom (cf. Lk 24:44; Jn 5:39; 1 Pet 1:10), and should indicate it by means of different types (cf. 1 Cor 10:11). [...] Christians should accept with veneration these writings which give expression to a lively sense of God, which are a storehouse of sublime teaching on God and of sound wisdom on human life, as well as a wonderful treasury of prayers; in them, too, the mystery of our salvation is present in a hidden way" (Vatican II, *Dei Verbum*, 15).

5:41–47. Jesus identifies three obstacles preventing his hearers from recognizing that he is the Messiah and Son of God—their lack of love of God, their striving after human glory and their prejudiced interpretation of sacred texts. His defence of his own actions and of his relationship with the Father might lead his adversaries to think that he was looking for human glory. But the testimonies he has

Jn 7:18
Mt 24:5

within you. ⁴³I have come in my Father's name, and you do not receive me; if another comes in his own name, him you will receive. ⁴⁴How can you believe, who receive glory from one another and do not seek the glory that comes from the only God?

Jn 12:43
Mt 23:5–7
Rom 2:29
Deut 31:26
Jn 7:19
Gen 3:15; 49:10
Deut 18:15
Lk 16:31

⁴⁵Do not think that I shall accuse you to the Father; it is Moses who accuses you, on whom you set your hope. ⁴⁶If you believed Moses, you would believe me, for he wrote of me. ⁴⁷But if you do not believe his writings, how will you believe my words?"

4. JESUS IS THE BREAD OF LIFE

Miracle of the loaves and fish

Mt 14:13–21
Mk 6:32–44
Lk 9:10–17

6 ¹After this Jesus went to the other side of the Sea of Galilee, which is the Sea of Tiberias. ²And a multitude followed him,

adduced (the Baptist, the miracles, the Father and the Scriptures) show clearly that it is not he who is seeking his glory, and that the Jews oppose him not out of love of God or in defence of God's honour, but for unworthy reasons or because of their merely human outlook.

The Old Testament, therefore, leads a person towards recognizing who Jesus Christ is (cf. Jn 1:45; 2:17, 22; 5:39, 46; 12:16, 41); yet the Jews remain unbelievers because their attitude is wrong: they have reduced the messianic promises in the sacred books to the level of mere nationalistic aspirations. This outlook, which is in no way supernatural, closes their soul to Jesus' words and actions and prevents them from seeing that the ancient prophecies are coming true in him (cf. 2 Cor 3:14–16).

6:1. This is the second lake formed by the river Jordan. It is sometimes described in the Gospels as the "lake of Gennesaret" (Lk 5:1), because that is the name of the area on the north-eastern bank of the lake, and sometimes as the "Sea of Galilee" (Mt 4:18; 15:29; Mk 1:16; 7:31), after the region in which it is

located. St John also calls it the "Sea of Tiberias" (cf. 21:1), after the city of that name which Herod Antipas founded and named after the Emperor Tiberius. In Jesus' time there were a number of towns on the shore of this lake—Tiberias, Magdala, Capernaum, Bethsaida, etc.— and the shore was often the setting for his preaching.

6:2. Although St John refers to only seven miracles and does not mention others which are reported in the Synoptics, in this verse and more expressly at the end of his Gospel (20:30; 21:25) he says that the Lord worked many miracles; the reason why the Evangelist, under God's inspiration, chose these seven must surely be because they best suited his purpose—to highlight certain facets of the mystery of Christ. He now goes on to recount the miracle of the multiplication of the loaves and the fish, a miracle directly connected with the discourses at Capernaum in which Jesus presents himself as "the bread of life" (6:35, 48).

6:4. St John's Gospel often mentions Jewish feasts when referring to events in

because they saw the signs which he did on those who were diseased. ³Jesus went up into the hills, and there sat down with his disciples. ⁴Now the Passover, the feast of the Jews, was at hand. ⁵Lifting up his eyes, then, and seeing that a multitude was coming to him, Jesus said to Philip, "How are we to buy bread, so that these people may eat?" ⁶This he said to test them, for he himself knew what he would do. ⁷Philip answered him, "Two hundred denarii[1] would not buy enough bread for each of them to get a little." ⁸One of his disciples, Andrew, Simon Peter's brother, said to him, ⁹"There is a lad here who has five barley loaves and two fish; but what are they among so many?" ¹⁰Jesus said, "Make the people sit down." Now there was much grass in the place; so the men sat down, in number about five thousand. ¹¹Jesus then took the loaves, and when he had given thanks, he distributed them to those who were seated; so also the fish, as much as they wanted.

Mt 5:1
Jn 2:13
Jn 11:15

Lk 22:1

2 Kings
4:42–44

---

our Lord's public ministry—as is the case here (cf. pp. 22–24).

Shortly before this Passover Jesus works the miracle of the multiplication of the loaves and the fish, which prefigures the Christian Easter and the mystery of the Blessed Eucharist, as he himself explains in the discourse, beginning at v. 26 in which he promises himself as nourishment for our souls.

6:5–9. Jesus is sensitive to people's material and spiritual needs. Here we see him take the initiative to satisfy the hunger of the crowd of people who have been following him.

Through these conversations and the miracle he is going to work, Jesus also teaches his disciples to trust in him whenever they meet up with difficulties in their apostolic endeavours in the future: they should engage in them using whatever resources they have—even if they are plainly inadequate, as was the case with the five loaves and two fish. He will supply what is lacking. In the Christian life we must put what we have at the service of our Lord, even if we do

not think it amounts to very much. He can make meagre resources productive.

"We must, then, have faith and not be dispirited. We must not be stopped by any kind of human calculation. To overcome the obstacles we have to throw ourselves into the task so that the very effort we make will open up new paths" (St J. Escrivá, *Christ Is Passing By*, 160).

6:10. The Evangelist gives us an apparently unimportant piece of information: "there was much grass in the place." This indicates that the miracle took place in the height of the Palestinian spring, very near the Passover, as mentioned in v. 4. There are very few big meadows in Palestine; even today there is one on the eastern bank of the lake of Gennesaret, called el-Batihah, where five thousand people could fit seated: it may have been the site of this miracle.

6:11. The account of the miracle begins with almost the very same words as those which the Synoptics and St Paul use to describe the institution of the Eucharist (cf. Mt 26:26; Mk 14:22; Lk 22:19; 1

1. The denarius was a day's wage for a labourer

Deut 18:15

Jn 12:13; 18:36

[12]And when they had eaten their fill, he told his disciples, "Gather up the fragments left over, that nothing may be lost." [13]So they gathered them up and filled twelve baskets with fragments from the five barley loaves, left by those who had eaten. [14]When the people saw the sign which he had done, they said, "This is indeed the prophet who is to come into the world!"

[15]Perceiving then that they were about to come and take him by force to make him king, Jesus withdrew again to the hills by himself.

Jesus walks on water

Mt 14:22f
Mk 6:45–52

[16]When evening came, his disciples went down to the sea, [17]got into a boat, and started across the sea to Capernaum. It was now

---

Cor 11:25). This indicates that the miracle, in addition to being an expression of Jesus' mercy towards the needy, is a symbol of the Blessed Eucharist, about which our Lord will speak a little later on (cf. Jn 6:26–58).

6:12–13. The profusion of detail shows how accurate this narrative is—the names of the apostles who address our Lord (vv. 5, 8), the fact that they were barley loaves (v. 9), the boy who provided the wherewithal (v. 9) and, finally, Jesus telling them to gather up the leftovers.

This miracle shows Jesus' divine power over matter, and his largesse recalls the abundance of messianic benefits which the prophets had foretold (cf. Jer 31:14).

Christ's instruction to pick up the left-overs teaches us that material resources are gifts of God and should not be wasted: they should be used in a spirit of poverty (cf. the note on Mk 6:42). In this connexion Paul VI pointed out that "after liberally feeding the crowds, the Lord told his disciples to gather up what was left over, lest anything should be lost (cf. Jn 6:12). What an excellent lesson in thrift—in the finest and fullest meaning of the term—for our age, given as it is to

wastefulness! It carries with it the condemnation of a whole concept of society wherein consumption tends to become an end in itself, with contempt for the needy, and to the detriment, ultimately, of those very people who believed themselves to be its beneficiaries, having become incapable of perceiving that man is called to a higher destiny" (Paul VI, Address to participants at the World Food Conference, 9 November 1974).

6:14–15. The faith which the miracle causes in the hearts of these people is still very imperfect: they recognize him as the Messiah promised in the Old Testament (cf. Deut 18:15), but they are thinking in terms of an earthly, political messianism; they want to make him king because they think the Messiah's function is to free them from Roman domination.

Our Lord, who later on (vv. 26–27) will explain the true meaning of the multiplication of the loaves and the fish, simply goes away, to avoid the people proclaiming him for what he is not. In his dialogue with Pilate (cf. Jn 18:36) he will explain that his kingship "is not of this world": "The Gospels clearly show that for Jesus anything that would alter his mission as the Servant of Yahweh was a temptation (cf. Mt 4:8; Lk 4:5). He does

dark, and Jesus had not yet come to them. [18]The sea rose because Mt 8:24
a strong wind was blowing. [19]When they had rowed about three or Ps 77:19
four miles,[m] they saw Jesus walking on the sea and drawing near
to the boat. They were frightened, [20]but he said to them, "It is I; do
not be afraid." [21]Then they were glad to take him into the boat,
and immediately the boat was at the land to which they were
going.

The people look for Jesus

[22]On the next day the people who remained on the other side of
the sea saw that there had been only one boat there, and that Jesus
had not entered the boat with his disciples, but that his disciples
had gone away alone. [23]However, boats from Tiberias came near Jn 6:11

---

not accept the position of those who
mixed the things of God with merely
political attitudes (cf. Mt 22:21; Mk
12:17; Jn 18:36). [...] The perspective of
his mission is much deeper. It consists in
complete salvation through transforming,
peacemaking, pardoning, and reconciling
love. There is no doubt, moreover, that
all this makes many demands on the
Christian who wishes truly to serve his
least brethren, the poor, the needy, the
outcast; in a word, all those who in their
lives reflect the sorrowing face of the
Lord (cf. *Lumen gentium*, 8)" (John Paul
II, Opening Address to the third general
conference of Latin American Bishops,
28 January 1979).

Christianity, therefore, must not be
confused with any social or political ide-
ology, however excellent. "I do not app-
rove of committed Christians in the
world forming a political-religious movement. That would be madness, even if it
were motivated by a desire to spread the
spirit of Christ in all the activities of
men. What we have to do is put God in
the heart of every single person, no
matter who he is. Let us try to speak then
in such a way that every Christian is able
to bear witness to the faith he professes

by example and word in his own circum-
stances, which are determined alike by
his place in the Church and in civil life,
as well as by ongoing events.

"By the very fact of being a man, a
Christian has a full right to live in the
world. If he lets Christ live and reign in
his heart, he will feel—quite noticeably
—the saving effectiveness of our Lord
in everything he does" (St Josemaría
Escrivá, *Christ Is Passing By*, 183).

6:16–21. It seems the disciples were disconcerted because darkness had fallen,
the sea was getting rough and Jesus had
still not appeared. But our Lord does not
abandon them; when they had been
rowing for some five kilometres (three
miles), he arrives unexpectedly, walking
on the water—to strengthen their faith,
which was still weak (cf. the notes on Mt
14:22–23 and Mk 6:48, 52).

In meditating on this episode Christian tradition has seen the boat as symbolizing the Church, which will have to
cope with many difficulties and which
our Lord has promised to help all
through the centuries (cf. Mt 28:20); the
Church, therefore, will always remain
firm. St Thomas Aquinas comments:

m. Greek *twenty-five or thirty stadia*

the place where they ate the bread after the Lord had given thanks. [24]So when the people saw that Jesus was not there, nor his disciples, they themselves got into the boats and went to Capernaum, seeking Jesus. [25]When they found him on the other side of the sea, they said to him, "Rabbi, when did you come here?"

The discourse on the Bread of Life

[26]Jesus answered them, "Truly, truly, I say to you, you seek me, not because you saw signs, but because you ate your fill of the loaves. [27]Do not labour for the food which perishes, but for the food which endures to eternal life, which the Son of man will give

Jn 4:14; 5:36
Mt 16:12

"The wind symbolizes the temptations and persecution the Church will suffer due to lack of love. For, as St Augustine says, when love grows cold, the sea becomes rougher and the boat begins to founder. Yet the wind, the storm, the waves and the darkness will fail to put it off course and wreck it" (*Comm. on St John*, in loc.).

6:26. Our Lord begins by pointing out that their attitudes are wrong: if they have the right attitude they will be able to understand his teaching in the eucharistic discourse. "You seek me", St Augustine comments, "'for the flesh, not for the spirit. How many seek Jesus for no other purpose than that he may do them good in this present life! [...] Scarcely ever is Jesus sought for Jesus' sake" (*In Ioann. Evang.*, 25, 10).

This verse marks the beginning of the discourse on the bread of life which goes up to v. 58. It opens with an introduction in the form of a dialogue between Jesus and the Jews (vv. 25–34), in which our Lord reveals himself as the bringer of the messianic gifts. Then comes the first part of the discourse (vv. 35–47), in which Jesus presents himself as the Bread of Life, in the sense that faith in him is food for eternal life. In the second part (vv.

48–58) Christ reveals the mystery of the Eucharist: he is the Bread of Life who gives himself sacramentally as genuine food.

6:27. Bodily food helps keep us alive in this world; spiritual food sustains and develops supernatural life, which will last forever in heaven. This food, which only God can give us, consists mainly in the gift of faith and sanctifying grace. Through God's infinite love we are given, in the Blessed Eucharist, the very author of these gifts, Jesus Christ, as nourishment for our souls.

"On him has God the Father set his seal": our Lord here refers to the authority by virtue of which he can give men the gifts he has referred to: for, being God and man, Jesus' human nature is the instrument by means of which the second Person of the Blessed Trinity acts. St Thomas Aquinas comments on this sentence as follows: "What the Son of Man will give he possesses through his superiority over all other men in his singular and outstanding fulness of grace ... . When a seal is impressed on wax, the wax receives the complete form of the seal. So it is that the Son received the entire form of the Father. This occurred in two ways; eternally (eternal genera-

to you; for on him has God the Father set his seal." [28]Then they said to him, "What must we do, to be doing the works of God?" [29]Jesus answered them, "This is the work of God, that you believe in him whom he has sent." [30]So they said to him, "Then what sign do you do, that we may see, and believe you? What work do you perform? [31]Our fathers ate the manna in the wilderness; as it is written, 'He gave them bread from heaven to eat.'" [32]Jesus then said to them, "Truly, truly, I say to you, it was not Moses who gave you the bread from heaven; my Father gives you the true bread from heaven. [33]For the bread of God is that which comes down from heaven, and gives life to the world." [34]They said to him, "Lord, give us this bread always."

1 Jn 3:23

Jn 2:18
Mk 8:11
Ex 16:13–14
Ps 78:24f
Wis 16:20

Jn 6:49

Jn 6:51

---

tion), which is not referred to here because the seal and the sealed are different in nature from one another; what is referred to here is the other manner, that is, the mystery of the Incarnation, whereby God the Father impressed on human nature the Word, who is the reflection and the very stamp of God's nature, as Hebrews 1:3 says" (*Comm. on St John*, in loc.).

6:28–34. This dialogue between Jesus and his hearers is reminiscent of the episode of the Samaritan woman (cf. Jn 4:11–15). On that occasion Jesus was speaking about water springing up to eternal life; here, he speaks of bread coming down from heaven to give life to the world. There, the woman was asking Jesus if he was greater than Jacob; here the people want to know if he can compare with Moses (cf. Ex 16:13). "The Lord spoke of himself in a way that made him seem superior to Moses, for Moses never dared to say that he would give food which would never perish but would endure to eternal life. Jesus promises much more than Moses. Moses promised a kingdom, and a land flowing with milk and honey, good health and other temporal blessings [...], plenty for the belly, but food which perishes; whereas Christ promised food which

never perishes but which endures forever" (St Augustine, *In Ioann. Evang.*, 25:12).

These people know that the manna—food which the Jews collected every day during their journey through the wilderness (cf. Ex 16:13ff)—symbolized messianic blessings; which was why they asked our Lord for a dramatic sign like the manna. But there was no way they could suspect that the manna was a figure of a great supernatural messianic gift which Christ was bringing to mankind—the Blessed Eucharist. In this dialogue and in the first part of the discourse (vv. 35–47), the main thing Jesus is trying to do is bring them to make an act of faith in him, so that he can then openly reveal to them the mystery of the Blessed Eucharist—that he is the bread "which comes down from heaven, and gives life to the world" (v. 33). Also, St Paul explains that the manna and the other marvels which happened in the wilderness were a clear prefiguring of Jesus Christ (cf. 1 Cor 10:3–4). The disbelieving attitude of these Jews prevented them from accepting what Jesus revealed. To accept the mystery of the Eucharist, faith is required, as Paul VI stressed: "In the first place we want to remind you that the Eucharist is a very great mystery; strictly speaking, to use

Jesus is the one who reveals the Father

Jn 4:14; 6:48; 7:37

Jn 6:26–29

Jn 17:6–8
Mt 11:28

Jn 4:34
Mt 26:39
Jn 10:28f; 17:12

Jn 5:29; 11:42

35Jesus said to them, "I am the bread of life; he who comes to me shall not hunger, and he who believes in me shall never thirst. 36But I said to you that you have seen me and yet do not believe. 37All that the Father gives me will come to me; and him who comes to me I will not cast out. 38For I have come down from heaven, not to do my own will, but the will of him who sent me; 39and this is the will of him who sent me, that I should lose nothing of all that he has given me, but raise it up on the last day. 40For this is the will of my Father, that every one who sees the Son and believes in him should have eternal life; and I will raise him up at the last day."

the words of sacred liturgy, it is 'the mystery of faith'. This is something well known to you but it is essential to the purpose of rejecting any poisonous rationalism. Many martyrs have witnessed to it with their blood. Distinguished Fathers and Doctors of the Church in unbroken succession have taught and professed it. [...] We must, therefore, approach this mystery, above all, with humble reverence, not following human arguments, which ought to be hushed, but in steadfast adherence to divine revelation" (*Mysterium fidei*).

6:35. Going to Jesus means believing in him, for it is through faith that we approach our Lord. Jesus uses the metaphor of food and drink to show that he is the one who really meets all man's noblest aspirations: "How beautiful is our Catholic faith! It provides a solution for all our anxieties, calms our minds and fills our hearts with hope" (St Josemaría Escrivá, *The Way*, 582).

6:37–40. Jesus clearly reveals that he is the one sent by the Father. This is something St John the Baptist proclaimed earlier on (Jn 3:33–36), and Jesus himself stated it in his dialogue with Nicodemus (3:17–21) and announced publicly in Jerusalem (5:20–30). Since Jesus is the one sent by the Father, the bread of life

come down from heaven to give life to the world, everyone who believes in him has eternal life, for it is God's will that everyone should be saved through Jesus Christ. These words of Jesus contain three mysteries: 1) that of faith in Jesus Christ, which means "going to Jesus", accepting his miracles (signs) and his words; 2) the mystery of the resurrection of believers, something which begins in this life through faith and becomes fully true in heaven; 3) the mystery of predestination, the will of our Father in heaven that all men be saved. These solemn words of our Lord fill the believer with hope.

St Augustine, commenting on vv. 37 and 38, praises the humility of Jesus: Jesus chose not to do his own will but that of the Father who sent him: "Humbly am I come, to teach humility am I come, as the master of humility am I come; he who comes to me is incorporated in me; he who comes to me, becomes humble; he who cleaves to me will be humble, for he does not his will but God's" (*In Ioann. Evang.*, 25, 15 and 16).

6:42. This is the second and last time St John mentions St Joseph in his Gospel, putting on record the general, though mistaken, opinion of those who knew Jesus and regarded him as the son of Joseph (cf. Jn 1:45; Lk 3:23; 4:22; Mt 13:55). Conceived in the virginal womb

⁴¹The Jews then murmured at him, because he said, "I am the bread which came down from heaven." ⁴²They said, "Is not this Jesus, the son of Joseph, whose father and mother we know? How does he now say, 'I have come down from heaven'?" ⁴³Jesus answered them, "Do not murmur among yourselves. ⁴⁴No one can come to me unless the Father who sent me draws him; and I will raise him up on the last day. ⁴⁵It is written in the prophets, 'And they shall all be taught by God.' Every one who has heard and learned from the Father comes to me. ⁴⁶Not that any one has seen the Father except him who is from God; he has seen the Father.

Jn 6:61

Lk 4:22

Jn 6:65

Is 54:13
Jer 31:33f

Jn 1:18

---

of Mary by the action of the Holy Spirit, our Lord's only Father was God himself (cf. the note on Jn 5:18). However, St Joseph acted as Jesus' father on earth, as God had planned (cf. the notes on Mt 1:16, 18). Therefore, Joseph was called the father of Jesus and he certainly was extremely faithful in fulfilling his mission to look after Jesus. St Augustine explains St Joseph's fatherhood in this way: "Not only does Joseph deserve the name of father: he deserves it more than anyone else. In what way was he a father? As profoundly as his fatherhood was chaste. Some people thought that he was the father of our Lord Jesus Christ in the same way as others are fathers, begetting according to the flesh and not receiving their children as fruit of their spiritual affection. That is why St Luke says that they supposed he was the father of Jesus. Why does he say that they only supposed it? Because human thoughts and judgments are based on what normally happens. And our Lord was not born of the seed of Joseph. However, to the piety and charity of Joseph a son was born to him of the Virgin Mary, who was the Son of God" (*Sermons*, 51, 20).

In this verse, as elsewhere (cf. Jn 4:29; 7:42), St John put on record the people's ignorance, whereas he and his readers knew the truth about Jesus. The Jews' objection is not directly refuted; it is simply reported, on the assumption that it presents no difficulty to the Christian reader, to whom the Gospel is addressed.

6:44–45. Seeking Jesus until one finds him is a free gift which no one can obtain through his own efforts, although everyone should try to be well disposed to receiving it. The Magisterium of the Church has recalled this teaching in Vatican II: "Before this faith can be exercised, man must have the grace of God to move and assist him; he must have the interior help of the Holy Spirit, who moves the heart and converts it to God, who opens the eyes of the mind and makes it easy for all to accept and believe the truth" (*Dei Verbum*, 5).

When Jesus says "They shall all be taught by God", he is evoking Isaiah 54:13 and Jeremiah 31:33ff, where the prophets refer to the future Covenant which God will establish with his people when the Messiah comes, the Covenant which will be sealed forever with the blood of the Messiah and which God will write on their hearts (cf. Is 53:10–12; Jer 31:31–34).

The last sentence of v. 45 refers to God's revelation through the prophets and especially through Jesus Christ.

6:46. Men can know God the Father only through Jesus Christ, because only he has seen the Father, whom he has

Jn 3:16
Jn 6:35

⁴⁷Truly, truly, I say to you, he who believes has eternal life.

Jesus is the Bread of Life in the Eucharist

Jn 6:31f
1 Cor 10:3–5

Heb 10:5–10

⁴⁸I am the bread of life. ⁴⁹Your fathers ate the manna in the wilderness, and they died. ⁵⁰This is the bread which comes down from heaven, that a man may eat of it and not die. ⁵¹I am the living bread* which came down from heaven; if any one eats of this bread, he will live for ever; and the bread which I shall give for the life of the world is my flesh."

---

come to reveal to us. In his prologue St John has already said: "No one has ever seen God; the only Son, who is in the bosom of the Father, he has made him known" (Jn 1:18). Later on Jesus will say to Philip at the Last Supper: "He who has seen me has seen the Father" (Jn 14:9), for Christ is the Way, the Truth and the Life, and no one goes to the Father except through him (cf. Jn 14:6).

In other words, in Christ God's revelation to men reaches its climax: "For he sent his Son, the eternal Word who enlightens all men, to dwell among men and to tell them about the inner life of God (cf. Jn 1:1–18). Hence, Jesus Christ, sent as 'a man among men', 'utters the words of God' (Jn 3:34), and accomplishes the saving work which the Father gave him to do (cf. Jn 5:36; 17:4). To see Jesus is to see his Father (cf. Jn 14:9)" (Vatican II, *Dei Verbum*, 4).

6:48. With this solemn declaration, which he repeats because of his audience's doubts (cf. Jn 6:35, 41), Jesus begins the second part of his discourse, in which he explicitly reveals the great mystery of the Blessed Eucharist. Christ's words have such a tremendous realism about them that they cannot be interpreted in a figurative way: if Christ were not really present under the species of bread and wine, this discourse would make absolutely no sense. But if his real presence in the Eucharist is accepted on faith, then his meaning is quite clear and we can see

how infinite and tender his love for us is.

This is so great a mystery that it has always acted as a touchstone for Christian faith: it is proclaimed as "the mystery of our faith" immediately after the Consecration of the Mass. Some of our Lord's hearers were scandalized by what he said on this occasion (cf. vv. 60–66). Down through history people have tried to dilute the obvious meaning of our Lord's words. In our own day the church Magisterium has explained this teaching in these words: "When transubstantiation has taken place, there is no doubt that the appearance of the bread and the appearance of the wine take on a new expressiveness and a new purpose since they are no longer common bread and common drink, but rather the sign of something sacred and the sign of spiritual food. But they take on a new expressiveness and a new purpose for the very reason that they contain a new 'reality' which we are right to call *ontological*. For beneath these appearances there is no longer what was there before but something quite different [...] since on the conversion of the bread and wine's substance, or nature, into the body and blood of Christ, nothing is left of the bread and the wine but the appearances alone. Beneath these appearances Christ is present whole and entire, bodily present too, in his physical 'reality', although not in the manner in which bodies are present in place.

"For this reason the Fathers have had to issue frequent warnings to the faithful, when they consider this august sacra-

⁵²The Jews then disputed among themselves, saying, "How can this man give us his flesh to eat?"* ⁵³So Jesus said to them, "Truly, truly, I say to you, unless you eat the flesh of the Son of man and drink his blood, you have no life in you; ⁵⁴he who eats my flesh and drinks my blood has eternal life, and I will raise him up on the last day. ⁵⁵For my flesh is food indeed, and my blood is

Jn 6:60

Jn 5:26

---

ment, not to be satisfied with the senses which announce the properties of bread and wine. They should rather assent to the words of Christ: these are of such power that they change, transform, 'tran-selement' the bread and the wine into his body and blood. The reason for this, as the same Fathers say more than once, is that the power which performs this action is the same power of almighty God that created the whole universe out of nothing at the beginning of time" (Paul VI, *Mysterium fidei*).

Concerning the Blessed Eucharist cf. also the notes on Mt 26:26–29; Mk 14:22, 24, 25; and Lk 22:16–20.

6:49–51. The manna during the Exodus was a figure of this bread—Christ himself—which nourishes Christians on their pilgrimage through this world. Communion is the wonderful banquet at which Christ gives himself to us: "the bread which I shall give for the life of the world is my flesh". These words promise the manifestation of the Eucharist at the Last Supper: "This is my body which is for you" (1 Cor 11:24). The words "for the life of the world" and "for you" refer to the redemptive value of the sacrifice of Christ on the cross. In some sacrifices of the Old Testament, which were a figure of the sacrifice of Christ, part of the animal offered up was later used for food, signifying participation in the sacred rite (cf. Ex 11:3–4). So, by receiving Holy Communion, we are sharing in the sacrifice of Christ: which is why the Church sings in the Divine Office on the

feast of Corpus Christi: "O sacred feast in which we partake of Christ: his sufferings are remembered, our minds are filled with his grace and we receive a pledge of the glory that is to be ours" (*Magnificat* antiphon, evening prayer II).

6:52. Christ's hearers understand perfectly well that he means exactly what he says; but they cannot believe that what he says could be true. If they had understood him in a metaphorical, figurative or symbolic sense there would be no reason for them to be so surprised and nothing to cause an argument. Later, Jesus reaffirms what he has said—confirming what they have understood him to say (cf. vv. 54–56).

6:53. Once again Jesus stresses very forcefully that it is necessary to receive him in the Blessed Eucharist in order to share in divine life and develop the life of grace received in Baptism. No parent is content to bring children into the world: they have to be nourished and looked after to enable them to reach maturity. "We receive Jesus Christ in Holy Communion to nourish our souls and to give us an increase of grace and the gift of eternal life" (St Pius X, *Catechism*, 289).

6:54. Jesus clearly states that his body and blood are a pledge of eternal life and a guarantee of the resurrection of the body. St Thomas Aquinas gives this explanation: "The Word gives life to our souls, but the Word made flesh nourishes our bodies. In this sacrament is contained the Word not only in his divinity but also in

drink indeed. ⁵⁶He who eats my flesh and drinks my blood abides in me, and I in him. ⁵⁷As the living Father sent me, and I live because of the Father, so he who eats me will live because of me.

Jn 15:4; 17:21, 26
1 Jn 2:24; 3:24

his humanity; therefore, it is the cause not only of the glorification of our souls but also of that of our bodies" (*Comm. on St John*, in loc.).

Our Lord uses a stronger word than just "eating" (the original verb could be translated as "chewing") which shows that Communion is a real meal. There is no room for saying that he was speaking only symbolically, which would mean that Communion was only a metaphor and not really eating and drinking the body and the blood of Christ.

"All these invitations, promises and threats sprang from the great desire which (Jesus) had of giving us himself in the holy sacrament of the altar. But why should Jesus so ardently desire us to receive him in holy communion? It is because love always sighs for, and tends to a union with, the object beloved. True friends wish to be united in such a manner as to become only one. The love of God for us being immense, he destined us to possess him not only in heaven, but also here below, by the most intimate union, under the appearance of bread in the Eucharist. It is true we do not see him; but he beholds us, and is really present; yes, he is present in order that we may possess him and he conceals himself, that we may desire him, and until we reach our true homeland Jesus Christ wishes in this way to be entirely ours, and to be perfectly united to us" (St Alphonsus Liguori, *The Love of Our Lord Jesus Christ*, chap. 2).

6:55. In the same way as bodily food is necessary for life on earth, Holy Communion is necessary for maintaining the life of the soul, which is why the Church exhorts us to receive this sacrament frequently:

"Every day, as is desirable, and in the greatest possible numbers, the faithful must take an active part in the sacrifice of the Mass, avail themselves of the pure, holy refreshment of Holy Communion and make a suitable thanksgiving in return for this great gift of Christ the Lord. Here are words they should keep in mind: 'Jesus Christ and the Church desire all Christ's faithful to approach the sacred banquet every day. The basis of this desire is that they should be united to God by the sacrament and draw strength from it to restrain lust, to wash away the slight faults of daily occurrence and to take precautions against the more serious sins to which human frailty is liable' (Decree of the S.C. of the Council, 20 December 1905)" (Paul VI, *Mysterium fidei*).

"The Saviour has instituted the most august sacrament of the Eucharist, which truly contains his flesh and his blood, so that he who eats this bread may live forever; whosoever, therefore, makes use of it often with devotion so strengthens the health and the life of his soul, that it is almost impossible for him to be poisoned by any kind of evil affection. We cannot be nourished with this flesh of life, and live with the affections of death. [...] Christians who are damned will be unable to make any reply when the just Judge shows them how much they are to blame for dying spiritually, since it was so easy for them to maintain themselves in life and in health by eating his Body which he had left them for this purpose. Unhappy souls, he will say, why did you die, seeing that you had at your com-

⁵⁸This is the bread which came from heaven, not such as the fathers ate and died; he who eats this bread will live for ever." ⁵⁹This he said in the synagogue, as he taught in Capernaum.

---

mand the fruit and the food of life?" (St Francis de Sales, *Introduction to the Devout Life*, 2, 20, 1).

6:56. The most important effect of the Blessed Eucharist is intimate union with Jesus Christ. The very word "communion" suggests sharing in the life of our Lord and becoming one with him; if our union with Jesus is promoted by all the sacraments through the grace which they give us, this happens more intensely in the Eucharist, for in it we receive not only grace but the very Author of grace: "Really sharing in the body of the Lord in the breaking of the eucharistic bread, we are taken up into communion with him and with one another. 'Because the bread is one, we, though many, are one body, all of us who partake of the one bread' (1 Cor 10:17)" (Vatican II, *Lumen gentium*, 7). Precisely because the Eucharist is the sacrament which best signifies and effects our union with Christ, it is there that the whole Church manifests and effects its unity: Jesus Christ "instituted in his Church the wonderful sacrament of the Eucharist, by which the unity of the Church is both signified and brought about" (Vatican II, *Unitatis redintegratio*, 2).

6:57. In Christ, the Incarnate Word sent to mankind, "the whole fullness of deity, dwells bodily" (Col 2:9) through the ineffable union of his human nature and his divine nature in the Person of the Word. By receiving in this sacrament the body and blood of Christ indissolubly united to his divinity, we share in the divine life of the second Person of the Blessed Trinity. We will never be able to appreciate enough the intimacy with God himself—Father, Son and Holy Spirit—that we are offered in the eucharistic banquet.

"We can therefore do nothing more agreeable to Jesus Christ than to go to Communion with the dispositions suitable to so great an action, since we are then united to Jesus Christ, according to the desire of this all-loving God. I have said with 'suitable' and not 'worthy' disposition, for who could communicate if it was necessary to be worthy of so great a Saviour? No one but a God would be worthy to receive a God. But by this word suitable, or convenient, I mean such a disposition as becomes a miserable creature, who is clothed with the unhappy flesh of Adam. Ordinarily speaking, it is sufficient that we communicate in a state of grace and with an anxious desire of advancing in the love of Jesus Christ" (St Alphonsus Liguori, *The Love of Our Lord Jesus Christ*, chap. 2).

6:58. For the third time (cf. 6:31–32 and 6:49) Jesus compares the true bread of life, his own body, with the manna God used to feed the Israelites every day during their forty years in the wilderness—thereby, inviting us to nourish our soul frequently with the food of his body.

"'Going to Communion every day for so many years! Anybody else would be a saint by now', you told me, 'and I ... I'm always the same!' 'Son,' I replied, 'keep up your daily Communion, and think: what would I be if I had not gone'" (St Josemaría Escrivá, *The Way*, 534).

The disciples' reaction

⁶⁰Many of his disciples, when they heard of it, said, "This is a hard saying; who can listen to it?" ⁶¹But Jesus, knowing in himself that his disciples murmured at it, said to them, "Do you take offence at this? ⁶²Then what if you were to see the Son of man ascending where he was before?* ⁶³It is the spirit that gives life, the flesh is of no avail; the words that I have spoken to you are spirit and life. ⁶⁴But there are some of you that do not believe." For Jesus knew from the first who those were that did not believe, and who it was that should betray him. ⁶⁵And he said, "This is why I told you that no one can come to me unless it is granted him by the Father."

Jn 6:41

Jn 3:13
2 Cor 3:6

Jn 13:11

Jn 6:44

6:60–62. Many of his listeners find the eucharistic mystery completely incomprehensible. Jesus Christ requires his disciples to accept his words because it is he who has spoken them. That is what the supernatural act of faith involves— that act "whereby, inspired and assisted by the grace of God, we believe that the things which he has revealed are true; not because of the intrinsic truth of the things, viewed by the natural light of reason, but because of the authority of God himself who reveals them, and who can neither be deceived nor deceive" (Vatican I, *Dei Filius*, chap. 3).

As on other occasions, Jesus speaks about future events to help his disciples believe: "I have told you before it takes place, so that when it does take place, you may believe" (Jn 14:29).

6:63. Jesus says that we cannot accept this mystery if we think of it in too human a way, in other words, by just seeking to indulge our senses or having too earthbound a view of things. Only someone who listens to his words and receives them as God's revelation, which is "spirit and life", is in a position to accept them.

6:66. The promise of the Eucharist, which caused arguments (v. 52) among Christ's

hearers at Capernaum and scandalized some of them (v. 61), led many people to give up following him. Jesus had outlined a wonderful and salvific truth, but those disciples closed themselves to divine grace; they were not ready to accept anything which went beyond their very limited horizons. The mystery of the Eucharist does call for a special act of faith. St John Chrysostom therefore advised Christians: "Let us in everything believe God, and gainsay him in nothing, though what is said be contrary to our thoughts and senses. [...] Let us act likewise in respect to the [eucharistic] mysteries, not looking at the things set before us, but keeping in mind his words. For his word cannot deceive" (St John Chrysostom, *Hom. on St Matthew*, 82).

6:67–71. This passage is similar to that at Capernaum where Peter again, in the name of the Twelve, takes the initiative in expressing his faith in Jesus as Messiah (cf. Mt 16:13–20; Mk 8:27–30). Other people present may have been unbelieving, but the apostles are not scandalized by our Lord's words: they say that they have already a deep-rooted confidence in him; they do not want to leave him. What St Peter says (v. 68) is not just a statement of human solidarity

⁶⁶After this many of his disciples drew back and no longer went with him. ⁶⁷Jesus said to the twelve, "Will you also go away?" ⁶⁸Simon Peter answered him, "Lord, to whom shall we go? You have the words of eternal life; ⁶⁹and we have believed, and have come to know, that you are the Holy One of God." ⁷⁰Jesus answered them, "Did I not choose you, the twelve, and one of you is a devil?" ⁷¹He spoke of Judas the son of Simon Iscariot, for he, one of the twelve, was to betray him.

Lk 2:28
Jn 6:63
Jn 1:49; 11:27
Mt 14:33; 16:16

Jn 6:64

5. JESUS, SENT BY THE FATHER, IS THE LIGHT OF THE WORLD AND THE GOOD SHEPHERD

Jesus goes up to Jerusalem during the feast of Tabernacles

7 ¹After this Jesus went about in Galilee; he would not go about in Judea, because the Jews[n] sought to kill him. ²Now the

Jn 5:18
Mk 9:30

but an expression of genuine supernatural faith—as yet imperfect—which is the result of the influence of divine grace on his soul (cf. Mt 16:17).

Although the Twelve stay with him at this point, Judas will later betray the Master. Jesus' foreknowledge of this future infidelity throws a shadow over his joy at the loyalty of the Twelve. We Christians should be humble enough to realize that we are capable of betraying our Lord if we give up using the means he has left us to cleave to him. St Peter's words (v. 68) are a beautiful aspiration we can use whenever we feel tempted.

6:68. Simon Peter expresses the feelings of the apostles who, through staying loyal to Jesus, are getting to know him much better and becoming more closely involved with him: "Seek Jesus; endeavouring to acquire a deep personal faith that will inform and direct your whole life. But, above all, let it be your commitment and your programme to love Jesus, with a sincere, authentic and personal love. He must be your friend and your support along the

path of life. He alone has words of eternal life" (John Paul II, Address to students in Guadalajara, 30 January 1979).

6:69. "The Holy One of God": this is what the original text must have said, according to most of the Greek codexes and the most important early translations. "The Holy One" is one of the expressions which designate the Messiah (cf. Mk 1:24; Lk 1:35; 4:34; Acts 2:27; Ps 16:10), or God himself (cf. Is 6:3; 43:15; 1 Pet 1:15; 1 Jn 2:20; etc.). The rendering "the Christ, the Son of God" found in some translations, including the Vulgate, is supported by less important Greek manuscripts, and would seem to be an explanation of the messianic significance of the original phrase.

7:1–3. The Jewish custom was for closer relatives to be called "brothers", brethren (cf. the notes on Mt 12:46–47 and Mk 6:1–3). These relatives of Jesus followed him without understanding his teaching or his mission (cf. Mk 3:31); but, because he worked such obvious miracles in Galilee (cf. Mt 15:32–39; Mk 8:1–10,

n. Or *Judeans*

93

Ex 23:15
Lev 23:34
Zech 14:16–19
Jn 2:11–12
Mt 12:46

Jews' feast of Tabernacles was at hand. ³So his brethren* said to him, "Leave here and go to Judea, that your disciples may see the works you are doing. ⁴For no man works in secret if he seeks to be known openly. If you do these things, show yourself to the world." ⁵For even his brethren did not believe in him. ⁶Jesus said

Jn 2:4; 17:1

Jn 3:19; 15:18

to them, "My time has not yet come, but your time is always here. ⁷The world cannot hate you, but it hates me because I testify of it that its works are evil. ⁸Go to the feast yourselves; I am not ° going up to this feast, for my time has not fully come." ⁹So saying, he remained in Galilee.

Mt 27:63

¹⁰But after his brethren had gone up to the feast, then he also went up, not publicly but in private. ¹¹The Jews were looking for

---

22–26) they suggest to him that he show himself publicly in Jerusalem and throughout Judea. Perhaps they wanted him to be a big success, which would have indulged their family pride.

7:2. The name of the feast recalls the time the Israelites spent living under canvas in the wilderness (cf. Lev 23:34–36). During the eight days the feast lasted (cf. Neh 8:13–18), around the beginning of autumn, the Jews commemorated the protection God had given the Israelites over the forty years of the Exodus. Because it coincided with the end of the harvest, it was also called the feast of ingathering (cf. Ex 23:16).

7:6–8. When the Jews who lived far away went up to Jerusalem to celebrate the main religious festivals, they usually went in caravans. Jesus had joined such caravans on other occasions (cf. Lk 2:41–45); but this time he does not want to go up to the Holy City with the crowd. He knows that the time is not ripe for him to show himself publicly in Jerusalem, for the teachers of the Law, whom he had severely taken to task (cf. 5:42–47) wanted to discredit him before the people and get rid of him (cf. 7:1).

Our Lord does not want to advance the time fixed by his Father, whose will he has come to do (cf. 4:34; 12:33; 13:1). However, his adherents could go up to Jerusalem because they had nothing to fear.

On the concept of "world" cf. the notes on Jn 1:10 and 15:18–19.

7:10. Because he had not arrived in advance of the feast (which was what people normally did), the first caravans would have reported that Jesus was not coming up, and therefore the members of the Sanhedrin would have stopped planning anything against him (cf. 7:1). By going up later, the religious authorities would not dare make any move against him for fear of hostile public reaction (cf. Mt 26:5). Jesus, possibly accompanied by his disciples, arrives unnoticed at Jerusalem, "in private", almost in a hidden way. Half-way through the feast, on the fourth or fifth day, he begins to preach in the temple (cf. 7:14).

7:12. Once again Jesus appears as a sign of contradiction, in line with the prophecy of Simeon in the temple (cf. Lk 2:34). People are divided in their opinions of him, but no one is indifferent. A Christian

---

o. Other ancient authorities add *yet*

him at the feast, and saying, "Where is he?" ¹²And there was much muttering about him among the people. While some said, "He is a good man," others said, "No, he is leading the people astray." ¹³Yet for fear of the Jews no one spoke openly of him.

Jn 9:22; 12:42; 19:38
Mt 13:54–57
Lk 2:47
Jn 3:11; 12:49

Jesus' teaching comes from God

¹⁴About the middle of the feast Jesus went up into the temple and taught. ¹⁵The Jews marvelled at it, saying, "How is it that this man has learning,ᵖ when he has never studied?" ¹⁶So Jesus answered them, "My teaching is not mine, but his who sent me; ¹⁷if any man's will is to do his will, he shall know whether the teaching is from God or whether I am speaking on my own authority. ¹⁸He who speaks on his own authority seeks his own glory; but he who seeks the glory of him who sent him is true, and in him there is no

Jn 5:41–44; 8:50

---

who takes his faith seriously may well have the same experience. "Of anyone in whom any grace shines," St Augustine comments, "some say that he is good; others that he is not, that he is deceiving the people. If this is said of God, it should console every Christian of whom the same is said" (*In Ioann. Evang.*, 28, 12).

7:15–16. The Evangelist does not stop here to tell us what exactly Jesus was preaching about; but he does repeat how impressed the Jews were, teachers of the Law included. They marvelled at the teaching of this man, whom they had never seen attending the schools run by the teachers of the Law, and they asked him this question, which is really quite malicious: Is he not interpreting the Law for himself, without having regard to the official teaching of the "masters"? At this point our Lord uses the opportunity to give a brief outline of his messianic dignity (7:16–24): he has not invented anything; his teaching is divine; the Father has revealed it to him (cf. 5:30; 8:28; 12:49; 14:10, 24). Because he is true God and true Man, he can speak about the

things of God with singular authority. (see 1:18).

7:17–18. An upright intention is needed if one is to discern that Jesus' doctrine comes from God. Jesus, for his part, suggests a criterion for recognizing that he is acting rightly: he should be judged not by the sublimity of his teaching and his works (cf. 8:54) but by the fact that he seeks the glorification of his Father, and is expounding the teaching that has been given him (cf. 7:16). Jesus worked spectacular miracles, the prophecies are being fulfilled in him and even his enemies can find nothing wrong with his doctrine or with his behaviour: why, then, do they not believe in him? The reason is that they are very prejudiced; they do not weigh the evidence calmly: that is the only explanation for their attributing to devils the things that Jesus has done (cf. v. 20). But if a person makes an effort to faithfully fulfil the will of God according to his lights, he will be well disposed to receive from God new light to allow him to discover Christ and his teaching.

Following Christ's example, the Church does not seek human success,

p. Or *this man knows his letters*

95

Rom 2:17–23

Jn 10:20
Mk 3:22–27

Gen 17:10–12
Lev 12:3

Jn 5:16
Mt 12:1–5

Jn 8:15
Zech 7:9

Jn 5:18

falsehood. ¹⁹Did not Moses give you the law? Yet none of you keeps the law. Why do you seek to kill me?" ²⁰The people answered, "You have a demon! Who is seeking to kill you?" ²¹Jesus answered them, "I did one deed, and you all marvel at it. ²²Moses gave you circumcision (not that it is from Moses, but from the fathers), and you circumcise a man upon the sabbath. ²³If on the sabbath a man receives circumcision, so that the law of Moses may not be broken, are you angry with me because on the sabbath I made a man's whole body well? ²⁴Do not judge by appearances, but judge with right judgment."

Jesus comes from God

²⁵Some of the people of Jerusalem therefore said, "Is not this the man whom they seek to kill? ²⁶And here he is, speaking openly, and they say nothing to him! Can it be that the authorities really know that this is the Christ? ²⁷Yet we know where this man comes

---

but the good of souls and the glory of God. "God is fully glorified, when men fully and consciously accept the work of salvation which he accomplished in Christ. By means of it God's plan is realized, a plan to which Christ lovingly and obediently submitted for the glory of the Father who sent him in order that the whole human race might become one people of God, form one body of Christ, and be built up into one temple of the Holy Spirit" (Vatican II, *Ad gentes*, 7).

7:19–24. Jesus is justifying the cures he has worked on the sabbath. On that day, for example, he cured the paralyzed man at the pool of Bethzatha (Jn 5:1–18), the man with the withered hand (Mt 12:10–13 and par.), the woman who was bent over (Lk 13:10–17), and a man with dropsy (Lk 14:1–6). Our Lord compares his behaviour with keeping two apparently opposed precepts of the Law: the sabbath is a day of rest, and yet the obligation of circumcision on the eighth day applies even if that day falls on a sabbath. Clearly, if it is lawful to circumcise on the sabbath, it must be even more so

to work a miraculous cure on the sabbath. That is why he asks them to judge rightly and recognize his saving power— to try to grasp the profound significance of the things that he is doing, even if they at first seem to go against the Law.

7:27. In this chapter we often see the Jews disconcerted, in two minds. They argue with one another over whether Jesus is the Messiah, or a prophet, or an imposter (v. 12); they do not know where he gets his wisdom from (v. 15); they are short-tempered (vv. 19–20); and they are surprised by the attitudes of the Sanhedrin (v. 26). Despite the signs they have seen (miracles, teaching) they do not want to believe that Jesus is the Messiah. Perhaps some, thinking that he came from Nazareth and was the son of Joseph and Mary, cannot see how this fits in with the notion usually taken from Isaiah's prophecy (Is 53:1–9) about the Messiah's origin being unknown —except for his coming from the line of David and being born in Bethlehem (cf. Mt 2:5 which quotes Mic 5:2; cf. Jn 7:42). In fact Jesus did fulfil those prophetic predictions, though most Jews did not know

from; and when the Christ appears, no one will know where he comes from." [28]So Jesus proclaimed, as he taught in the temple, "You know me, and you know where I come from? But I have not come of my own accord; he who sent me is true, and him you do not know. [29]I know him, for I come from him, and he sent me." [30]So they sought to arrest him; but no one laid hands on him, because his hour had not yet come.

Jn 8:19; 19:9

Jn 1:1; 8:55
Mt 11:27
Jn 7:44; 8:20
Lk 4:29; 22:53

Jesus must return to the Father

[31]Yet many of the people believed in him; they said, "When the Christ appears, will he do more signs than this man has done?" [32]The Pharisees heard the crowd thus muttering about him, and the chief priests and Pharisees sent officers to arrest him. [33]Jesus then said, "I shall be with you a little longer, and then I go to him who sent me; [34]you will seek me and you will not find me; where

Jn 8:30

Jn 13:33

Jn 8:21; 17:24

---

it because they knew nothing about his virginal birth in Bethlehem or his descent from David. Others must have known that he was of the house of David and had been born in Bethlehem, but even so they did not want to accept his teaching because it demanded a mental and moral conversion.

7:28–29. Not without a certain irony, Jesus refers to the superficial knowledge these Jews had of him: however, he asserts that he comes from the Father who has sent him, whom only he knows, precisely because he is the Son of God (cf. Jn 1:18).

7:30. The Jews realized that Jesus was making himself God's equal, which was regarded as blasphemy and, according to the Law, was something punishable by death by stoning (cf. Lev 24:15–16, 23).

This is not the first time St John refers to the Jews' hostility (cf. Jn 5:10), nor will it be the last (8:59; 10:31–33). He stresses this hostility because it was a fact and perhaps also to show that Jesus acts freely when, to fulfil his Father's will he gives himself over to his enemies when his "hour" arrives (cf. Jn 18:4–8). "He did not therefore mean an hour when

he would be forced to die, but one when he would allow himself to be put to death. For he was waiting for the time in which he should die, even as he waited for the time in which he should be born" (St Augustine, *In Ioann. Evang.*, 31, 5).

7:31–32. In Jesus the prophecy of Simeon to the Virgin Mary is being fulfilled: he is a sign of contradiction for his own people (cf. Lk 2:34). Some believe in him (v. 31), others are in two minds (vv. 41–42), others violently reject him (vv. 44–48). The poor and the humble believe, says St Augustine,—those who recognize that they are ailing and are keen to have medicine; whereas the powerful and the proud are angry with him. Not only do they not recognize the physician, they want to kill him (cf. *In Ioann. Evang.*, 31, 7).

7:33–34. This prophecy refers to the death and ascension of Jesus. He says "where I am" to indicate the glorious state of his soul, which his body also will enjoy after its resurrection. The Jews who reject him have blocked their route to heaven. However, later on, Jesus, moved by infinite charity, will ask the Father to forgive them because they do

Is 55:6

Deut 4:29
Prov 1:28
Hos 5:6

Jn 4:10–14
Is 55:1–3
Ezek 47:1–12
Jn 19:34
Acts 2:1–13;
5:32

I am you cannot come." ³⁵The Jews said to one another, "Where does this man intend to go that we shall not find him? Does he intend to go to the Dispersion among the Greeks and teach the Greeks? ³⁶What does he mean by saying, 'You will seek me and you will not find me,' and, 'Where I am you cannot come'?"

³⁷On the last day of the feast, the great day, Jesus stood up and proclaimed, "If any one thirst, let him come to me and drink. ³⁸He who believes in me, asq the scripture has said, 'Out of his heart shall flow rivers of living water.'" ³⁹Now this he said about the

---

not know what they are doing (Lk 23:34). And so, at Pentecost, many will repent of their sin and God will pardon them (cf. Acts 2:38) and the gates of heaven will be open to them again; but others will remain adamant in their unbelief.

7:37–39. On each of the eight days of the feast of Tabernacles the high priest went to the pool of Siloam and used a golden cup to bring water to the temple and sprinkle it on the altar, in remembrance of the water which sprang up miraculously in the desert, asking God to send rain in plenty (cf. Ex 17:1–7). Meanwhile, a passage from the prophet Isaiah was chanted (cf. Is 12:3) which told of the coming of the Saviour and of the outpouring of heavenly gifts that would accompany him; Ezekiel 47 was also read, in which it spoke of the torrents of water which would pour out of the temple. Jesus, who would have been at this ceremony, now proclaims—in the presence of a huge crowd, undoubtedly, because it was the most solemn day of the festival—that that time has come: "If any one thirst, let him come to me and drink ...". This invitation recalls the words of divine wisdom: "Come to me, you who desire me, and eat your fill" (Sir 24:19; cf. Prov 9:4–5). Our Lord presents himself as him who can fill man's heart and bring him peace (cf. also Mt 11:28). In this connexion St Augustine exclaims:

"You made us for yourself, Lord, and our hearts find no peace until they rest in you" (*Confessions*, 1, 1, 1).

Jesus' words as preserved in v. 37 led St Alphonsus to write this tender commentary full of love for our Saviour: "In Jesus Christ we have three fountains of grace. The first is the fountain of mercy, where we can be purified of all the stains of our sins. [...] The second is that of love: no one who meditates on the suffering and shame that Jesus Christ undergoes out of love for us, from his birth to his death, can fail to be kindled by that happy fire which comes down on earth to set on fire the hearts of all men. [...] The third is the fountain of peace: let him who seeks peace of heart come to me, who is the God of peace" (*Meditations for Advent*, med. 8).

Furthermore, when Jesus speaks of "rivers of living water" flowing out of his heart, he is probably referring to Ezekiel 36:25ff where it is announced that in messianic times the people will be sprinkled with clean water and will be given a new spirit and their heart of stone will be changed for a heart of flesh. In other words, Jesus, once he has been exalted as befits his position as Son of God, will send at Pentecost the Holy Spirit, who will change the hearts of those who believe in him. "For this reason, Christian tradition has summarized the attitude we should adopt

q. Or *let him come to me, and let him who believes in me drink. As*

Spirit, which those who believed in him were to receive; for as yet the Spirit had not been given, because Jesus was not yet glorified.

Different opinions about Jesus

⁴⁰When they heard these words, some of the people said, "This is really the prophet." ⁴¹Others said, "This is the Christ." But some said, "Is the Christ to come from Galilee? ⁴²Has not the scripture said that the Christ is descended from David, and comes from Bethlehem, the village where David was?" ⁴³So there was a division among the people over him. ⁴⁴Some of them wanted to arrest him, but no one laid hands on him.

⁴⁵The officers then went back to the chief priests and Pharisees, who said to them, "Why did you not bring him?" ⁴⁶The

1 Cor 10:4
2 Cor 3:17
Deut 18:15
Jn 1:46
2 Sam 7:12
Mic 5:2
Mt 2:6; 22:42
Lk 2:4–11
Jn 9:16
Jn 7:30
Mt 7:28;
13:54–56

---

towards the Holy Spirit in just one idea—docility. That means we should be aware of the work of the Holy Spirit all around us, and in our own selves we should recognize the gifts he distributes, the movements and institutions he inspires, the affections and decisions he provokes in our hearts" (St J. Escrivá, *Christ Is Passing By*, 130).

To say that the Holy Spirit will come visibly at Pentecost does not mean that he has not been active before: when the Old Testament prophets speak they are inspired by the Holy Spirit (cf. 2 Pet 1:21) and there are countless passages in the New Testament where we are told that he is acting: for example, he overshadows the Blessed Virgin at the Annunciation; he moves Zechariah to prophesy the wonders of the Lord, and Simeon to proclaim that the Saviour of the world has come.

But, asks St Augustine, "how are the words of the Evangelist to be understood: 'The Spirit had not yet been given, since Jesus was not yet glorified', if not in the sense that, after the glorification of Christ, there would certainly be a giving or sending of the Holy Spirit of such a kind as there had never been before?" (*De Trinitate*, 4, 20). Our Lord was referring, therefore, to the coming of the Holy Spirit after his ascension into heaven, an outpouring which St John sees as sym-

bolically anticipated when Christ's side is pierced by a lance and blood and water flow out (Jn 19:34). The Fathers saw in this the birth of the Church and the sanctifying power of the sacraments, especially those of Baptism and the Eucharist.

7:40–43. "The prophet" refers to Deuteronomy 18:18, which predicts the coming of a prophet during the last times, a prophet to whom all must listen (cf. Jn 1:21; 6:14); and "the Christ" ("the Messiah") was the title most used in the Old Testament to designate the future Saviour whom God would send. This passage shows us, once again, the range of people's attitudes towards Jesus. Many Jews—not taking the trouble to check— did not know that he had been born in Bethlehem, the city of David, where Micah (5:2) says the Lord will be born. It was their own fault that they used this ignorance as an excuse for not accepting Christ. Others, however, realized from his miracles that he must be the Messiah. The same pattern prevails throughout history: some people see him simply as an extraordinary man, not wanting to admit that his greatness comes precisely from the fact that he is the Son of God.

7:46. The truth begins to influence the straightforward souls of the servants of

officers answered, "No man ever spoke like this man!" [47]The
Pharisees answered them, "Are you led astray, you also? [48]Have
any of the authorities or of the Pharisees believed in him? [49]But
this crowd, who do not know the law, are accursed." [50]Nicodemus,
who had gone to him before, and who was one of them, said to
them, [51]"Does our law judge a man without first giving him a hearing and learning what he does?" [52]They replied, "Are you from
Galilee too? Search and you will see that no prophet is to rise from
Galilee." [53]They went each to his own house, [1]but Jesus went to the
Mount of Olives.

Jn 12:42

Jn 3:1–2
Deut 1:16–7

Jn 1:46; 7:41

the Sanhedrin but it cannot make head-
way against the obstinacy of the
Pharisees. "Notice that the Pharisees and
scribes derive no benefit either from witnessing miracles or reading the Scriptures; whereas their servants, without
these helps, were captivated by a single
discourse, and those who set out to arrest
Jesus went back under the influence of
his authority. And they did not say, 'We
cannot arrest him, the people will not let
us'; instead they extolled Christ's wisdom. Not only is their prudence admirable, for they did not need signs; it is also
impressive that they were won over by
his teaching on its own; they did not say,
in effect, 'No man has ever worked such
miracles,' but 'No man ever spoke like
this man.' Their conviction also is worthy
of admiration: they go to the Pharisees,
who were opposed to Christ, and address
them in the way they do" (St John
Chrysostom, *Hom. on St John*, 9).

8:1–11. This passage is absent from many
ancient codexes, but it was in the Vulgate
when the Magisterium, at the Council
of Trent, defined the canon of Holy
Scripture. Therefore, the Church regards it
as canonical and inspired, and has used it
and continues to use it in the liturgy. It is
also included in the New Vulgate, in the
same position as it occupied before. It may
be that some people of a very strict frame
of mind thought that because it showed

Jesus to be so merciful, it might lead to a
relaxation of moral standards. In any
event, the episode demonstrates how Jesus
sees his role as Judge (see 8:15): he is the
Just One, but he does not condemn;
whereas these critics, even though they are
sinners, want to apply the death penalty.

In commenting on the episode of the
woman caught in adultery Fray Luis de
Granada gives these general considera-
tions on the mercy of Christ: "Your feelings, your deeds and your words should
be akin to these, if you desire to be a
beautiful likeness of the Lord. And therefore the Apostle is not content with telling us to be merciful; he tells us, as
God's sons, to put on 'the bowels of
mercy' (cf. Col 3:12). Imagine, then,
what the world would be like if everyone
arrayed themselves in this way.

"All this is said to help us understand
to some degree the great abundance of
the goodness and compassion of our
Saviour, which shine forth so clearly in
these actions of his, for [...] in this life
we cannot know God in himself; we can
know him only through his actions. [...]
But it should also be pointed out that we
should never act in such a way in view of
God's mercy, that we forget about his
justice; nor should we attend to his justice forgetting about his mercy; for hope
should have in it an element of fear, and
fear an element of hope" (*Life of Jesus
Christ*, 13, 4).

The adulterous woman — Jesus as judge

8 ²Early in the morning he came again to the temple; all the people came to him, and he sat down and taught them. ³The scribes and the Pharisees brought a woman who had been caught in adultery, and placing her in the midst ⁴they said to him, "Teacher, this woman has been caught in the act of adultery. ⁵Now in the law Moses commanded us to stone such. What do you say about her?" ⁶This they said to test him, that they might have some charge to bring against him. Jesus bent down and wrote with his finger on the ground. ⁷And as they continued to ask him, he stood up and said to them, "Let him who is without sin among you be the first to throw a stone at her." ⁸And once more he bent down

Lk 21:37f

Lev 20:10
Deut 22:22–24

Mt 22:15
Lk 20:20

Deut 17:7
Rom 2:1, 22

8:1. We know that on a number of occasions our Lord withdrew to the Mount of Olives to pray (cf. Jn 18:1; Lk 22:39). This place was to the east of Jerusalem; the Kidron valley (cf. Jn 18:1) divided it from the hill on which the temple was built. It had from ancient times been a place of prayer: David went there to adore God during the difficult period when Absalom was in revolt (2 Sam 15:32), and there the prophet Ezekiel contemplated the glory of Yahweh entering the temple (Ezek 43:1–5). At the foot of the hill there was a garden, called Gethsemane or "the place of the oil-press", an enclosed plot containing a plantation of olive trees. Christian tradition has treated this place with great respect and has maintained it as a place of prayer. Towards the end of the fourth century a church was built there, on whose remains the present church was built. There are still some ancient olive trees growing there which could well derive from those of our Lord's time.

8:6. The question put by the scribes and Pharisees has a catch: our Lord had often shown understanding to people whom they considered sinners; they come to him now with this case to see if he will be equally indulgent — which will allow them to accuse him of infringing a very clear precept of the Law (cf. Lev 20:10).

8:7. Jesus' reply refers to the way stoning was carried out: those who witnessed the crime had to throw the first stones, and then others joined in, to erase the slur on the people which the crime implied (cf. Deut 17:7). The question put to Jesus was couched in legal terms; he raises it to the moral plane (the basis and justification of the legal plane), appealing to the people's conscience. He does not violate the law, St Augustine says, and at the same time he does not want to lose what he is seeking — for he has come to save that which was lost: "His answer is so full of justice, gentleness and truth. [...] O true answer of Wisdom. You have heard: Keep the Law, let the woman be stoned. But how can sinners keep the Law and punish this woman? Let each of them look inside himself and enter the tribunal of his heart and conscience; there he will discover that he is a sinner. Let this woman be punished, but not by sinners; let the Law be applied, but not by its transgressors" (St Augustine, *In Ioann. Evang.*, 33, 5).

and wrote with his finger on the ground. [9]But when they heard it, they went away, one by one, beginning with the eldest, and Jesus was left alone with the woman standing before him. [10]Jesus looked up and said to her, "Woman, where are they? Has no one condemned you?" [11]She said, "No one, Lord." And Jesus said, "Neither do I condemn you; go, and do not sin again."[r*]

Jn 5:14
Ezek 33:11

Jesus, the light of the world

Jn 1:5–9; 12:46
Is 49:6
Mt 5:14

[12]Again Jesus spoke to them, saying, "I am the light of the world; he who follows me will not walk in darkness, but will have the

---

8:11. "The two of them were left on their own, the wretched woman and Mercy. But the Lord, having smitten them with the dart of justice, does not even deign to watch them go but turns his gaze away from them and once more writes on the ground with his finger. But when the woman was left alone and they had all gone, he lifted up his eyes to the woman. We have already heard the voice of justice; let us now hear the voice of gentleness. I think that woman was the more terrified when she heard the Lord say, 'Let him who is without sin among you be the first to throw a stone at her,' [...] fearing now that she would be punished by him, in whom no sin could be found. But he, who had driven away her adversaries with the tongue of justice, now looking at her with the eyes of gentleness asks her, 'Has no one condemned you?' She replies, 'No one, Lord.' And he says, 'Neither do I condemn you; I who perhaps you feared would punish you, because in me you have found no sin.' Lord, can it be that you favour sinners? Assuredly not. See what follows: 'Go and sin no more.' Therefore, the Lord also condemned sin, but not the woman" (St Augustine, *In Ioann. Evang.*, 33, 5–6).

Jesus, who is the Just One, does not condemn the woman; whereas these people are sinners, yet they pass sentence of death. God's infinite mercy should move us always to have compassion on those who commit sins, because we ourselves are sinners and in need of God's forgiveness.

8:12. This is the beginning of another dispute between Jesus and the Pharisees. The scene is the precincts of the temple —to be more precise, what was called the "court of the women"; this came before the court of the people, which in turn came before the court of the priests, which contained the altar of holocausts (cf. the note to Mk 1:21).

It is still the feast of Tabernacles (cf. Jn 7:2); and it was the custom on the first night to fill the court of the women with the bright light of huge lamps which lit up the sky. This brought to mind the bright cloud of God's presence which guided the Israelites through the wilderness during the Exodus. It was probably during this feast that Jesus spoke of himself as "the Light". In any event, the image of light is often found in the Old Testament to designate the Messiah: the prophet Isaiah predicted that a great light would shine for the people who walked in darkness, beginning with the tribes of the North (Is 9:1–6; cf. Mt 4:15–16), and

---

r. Some ancient authorities insert 7:53—8:11 either at the end of this gospel or after Lk 21:38, with variations of the text. Others omit it altogether

light of life." [13]The Pharisees then said to him, "You are bearing witness to yourself; your testimony is not true." [14]Jesus answered, "Even if I do bear witness to myself, my testimony is true, for I know whence I have come and whither I am going, but you do not know whence I have come or whither I am going. [15]You judge according to the flesh, I judge no one. [16]Yet even if I do judge, my judgment is true, for it is not I alone that judge, but I and he[s] who sent me. [17]In your law it is written that the testimony of two men is true; [18]I bear witness to myself, and the Father who sent me bears witness to me." [19]They said to him therefore, "Where is

Is 5:31

Jn 7:24; 12:47

Jn 5:30; 8:29

Deut 17:6; 19:15

1 Jn 5:9

Jn 12:45; 14:7

---

that the Messiah would not only be the King of Israel but the light of the nations (Is 42:6; 49:6); and David spoke of God as a light enlightening the soul of the righteous man and giving him strength (Ps 27:1). This image, therefore, was well understood during Jesus' time: Zechariah uses it (Lk 1:78), as does Simeon (Lk 2:30–32), to show his joy on seeing the ancient prophecies fulfilled.

Our Lord applies this image to himself in two ways: he is the light which enlightens our minds, for he is the fulness of divine revelation (cf. Jn 1:9, 18); and he is also the light which enlightens our hearts to enable us to accept this Revelation and live according to it (cf. Jn 1:4–5). This is why Jesus asks them to follow him and "become sons of light" (Jn 12:36), although he knows that many will reject this light because they do not want their evil deeds to be uncovered (cf. Jn 3:20).

"See how the words of the Lord accord with the truth of the Psalm: 'With thee is the fountain of life; in thy light do we see light' (Ps 36:9). The psalmist connects light with the source of life, and the Lord speaks of a 'light of life'. When we are thirsty we look for a fountain; when we are in darkness we look for light. [...] Not so with God: he is light and fountain. He who shines for you to

enable you to see, flows for you to enable you to drink" (St Augustine, *In. Ioann. Evang.*, 34, 6).

8:13–18. The Pharisees try to dilute the force of Jesus' arguments: they make out that he has only his own word to go on and no one can bear witness on his own behalf: so what he says has no validity.

In a similar situation (cf. Jn 5:31ff) Jesus had cited four witnesses to support him—John the Baptist's teaching, the miracles he himself performed, the words his Father spoke when he was baptized in the Jordan, and Holy Scripture. Here Jesus affirms the validity of his own testimony (v. 14) on the grounds that he is one with the Father. This is the same as saying that his is a more than human testimony. "He speaks to tell them that he comes from God, that he is God, and that he is the Son of God, but he does not say so openly, because he always connects humility with profundity. God deserves that we should believe in him" (St John Chrysostom, *Hom. on St John*, 51).

8:19. The Pharisees, who did not want to admit Jesus' divine origin, now ask him for proof that what he says is true. Their question is insidious and malicious, for they do not think he can show them the Father.

---

s. Other ancient authorities read *the Father*

your Father?" Jesus answered, "You know neither me nor my Father; if you knew me, you would know my Father also."

Jn 13:1
Lk 22:53

²⁰These words he spoke in the treasury, as he taught in the temple; but no one arrested him, because his hour had not yet come.

Jn 7:32–36;
13:33, 36
Prov 1:28

Jn 7:35

Jesus says he has been sent by the Father

²¹Again he said to them, "I go away, and you will seek me and die in your sin;* where I am going, you cannot come." ²²Then said the Jews, "Will he kill himself, since he says, 'Where I am going,

---

Knowing Jesus, that is, believing in him and accepting the mystery of his divinity, means knowing the Father. John 12:44–45 repeats the same teaching in other words. And Jesus is saying the same when he reproaches Philip: "Have I been with you so long, and yet you do not know me, Philip? He who has seen me has seen the Father" (Jn 14:9). Jesus is the visible manifestation of the invisible God, the ultimate, definitive revelation of God to men (cf. Heb 1:1–3). Jesus Christ "by the total fact of his presence and self-manifestation—by words and works, signs and miracles, but above all by his death and glorious resurrection from the dead, and finally by sending the Spirit of truth [...]] revealed that God was with us, to deliver us from the darkness of sin and death, and to raise us up to eternal life" (Vatican II, *Dei Verbum*, 4).

8:20. "The treasury", where money for the poor was collected, was located in the women's courtyard. For more information see the note on Lk 21:1–4.

8:21–24. At the outset of his public ministry, Jesus could be seen to have all the features of the promised Messiah; some people recognized him as such and became his followers (cf. Jn 1:12–13; 4:42; 6:69; 7:41); but the Jewish authorities, although they were expecting the

Messiah (cf. Jn 1:19ff), persisted in their rejection of Jesus. Hence the warning to them: he is going where they cannot follow, that is, he is going to heaven, which is where he has come from (cf. Jn 6:41ff), and they will keep on looking out for the Messiah foretold by the prophets; but they will not find him because they look for him outside of Jesus, nor can they follow him, for they do not believe in him. You are of the world, our Lord is saying to them, not because you are on earth but because you are living under the influence of the prince of this world (cf. Jn 12:31; 14:30; 16:11); you are his vassals and you do his deeds (cf. 8:44); therefore, you will die in your sin. "We were all born with sin", St Augustine comments, "all by our living have added to what we were by nature, and have become more of this world than we then were, when we were born of our parents. Where would we be if he had not come, who had no sin at all, to loose all sin? The Jews, because they did not believe in him, deserved to have it said to them, You will die in your sin" (*In Ioann. Evang.*, 38, 6).

The salvation which Christ brings will be applied to those who believe in his divinity. Jesus declares his divinity when he says "I am he", for this expression, which he repeats on other occasions (cf. Jn 8:28; 13:19), is reserved to Yahweh in the Old Testament (cf. Deut

you cannot come'?" ²³He said to them, "You are from below, I am from above; you are of this world, I am not of this world. ²⁴I told you that you would die in your sins, for you will die in your sins unless you believe that I am he." ²⁵They said to him, "Who are you?" Jesus said to them, "Even what I have told you from the beginning.ᵗ ²⁶I have much to say about you and much to judge; but he who sent me is true, and I declare to the world what I have heard from him." ²⁷They did not understand that he spoke to them

Jn 3:31

Ex 3:14

Jn 7:28;
12:48–50

32:39; Is 43:10–11), where God, in revealing his name and therefore his essence, says to Moses "I AM WHO I AM" (Ex 3:14). In this profound way God says that he is the Supreme Being in a full, absolute sense, that he is dependent on no other being, that all other things depend on him for their being and existence. Thus, when Jesus says of himself "I am he", he is revealing that he is God.

8:25. A little before this Jesus had spoken about his heavenly origin and his divine nature (cf. vv. 23–24); but the Jews do not want to accept this revelation; which is why they ask him for an even more explicit statement: "Who are you?" Our Lord's reply can be understood in different ways, because the Greek text has two meanings: 1) our Lord is confirming what he has just asserted (cf. vv. 23–24) and what he has been teaching throughout this visit to Jerusalem—in which case it may be translated "precisely what I am telling you" or else "in the first place what I am telling you". This is the interpretation given in the New Vulgate. 2) Jesus is indicating that he is the "Beginning", which is the word St John also uses in the Apocalypse to designate the Word, the cause of all creation (Rev 3:14; cf. Rev 1:8). In this way Jesus states his divine origin. This is the interpretation given in the Vulgate. Either way, Christ is once more revealing his divinity; he is reaf-

firming what he said earlier, but without saying it all over again.

"Many people in our own days ask the same question: 'Who are you?' [...] Who, then, was Jesus? Our faith exults and cries out: it is he, it is he, the Son of God made man. He is the Messiah we were expecting: he is the Saviour of the world, the Master of our lives; he is the Shepherd that guides men to their pastures in time, to their destinies beyond time. He is the joy of the world; he is the image of the invisible God; he is the way, the truth and the life; he is the interior friend; he is the One who knows us even from afar; he knows our thoughts; he is the One who can forgive us, console, cure, even raise from the dead; and he is the One who will return, the judge of one and all, in the fullness of his glory and our eternal happiness" (Paul VI, *General Audience*, 11 December 1974).

8:26–27. "He who sent me": an expression very often found in St John's Gospel, referring to God the Father (cf. 5:37; 6:44; 7:28; 8:16).

The Jews who were listening to Jesus did not understand whom he was referring to; but St John, in recounting this episode, explains that he meant his Father, from whom he came.

"He spoke to them of the Father": this is the reading in most of the Greek codexes, including the more important

t. Or *Why do I talk to you at all?*

Jn 3:14; 12:32   of the Father. [28]So Jesus said, "When you have lifted up the Son of man, then you will know that I am he, and that I do nothing on
Jn 4:34; 16:32   my own authority but speak thus as the Father taught me. [29]And he who sent me is with me; he has not left me alone, for I always

---

ones. Other Greek codexes and some translations, including the Vulgate, read "he was calling God his Father".

"What I have heard from him": Jesus had connatural knowledge of his Father, and it is from this knowledge that he speaks to men; he knows God not through revelation or inspiration as the prophets and sacred writers did, but in an infinitely higher way: which is why he can say that no one knows the Father but the Son and he to whom the Son chooses to reveal him (cf. Mt 11:27). On the type of knowledge Jesus had during his life on earth, see the note on Luke 2:52.

8:28. Our Lord is referring to his passion and death: (see Jn 12:32–33). Rounding out the Synoptics and the letters of St Paul, the Fourth Gospel presents the cross, above all, as a royal throne on which Christ is "lifted up" and from which he offers all men the fruits of salvation (cf. Jn 3:14–15; Num 21:9ff; Wis 16:6).

Jesus says that when that time comes, the Jews will know who he is and his intimate union with the Father, because many of them will discover, thanks to his death and resurrection, that he is the Messiah, the Son of God (cf. Mk 15:39; Lk 23:48). After the coming of the Holy Spirit many thousands will believe in him.

8:30–32. Of those Jews who do believe in him Jesus asks much more than a shallow faith resulting from superficial enthusiasm: they should be true disciples; Jesus' words should imbue their whole life. That kind of faith will bring them to know the truth and to become really free persons.

The knowledge of the truth which Christ is speaking about is not just intel-lectual knowledge; it is rather the maturing in the soul of the seed of divine revelation. That revelation's climax is to be found in Christ's teaching, and it constitutes a genuine communication of supernatural life (cf. Jn 5:24): he who believes in Jesus, and through him in the Father, receives the wonderful gift of eternal life. Knowing the truth is, in the last analysis, knowing Christ himself, God become man to save us; it means realizing that the inaccessible God has become man, our Friend, our Life.

This is the only kind of knowledge which really sets us free, because it removes us from a position of alienation from God—the state of sin and therefore of slavery to the devil and to all the attachments of our fallen nature—and puts us on the path of friendship with God, the path of grace, of the Kingdom of God. Therefore, the liberation we obtain is not just light which shows us the way; it is grace, which empowers us to keep to that way despite our limitations.

"Jesus Christ meets the man of every age, including our own, with the same words: 'You will know the truth, and the truth will make you free' (Jn 8:32). These words contain both a fundamental requirement and a warning: the requirement of an honest relationship with regard to truth as a condition for authentic freedom, and the warning to avoid every kind of illusory freedom, every superficial unilateral freedom, every freedom that fails to enter into the whole truth about man and the world. Today also, even after two thousand years, we see Christ as the one who brings man freedom based on truth, frees

do what is pleasing to him." [30]As he spoke thus, many believed in him.

"The truth will set you free"

[31]Jesus then said to the Jews who had believed in him, "If you continue in my word, you are truly my disciples, [32]and you will know the truth, and the truth will make you free." [33]They

Jn 15:14

---

man from what curtails, diminishes and as it were breaks off this freedom at its root, in man's soul, his heart and his conscience. What a stupendous confirmation of this has been given and is still being given by those who, thanks to Christ and in Christ, have reached true freedom and have manifested it even in situations of external constraint!" (John Paul II, *Redemptor hominis*, 12).

"Christ himself links liberation particularly with knowledge of the truth; 'You will know the truth and the truth will make you free' (Jn 8:32). This sentence testifies above all to the intimate significance of the freedom for which Christ liberates us. Liberation means man's inner transformation, which is a consequence of the knowledge of truth. The transformation is, therefore, a spiritual process, in which man matures 'in true righteousness and holiness' (Eph 4:24). [...] Truth is important not only for the growth of human knowledge, deepening man's interior life in this way; truth has also a prophetic significance and power. It constitutes the content of testimony and it calls for testimony. We find this prophetic power of truth in the teaching of Christ. As a prophet, as a witness to truth, Christ repeatedly opposes non-truth; he does so with great forcefulness and decision and often he does not hesitate to condemn falsehood" (John Paul II, General Audience, 21 February 1979).

St Thomas Aquinas says: "In this passage, being made free does not refer to being freed of every type of wrong [...]; it means being freed in the proper sense of the word, in three ways: first, the truth of his teaching will free us from the error of untruth [...]; second, the truth of grace will liberate us from the slavery of sin: 'the law of the Spirit of life in Christ Jesus has set me free from the law of sin and death' (Rom 8:2); third, the truth of eternity in Christ Jesus will free us from decay (cf. Rom 8:21)" (*Comm. on St John*, in loc.).

"The truth will set you free. How great a truth is this, which opens the way to freedom and gives it meaning throughout our lives. I will sum it up for you, with the joy and certainty which flow from knowing there is a close relationship between God and his creatures. It is the knowledge that we have come from the hands of God, that the Blessed Trinity looks upon us with predilection, that we are children of so wonderful a Father. I ask my Lord to help us decide to take this truth to heart, to dwell upon it day by day; only then will we be acting as free men. Do not forget: anyone who does not realize that he is a child of God is unaware of the deepest truth about himself. When he acts he lacks the dominion and self-mastery we find in those who love our Lord above all else" (St Josemaría Escrivá, *Friends of God*, 26).

8:33–34. For centuries the people of Israel were ruled by other nations (Egypt, Babylon, Persia ...), and now they were

Mt 3:9   answered him, "We are descendants of Abraham, and have never
been in bondage to any one. How is it that you say, 'You will be
made free'?"

Rom 6:17–20   34Jesus answered them, "Truly, truly, I say to you, every one
Gen 21:10   who commits sin is a slave of sin. 35The slave does not continue
Gal 4:30   in the house for ever; the son continues for ever. 36So if the Son
Gal 5:1
Jn 5:38   makes you free, you will be free indeed. 37I know that you are
Mt 21:36–46   descendants of Abraham; yet you seek to kill me, because my
word finds no place in you. 38I speak of what I have seen with my
Father, and you do what you have heard from your father."

The true children of Abraham
39They answered him, "Abraham is our father." Jesus said to
them, "If you were Abraham's children, you would do what

---

under the dominion of Rome. The Jews think Jesus is referring to political bondage or dominion—which in fact they had experienced but never accepted. In addition, since they belong to the people chosen by God, they regard themselves as free of the moral errors and aberrations of Gentile nations.

They thought that true freedom was a matter of belonging to the chosen people. Our Lord replies that it is not enough to belong to the line of Abraham: true freedom consists in not being slaves of sin. Both Jews and Gentiles were subject to the slavery of original sin and personal sin (cf. Rom 5:12; 6:20 and 8:2). Only Christ, the Son of God, can liberate man from that sorry state (cf. Gal 4:21–31); but these Jews do not understand the redemptive work which Christ is doing and which will reach its climax in his death and resurrection.

"The Saviour", St Augustine comments, "is here explaining that we will not be freed from overlords, but from the devil; not from captivity of the body but from malice of soul" (*Sermons*, 48).

8:35–36. The words "slave" and "son" are reminiscent of the two sons of Abraham: Ishmael, born of the slave woman Hagar, who would be given no part in the inheritance; and Isaac, son of the free woman Sarah, who would be the heir to God's promises (cf. Gen 21:10–12; Gal 4:28–31). Physical descent from Abraham is not enough for inheriting God's promises and attaining salvation: by faith and charity one must identify oneself with Jesus Christ, the true and only Son of the Father, the only one who can make us sons of God and thereby bring us true freedom (cf. Rom 8:21; Gal 4:31). Christ gives "power to become children of God [to those] who were born, not of blood nor of the will of the flesh nor of the will of man, but of God" (Jn 1:12–13). Thus, a person who identifies himself with Christ becomes a son of God and obtains the freedom proper to sons.

"Freedom finds its true meaning when it is put to the service of the truth which redeems, when it is spent in seeking God's infinite Love which liberates us from all forms of slavery. Each passing day increases my yearning to proclaim to the four winds this inexhaustible treasure that belongs to Christianity: 'the glorious freedom of the children of God!' (Rom 8:21). [...] Where does our free-

108

Abraham did, [40]but now you seek to kill me, a man who has told you the truth which I heard from God; this is not what Abraham did. [41]You do what your father did." They said to him, "We were not born of fornication; we have one Father, even God."* [42]Jesus said of them, "If God were your Father, you would love me, for I proceeded and came forth from God; I came not of my own account, but he sent me. [43]Why do you not understand what I say? It is because you cannot bear to hear my word. [44]You are of your father the devil, and your will is to do your father's desires. He was a murderer from the beginning, and has nothing to do with the truth, because there is no truth in him. When he lies, he speaks according to his own nature, for he is a liar and the father of lies. [45]But, because I tell the truth, you do not believe me. [46]Which of you convicts me of sin? If I tell the truth, why do you not believe

Ex 4:22
Deut 32:6

1 Jn 5:1

Jn 12:39
Mt 12:34
1 Jn 3:8–15
Gen 3:1–4
Wis 2:24
2 Pet 2:4

2 Cor 5:21
1 Pet 2:22

---

dom come from? It comes from Christ our Lord. This is the freedom with which he has ransomed us (cf. Gal 4:31). That is why he teaches, 'if the Son makes you free, you will be free indeed' (Jn 8:36)" (St J. Escrivá, *Friends of God*, 27 and 35).

8:37–41. Our Lord replies to the Jews' objection: yes indeed, they are Abraham's children, but only in a natural sense, according to the flesh; that does not count any more; what matters now is acceptance of Jesus as the One sent by the Father. Jesus' questioners are spiritually very far away from being true children of Abraham: Abraham rejoiced to see the Messiah (cf. Jn 8:56); through his faith he was reckoned righteous (cf. Rom 4:1ff), and his faith led him to act consequentially (cf. Jas 2:21–24); this was how he attained the joy of eternal blessedness (cf. Mt 8:11; Lk 16:24). Although those Jews "derived from him the generation of the flesh, they had become degenerate, by not imitating the faith of him whose sons they were" (St Augustine, *In Ioann. Evang.*, 42, 1). Those who live by faith are the true sons of Abraham and like him they will be blessed by God (cf. Gal 3:7–9). In fact, the people

who are arguing with our Lord have not only rejected his teaching: their own deeds indicate that they have a radically different affiliation: "You do what your father did" is a veiled accusation that they are children of the devil (cf. v. 44).

The false security Jews felt in being descended from Abraham has its parallel in a Christian who is content with being baptized and with a few religious observances, but does not live up to the requirements of faith in Christ.

8:42–44. In claiming to be children of God, the Jews appeal to statements in the Old Testament (cf. Ex 4:22; Deut 32:6; Is 63:16; Jer 3:4; 31:9; Mal 1:6). However, the attitude they adopt towards Jesus is in contradiction with this condition of being children of God—for that should lead them to accept Jesus, since he is the One sent by the Father. Because they reject the Only-begotten Son they are acting like partisans or sons of God's enemy, the devil. The devil, because he opposes our Lord, who is the Truth, is the father of lies: by lying he seduced our first parents and he deceives all those who yield to his temptations.

Jn 8:37
1 Jn 4:6

Jn 7:20
Mk 3:21ff

Jn 5:41; 7:18

Jn 5:24–28;
6:40, 47, 11:25
me? [47]He who is of God hears the words of God; the reason why you do not hear them is that you are not of God."

[48]The Jews answered him, "Are we not right in saying that you are a Samaritan and have a demon?" [49]Jesus answered, "I have not a demon; but I honour my Father, and you dishonour me. [50]Yet I do not seek my own glory; there is One who seeks it and he will be the judge. [51]Truly, truly, I say to you, if any one keeps my word, he will never see death."

"Before Abraham was, I am"

Jn 7:20

Jn 4:12
[52]The Jews said to him, "Now we know that you have a demon. Abraham died, as did the prophets; and you say, 'If any one keeps my word, he will never taste death.' [53]Are you greater than our

---

8:48. Instead of replying to Jesus' line of argument, the Jews attack him by insulting him. Before all this, they had spread the calumny that he was possessed by the devil, that he was out of his mind (cf. Mk 3:21) and that he cast out demons in the name of the prince of demons (cf. Mk 3:22; Mt 12:24). By calling him a Samaritan they accuse him of being a heretic, a violator of the Law, a semi-pagan: the Jews regarded the Samaritans as the prototypes of religious perversion. (On the origin of the Samaritan people and why there was such hostility between them and the Jews, cf. the notes on Lk 9:52–53 and Jn 4:20, 21–24).

8:50. Faced with these wild accusations, Jesus acts with great patience, while still firmly defending divine truth. "When it was necessary for him to teach", St John Chrysostom says, "and bend his enemies' pride, he acted very resolutely; whereas, when he had to bear an insult, he acted with great meekness, thus teaching us to defend God's rights and be forgetful of our own" (*Hom. on St John*, 54).

Jesus leaves this argument to the judgment of God, for he is not seeking human fame. St Paul will reiterate this teaching of our Lord, to underline his

own upright intention and the kindness with which we should treat everyone (cf. Rom 12:19–20).

8:51–53. "He will never see death": our Lord promises eternal life to those who accept and remain faithful to his teaching.

Sin, as the Fourth Gospel teaches, is death of the soul; and sanctifying grace, life (cf. Jn 1:4, 13; 3:15, 16, 36; etc.). Through grace we enter eternal life, a pledge of the glory we shall attain beyond this earthly life and which is the true Life. Blinded by their hostility, the Jews do not want to listen to the Lord and therefore they fail to understand him.

8:55. The knowledge our Lord is speaking about is more than intellectual knowledge. The Old Testament speaks of this "knowing" in the sense of love, faithfulness, generous self-surrender. Love for God comes from the certain knowledge we have of him, and the more we love him, the better we get to know him.

Jesus, whose holy human nature was intimately united (though not mixed) with his divinity in the one Person of the Word, continues to assert his singular and ineffable knowledge of the Father. But this accurate language of Jesus is absol-

father Abraham, who died? And the prophets died! Who do you claim to be?" [54]Jesus answered, "If I glorify myself, my glory is nothing; it is my Father who glorifies me, of whom you say that he is your God. [55]But you have not known him; I know him. If I said, I do not know him, I should be a liar like you; but I do know him and I keep his word. [56]Your father Abraham rejoiced that he was to see my day; he saw it* and was glad." [57]The Jews then said to him, "You are not yet fifty years old, and have you seen Abraham?"u [58]Jesus said to them, "Truly, truly, I say to you, before Abraham was, I am."* [59]So they took up stones to throw at him; but Jesus hid himself, and went out of the temple.

Jn 7:28–29

Gen 17:17
Mt 13:17–18

Jn 8:24
Jn 10:31
Lk 4:29ff

---

utely incomprehensible to those who close themselves to faith: they even think he is blaspheming (cf. v. 59).

8:56. Jesus presents himself as the fulfilment of the hopes of the Old Testament patriarchs. They had stayed faithful, eager to see the Day of Salvation. Referring to their faith, St Paul exclaims: "These all died in faith, not having received what was promised, but having seen it and greeted it from afar, and having acknowledged that they were strangers and exiles on the earth" (Heb 11:13). The most outstanding of those patriarchs was Abraham, our father in faith (cf. Gal 3:7), who received the promise of being father of an immense people, the chosen people from whom would be born the Messiah.

The future fulfilment of the messianic promises was a source of great joy for Abraham: "Abraham, our father, who was set apart for the future accomplishment of the Promise, and who hoped against hope, receives when his son Isaac is born the prophetic firstfruits of this joy. This joy becomes transfigured through a trial touching death, when this only son is restored to him alive, a prefiguring of the resurrection of the one who was to

come: the only son of God, promised for the redeeming sacrifice. Abraham rejoiced at the thought of seeing the Day of Christ, the Day of Salvation: 'he saw it and was glad'" (Paul VI, *Gaudete in Domino*, 2).

Jesus moves on a plane superior to that of the patriarchs, for they only saw prophetically, from "afar", the Day of Christ, that is, the actual event of the Redemption, whereas it is Christ who brings it to pass.

8:58. Jesus' reply to the sceptical remarks of the Jews contains a revelation of his divinity. By saying "Before Abraham was, I am" our Lord is referring to his being eternal, because he is God. Therefore, St Augustine explains: "Acknowledge the Creator, discern the creature. He who was speaking was a descendant of Abraham, but that Abraham might be made, before Abraham he was" (*In Ioann. Evang.*, 43, 17). The Fathers recall, in connexion with the words of Christ, the solemn theophany of Sinai: "I AM WHO I AM" (Ex 3:14), and also St John's distinction, in the prologue to his Gospel, between the world which "was made" and the Word which "was" from all eternity (cf. Jn 1:1–3). The words "I

u. Other ancient authorities read *has Abraham seen you?*

Curing of the man born blind

Ex 20:5
Lk 13:2

Jn 11:4

Jn 5:17–20;
11:9–10
Jn 8:12; 12:35

Mk 8:23

9 ¹As he passed by, he saw a man blind from his birth. ²And his disciples asked him, "Rabbi, who sinned, this man or his parents, that he was born blind?" ³Jesus answered, "It was not that this man sinned, or his parents, but that the works of God might be made manifest in him. ⁴We must work the works of him who sent me, while it is day; night comes, when no one can work.* ⁵As long as I am in the world, I am the light of the world." ⁶As he said this, he spat on the ground and made clay of the spittle and

---

am", used by Jesus so absolutely, are the equivalent therefore, of his affirming his eternity and his divinity. Cf. the note on Jn 8:21–24.

9:2–3. The disciples' question echoes general Jewish views on the causes of illness and of misfortunes in general: they regarded them as punishment for personal sins (cf. Job 4:7–8; 2 Mac 7:18), or as the sins of parents being visited on their children (cf. Tob 3:3).

We know through Revelation (cf. Gen 3:16–19; Rom 5:12; etc.) that the origin of all the misfortunes which afflict mankind is sin—original sin and later personal sin. However, this does not mean that each misfortune or illness has its immediate cause in a personal sin, as if God inflicted or allowed evils to happen in direct proportion to every sin committed. Suffering, which is so often a factor in the life of the just man, can be a resource God sends him to cleanse him of his imperfections, to exercise him in virtue and to unite him to the sufferings of Christ the Redeemer who, although he was innocent, bore in himself the punishment our sins merited (cf. Is 53:4; 1 Pet 2:24; 1 Jn 3:5). For example, our Lady and St Joseph and all the saints have experienced intense suffering, thereby sharing in the redemptive suffering of Christ.

9:4–5. The "day" refers to Jesus' life on earth. Hence the urgency with which he approaches the task of doing the will of the Father until he reaches his death, which he compares with "night". This "night" can also be understood as referring to the end of the world; in this passage it means that the Redemption of men brought about by Christ needs to be continued by the Church throughout the centuries, and also that Christians should strive to spread the Kingdom of God.

"Time is precious, time passes, time is a phase of experiment with regard to our decisive and definitive fate. Our future and eternal destiny depends on the proof we give of faithfulness to our duties. Time is a gift from God; it is a question posed by God's love to our free and, it can be said, fateful answer. We must be sparing of time, in order to use it well, in the intense activity of our life of work, love and suffering. Idleness or boredom have no place in the life of a Christian! Rest, yes, when necessary (cf. Mk 6:31), but always with a view to vigilance, which only on the last day will open to a light on which the sun will never set" (Paul VI, Homily, 1 January 1976).

Jesus proclaims that he is the light of the world because his life among men has given us the ultimate meaning of the world, of the life of every man and every woman, and of mankind as a whole. Without Jesus all creation is in darkness, it does not understand itself, it does not know where it is going. "Only in the

anointed the man's eyes with the clay, [7]saying to him, "Go, wash
in the pool of Siloam" (which means Sent). So he went and washed and came back seeing. [8]The neighbours and those who had
seen him before as a beggar, said, "Is not this the man who used
to sit and beg?" [9]Some said, "It is he"; others said, "No, but he is
like him." He said, "I am the man." [10]They said to him, "Then
how were your eyes opened?" [11]He answered, "The man called
Jesus made clay and anointed my eyes and said to me, 'Go to
Siloam and wash'; so I went and washed and received my sight."
[12]They said to him, "Where is he?" He said, "I do not know."

Is 8:6

---

mystery of the Incarnate Word does the
mystery of man take on light. [...]
Through Christ and in Christ, the riddles
of sorrow and death grow meaningful;
apart from his Gospel they overwhelm
us" (Vatican II, *Gaudium et spes*, 22).
Jesus warns us—as he will do more
clearly in John 12:35–36—of the need to
let ourselves be enlightened by the light,
which is he himself (cf. Jn 1:9–12).

9:6–7. This cure is done in two stages—
Jesus' action on the eyes of the blind
man, and the man being told to go and
wash in the pool of Siloam. Our Lord
also used saliva to cure a man who was
deaf and dumb (cf. Mk 7:33) and another
blind man (cf. Mk 8:23). The pool of
Siloam was a reservoir built by King
Hezekiah, in the seventh century BC, to
supply Jerusalem with water (cf. 2 Kings
20:20; 2 Chron 32:30); the prophets
regarded these waters as a sign of divine
favour (cf. Is 8:6; 22:11). St John, using
the broader etymology of the word
"Siloam", applies it to Jesus who is the
"One sent" by the Father. Our Lord works
through the medium of matter to produce
effects which exceed anything matter can
do. Something similar will occur with the
sacraments: through his word he will
confer on material media the power of
spiritually regenerating man.

Our Lord's instruction to the blind
man is reminiscent of the miracle of

Naaman, the Syrian general who was
cured of leprosy when, on the instruction
of the prophet Elisha, he washed seven
times in the waters of the Jordan (cf. 2
Kings 5:1ff). Naaman had hesitated
before obeying, whereas the blind man
obeys promptly without asking questions
or raising objections.

"What an example of firm faith the
blind man gives us! A living, operative
faith. Do you behave like this when God
commands, when so often you cannot
see, when your soul is worried and the
light is gone? What power could the
water possibly contain that when the
blind man's eyes were moistened with it
they were cured? Surely some mysterious eye salve, or a precious medicine
made up in the laboratory of some wise
alchemist, would have done better? But
the man believed; he acted upon the
command of God, and he returned with
eyes full of light" (St Josemaría Escrivá,
Friends of God, 193).

9:8–34. After recounting the miracle, the
Evangelist reports the doubts of the
man's friends and neighbours (vv. 8–12)
and the inquiry made by the Pharisees:
they question the man (vv. 13–17), his
parents (vv. 18–23), and then the man
again, whom they end up condemning
and expelling from their presence (vv.
24–34). This passage is so full of detail
that it looks like an eyewitness account.

Jn 5:9
Mt 12:10–11
Lk 3:10ff

Jn 3:2; 7:43;
9:31, 33

Jn 4:19
Mt 16:14

[13]They brought to the Pharisees the man who had formerly been blind. [14]Now it was a sabbath day when Jesus made the clay and opened his eyes. [15]The Pharisees again asked him how he had received his sight. And he said to them, "He put clay on my eyes, and I washed, and I see." [16]Some of the Pharisees said, "This man is not from God, for he does not keep the sabbath." But others said, "How can a man who is a sinner do such signs?" There was a division among them. [17]So they again said to the blind man, "What do you say about him, since he has opened your eyes?" He said, "He is a prophet."

[18]The Jews did not believe that he had been blind and had received his sight, until they called the parents of the man who had received his sight, [19]and asked them, "Is this your son, who you say was born blind? How then does he now see?" [20]His par-

---

The Fathers and Doctors of the Church have seen this miracle as symbolizing the sacrament of Baptism in which, through the medium of water, the soul is cleansed and receives the light of faith: "He sent the man to the pool called the pool of Siloam, to be cleansed and to be enlightened, that is, to be baptized and receive in baptism full enlightenment" (St Thomas Aquinas, *Comm. on St John*, in loc.).

This episode also reflects the different attitudes of people to our Lord and his miracles. The blind man, a straightforward person, believes in Jesus as envoy, prophet (vv. 17, 33) and Son of God (vv. 17, 33, 38); whereas the Pharisees persist in not wanting to see or believe, despite the clear evidence before them (vv. 24–34).

In this miracle Jesus once again reveals himself as the light of the world. This bears out the statement in the prologue: "The true light that enlightens every man was coming into the world" (1:9). Not only does he give light to the eyes of the blind man: he enlightens his soul, leading him to make an act of faith in his divinity (v. 38). At the same time we can see the obvious drama of those whose blindness darkens their minds, as our Lord said in his dialogue with Nicodemus: "The light has come into the world, and men loved darkness rather than light, because their deeds were evil" (Jn 3:19).

9:14–16. The Pharisees bring up the same accusation as they did when the paralyzed man was cured beside the pool (Jn 5:10) and as on other occasions: Jesus has broken the Law because he cures the sick on the sabbath (cf. Lk 13:16; 14:5; etc.). Christ had often taught that observance of the law of sabbath rest (cf. Ex 20:8, 11; 21:13; Deut 5:14) was compatible with the duty to do good (cf. Mt 12:3–8; Mk 2:28; Lk 6:5). Charity, the good of others, takes precedence over all the other commandments (cf. the note on Mt 12:3–8). If rules are given precedence in a blind sort of way over the inescapable obligations of justice and charity, the result is fanaticism, which always goes against the Gospel and even against right reason— as happens in this instance with the Pharisees. Their minds are so closed that they do not want to see God's hand in something which simply could not be done without divine power. The dilemma

ents answered, "We know that this is our son, and that he was
born blind; [21]but how he now sees we do not know, nor do we
know who opened his eyes. Ask him; he is of age, he will speak
for himself." [22]His parents said this because they feared the Jews, Jn 7:13; 14:22;
16:2
for the Jews had already agreed that if any one should confess
him to be Christ, he was to be put out of the synagogue. [23]There-
fore his parents said, "He is of age, ask him."

The blindness of the Jews
[24]So for the second time they called the man who had been blind, Josh 7:19
and said to him, "Give God the praise; we know that this man is a
sinner." [25]He answered, "Whether he is a sinner, I do not know;
one thing I know, that though I was blind, now I see." [26]They said
to him, "What did he do to you? How did he open your eyes?"

---

they pose themselves—Is he a man of
God, as his miracles imply; or a sinner,
because he does not keep the sabbath (cf.
Mk 3:23–30)?—can only arise in people
whose outlook is that of religious fanat-
ics. Their mistaken interpretation of how
certain precepts should be kept leads
them to forget the essence of the Law—
love of God and love of neighbour.

To avoid accepting Jesus' divinity,
the Pharisees reject the only possible correct interpretation of the miracle; whereas the blind man—like all unprejudiced
people open to the truth— finds solid
grounds in the miracle for confessing that
Christ works through the power of God
(Jn 9:33): "He supported and confirmed
his preaching by miracles to arouse the
faith of his hearers and give them assurance, but not to coerce them" (Vatican II,
Dignitatis humanae, 11).

9:24. "Give God the praise": a solemn
declaration, like an oath, exhorting a
person to tell the truth. But the Pharisees
are not looking for the truth: they want to
intimidate the man to get him to with-
draw his statement. They try to pressure
him by warning him: "We know this man
is a sinner." St Augustine comments:

"What do they mean, Give God the
praise? They mean, deny what you have
received. Clearly, this is not to give God
the praise, but rather to blaspheme
against God" (*In Ioann. Evang.*, 44, 11).

9:25–34. This interrogation shows that
the miracle was so patent that not even
his enemies could deny it. Our Lord
worked many miracles during his public
ministry, showing that he had complete
power over everything, in other words
that he was divine.

Rationalism, basing itself on an erro-
neous philosophical principle, refuses to
accept that God can intervene in a supernatural way in this world; it therefore
denies the possibility of miracles: but the
Church has always taught that miracles
do happen and that they serve a purpose:
"If any one shall say that miracles are
impossible, and that therefore all the
accounts regarding them, even those contained in Holy Scripture, are to be dis-
missed as fabulous or mythical; or that
miracles can never be known with certainty, and that the divine origin of
Christianity cannot be proved by them—
let him be *anathema*" (Vatican I, *Dei
Filius*, chap. 3 and can. 4).

27He answered them, "I have told you already, and you would not listen. Why do you want to hear it again? Do you too want to become his disciples?" 28And they reviled him, saying, "You are his disciple, but we are disciples of Moses. 29We know that God has spoken to Moses, but as for this man, we do not know where he comes from." 30The man answered, "Why, this is a marvel! You do not know where he comes from, and yet he opened my eyes. 31We know that God does not listen to sinners, but if any one is a worshipper of God and does his will, God listens to him. 32Never since the world began has it been heard that any one opened the eyes of a man born blind. 33If this man were not from God, he could do nothing." 34They answered him, "You were born in utter sin, and would you teach us?" And they cast him out.

35Jesus heard that they had cast him out and having found him he said, "Do you believe in the Son of man?"v 36He answered,

Is 1:15
Prov 15:29
Acts 10:35

Jn 9:16

Jn 9:2

9:29. Everyone saw the miracle, but the Pharisees are so stubborn that they will not accept the significance of the event, not even after questioning the man himself and his parents. "The sin of the Pharisees did not consist in not seeing God in Christ, but in voluntarily shutting themselves up within themselves, in not letting Jesus, who is the light, open their eyes (cf. Jn 9:39–41)" (St Josemaría Escrivá, *Christ Is Passing By*, 71). As this episode proceeds, the faith of the man himself deepens. He begins by recognizing Jesus as a prophet (v. 17) and he ends up acknowledging his divinity (v. 35); whereas over the same course of events the authorities become more and more obstinate—moving from doubt (v.16), through the blasphemous assertion that Jesus is a sinner, to eventually expelling the beggar (v. 34)—a useful warning about the danger of pride which can blind one to the obvious.

9:34. After the Babylonian exile (sixth century BC), a Jewish custom developed of expelling from the synagogue those who had committed certain crimes. This took two forms—temporary expulsion for thirty days as a disciplinary measure, and permanent expulsion, which later was often imposed on Jews who became Christians. What is being referred to here is probably permanent expulsion, which was what was planned (v. 22) and which is noted elsewhere in the Gospels (cf. Jn 12:42; 16:2; Lk 6:22).

9:35–38. This does not seem to have been an accidental meeting. The Pharisees have cast the man out of the synagogue; our Lord not only receives him but helps him make an act of faith in his divinity: "Now with the face of his heart washed and with his conscience cleansed, he acknowledges him to be not only Son of man but Son of God" (St Augustine, *In Ioann. Evang.*, 44, 15). This dialogue reminds us of Jesus' conversation with the Samaritan woman (cf. Jn 4:26).

9:39. This judgment which our Lord pronounces follows on the act of faith of the man who has been cured, and the persistent obstinacy of the Pharisees. He has not come to condemn the world but to

---

v. Other ancient authorities read *the Son of God*

"And who is he, sir, that I may believe in him?" [37]Jesus said to him, "You have seen him, and it is he who speaks to you." [38]He said, "Lord, I believe"; and he worshipped him. [39]Jesus said, "For judgment I came into this world, that those who do not see may see, and that those who see may become blind." [40]Some of the Pharisees near him heard this, and they said to him, "Are we also blind?" [41]Jesus said to them, "If you were blind, you would have no guilt; but now that you say, 'We see,' your guilt remains."

Jn 4:26

Jn 8:12
Mt 13:13

Mt 15:14

Jn 3:36
Prov 26:12

The Good Shepherd

10 [1]"Truly, truly, I say to you, he who does not enter the sheepfold by the door but climbs in by another way, that man is a thief and a robber; [2]but he who enters by the door is the shep-

Ezek 34:1–31
Jer 23:1–3

---

save it (cf. Jn 3:17), but his presence among us already involves a judgment, because each of us has to take a stand on whether to reject or accept Jesus. Christ's coming implies the fall of some and the salvation of others (cf. Lk 2:34). In this sense, we will fall into one of two categories (cf. Jn 3:18–21; 12:47–48): on the one hand, the humble of heart (cf. Mt 11:25), who recognize their failings and who go to Jesus in search of forgiveness (these will receive the light he is speaking of); on the other hand, those who are satisfied with themselves and think that they do not need Christ or his word (they say they see but they are blind). Thus we ourselves decide our ultimate fate, depending on whether we accept or reject Jesus.

9:40–41. Jesus' words sting the Pharisees, who are always looking to catch him in something he says. They realize that he is referring to them and they ask him, "Are we also blind?" Jesus' answer is quite clear: they can see but they do not want to: therefore they are unworthy. "If you realized you were blind, if you admitted you were blind and ran to the physician, you would have no sin, for I have come to take away sin; but because you say that you can see, you remain in your

blindness" (St Augustine, *In Ioann. Evang.*, 45, 17).

10:1–18. The image of the Good Shepherd recalls a favourite theme of Old Testament prophetic literature: the chosen people is the flock, and Yahweh is their shepherd (cf. Ps 23). Kings and priests are also described as shepherds or pastors. Jeremiah inveighs against those pastors who had let their sheep go astray and in God's name promises new pastors who will graze their flocks properly so that they will never again be harassed or anxious (cf. 23:1–6; also 2:8; 3:15; 10:21; Is 40:1–11). Ezekiel reproaches pastors for their misdeeds and sloth, their greed and neglect of their responsibility: Yahweh will take the flock away from them and he himself will look after their sheep; indeed, a unique shepherd will appear, descended from David, who will graze them and protect them (Ezek 34). Jesus presents himself as this shepherd who looks after his sheep, seeks out the strays, cures the crippled and carries the weak on his shoulders (cf. Mt 18:12–14; Lk 15:4–7), thereby fulfilling the ancient prophecies.

From earliest times, Christian art found its inspiration in this touching image of the Good Shepherd, thereby

herd of the sheep. ³To him the gatekeeper opens; the sheep hear his voice, and he calls his own sheep by name and leads them out.

Jn 10:27

⁴When he has brought out all his own, he goes before them, and the sheep follow him, for they know his voice. ⁵A stranger they will not follow, but they will flee from him, for they do not know the voice of strangers." ⁶This figure Jesus used with them, but they did not understand what he was saying to them.

Ps 118:20

⁷So Jesus again said to them, "Truly, truly, I say to you, I am the door of the sheep. ⁸All who came before me are thieves and robbers; but the sheep did not heed them. ⁹I am the door; if any

---

leaving us a representation of Christ's love for each of us.

In addition to the title of Good Shepherd, Christ applies to himself the image of the door into the sheepfold of the Church. "The Church," Vatican II teaches, "is a sheepfold, the sole and necessary gateway to which is Christ (cf. Jn 10:1–10). It is also a flock, of which God foretold that he himself would be the shepherd (cf. Is 40:11; Ezek 34:11ff), and whose sheep, although watched over by human shepherds, are nevertheless at all times led and brought to pasture by Christ himself, the Good Shepherd and prince of shepherds (cf. Jn 10:11; 1 Pet 5:4), who gave his life for his sheep (cf. Jn 10:11–15)" (*Lumen gentium*, 6).

10:1–2. The flock can be harmed in a subtle, hidden way, or in a blatant way through abuse of authority. The history of the Church shows that its enemies have used both methods: sometimes they enter the flock in a secretive way to harm it from within; sometimes they attack it from outside, openly and violently. "Who is the good shepherd? 'He who enters by the door' of faithfulness to the Church's doctrine and does not act like the hireling 'who sees the wolf coming and leaves the sheep and flees'; whereupon 'the wolf snatches them and scatters them (cf. Jn 10:1–21)'" (St Josemaría Escrivá, *Christ Is Passing By*, 34).

10:3–5. In those times it was usual at nightfall to bring a number of flocks together into one sheepfold, where they would be kept for the night with someone acting as lookout. Then at dawn the shepherds would come back and open the sheepfold and each would call his sheep which would gather round and follow him out of the pen (they were used to his voice because he used to call them to prevent them from going astray) and he would then lead them to pasture. Our Lord uses this image—one very familiar to his listeners—to teach them a divine truth: since there are strange voices around, we need to know the voice of Christ—which is continually addressing us through the Magisterium of the Church—and to follow it, if we are to get the nourishment our soul needs. "Christ has given his Church sureness in doctrine and a fountain of grace in the sacraments. He has arranged things so that there will always be people to guide and lead us, to remind us constantly of our way. There is an infinite treasure of knowledge available to us: the word of God kept safe by the Church, the grace of Christ administered in the sacraments and also the witness and example of those who live by our side and have known how to build with their good lives a road of faithfulness to God" (*Christ Is Passing By*, 34).

one enters by me, he will be saved, and will go in and out and find pasture. ¹⁰The thief comes only to steal and kill and destroy; I came that they may have life, and have it abundantly. ¹¹I am the good shepherd. The good shepherd lays down his life for the sheep. ¹²He who is a hireling and not a shepherd, whose own the sheep are not, sees the wolf coming and leaves the sheep and flees; and the wolf snatches them and scatters them. ¹³He flees because he is a hireling and cares nothing for the sheep. ¹⁴I am the good shepherd;* I know my own and my own know me, ¹⁵as the Father knows me and I know the Father; and I lay down my life

Jn 3:17
Is 49:9–10

Ps 23:1ff
Lk 15:4–7

Acts 20:29
1 Pet 2:25

2 Tim 2:19

Mt 11:25–27

10:6. Christ develops and interprets the image of the shepherd and the flock, to ensure that everyone who is well-disposed can understand his meaning. But the Jews fail to understand—as happened also when he promised the Eucharist (Jn 6:41–43) and spoke of the "living water" (Jn 7:40–43), or when he raised Lazarus from the dead (Jn 11:45–46).

10:7. After describing his future Church through the image of the flock, Christ extends the simile and calls himself the "door of the sheep". The shepherds and the sheep enter the sheepfold: both must enter through the door, which is Christ. "I", St Augustine preached, "seeking to enter in among you, that is, into your heart, preach Christ: if I were to preach other than that, I should be trying to enter by some other way. Through Christ I enter in, not to your houses but to your hearts. Through him I enter and you have willingly heard me speak of him. Why? Because you are Christ's sheep and you have been purchased with Christ's blood" (*In Ioann. Evang.*, 47, 2–3).

10:8. The severe reproach Jesus levels against those who came before him does not apply to Moses or the prophets (cf. Jn 5:39, 45; 8:56; 12:41), nor to the Baptist (cf. Jn 5:33), for they proclaimed the future Messiah and prepared the way for him. He is referring to the false prophets

and deceivers of the people, among them some teachers of the Law—blind men and blind guides (cf. Mt 23:16–24) who block the people's way to Christ, as happened just a little before when the man born blind was cured (cf. Jn 9).

10:11–15. "The good shepherd lays down his life for the sheep": "Here," says St John Chrysostom, "he is speaking of his passion, making it clear this would take place for the salvation of the world and that he would go to it freely and willingly" (*Hom. on St John*, 59, 3). Our Lord spoke further about giving abundant pasture; now he speaks about giving his very life: "He did what he said he would do," St Gregory comments; "he gave his life for his sheep, and he gave his body and blood in the Sacrament to nourish with his flesh the sheep he had redeemed" (*In Evangelia homiliae*, 14, ad loc.). Hired men, on the other hand, run away if there is any danger, leaving the flock at risk. "Who is the hireling? He who sees the wolf coming and flees. The man who seeks his own glory, not the glory of Christ; the man who does not dare to reprove sinners. You are the hireling; you have seen the wolf coming and have fled [...] because you held your peace; and you held your peace, because you were afraid" (St Augustine, *In Ioann. Evang.*, 46, 8).

"Let them remember that their priestly ministry ... is—in a special way —'ordered' to the great solicitude of the

Jn 11:52
Ezek 37:24
Eph 4:4–5

for the sheep. ¹⁶And I have other sheep, that are not of this fold; I must bring them also, and they will heed my voice. So there shall be one flock, one shepherd. ¹⁷For this reason the Father loves me,

Phil 2:8–9

because I lay down my life, that I may take it again. ¹⁸No one

Jn 5:26

takes it from me, but I lay it down of my own accord. I have power to lay it down, and I have power to take it again; this charge I have received from my Father."*

Jn 7:43; 9:16
Jn 7:20; 8:48

¹⁹There was again a division among the Jews because of these words. ²⁰Many of them said, "He has a demon, and he is mad;

Good Shepherd, solicitude for the salvation of every human being. And this we must all remember: that it is not lawful for any one of us to deserve the name of 'hireling', that is to say, the name of one 'to whom the sheep do not belong', one who, 'since he is not the shepherd and the sheep do not belong to him, abandons the sheep and runs away as soon as he sees the wolf coming, and then the wolf attacks and scatters the sheep; this is because he is only a hired man and has no concern for the sheep.' The solicitude of every good shepherd is that all people 'may have life and have it to the full', so that none of them may be lost, but should have eternal life. Let us endeavour to make this solicitude penetrate deeply into our souls; let us strive to live it. May it characterize our personality, and be at the foundation of our priestly identity" (John Paul II, *Letter to priests*, 8 April 1979).

The Good Shepherd knows each of his sheep and calls it by name. This touching simile seems to be an exhortation to future pastors of the Church, as St Peter will later on explain: "Tend the flock of God that is your charge, not for shameful gain but eagerly, not as domineering over those in your charge but being examples to the flock" (1 Pet 5:2).

"The holiness of Christ's Spouse has always been shown—as it can be seen today—by the abundance of good shepherds. But our Christian faith, which teaches us to be simple, does not bid us be simple-minded. There are hirelings who keep silent, and there are hirelings who speak with words which are not those of Christ. That is why, if the Lord allows us to be left in the dark even in little things, if we feel that our faith is not firm, we should go to the good shepherd. He enters by the door as of right. He gives his life for others and wants to be in word and behaviour a soul in love. He may be a sinner too, but he trusts always in Christ's forgiveness and mercy" (St Josemaría Escrivá, *Christ Is Passing By*, 34).

10:16. "One flock, one shepherd." Christ's mission extends to everyone even though his own preaching is addressed, in the first instance, to the sheep of the house of Israel, as he himself revealed to the Canaanite woman (cf. Mt 15:24), and even though he sent the apostles on their first mission to preach to the people of Israel (cf. Mt 10:6). Now, however, foreseeing the fruits of his redemptive death (v. 15), he reveals that these will be applied to "other sheep, that are not of this fold", that is, Israel, and, after the resurrection, he does send the apostles to all nations (cf. Mt 28:19), to preach the Gospel to all creation (cf. Mk 16:15), beginning in Jerusalem and extending to all Judea, Samaria and the ends of the earth (cf. Acts 1:8). This fulfils the ancient promises about the rule of the Messiah covering the whole world (cf. Ps 2:8; Is 2:2–6; 66:17–19). The universal

why listen to him?" ²¹Others said, "These are not the sayings of one who has a demon. Can a demon open the eyes of the blind?"

Mk 3:21

6. JESUS AND THE FATHER

Jesus and the Father are one

²²It was the feast of the Dedication at Jerusalem; ²³it was winter, and Jesus was walking in the temple, in the portico of Solomon.

1 Mac 4:36, 59
Acts 3:11

---

scope of salvation caused St Paul to exclaim: "Remember that at one time you ... were ... separated from Christ, alienated from the commonwealth of Israel, and strangers to the covenants of promise, having no hope and without God in the world. But now in Christ Jesus you who once were far off have been brought near in the blood of Christ" (Eph 2:11–13; cf. Gal 3:27–28; Rom 3:22).

The unity of the Church is to be found under one visible head, for "it was to the Apostolic College alone, of which Peter is the head, that we believe that our Lord entrusted all the blessings of the New Covenant, in order to establish on earth the one Body of Christ into which all those should be fully incorporated who belong in any way to the people of God" (Vatican II, *Unitatis redintegratio*, 3). It is a Catholic's constant yearning that everyone should come to the true Church, "God's only flock, which like a standard lifted high for the nations to see, ministers the Gospel of peace to all mankind, as it makes its pilgrim way in hope towards its goal, the fatherland above" (ibid., 2).

10:17–18. Jesus shows that of his own free will he will give himself up to death for the sake of the flock (cf. Jn 6:51). Having been given supreme authority, Christ is free to offer himself as a sacrifice of expiation, and he voluntarily accepts his Father's commandment, in an act of perfect obedience. "We will never

fully understand Jesus' freedom. It is immense, infinite, as is his love. But the priceless treasure of his generous holocaust should move us to ask, 'Why, Lord, have you granted me this privilege which I can use to follow in your footsteps, but also offend you?' Thus we come to appreciate that freedom is used properly when it is directed towards the good; and that it is misused when men are forgetful and turn away from the Love of loves" (St Josemaría Escrivá, *Friends of God*, 26).

10:19–21. The evangelist has reported a number of instances (cf. Jn 6:52; 7:12, 25–27, 31, 40–43) where people argued with each other about something our Lord said. On this occasion some people reject his teaching and repeat the calumny that he is possessed (Jn 7:20; 8:48) and does miracles through the power of the prince of demons (cf. Mt 9:34; 12:24; Mk 3:22; Lk 11:15); while others open their minds to the light and recognize that he must have divine powers if he can cure a blind man (cf. Jn 9).

The scene is forever being repeated. "Jesus: wherever you have passed no heart remains indifferent. You are either loved or hated. When an apostle follows you, carrying out his duty, is it surprising that—if he is another Christ—he should arouse similar murmurs of aversion or of love?" (St J. Escrivá, *The Way*, 687).

10:22. This feast commemorates an

121

Lk 22:67

Jn 5:36

Jn 6:64; 8:45
Jn 10:3–4:14
Prov 28:5
1 Cor 2:14
Jn 6:39; 10:10;
17:12
Rom 8:33–39
Deut 32–39
Is 43:13
1 Jn 4:4
Jn 1:1; 14:10–11

²⁴So the Jews gathered round him and said to him, "How long will you keep us in suspense? If you are the Christ, tell us plainly." ²⁵Jesus answered them, "I told you, and you do not believe. The works that I do in my Father's name, they bear witness to me; ²⁶but you do not believe, because you do not belong to my sheep. ²⁷My sheep hear my voice, and I know them, and they follow me; ²⁸and I give them eternal life, and they shall never perish, and no one shall snatch them out of my hand. ²⁹My Father, who has given them to me,ʷ is greater than all, and no one is able to snatch them out of the Father's hand. ³⁰I and the Father are one."

episode in Jewish history (cf. 1 Mac 4:36–59; 2 Mac 1–2, 19; 10:1–8) when Judas Maccabeus, in the year 165 BC, after liberating Jerusalem from the control of the Seleucid kings of Syria, cleansed the temple of the profanations of Antiochus Epiphanes (1 Mac 1:54). From then onwards, on the twenty-fifth day of the month of Kisleu (November-December) and throughout the following week, all Judea celebrated the anniversary of the dedication of the new altar. It was also known as the "festival of lights" because it was customary to light lamps, a symbol of the Law, and put them in the windows of the houses (cf. 2 Mac 1:18).

10:24–25. When these Jews ask Jesus if he is the Messiah, "they speak in this way", St Augustine comments, "not because they desire truth, but to prepare the way for calumny" *(In Ioann. Evang.*, 48, 3). We have already seen Jesus reveal, by his words and deeds, that he is the only Son of God (5:19ff; 7:16ff; 8:25ff). In view of their good dispositions, he explicitly told the Samaritan woman (4:26) and the man born blind (9:37) that he was the Messiah and Saviour. Now he reproaches his listeners for refusing to recognize the works he does in his Father's name (cf. 5:36; 10:38). On other occasions he referred to

works as a way to distinguish true prophets from false ones: "You will know them by their fruits" (Mt 7:16; cf. Mt 12:33).

10:26–29. Certainly faith and eternal life cannot be merited by man's own efforts: they are a gift of God. But the Lord does not deny anyone grace to believe and be saved, because he "desires all men to be saved and to come to the knowledge of the truth" (1 Tim 2:4). If someone tries to avoid receiving the gift of faith, his unbelief is blameworthy. On this point St Thomas Aquinas teaches: "I can see, thanks to the light of the sun; but if I close my eyes, I cannot see: this is no fault of the sun, it is my own fault, because by closing my eyes, I prevent the sunlight from reaching me" *(Comm. on St John,* ad loc.).

But those who do not oppose divine grace do come to believe in Jesus. They are known to and loved by him, enter under his protection and remain faithful with the help of his grace, which is a pledge of the eternal life which the Good Shepherd will eventually give them. It is true that in this world they will have to strive and in the course of striving they will sustain wounds; but if they stay united to the Good Shepherd nothing and no one will snatch Christ's sheep from

w. Other ancient authorities read *What my Father has given to me*

An attempt to stone Jesus

³¹The Jews took up stones again to stone him. ³²Jesus answered them, "I have shown you many good works from the Father; for which of these do you stone me?" ³³The Jews answered him, "We stone you for no good work but for blasphemy; because you, being a man, make yourself God." ³⁴Jesus answered them, "Is it

Jer 8:59

Jn 5:18
Mt 26:65f

Ps 82:6

---

him, because our Father, God, is stronger than the Evil One. Our hope that God will grant us final perseverance is not based on our strength but on God's mercy: this hope should always motivate us to strive to respond to grace and to be ever more faithful to the demands of our faith.

10:30. Jesus reveals that he and the Father are one in substance. Earlier he proclaimed that God was his Father, "making himself equal with God"—which is why a number of times the Jewish authorities think of putting him to death (cf. 5:18; 8:59). Now he speaks about the mystery of God, which is something we can know about only through Revelation. Later on he will reveal more about this mystery, particularly at the Last Supper (14:10; 17:21–22). It is something the evangelist reflects on at the very beginning of the Gospel, in the prologue (cf. Jn 1:1 and note).

"Listen to the Son himself", St Augustine invites us. "'I and the Father are one.' He did not say, 'I am the Father' or 'I and the Father are one [Person].' But when he says 'I and the Father are one,' notice the two words '[we are]' and 'one' ... For if they are one, then they are not diverse; if '[we] are', then there is both a Father and a Son" (*In Ioann. Evang.*, 36, 9). Jesus reveals that he is one in substance with the Father as far as divine essence or nature is concerned, but he also reveals that the Father and the Son are distinct Persons: "We believe then in the Father who eternally begets the Son; in the Son, the Word of God, who is eternally begotten; in the Holy Spirit, the uncreated

Person who proceeds from the Father and the Son as their eternal Love. Thus in the three divine Persons, *coaeternae sibi et coaequales*, the life and beatitude of God perfectly One superabound and are consummated in the supreme excellence and glory proper to uncreated Being, and always 'there should be venerated Unity in the Trinity and Trinity in the Unity'" (Paul VI, *Creed of the People of God*, 10).

10:31–33. The Jews realize that Jesus is saying that he is God, but they interpret his words as blasphemy. He was called a blasphemer when he forgave the sins of the paralytic (Mt 9:1–8), and he will also be accused of blasphemy when he is condemned after solemnly confessing his divinity before the Sanhedrin (Mt 26:63–65). Our Lord, then, did reveal that he was God; but his hearers rejected this revelation of the mystery of the Incarnate God, refusing to examine the proof Jesus offered them; consequently, they accuse him, a man, of making himself God. Faith bases itself on reasonable evidence—miracles and prophecies—for believing that Jesus is really man and really God, even though our limited minds cannot work out how this can be so. Thus, our Lord, in order to affirm his divinity once more, uses two arguments which his adversaries cannot refute—the testimony of Holy Scripture (prophecies) and that of his own works (miracles).

10:34–36. On a number of occasions the Gospel has shown our Lord replying to the Jews' objections. Here he patiently

Mt 5:17

Jer 1:5

Jn 2:11

Jn 8:59
Lk 4:30

Jn 1:28
Mt 19:1

not written in your law, 'I said, you are gods'? ³⁵If he called them gods to whom the word of God came (and scripture cannot be broken), ³⁶do you say of him whom the Father consecrated and sent into the world, 'You are blaspheming,' because I said, 'I am the Son of God'? ³⁷If I am not doing the works of my Father, then do not believe me; ³⁸but if I do them, even though you do not believe me, believe the works, that you may know and understand that the Father is in me and I am in the Father." ³⁹Again they tried to arrest him, but he escaped from their hands.

⁴⁰He went away again across the Jordan to the place where John at first baptized, and there he remained. ⁴¹And many came to

---

uses a form of argument which they regard as decisive—the authority of Holy Scripture. He quotes Psalm 82 in which God upbraids certain judges for acting unjustly despite his reminding them that "You are gods, sons of the Most High, all of you" (Ps 82:6). If this psalm calls the sons of Israel gods and sons of God, with how much more reason should he be called God who has been sanctified and sent by God? Christ's human nature, on being assumed by the Word, is sanctified completely and comes to the world to sanctify men. "The Fathers of the Church constantly proclaim that what was not assumed by Christ was not healed. Now Christ took a complete human nature just as it is found in us poor unfortunates, but one that was without sin, for Christ said of himself that he was the one 'whom the Father consecrated and sent into the world'" (Vatican II, *Ad gentes*, 3).

By using Sacred Scripture (cf. Mt 4:4, 7, 10; Lk 4:1) Jesus teaches us that Scripture comes from God. Therefore, the Church believes and affirms that "those divinely revealed realities which are contained and presented in Sacred Scripture have been committed to writing under the inspiration of the Holy Spirit. Holy Mother Church, relying on the belief of the Apostles, holds that the books of both the Old and New Testa-

ment in their entirety, with all their parts, are sacred and canonical because, having been written under the inspiration of the Holy Spirit (cf. Jn 20:31; 2 Tim 3:16; 2 Pet 1:19–21) they have God as their author and have been handed on as such to the Church. [...] Therefore, since everything is asserted by the Holy Spirit, it follows that the books of Scripture must be acknowledged as teaching firmly, faithfully, and without error that truth which God wanted to put into the sacred writings for the sake of our salvation" (Vatican II, *Dei Verbum*, 11).

10:37–38. The works which our Lord is referring to are his miracles, through which God's power is made manifest. Jesus presents his words and his works as forming a unity, with the miracles confirming his words and his words explaining the meaning of miracles. Therefore, when he asserts that he is the Son of God, this revelation is supported by the credentials of the miracles he works: hence, if no one can deny the fact of the miracles, it is only right for him to accept the truth of the words.

10:41–42. The opposition offered by some people (cf. Jn 10:20, 31, 39) contrasts with the way other people accept him and follow him to where he goes after this. St John the Baptist's preparatory work is still

him; and they said, "John did no sign, but everything that John
said about this man was true." [42]And many believed in him there.

Jn 8:30

7. JESUS IS THE RESURRECTION AND THE LIFE

Jesus' reaction to the death of Lazarus

11 [1]Now a certain man was ill, Lazarus of Bethany, the village
of Mary and her sister Martha. [2]It was Mary who anointed
the Lord with ointment and wiped his feet with her hair, whose
brother Lazarus was ill. [3]So the sisters sent to him, saying, "Lord,

Lk 10:38

Jn 12:3
Lk 7:37

producing results: those who accepted the
Baptist's message now look for Christ and
they believe when they see the truth of
what the Precursor said: Jesus is the
Messiah, the Son of God (cf. Jn 1:34).

Work done in the Lord's name is
never useless: "Therefore, my beloved
brethren, be steadfast, immovable, always
abounding in the work of the Lord, knowing that in the Lord your labour is not in
vain" (1 Cor 15:58). Just as the Baptist's
word and example had the effect of helping many people later to believe in Jesus,
the apostolic example given by Christians
will never be in vain, even though the
results may not come immediately. "To
sow. The sower went out ... Scatter your
seed, apostolic soul. The wind of grace
will bear it away if the furrow where it
falls is not worthy ... Sow, and be certain
that the seed will take root and bear fruit"
(St Josemaría Escrivá, *The Way*, 794).

11:1–45. This chapter deals with one of
Jesus' most outstanding miracles. The
Fourth Gospel, by including it, demonstrates Jesus' power over death, which
the Synoptic Gospels showed by report-
ing the raising of the daughter of Jairus
(Mt 9:255 and par.) and of the son of the
widow of Nain (Lk 7:12).

The evangelist first sets the scene (vv.
1–16); then he gives Jesus' conversation
with Lazarus' sisters (vv. 17–37); finally,

he reports the raising of Lazarus four
days after his death (vv. 38–45). Bethany
was only about three kilometres (two
miles) from Jerusalem (v. 18). On the
days prior to his passion, Jesus often visited this family, to which he was very
attached. St John records Jesus' affection
(vv. 3, 5, 36) by describing his emotion
and sorrow at the death of his friend.

By raising Lazarus our Lord shows
his divine power over death and thereby
gives proof of his divinity, in order to
confirm his disciples' faith and reveal
himself as the Resurrection and the Life.
Most Jews, but not the Sadducees,
believed in the resurrection of the body.
Martha believed in it (cf. v. 24).

Apart from being a real, historical
event, Lazarus' return to life is a sign of
our future resurrection: we too will return
to life. Christ, by his glorious resurrection through which he is the "first-born
from the dead" (Col 1:18; 1 Cor 15:20;
Rev 1:5), is also the cause and model of
our resurrection. In this his resurrection
is different from that of Lazarus, for
"Christ being raised from the dead will
never die again" (Rom 6:9), whereas
Lazarus returned to earthly life, later to
die again.

11:2. There are a number of women in
the Gospels who are called Mary. The
Mary here is Mary of Bethany, the sister

125

Jn 9:3 he whom you love is ill." ⁴But when Jesus heard it he said, "This illness is not unto death; it is for the glory of God, so that the Son of God may be glorified by means of it."

⁵Now Jesus loved Martha and her sister and Lazarus. ⁶So when he heard that he was ill, he stayed two days longer* in the place where he was. ⁷Then after this he said to the disciples, "Let us go Jn 8:59; 10:31 into Judea again." ⁸The disciples said to him, "Rabbi, the Jews were but now seeking to stone you, and are you going there 1 Jn 2:10f again?" ⁹Jesus answered, "Are there not twelve hours in the day? If any one walks in the day, he does not stumble, because he sees Jn 12:35 the light of this world. ¹⁰But if any one walks in the night, he Mt 9:24 stumbles, because the light is not in him." ¹¹Thus he spoke, and then he said to them, "Our friend Lazarus has fallen asleep, but I go to awake him out of sleep." ¹²The disciples said to him, "Lord,

---

of Lazarus (v. 2), the woman who later anointed our Lord, again in Bethany, at the house of Simon the leper (cf. Jn 12:1–8; Mk 14:3): the indefinite or aorist "(she) anointed" expresses an action which occurred prior to the time of writing, but the anointing took place after the resurrection of Lazarus.

Were Mary of Bethany, Mary Magdalene and the "sinful" woman who anointed Jesus' feet in Galilee (cf. Lk 7:37) one, two or three women? Although sometimes it is argued that they are one and the same, it seems more likely that they were all different people. Firstly, we must distinguish the Galilee anointing (Lk 7:38) by the "sinner" from the Bethany anointing done by Lazarus' sister (Jn 12:1): because of the time they took place and particular details reported, they are clearly distinct (cf. the note on Jn 12:1). Besides, the Gospels give us no positive indication that Mary of Bethany was the same person as the "sinner" of Galilee. Nor are there strong grounds for identifying Mary Magdalene and the "sinner", whose name is not given; Mary Magdalene appears among the women who follow Jesus in Galilee as the woman out of whom seven demons were cast

(cf. Lk 8:2), and Luke presents her in his account as someone new: no information is given which could link her with either of the two other women.

Nor can Mary of Bethany and Mary Magdalene be identified, for John differentiates between the two: he never calls Lazarus' sister Mary Magdalene, nor does he in any way link the latter (who stays beside the cross—Jn 19:25—and who goes to the tomb and sees the risen Lord) with Mary of Bethany.

The reason why Mary of Bethany has sometimes been confused with Mary Magdalene is due (1) to the identification of the latter with the "sinner" of Galilee through connecting Magdalene's possession by the devil with the sinfulness of the woman who did the anointing in Galilee; and (2) to confusing the two anointings, which would make Lazarus' sister the "sinner" who does the first anointing. This was how the three women were made out to be one, but there are no grounds for that interpretation. The best-grounded and most common interpretation offered by exegetes is that they are three distinct women.

11:4. The glory which Christ speaks of

if he has fallen asleep, he will recover." [13]Now Jesus had spoken of his death, but they thought that he meant taking rest in sleep. [14]Then Jesus told them plainly, "Lazarus is dead; [15]and for your sake I am glad that I was not there, so that you may believe. But let us go to him." [16]Thomas, called the Twin, said to his fellow disciples, "Let us also go, that we may die with him."

Jn 14:5;
20:24–29
Mk 10:32

[17]Now when Jesus came, he found that Lazarus[x] had already been in the tomb four days. [18]Bethany was near Jerusalem, about two miles[y] off, [19]and many of the Jews had come to Martha and Mary to console them concerning their brother. [20]When Martha heard that Jesus was coming, she went to meet him, while Mary sat in the house. [21]Martha said to Jesus, "Lord, if you had been here, my brother would not have died. [22]And even now I know that whatever you ask from God, God will give you." [23]Jesus said

Lk 10:39ff

Mt 11:43
Mk 11:24

here, St Augustine says, "was no gain to Jesus; it was only for our good. Therefore, Jesus says that his illness is not unto death, because the particular death was not for death but rather for a miracle, which being wrought men should believe in Christ and thereby avoid the true death" (*In Ioann. Evang.*, 49, 6).

11:8–10. Stoning was the form of capital punishment applying to blasphemy (cf. Lev 24:16). We have seen that people tried to stone Jesus at least twice: first, when he proclaimed that he was the Son of God and that he existed from eternity (by saying that he "was" before Abraham lived)—Jn 8:58–59; second, when he revealed that he and the Father were one (cf. Jn 10:30–31).

These attempts by the Jewish authorities failed because Jesus "hour" had not yet arrived—that is, the time laid down by his Father for his death and resurrection. When the crucifixion comes, it will be the hour of his enemies and of "the power of darkness" (Lk 22:53). But until that moment it is daytime, and our Lord can walk without his life being in danger.

11:16. Thomas' words remind us of the apostles saying at the Last Supper that they would be ready to die for their Master (cf. Mt 2:31–35). We have seen how the apostles stayed loyal when many disciples left our Lord after his discourse on the Bread of Life (Jn 6:67–71), and how they remained faithful to him despite their personal weaknesses. But when, after Judas Iscariot's betrayal, Jesus lets himself be arrested without offering resistance—in fact, forbidding the use of weapons (cf. Jn 18:11)—they become disconcerted and run away. Only St. John will stay faithful in Jesus' hour of greatest need.

11:18. Fifteen stadia, in Greek measurement: three kilometres (two miles).

11:21–22. According to St Augustine, Martha's request is a good example of confident prayer, a prayer of abandonment into the hands of God, who knows better than we what we need. Therefore, "she did not say, But now I ask you to raise my brother to life again. [...] All she said was, I know that you can do it; if you will, do it; it is for you to judge

x. Greek *he*   y. Greek *fifteen stadia*

127

Jn 5:25; 6:40
to her, "Your brother will rise again." ²⁴Martha said to him, "I know that he will rise again in the resurrection at the last day."

Jn 5:25; 8:51
²⁵Jesus said to her, "I am the resurrection and the life,ᶻ he who believes in me, though he die, yet shall he live, ²⁶and whoever

Jn 6:69
Mt 16:16
lives and believes in me shall never die. Do you believe this?" ²⁷She said to him, "Yes, Lord; I believe that you are the Christ, the son of God, he who is coming into the world."

²⁸When she had said this, she went and called her sister Mary, saying quietly, "The Teacher is here and is calling for you." ²⁹And when she heard it, she rose quickly and went to him. ³⁰Now Jesus had not yet come to the village, but was still in the place where Martha had met him. ³¹When the Jews who were with her in the house, consoling her, saw Mary rise quickly and go out, they followed her, supposing that she was going to the tomb to weep

Jn 11:21
there. ³²Then Mary, when she came to where Jesus was and saw

---

whether to do it, not for me to presume" (*In Ioann. Evang.*, 49, 13). The same can be said of Mary's words, which St John repeats at v. 32.

11:24–26. Here we have one of the most concise definitions Christ gives of himself, and which St John faithfully passes on to us (cf. Jn 10:9; 14:6; 15:1): Jesus is the Resurrection and the Life. He is the Resurrection because by his victory over death he is the cause of the resurrection of all men. The miracle he works in raising Lazarus is a sign of Christ's power to give life to people. And so, by faith in Jesus Christ, who arose first from among the dead, the Christian is sure that he too will rise one day, like Christ (cf. 1 Cor 15:23; Col 1:18). Therefore, for the believer death is not the end; it is simply the step to eternal life, a change of dwelling place, as one of the *Roman Missal*'s Prefaces of Christian Death puts it: "Lord, for your faithful people life is changed, not ended. When the body of our earthly dwelling lies in death, we gain an everlasting dwelling place in heaven".

By saying that he is Life, Jesus is referring not only to that life which begins beyond the grave, but also to the supernatural life which grace brings to the soul of man when he is still a wayfarer on this earth.

"This life, which the Father has promised and offered to each man in Jesus Christ, his eternal and only Son, who 'when the time had fully come' (Gal 4:4), became incarnate and was born of the Virgin Mary, is the final fulfilment of man's vocation. It is in a way the fulfilment of the 'destiny' that God has prepared for him from eternity. This 'divine destiny' is advancing, in spite of all the enigmas, the unsolved riddles, the twists and turns of 'human destiny' in the world of time. Indeed, while all this, in spite of all the riches of life in times, necessarily and inevitably leads to the frontiers of death and the goal of the destruction of the human body, beyond that goal we see Christ. 'I am the resurrection and the life, he who believes in me ... shall never die.' In Jesus Christ, who was crucified and laid in the tomb and then rose again, 'our hope of resurrection dawned ... the

z. Other ancient authorities omit *and the life*

him, fell at his feet, saying to him, "Lord, if you had been here, my brother would not have died." ³³When Jesus saw her weeping, and the Jews who came with her also weeping, he was deeply moved in spirit and troubled; ³⁴and he said, "Where have you laid him?" They said to him, "Lord, come and see." ³⁵Jesus wept. ³⁶So the Jews said, "See how he loved him!" ³⁷But some of them said, "Could not he who opened the eyes of a blind man have kept this man from dying?"

Jn 11:38;
13:21
Mt 9:36
Mk 6:34

Lk 19:41

The raising of Lazarus

³⁸Then Jesus, deeply moved again, came to the tomb; it was a cave, and a stone lay upon it. ³⁹Jesus said, "Take away the stone." Martha, the sister of the dead man, said to him, "Lord, by this time there will be an odour, for he has been dead four days." ⁴⁰Jesus said to her, "Did I not tell you that if you would believe you would see the glory of God?" ⁴¹So they took away the stone. And Jesus lifted his eyes and said, "Father, I thank thee that thou

Jn 17:1
Mt 14:19

bright promise of immortality' (*Roman Missal*, Preface of Christian Death, I), on the way to which man, through the death of the body, shares with the whole of visible creation the necessity to which matter is subject" (John Paul II, *Redemptor hominis*, 18).

11:33–36. This passage gives us an opportunity to reflect on the depth and tenderness of Jesus' feelings. If the physical death of his friend can move him to tears, what will he not feel over the spiritual death of a sinner who has brought about his eternal condemnation? "Christ wept: let man also weep for himself. For why did Christ weep, but to teach men to weep" (St Augustine, *In Ioann. Evang.*, 49, 19). We also should weep—but for our sins, to help us return to the life of grace through conversion and repentance. We should appreciate our Lord's tears: he is praying for us, who are sinners: "Jesus is your friend. The Friend. With a human heart, like yours. With loving eyes that wept for Lazarus. And he loves you as much as he loved Lazarus" (St Josemaría Escrivá, *The Way*, 422).

11:41–42. Through his sacred humanity Jesus is expressing himself as the natural Son of God, that is, he is the metaphysical Son of God, not adopted like the rest of men. This is the source of Jesus' feelings, which helps us to understand that when he says "Father" he is speaking with a unique and indescribable intensity. When the Gospels let us see Jesus praying, they always show him beginning with the invocation "Father", which reflects his singular trust and love. These sentiments should also in some way find a place in our prayer, for through Baptism we are joined to Christ and in him we became children of God (cf. Jn 1:12; Rom 6:1–11; 8:14–17), and so we should always pray in a spirit of sonship and gratitude for the many good things our Father God has given us.

The miracle of the raising of Lazarus, which really is an extraordinary miracle, is a proof that Jesus is the Son of God, sent into the world by his Father. And so it is, that when Lazarus is brought back to life, people's faith in Jesus is increased—the disciples' (v. 15), Martha's and Mary's (vv. 26, 40) and that of the people at large (vv. 36, 45).

Jn 12:30
Mt 14:23

Jn 5:27–29

hast heard me. ⁴²I knew that thou hearest me always, but I have said this on account of the people standing by, that they may believe that thou didst send me." ⁴³When he had said this, he cried with a loud voice, "Lazarus, come out." ⁴⁴The dead man came out, his hands and feet bound with bandages, and his face wrapped with a cloth. Jesus said to them, "Unbind him, and let him go."

The Sanhedrin decides on the death of Jesus

⁴⁵Many of the Jews therefore, who had come with Mary and had seen what he did, believed in him; ⁴⁶but some of them went to the Pharisees and told them what Jesus had done. ⁴⁷So the chief priests and the Pharisees gathered the council, and said, "What are

Lk 16:31

Mt 26:3–5

11:43. Jesus calls Lazarus by name. Although he is really dead, he has not thereby lost his personal identity: dead people continue to exist, but they have a different mode of existence, because they have changed from mortal life to eternal life. This is why Jesus states that God "is not God of the dead, but of the living", for to him all are alive (cf. Mt 22:32; Lk 20:38).

This passage can be applied to the spiritual resurrection of the soul who has sinned and recovers grace. God wants us to be saved (cf. 1 Tim 2:4); therefore we should never lose heart; we should always desire and hope to reach this goal: "Never despair. Lazarus was dead and decaying: 'Iam foetet, quatriduanus enim est. By now he will smell; this is the fourth day,' says Martha to Jesus. If you hear God's inspiration and follow it— 'Lazare, veni foras!: Lazarus, come out!'—you will return to Life" (St Josemaría Escrivá, *The Way*, 719).

11:44. The Jews prepared the body for burial by washing it and anointing it with aromatic ointments to delay decomposition and counteract offensive odours; they then wrapped the body in linen cloths and bandages, covering the head with a napkin—a method very like the

Egyptians', but not entirely extending to full embalming, which involved removing certain internal organs.

Lazarus' tomb would have consisted of a subterranean chamber linked to the surface by steps, with the entrance blocked by a slab. Lazarus was moved out to the entrance by a supernatural force. As happened in the case of the raising of Jairus' daughter (Mk 5:42–43), due to their astonishment no one moved until our Lord's words broke the atmosphere of silence and terror which had been created. St Augustine sees in the raising of Lazarus a symbol of the sacrament of Penance: in the same way as Lazarus comes out of the tomb, "when you confess, you come forth. For what does 'come forth' mean if not emerging from what is hidden, to be made manifest. But for you to confess is God's doing; he calls you with an urgent voice, by an extraordinary grace. And just as the dead man came out still bound, so you go to confession still guilty. In order that his sins be loosed, the Lord said this to his ministers: 'Unbind him and let him go'. What you will loose on earth will be loosed also in heaven" (St Augustine, *In Ioann. Evang.*, 49, 24). Christian art has used this comparison from very early on; in the catacombs we find some one hun-

we to do? For this man performs many signs. [48]If we let him go
on thus, every one will believe in him, and the Romans will come
and destroy our holy place[a] and our nation." [49]But one of them,
Caiaphas, who was high priest that year, said to them, "You know
nothing at all; [50]you do not understand that it is expedient for you
that one man should die for the people, and that the whole nation
should not perish."* [51]He did not say this of his own accord, but
being high priest that year he prophesied that Jesus should die for
the nation, [52]and not for the nation only, but to gather into one the
children of God who are scattered abroad. [53]So from that day on
they took counsel how to put him to death.

Jn 18:31
Lk 3:2

Num 27:21

Jn 10:6
1 Jn 2:2

Jn 5:18
Mt 12:14

---

dred and fifty representations of the raising of Lazarus, symbolizing thereby the
gift of the life of grace which comes
through the priest, who in effect repeats
these words to the sinner: "Lazarus,
come out."

11:45–48. Once again, as Simeon had
predicted, Jesus is a sign of contradiction
(cf. Lk 2:34; Jn 7:12, 31, 40; 9:16; etc.):
presented with the miracle of the raising
of Lazarus some people believe in Jesus
(cf. v. 45), and some denounce him to his
enemies (cf. vv. 46–47)—confirming
what is said in the parable of the rich
man: "neither will they be convinced if
someone should rise from the dead" (cf.
Lk 16:31).

"Our (holy) place": this expression or
similar expressions such as "the place",
"this place", was used to designate the
temple, the holy place par excellence
and, by extension, all the Holy City of
Jerusalem (cf. 2 Mac 5:19; Acts 6:14).

11:49–53. Caiaphas held the high priesthood from the year AD 18 to the year 36.
Caiaphas was the instrument God used to
prophesy the redemptive death of the
Saviour, for it was one of the functions of
the high priest to consult God on how to
lead the people (cf. Ex 28:30; Num

27:21; 1 Sam 23:9; 30:7–8). Here
Caiaphas' words have a dual meaning:
one, Caiaphas' meaning, is that he wants
to put Christ to death, on the pretext that
that will ensure the political peace and
survival of Israel; the other, the meaning
intended by the Holy Spirit, is the
announcement of the foundation of the
new Israel, the Church, through the death
of Christ on the cross (Caiaphas is
unaware of this meaning). And so it happens that the last high priest of the Old
Alliance prophesies the investiture of the
High Priest of the New Alliance, which
will be sealed with his own blood.

When the Evangelist states that
Christ was going to die "to gather into
one the children of God who are scattered abroad" (v. 52), he is referring to
what our Lord had said regarding the
salvific effects of his death (cf. Jn 10:14–
15). The prophets had already announced
the future assembly of Israelites faithful
to God to form the new people of Israel
(cf. Is 43:5; Jer 23:3–5; Ezek 34:23;
37:21–24). These prophecies are fulfilled
by the death of Christ, who, on being
raised up on the cross, draws and gathers
together the true people of God, composed of all believers, whether Israelites
or not. The Second Vatican Council uses
this passage as a source when speaking

a. Greek *our place*

131

Jn 7:1

⁵⁴Jesus therefore no longer went about openly among the Jews, but went from there to the country near the wilderness, to a town called Ephraim; and there he stayed with the disciples.

Jn 2:13; 6:4
2 Chron 30:17

⁵⁵Now the Passover of the Jews was at hand, and many went up from the country to Jerusalem before the Passover, to purify themselves. ⁵⁶They were looking for Jesus and saying to one another as they stood in the temple, "What do you think? That he will not come to the feast?" ⁵⁷Now the chief priests and the Pharisees had given orders that if any one knew where he was, he should let them know, so that they might arrest him.

Jn 7:11

---

of the universality of the Church: "All men are called to belong to the new people of God. This people therefore, whilst remaining one and only one, is to be spread throughout the whole world and to all ages in order that the design of God's will may be fulfilled: he made human nature one in the beginning and has decreed that all his children who were scattered should be finally gathered together as one (cf. Jn 11:52). It was for this purpose that God sent his Son; whom he appointed heir of all things (cf. Heb 1:2), that he might be teacher, king and priest of all, the head of the new and universal people of God's sons" (*Lumen gentium*, 13).

In the fourth century, St John Chrysostom explained the catholicity of the Church using these words: "What is the meaning of 'to gather into one those who are scattered abroad'? He made them one body. He who dwells in Rome knows that the Christians of India are his members" (Hom. on St John, 65, 1).

11:54. The time for him to die has not yet arrived; therefore Jesus acts prudently, taking the steps anyone would take not to precipitate events.

11:55. Since the Passover was the most solemn Jewish feast, the people used to arrive in Jerusalem some days in advance to prepare for it by washings, fasts and

offerings—practices established not by the Mosaic law but by popular piety; the rites of the Passover itself, with the sacrificing of the lamb, were a rite of purification and expiation for sins. The Passover of the Jews was a figure of the Christian Pasch or Easter, for, as St Paul the Apostle teaches us, our paschal lamb is Christ (cf. Cor 5:7), who offered himself once and for all to the eternal Father on the cross to atone for our sins. Paul VI recalled this happy truth of faith: "Gave himself for me? But does there still exist a religion which is expressed in sacrifices? No, the sacrifices of the ancient law and pagan religions have no longer any reason to exist; but the world always needs a sacrifice, a valid, unique and perennial one, for the redemption of human sin [...]; it is the sacrifice of Christ on the cross, which wipes out sin from the world; a sacrifice which the Eucharist actualizes in time and makes it possible for the men of this earth to take part in it" (*Homily on Corpus Christi*, 17 June 1976).

If the Jews prepared to celebrate the Passover with all these rites and ablutions, it is obvious what steps we should take to celebrate or participate in the Mass and to receive Christ—our Pasch—in the Eucharist. "On this earth, when we receive an important person, we bring out the best—lights, music, formal dress. How should we prepare to receive Christ

8. JESUS IS ACCLAIMED AS THE MESSIANIC KING

Mary anoints our Lord at Bethany

12 *¹Six days before the Passover, Jesus came to Bethany, where Lazarus was, whom Jesus had raised from the dead. ²There they made him a supper; Martha served, and Lazarus was one of those at table with him. ³Mary took a pound of costly ointment of pure nard and anointed the feet of Jesus and wiped his feet with her hair; and the house was filled with the fragrance of the ointment. ⁴But Judas Iscariot, one of his disciples (he who was

Jn 11:1ff
Mt 26:6–13
Mk 14:3–9

Lk 10:40

Lk 7:38

into our soul? Have we ever thought about how we would behave if we could only receive him once in a lifetime?" (St J. Escrivá, *Christ Is Passing By*, 91).

12:1. Jesus pays another visit to his friends in Bethany. It is very touching to see this friendship, at once divine and human, expressed in the form of frequent contact. "It's true that I always call our tabernacle 'Bethany'. Become a friend of the Master's friends—Lazarus, Martha, Mary— and then you won't ask me any more why I call our tabernacle 'Bethany'" (St Josemaría Escrivá, *The Way*, 322).

12:2–3. Apparently, our Lord was anointed on two different occasions— first, at the start of his public ministry, in Galilee, as recounted by St Luke (7:36– 50); and second, towards the end of his life, in Bethany, reported here by St John and undoubtedly the same incident as described by St Matthew (26:6–13) and St Mark (14:3–9). The two anointings are quite distinct: they occur at different times and the details of the accounts differ: the first is a demonstration of repentance followed by pardon; the second, a delicate expression of love, which Jesus further interprets as an anticipation of the anointing of his body in burial (v. 7).

Although these anointings of Jesus

had a particular significance, they should be seen in the context of eastern hospitality; cf. the note on Mk 14:3–9.

The pound was a measure of weight equivalent to three hundred grams; a denarius, as we have indicated elsewhere, was a day's wage of an agricultural labourer; therefore, the cost of the flask of perfume would have amounted to a year's wage.

"What a shining proof of magnanimity is this 'extravagance' on Mary's part! Judas on the other hand laments this 'waste' of so valuable a perfume; in his greed he had been calculating the price: it would have fetched at least 'three hundred silver pieces'.

"True detachment leads us to be very generous with God and with our fellow-men. [...] Don't be mean and grudging with people who, without counting the cost, have given of their all, everything they have, for your sake. Just ask yourselves, how much does it cost you—in financial terms as well—to be Christians? Above all, don't forget that 'God loves a cheerful giver' (2 Cor 9:7)" (St Josemaría Escrivá, *Friends of God*, 126).

12:4–6. From this passage and from John 13:29 we know that Judas was the person in charge of the money. His petty thefts—they could not have been any

Jn 13:29
Lk 8:3

Deut 15:11

Jn 11:56ff

Jn 7:31

to betray him), said, [5]"Why was this ointment not sold for three hundred denarii[b] and given to the poor?" [6]This he said, not that he cared for the poor, but because he was a thief, and as he had the money box he used to take what was put into it. [7]Jesus said, "Let her alone, let her keep it for the day of my burial. [8]The poor you always have with you, but you do not always have me."

[9]When the great crowd of the Jews learned that he was there, they came, not only on account of Jesus but also to see Lazarus, whom he had raised from the dead. [10]So the chief priests planned to put Lazarus also to death, [11]because on account of him many of the Jews were going away and believing in Jesus.

Mt 21:1–11
Mk 11:1–10
Lk 19:28–38

1 Mac 13:51

The Messiah's entry into Jerusalem

[12]The next day a great crowd who had come to the feast heard that Jesus was coming to Jerusalem. [13]So they took branches of palm

---

more than that, given the meagre resources of Jesus and the Twelve—played their part in disposing him to commit his eventual sin of betraying Jesus; his complaint about the woman's generosity was quite hypocritical. "Frequently the servants of Satan disguise themselves as servants of righteousness (cf. 2 Cor 11:14 –15). Therefore, (Judas) hid his malice under a cloak of piety" (St Thomas Aquinas, *Comm. on St John*, ad loc.).

12:7–8. As well as praising Mary's generous gesture, our Lord indirectly announces his death, even implying that it will happen so precipitously that there will hardly be time to prepare his body for burial in the normal way (cf. Lk 23:56; see also the note on Jn 11:44). He is not saying that almsgiving is not a good thing (he often recommended it: cf. Lk 11:41; 12:33); nor that people should have no concern for the poor (cf. Mt 25:40); what he is doing here is exposing the hypocrisy of people like Judas who deceitfully profess noble motives in order to avoid giving God the honour he is due (cf. also the notes on Mt 26:8–11; Mk 14:3–9).

12:9–11. The news of the raising of Lazarus has spread rapidly among the people of Judea and those travelling up to Jerusalem for the Passover; many believe in Jesus (cf. Jn 11:45); others look for him (cf. Jn 11:56) perhaps more out of curiosity (cf. Jn 12:9) than faith. Following Christ demands more of each of us than just superficial, short-lived enthusiasm. We should not forget those "who, when they hear the word, immediately receive it with joy; and they have no root in themselves, but endure for a while; then, when tribulation or persecution arises on account of the word, immediately they fall away" (Mk 4:16–17).

12:13. When the crowd uses the words "Blessed is he who comes in the name of the Lord", taken from Psalm 118:26, they are acclaiming Jesus as the Messiah. The words "the king of Israel", not included in the Synoptics, underline Christ's royalty: the Messiah is the King of Israel *par excellence*. However, Jesus had previously fled from those who wanted to make him king because they had an

b. The denarius was a day's wage for a labourer

trees and went out to meet him, crying, "Hosanna! Blessed is he who comes in the name of the Lord, even the King of Israel! ¹⁴And Jesus found a young ass and sat upon it; as it is written,

> ¹⁵"Fear not, daughter of Zion;
> behold, your king is coming,
> sitting on an ass's colt!"

¹⁶His disciples did not understand this at first; but when Jesus was glorified, then they remembered that this had been written of him and had been done to him. ¹⁷The crowd that had been with him when he called Lazarus out of the tomb and raised him from the dead bore witness. ¹⁸The reason why the crowd went to meet him was that they heard he had done this sign. ¹⁹The Pharisees then said to one another, "You see that you can do nothing; look, the world has gone after him."

Rev 7:9
Ps 118:26
Jn 1:49; 6:25
Zech 9:9
Is 40:9
Jn 2:22; 7:39
Jn 11:47f

Jesus announces his glorification

²⁰Now among those who went up to worship at the feast were some Greeks. ²¹So these came to Philip, who was from Bethsaida

Jn 1:44; 7:34f; 11:55

---

earth-bound view of his mission (Jn 6:14–15). Later on, before Pilate, he will explain that his kingship "is not of this world". "Christ", St Augustine teaches, "was not king of Israel for exacting tribute, or arming a host with the sword; but king of Israel to rule souls, to counsel them for eternal life, to bring to the Kingdom of heaven those that believe, hope and love" (*In Ioann. Evang.*, 51, 4).

"Christ should reign first and foremost in our soul. But how would we reply if he asks us: 'How do you go about letting me reign in you?' I would reply that I need lots of his grace. Only that way can my every heartbeat and breath, my least intense look, my most ordinary word, my most basic feeling be transformed into a hosanna to Christ my King" (St Josemaría Escrivá, *Christ Is Passing By*, 181).

12:14–16. After Jesus' resurrection, the apostles will grasp the meaning of many episodes in our Lord's life which they had not previously understood fully (cf.

Jn 2:22). For example, in his triumphal entry into Jerusalem with all the people acclaiming him as Messiah, they will see the fulfilment of the Old Testament prophecies (cf., e.g., in addition to Zech 9:9, which the Gospel quotes, Gen 49:10–11). See the notes on Mt 21:1–5; Mk 11:1–11; and Lk 19:39–35.

12:17–19. The Gospel records the part played by the raising of Lazarus in bringing about Jesus' death. Those who witnessed the miracle see Jesus as the Messiah sent by God, and their faith influences many of the pilgrims who have come up for the Passover; but the Pharisees persist in their blindness, which leads them to seek Christ's death (cf. Jn 11:53).

12:20–23. These "Greeks" approach Philip because seemingly this Apostle, who has a Greek name, must have understood Greek and been able to act as interpreter. If that was the case, then this is a very important moment because it means

in Galilee, and said to him, "Sir, we wish to see Jesus." ²³Philip
went and told Andrew; Andrew went with Philip and they told

Jn 2:4

Jesus. ²³And Jesus answered them, "The hour has come for the

Is 53:10–12
Rom 14:9
1 Cor 15:36

Son of man to be glorified. ²⁴Truly, truly, I say to you, unless a
grain of wheat falls into the earth and dies, it remains alone; but if

Mt 16:25
Mk 8:35
Lk 9:24

it dies, it bears much fruit. ²⁵He who loves his life loses it, and he
who hates his life in this world will keep it for eternal life. ²⁶If any
one serves me, he must follow me; and where I am, there shall my

Jn 14:3; 17:24

servant be also; if any one serves me, the Father will honour him.

---

that people of a non-Jewish culture came
in search of Christ: which would make
them the first-fruits of the spread of the
Christian faith in the hellenic world. This
would make it easier to understand our
Lord's exclamation in verse 23, about his
own glorification, which has to do not
only with his being raised up to the right
hand of the Father (cf. Phil 2:6–11) but
also with his attracting all men to himself
(cf. Jn 12:32).

Jesus refers to "the hour" on other
occasions also. Sometimes he means the
end of the world (cf. Mk 13:32; Jn 5:25);
sometimes, as is the case here, it means
the moment of redemption through his
death and glorification (cf. Mk 14:41; Jn
2:4; 4:23; 7:30; 8:20; 12:27; 13:1; 17:1).

12:24–25. There is an apparent paradox
here between Christ's humiliation and his
glorification. Thus, "it was appropriate
that the loftiness of his glorification
should be preceded by the lowliness of
his passion" (St Augustine, *In Ioann.
Evang.*, 51, 8). This is the same idea as
we find in St Paul, when he says that
Christ humbled himself and became obedient unto death, even death on a cross,
and that therefore God the Father exalted
him above all created things (cf. Phil
2:8–9). This is a lesson and an encour-
agement to the Christian, who should see
every type of suffering and contradiction
as a sharing in Christ's cross, which
redeems us and exalts us. To be supernat-

urally effective, a person has to die to
himself, forgetting his comfort and shed-
ding his selfishness. "If the grain of wheat
does not die, it remains unfruitful. Don't
you want to be a grain of wheat, to die
through mortification, and to yield a rich
harvest? May Jesus bless your wheat-
field!" (St J. Escrivá, *The Way*, 199).

12:26. Our Lord has spoken about his
sacrifice being a condition of his entering
his glory. And what holds good for the
Master applies also to his disciples (cf.
Mt 10:24; Lk 6:40). Jesus wants each of
us to be of service to him. It is a mystery
of God's plans that he—who is all, who
has all and who needs nothing and
nobody—should choose to need our help
to ensure that his teaching and the salvation wrought by him reaches all men.

"To follow Christ: that is the secret.
We must accompany him so closely that
we come to live with him, like the first
Twelve did; so closely, that we become
identified with him. Soon we will be able
to say, provided we have not put obstacles in the way of grace, that we have put
on, have clothed ourselves with, our Lord
Jesus Christ (cf. Rom 13:14). [...]

"I have distinguished as it were four
stages in our effort to identify ourselves
with Christ—seeking him, finding him,
getting to know him, loving him. It may
seem clear to you that you are only at the
first stage. Seek him then, hungrily; seek
him within yourselves with all your

27"Now is my soul troubled. And what shall I say? 'Father, save me from this hour'? No, for this purpose I have come to this hour. 28Father, glorify thy name." Then a voice came from heaven, "I have glorified it, and I will glorify it again." 29The crowd standing by heard it and said that it had thundered. Others said, "An angel has spoken to him." 30Jesus answered, "This voice has come for your sake, not for mine. 31Now is the judgment of this world,

Jn 11:33
Ps 6:3
Mt 26:38
Heb 5:7–8
Jn 5:37
Mt 17:5
Lk 22:43
Jn 11:42
Jn 3:19; 14:30
Lk 10:18

strength. If you act with determination, I am ready to guarantee that you have already found him, and have begun to get to know him and to love him, and to hold your conversation in heaven (cf. Phil 3:20)" (St Josemaría Escrivá, *Friends of God*, 299–300).

12:27. The thought of the death that awaits him saddens Jesus, and he turns to the Father in a prayer very similar to that of Gethsemane (cf. Mt 26:39; Mk 14:36; Lk 22:42): our Lord, as man, seeks support in the love and power of his Father God to be strengthened to fulfil his mission. We find this very consoling, for we often feel weak in moments of trial: like Jesus we should seek support in God's strength, for "thou art my rock and my fortress" (Ps 31:3).

12:28. "Glory" in Holy Scripture implies God's holiness and power; the "glory of God" dwelt in the sanctuary in the desert and in the temple of Jerusalem (cf. Ex 40:35; 1 Kings 8:11). The voice of the Father saying "I have glorified it, and I will glorify it again" is a solemn ratification that the fullness of divinity dwells in Jesus (cf. Col 2:9; Jn 1:14) and that, through his passion, death and resurrection, it will be made patent, in his human nature itself, that Jesus is the Son of God (cf. Mk 15:39).

This episode evokes other occasions—at Christ's baptism (cf. Mt 3:13–17 and par.) and his transfiguration (Mt 17:1–5 and par.)—when God the Father bears witness to the divinity of Jesus.

12:31–33. Jesus tells them the results that will flow from his passion and death. "Now is the judgment of this world", that is, of those who persist in serving Satan, the "prince of this world". Although "world" means the totality of mankind whom Christ comes to save (cf. Jn 3:16–17), it also often means all that is opposed to God (cf. the note on Jn 1:10) which is the sense it has here. On being nailed to the cross, Jesus is the supreme sign of contradiction for all men: those who recognize him as Son of God will be saved (cf. Lk 23:39–43); those who reject him will be condemned. Christ crucified is the maximum expression of the Father's love for us (cf. Jn 3:14–16; Rom 8:32), the sign raised on high which was prefigured in the bronze serpent raised up by Moses in the wilderness (cf. Jn 3:14; Num 21:9).

Our Lord on the cross, then, is the Judge who will condemn the world (cf. Jn 3:17) and the devil (cf. Jn 16:11); in fact they have provoked their own condemnation by not accepting or believing in God's love. From the cross the Lord will attract all men to himself, for all will be able to see him there, crucified

"Christ our Lord was crucified; from the height of the cross he redeemed the world, thereby restoring peace between God and men. Jesus reminds all of us: '*Et ego, si exaltatus fuero a terra, omnia traham ad meipsum*, and I, when I am

137

Rev 12:9
Jn 8:28

now shall the ruler of this world be cast out; [32]and I, when I am lifted up* from the earth, will draw all men to myself." [33]He said this to show by what death he was to die. [34]The crowd answered him, "We have heard from the law that the Christ remains for ever. How can you say that the Son of man must be lifted up? Who is this Son of man?" [35]Jesus said to them, "The light is with you for a little longer. Walk while you have the light, lest the darkness overtake you; he who walks in the darkness does not know where he goes. [36]While you have the light, believe in the light, that you may become sons of light."

Is 9:6f
Dan 7:14

Jn 8:12; 9:5;
11:10

Jer 13:16
Eph 5:8

When Jesus had said this, he departed and hid himself from them.

---

lifted up from the earth, will draw all things to myself' (Jn 12:32). If you put me at the centre of all earthly activities, he is saying, by fulfilling the duty of each moment, in what appears important and what appears unimportant, I will draw everything to myself. My kingdom among you will be a reality!" (St Josemaría Escrivá, *Christ Is Passing By*, 183). Every Christian, following Christ, has to be a flag raised aloft, a light on a lampstand— through prayer and mortification, a sign of the saving love of God the Father.

"Through his incarnation, through his work at Nazareth and his preaching and miracles in the land of Judea and Galilee, through his death on the cross, and through his resurrection, Christ is the centre of the universe, the firstborn and Lord of all creation.

"Our task as Christians is to proclaim this kingship of Christ, announcing it through what we say and do. Our Lord wants men and women of his own in all walks of life. Some he calls away from society, asking them to give up involvement in the world, so that they can remind the rest of us by their example that God exists. To others he entrusts the priestly ministry. But he wants the vast majority to stay right where they are, in all earthly occupations in which they work—the factory, the laboratory, the farm, the trades, the streets of the big cities and the trails of the mountains" (ibid., 105).

12:32. "I will draw all men to myself." The Vulgate, following important Greek manuscripts, translates this as *omnia*, "all things"; the New Vulgate, using equally important and more numerous manuscripts, opts for *omnes*, "everyone". There is no compelling reason for adopting one or other reading: both are theologically correct and neither excludes the other, for Christ attracts all creation to himself, but especially mankind (cf. Rom 8:18–23).

12:34–36. The question posed here touches on the mystery of the Messiah. Jesus does not provide a direct explanation, perhaps because they would be able to understand it only after his resurrection. He limits himself to suggesting that his presence among them is light enough for them to glimpse the mystery of Christ.

"To deserve this light from God, we must love. We must be humble enough to realize we need to be saved, and we must say with Peter: 'Lord, to whom shall we go? You have the words of life everlasting, and we have believed and have come to know that you are the Christ, the Son of God' (Jn 6:68–69). If we really do this, if we allow God's word to enter our

Jesus appeals for faith in himself

[37]Though he had done so many signs before them, yet they did not believe in him; [38]it was that the word spoken by the prophet Isaiah might be fulfilled:

> "Lord, who has believed our report,
> and to whom has the arm of the Lord been revealed?"

[39]Therefore they could not believe. For Isaiah again said,

> [40]"He has blinded their eyes and hardened their heart,
> lest they should see with their eyes and perceive with their heart,
> and turn for me to heal them."

Is 53:1
Rom 10:16

Is 6:9–10
Mt 13:14ff
Acts 28:26f

---

hearts, we can truly say that we do not walk in darkness, for the light of God will shine out over our weakness and our personal defects, as the sun shines above the storm" (St Josemaría Escrivá, *Christ Is Passing By*, 45).

12:37–40. The Evangelist here summarizes the rejection of Jesus by the Jews, giving the reason why many failed to believe in him despite witnessing his miracles and hearing him teach. He quotes two prophecies of Isaiah. From the first (Is 53:1) we can see that faith is a gift from God which we cannot merit by our works nor attain through reason, though this does not mean that the grounds on which it rests—miracles, prophecies etc.—are not evident, or that what faith teaches is opposed to reason. However, in addition to receiving this gift, we must cooperate with it freely and voluntarily; as the Magisterium of the Church teaches: "But though the assent of faith is by no means a blind action of the mind, still no man can 'assent to the Gospel teaching', as is necessary to obtain salvation 'without the illumination and inspiration of the Holy Spirit, who gives to all men sweetness in assenting to and believing in truth'. Wherefore, faith itself, even when it does not work by charity (cf. Gal 5:6), is in itself a gift of

God, and the act of faith is a work appertaining to salvation, by which man yields voluntary obedience to God himself by assenting to and cooperating with his grace, which he is able to resist" (Vatican I, *Dei Filius*, chap. 3, *Dz-Sch*, 3010).

With the second prophecy (Is 6:910), to which other books of the New Testament also refer (cf. Mt 13:14; Mk 4:12; Lk 8:10; Acts 28:26; Rom 9:1–13; 11:18), St John explains that the unbelief of the Jews, which could have been a source of scandal to the early Christians, was in fact something foreseen and predicted: "Some, then, mutter in themselves and, when they can, now and then cry out, saying, What did the Jews do or what was their faith, for it to be necessary for the words of the prophet Isaiah to be fulfilled? To this we answer that the Lord, who knows the future, predicted by the prophet the unbelief of the Jews; he predicted it, but he was not its cause. Just as God compels no one to sin, though he knows already man's future sins. [...] Consequently, what the Jews did was sin; but they were not compelled to do so by him who hates sin; and it was only predicted that they would sin, by him from whom nothing is hidden. If they had wished to do not evil but good, they would not have been hindered; but then God would have foreseen this, for he

Is 6:1 ⁴¹Isaiah said this because he saw his glory and spoke of him.
Jn 7:48; 9:22 ⁴²Nevertheless many even of the authorities believed in him, but for fear of the Pharisees they did not confess it, lest they should
Jn 5:44 be put out of the synagogue: ⁴³for they loved the praise of men more than the praise of God.
Mt 10:40 ⁴⁴And Jesus cried out and said, "He who believes in me,
Jn 14:7–9 believes not in me, but in him who sent me. ⁴⁵And he who sees
Jn 8:12; 12:53 me sees him who sent me. ⁴⁶I have come as light into the world,
Jn 3:17 that whoever believes in me may not remain in darkness. ⁴⁷If any
Lk 8:21 one hears my sayings and does not keep them, I do not judge him; for I did not come to judge the world but to save the world. ⁴⁸He
Lk 20:16 who rejects me and does not receive my sayings has a judge; the
Heb 4:12 word that I have spoken will be his judge on the last day. ⁴⁹For I
Deut 18:18f have not spoken on my own authority; the Father who sent me has himself given me commandment what to say and what to speak.
Jn 8:26–28 ⁵⁰And I know that his commandment is eternal life. What I say, therefore, I say as the Father has bidden me."

knows what each man will do, and what he will render him according to his works" (St Augustine, *In Ioann. Evang.*, 53, 4).

12:42–43. On a number of occasions our Lord praised individuals who confessed their faith in him, for example, the woman who had the flow of blood (Lk 8:43–48), the centurion (Mt 8:8–10), the Canaanite woman (Mt 15:21–28), St Peter (Mt 16:16–17). But now, in this very tense situation, these Jewish leaders are afraid to confess him publicly (cf. also Jn 7:13); they do not want to face being expelled from the Jewish community (cf. Jn 9:22) or compromise their social position (cf. Jn 5:44).

Christians can often experience contradiction because they act in a way consistent with the demands of their faith (cf. 1 Pet 5:9): "What does it matter if you have the whole world against you, with all its power? You ... keep going! Repeat the words of the psalm: 'The Lord is my light and my salvation: whom need I fear? *Si consistant adversum me castra,*

non timebit cor meum. Though an army pitched camp against me, my heart shall not be afraid'" (St Josemaría Escrivá, *The Way*, 482).

12:44–50. With these verses St John brings to an end his account of our Lord's public ministry. He brings together certain fundamental themes developed in previous chapters—the need for faith in Christ (v. 44); the Father and the Son are one yet distinct (v. 45); Jesus is Light and Life of the world (vv. 46, 50); men will be judged in accordance with whether they accept or reject the Son of God (vv. 47–49). The chapters which follow contain Jesus' teaching to his Apostles at the Last Supper, and the accounts of the Passion and Resurrection.

12:45. Christ, the Word Incarnate, is one with the Father (cf. Jn 10:30): "he reflects the glory of God" (Heb 1:3); "he is the image of the invisible God" (Col 1:15). In John 14:9 Jesus expresses himself in almost the same words: "He who has seen me has seen the Father". At the

Jesus is manifested as the Messiah Son of God in his passion, death and resurrection

9. THE LAST SUPPER

Jesus washes his disciples' feet

Jn 2:4; 7:30;
8:20; 15:13
Gal 2:20
1 Jn 3:16

13 *[1]Now before the feast of the Passover, when Jesus knew that his hour had come to depart out of this world to the

---

same time he speaks of his oneness with the Father, we are clearly shown the distinction of persons—the Father who sends, and the Son who is sent.

In Christ's holy human nature his divinity is, as it were, hidden, that divinity which he possesses with the Father in the unity of the Holy Spirit (cf. Jn 14:7–11). In theology "circumincession" is the word usually used for the fact that, by virtue of the unity among the three Persons of the Blessed Trinity, "the Father is wholly in the Son and wholly in the Holy Spirit; the Son wholly in the Father and wholly in the Holy Spirit; Holy Spirit wholly in the Father and wholly in the Son" (Council of Florence, Decree *Pro Jacobitis, Dz-Sch*, 1331).

12:47. Christ has come to save the world by offering himself in sacrifice for our sins and bringing us supernatural life (cf. Jn 3:17). But he has also been made Judge of the living and the dead (cf. Acts 10:42): he passes sentence at the particular judgment which happens immediately after death, and at the end of the world, at his second coming or Parousia, at the universal judgment (cf. Jn 5:22; 8:15–16; and see the note on Jn 15:22–25).

13:1–38. St John devotes a large part of his Gospel (chaps. 13–17) to recounting Jesus' teaching to his apostles at the Last Supper. This section also tells us things which are not reported in the Synoptics—the washing of feet, for example; and it omits the institution of the Eucharist, which the other Gospels and St Paul had already passed on (cf. Mt 26:26–28 and par.; 1 Cor 11:23–27), and which St John himself dealt with in chapter 6. In chapters 13 to 17 the Evangelist extensively reports our Lord's words on this exceptionally important occasion. Chapter 13 begins by describing just how important the occasion was (vv. 1–3). It goes on to narrate the washing of feet (vv. 4–11) and Jesus' explanation of why he did it (vv. 12–17). It then mentions the denunciation of the betrayer (vv. 18–32) and ends with the teaching of the new commandment (vv. 33–35) and the prediction of Peter's denial (vv. 36–38).

13:1. Jewish families sacrificed a lamb on the eve of the Passover, in keeping with God's command at the time of the exodus when God liberated them from the slavery of the Pharaoh (cf. Ex 12:3–14; Deut 16:1–8). This liberation prefig-

Jn 11:27
Lk 22:3

Jn 1:1; 3:35;
16:28; 17:2

Mt 11:29; 20:28
Lk 12:37

Father, having loved his own who were in the world, he loved them to the end. ²And during supper, when the devil had already put it into the heart of Judas Iscariot, Simon's son, to betray him, ³Jesus, knowing that the Father had given all things into his hands, and that he had come from God and was going to God, ⁴rose from supper, laid aside his garments, and girded himself with a towel. ⁵Then he poured water into a basin, and began to wash the disciples' feet, and to wipe them with the towel with which he was girded. ⁶He came to Simon Peter, and Peter said to him, "Lord, do

---

ured that which Jesus Christ would bring about—the redemption of men from the slavery of sin by means of his sacrifice on the cross (cf. 1:29). This is why the celebration of the Jewish Passover was the ideal framework for the institution of the new Christian Passover.

Jesus knew everything that was going to happen; he knew his death and resurrection were imminent (cf. 18:4); this is why his words acquire a special tone of intimacy and love towards those whom he is leaving behind in the world. Surrounded by those whom he has chosen and who have believed in him, he gives them his final teachings and institutes the Eucharist, the source and centre of the life of the Church. "He himself wished to give that encounter such a fulness of meaning, such a richness of memories, such a moving image of words and thoughts, such a newness of acts and precepts, that we can never exhaust our reflection and exploration of it. It was a testamentary supper, infinitely affectionate and immensely sad, and at the same time a mysterious revelation of divine promises, of supreme visions. Death was imminent, with silent omens of betrayal, of abandonment, of immolation; the conversation dies down but Jesus continues to speak in words that are new and beautifully reflective, in almost supreme intimacy, almost hovering between life and death" (Paul VI, Homily on Holy Thursday, 27 March 1975).

What Christ did for his own may be summed up in this sentence: "He loved them to the end." It shows the intensity of his love—which brings him even to give up his life (cf. Jn 15:13); but this love does not stop with his death, for Christ lives on after his resurrection and he continues loving us infinitely: "It was not only thus far that he loved us, who always and forever loves us. Far be it from us to imagine that he made death the end of his loving, who did not make death the end of his living" (St Augustine, *In Ioann. Evang.*, 55, 2).

13:2. The Gospels show us the presence and activity of the devil running right through Jesus' life (cf. Mt 4:1–11; Lk 22:3; Jn 8:44; 12:31; etc.). Satan is "the enemy" (Mt 13:39), "the evil one" (1 Jn 2:13). St Thomas Aquinas (cf. *Comm. on St John*, in loc.) points out that, in this passage, on the one hand we clearly see the malice of Judas, who fails to respond to this demonstration of love, and on the other hand great emphasis is laid on the goodness of Christ, who reaches out beyond Judas' malice by washing his feet also and by treating him as a friend right up to the moment when he betrays him (cf. Lk 22:48).

13:3–6. Aware that he is the Son of God, Jesus voluntarily humbles himself to the point of performing a service appropriate to household servants. This passage recalls

you wash my feet?" [7]Jesus answered him, "What I am doing you do not know now, but afterward you will understand." [8]Peter said to him, "You shall never wash my feet." Jesus answered him, "If I do not wash you, you have no part in me." [9]Simon Peter said to him, "Lord, not my feet only but also my hands and my head!" [10]Jesus said to him, "He who has bathed does not need to wash, except for his feet,[c] but he is clean all over; and you are clean, but not all of you." [11]For he knew who was to betray him; that was why he said, "You are not all clean."

Jn 13:12ff;
14:26

Jn 15:3

Jn 6:64, 70f

---

the Christological hymn in St Paul's Letter to the Philippians: "Christ Jesus, who, though he was in the form of God, did not count equality with God a thing to be grasped, but emptied himself, taking the form of a servant ..." (Phil 2:5–7).

Christ had said that he came to the world "not to be served but to serve" (Mk 10:45). In this scene he teaches us the same thing, through specific example, thereby exhorting us to serve each other in all humility and simplicity (cf. Gal 6:2; Phil 2:3). "Once again he preaches by example, by his deeds. In the presence of his disciples, who are arguing out of pride and vanity, Jesus bows down and gladly carries out the task of a servant [...] This tactfulness of our Lord moves me deeply. He does not say: 'If I do this, how much more ought you to do?' He puts himself at their level, and he lovingly chides those men for their lack of generosity.

"As he did with the first twelve, so also, with us, our Lord can and does whisper in our ear, time and again: *exemplum dedi vobis* (Jn 13:15), I have given you an example of humility. I have become a slave, so that you too may learn to serve all men with a meek and humble heart" (St Josemaría Escrivá, *Friends of God*, 103).

Peter understands particularly well how thoroughly our Lord has humbled himself, and he protests, in the same kind of way as he did on other occasions, that he will not hear of Christ suffering (cf. Mk 8:32 and par.). St Augustine comments: "Who would not shrink back in dismay from having his feet washed by the Son of God .... You? Me? Words to be pondered on rather than spoken about, lest words fail to express their true meaning" (*In Ioann. Evang.*, 56, 1).

13:7–14. Our Lord's gesture had a deeper significance than St Peter was able to grasp at this point; nor could he have suspected that God planned to save men through the sacrificing of Christ (cf. Mt 16:22ff). After the Resurrection the apostles understood the mystery of this service rendered by the Redeemer: by washing their feet, Jesus was stating in a simple and symbolic way that he had not come "to be served but to serve". His service, as he already told them, consists in giving "his life as a ransom for many" (Mt 20:28; Mk 10:45).

Our Lord tells the apostles that they are now clean, for they have accepted his words and have followed him (cf. 15:3)—all but Judas, who plans to betray him. St John Chrysostom comments as follows: "You are already clean because of the word that I have spoken to you. That is: You are clean only to that extent. You have already received the Light; you

---

c. Other ancient authorities omit *except for his feet*

Mt 23:8, 10
Sir 32:1
Lk 22:27
1 Tim 5:10
Phil 2:5
Col 3:13
1 Pet 2:21; 5:3
Mt 10:24
Lk 6:40
Mt 7:24
Jas 1:25
Jn 6:70
Ps 41:9

[12]When he had washed their feet, and taken his garments, and resumed his place, he said to them, "Do you know what I have done to you? [13]You call me Teacher and Lord; and you are right, for so I am. [14]If I then, your Lord and Teacher, have washed your feet, you also ought to wash one another's feet. [15]For I have given you an example, that you also should do as I have done to you. [16]Truly, truly, I say to you, a servant[d] is not greater than his master; nor is he who is sent greater than he who sent him. [17]If you know these things, blessed are you if you do them. [18]I am not speaking of you all; I know whom I have chosen; it is that the scripture may be fulfilled, 'He who ate my bread has lifted his

---

have already got rid of the Jewish error. The Prophet asserted: 'Wash yourselves; make yourselves clean; remove the evil from your souls' (Is 1:16)... . Therefore, since they had rooted out all evil from their souls and were following him with complete sincerity, he declared, in accordance with the Prophet's words: 'He who has bathed is clean all over'" (St John Chrysostom, *Hom. on St John*, 70, 3).

Also, when our Lord speaks about the apostles being clean, now, just before the institution of the Blessed Eucharist, he is referring to the need for the soul to be free from sin if it is to receive this sacrament. St Paul repeats this teaching when he says: "Whoever eats the bread or drinks the cup of the lord in an unworthy manner will be guilty of profaning the body and blood of the Lord" (1 Cor 11:27). On the basis of these teachings of Jesus and the apostles, the Church lays down that anyone who is conscious of having committed a grave sin, or who has any positive doubt on that score, must go to confession before receiving Holy Communion.

13:15–17. Jesus' whole life was an example of service towards men, fulfilling his Father's will to the point of dying on the cross. Here our Lord promises us that if

we imitate him, our Teacher, in disinterested service (which always implies sacrifice), we will find true happiness which no one can wrest from us (cf. 16:22; 17:13). "'I have given you an example', he tells his disciples after washing their feet, on the night of the Last Supper. Let us reject from our hearts any pride, any ambition, any desire to dominate; and peace and joy will reign around us and within us, as a consequence of our personal sacrifice" (St Josemaría Escrivá, *Christ Is Passing By*, 94).

13:18. Lifting one's heel against someone means hitting him brutally; metaphorically, therefore, it means violent enmity. Judas' treachery fulfils the words of Psalm 41:9 where the psalmist complains bitterly of a friend's treachery. Once again the Old Testament prefigures events which find their full expression in the New.

Through Baptism, the Christian has become a son of God and is called to share in God's good things, not only in heaven but also on earth: he has received grace, he shares in the eucharistic banquet, he shares with his brethren, other Christians, the friendship of Jesus. Therefore, if a person sins who has been born again through Baptism, in some

d. Or *slave*

144

heel against me.' [19]I tell you this now, before it takes place, that when it does take place you may believe that I am he. [20]Truly, truly, I say to you, he who receives any one whom I send receives me; and he who receives me receives him who sent me."

Jn 14:29; 16:4; 8:24
Mt 10:40
Mk 9:37
Lk 9:48

The treachery of Judas foretold

[21]When Jesus had thus spoken, he was troubled in spirit, and testified, "Truly, truly, I say to you, one of you will betray me." [22]The disciples looked at one another, uncertain of whom he spoke. [23]One of his disciples, whom Jesus loved, was lying close to the breast of Jesus; [24]so Simon Peter beckoned to him and said, "Tell

Mt 26:21–25
Mk 14:18, 21
Lk 22:21–23
Jn 12:27

Jn 19:26; 20:2;
21:7–20

---

sense his is a sort of treachery similar to that of Judas'. However, we have the recourse of repentance: if we trust in God's mercy we can set about recovering our friendship with God.

"Wake up! Listen to what the Holy Spirit tells you: '*Si inimicus meus maledixisset mihi, sustinuissem utique* — If it were an enemy who insulted me, I could put up with that.' But you ... '*tu vero homo unanimis, dux meus, et notus meus, qui simul mecum dulces capiebas cibos* — you, my friend, my apostle, who sit at my table and take sweet food with me!'" (St J. Escrivá, *The Way*, 244).

13:19. Jesus tells the Apostles in advance about Judas' treachery, so that when they see Christ's predictions come true, they will realize he has divine knowledge and that in him are fullfilled the Scriptures of the Old Testament (cf. Jn 2:22). On the words "I am", cf. the note on Jn 8:21–24.

13:21. Christ's sadness is proportionate to the gravity of the offence. Judas was one of those whom Jesus chose to be an apostle: he had been on intimate terms with him for three years, he had followed him everywhere, had seen his miracles, had heard his divine teaching, and experienced the tenderness of his affection. And despite all that, when the moment of truth comes, Judas not only abandons the

Master but betrays him and sells him. Betrayal by an intimate friend is something much more painful and cruel than betrayal by a stranger, for it involves a lack of loyalty. The spiritual life of the Christian is also true friendship with Jesus; this means it is based on loyalty and uprightness, and on being true to one's word.

Judas had already decided to hand Jesus over and had made arrangements with the chief priests (cf. Mt 26:14; Mk 14:10–11; Lk 22:3–6). Temptation had been burrowing its way into Judas' heart for some time back, as we saw at the anointing in Bethany when he protested against Mary's loving gesture; St John commented in that connexion that he did it not out of love for the poor but because he was a thief (cf. Jn 12:6).

13:23. In that period, on important occasions the customary thing was to eat reclining on a kind of divan called a *triclinium*. The diner rested on his left elbow and ate with his right hand. This meant it was easy to lean on the person on one's left and talk to him without people hearing. In this verse we can see the intimacy and trust which existed between the Master and his beloved disciple (cf. Jn 19:27; 20:2; 21:23), a model of Jesus' love for all his true disciples and of theirs for their Master.

us who it is of whom he speaks." ²⁵So lying thus, close to the breast of Jesus, he said to him, "Lord, who is it?" ²⁶Jesus answered, "It is he whom I shall give this morsel when I have dipped it." So when he had dipped the morsel, he gave it to Judas, the son of Simon Iscariot. ²⁷Then after the morsel, Satan entered into him. Jesus said to him, "What you are going to do, do quickly," ²⁸Now no one at the table knew why he said this to him. ²⁹Some thought that, because Judas had the money box, Jesus was telling him, "Buy what you need for the feast"; or, that he should give something to the poor. ³⁰So, after receiving the morsel, he immediately went out; and it was night.

Jn 13:2
Lk 22:3

Jn 12:6

Jn 8:12
Lk 22:53

13:26–27. The morsel which Jesus offers him is a sign of friendship and, therefore, an invitation to him to give up his evil plotting. But Judas rejects the chance he is offered. "What he received is good", St Augustine comments, "but he received it to his own perdition, because he, being evil, received in an evil manner what is good" (*In Ioann. Evang.*, 61, 6). Satan entering into him means that from that moment Judas gave in completely to the devil's temptation.

13:29. "These details have been recorded that we may not bear ill will against those who wrong us, but may reproach them and weep over them. Indeed, not those who are wronged, but those who do wrong deserve our tears. For the covetous man and the slanderer, and the man guilty of any other wrongdoing injure themselves most of all. [...] Christ repaid the man who was going to betray him with just the opposite. For example, he washed his feet, reproved him without bitterness, censured him in private, ministered to him, allowed him to share in his table and his kiss. Yet, though Judas did not become better because of these things, Jesus himself persevered in his course of action" (St John Chrysostom, *Hom. on St John*, 71, 4).

13:30. The indication that "it was night" is not just a reference to the time of day

but to darkness as an image of sin, an image of the power of darkness whose hour was beginning at that very moment (cf. Lk 22:53). The contrast between light and darkness, the opposition of good and evil, is frequently met with in the Bible, especially in the Fourth Gospel: even in the prologue we are told that Christ is the true Light which the darkness has not overcome (cf. Jn 1:5).

13:31–32. This glorification refers above all to the glory which Christ will receive once he is raised up on the cross (Jn 3:14; 12:32). St John stresses that Christ's death is the beginning of his victory: his very crucifixion can be considered the first step in his ascension to his Father. At the same time it is glorification of the Father, because Christ, by voluntarily accepting death out of love, as a supreme act of obedience to the will of God, performs the greatest sacrifice man can offer for the glorification of God. The Father will respond to this glorification which Christ offers him by glorifying Christ as Son of man, that is, in his holy human nature, through his resurrection and ascension to God's right hand. Thus the glory which the Son gives the Father is at the same time glory for the Son. Christ's disciple will also find his highest motivation by identifying himself with Christ's obedience. St Paul teaches

The new commandment. The disciples' desertion foretold

[31]When he had gone out, Jesus said, "Now is the Son of man glorified, and in him God is glorified; [32]if God is glorified in him, God will also glorify him in himself, and glorify him at once. [33]Little children, yet a little while I am with you. You will seek me; and as I said to the Jews so now I say to you, 'Where I am going you cannot come.' [34]A new commandment* I give to you, that you love one another; even as I have loved you, that you also love one another. [35]By this all men will know that you are my disciples, if you have love for one another."

[36]Simon Peter said to him, "Lord, where are you going?" Jesus answered, "Where I am going you cannot follow me now; but you

Jn 12:23;
17:1–5

Jn 7:33; 8:21

Jn 15:12, 13, 17
1 Jn 2:8
Lev 19:18

Jn 17:23
Acts 4:32

Jn 21:18f
Mt 26:33–35
Mk 14:29, 31
Lk 22:31–34

---

this very clearly when he says: "Far be it from me to glory except in the cross of the Lord Jesus Christ" (Gal 6:14).

13:33. From this verse onward the Evangelist recounts what is usually called the discourse of the Last Supper; in it we can distinguish three parts. In the first, our Lord begins by proclaiming the New Commandment (vv. 33–35) and predicts Peter's denials (vv. 36–38); he tells them that his death means his going to his Father (chap. 14), with whom he is one because he is God (vv. 1–14); and he announces that after his resurrection he will send them the Holy Spirit, who will guide them by teaching them and reminding them of everything he told them (vv. 15–31).

The second part of the discourse is contained in chapters 15 and 16. Jesus promises to those who believe in him a new life of union with him, as intimate as that of a vine and its branches (15:1–8). To attain this union one must keep his New Commandment (vv. 9–17). He forewarns them about the contradictions they will suffer, and he encourages them by promising the Holy Spirit who will protect them and console them (vv. 18–27). The action of the Paraclete or Consoler will lead them to fulfil the mission Jesus has entrusted to them (16:1–15). The

fruit of the presence of the Holy Spirit will be fullness of joy (vv. 16–33).

The third part (chap. 17) gives Jesus' priestly prayer, in which he asks the Father to glorify him through the cross (vv. 1–5). He prays also for his disciples (vv. 6–19) and for all those who through them will believe in him, so that, staying in the world without being in the world, the love of God should be in them and they should bear witness to Christ being the envoy of the Father (vv. 20–26).

13:34–35. After announcing that he is leaving them (v. 33). Christ summarizes his commandments in one—the New Commandment. He will repeat it a number of times during the discourse of the Supper (cf. Jn 15:12, 17), and St John in his First Letter will insist on the need to practise this commandment of the Lord and on the demands it implies (cf. 1 Jn 2:8; 3:7–21).

Love of neighbour was already commanded in the Old Testament (cf. Lev 19:18)—and Jesus ratified this when he specified that it was the second precept of the whole Law and similar to the first: Love God with all your heart and soul and mind (cf. Mt 22:37–40). But Jesus gives the precept of brotherly love new meaning and content by saying "even as I have loved you".

shall follow afterward." ³⁷Peter said to him, "Lord, why cannot I follow you now? I will lay down my life for you." ³⁸Jesus answered, "Will you lay down your life for me? Truly, truly, I say to you, the cock will not crow, till you have denied me three times.

The love of neighbour called for by the Old Law did also in some way extend to one's enemies (Ex 23:4–5); however, the love which Jesus preaches is much more demanding and includes returning good for evil (cf. Mt 5:43–44), because Christian love is measured not by man's heart but by the heart of Christ, who gives up his life on the cross to redeem all men (cf. 1 Jn 4:9–11). Here lies the novelty of Jesus' teaching, and our Lord can rightly say that it is his commandment, the principal clause of his last will and testament. Love of neighbour cannot be separated from love of God: "The greatest commandment of the law is to love God with one's whole heart and one's neighbour as oneself (cf. Mt 22:37–40). Christ has made this love of neighbour his personal commandment and has enriched it with a new meaning when he willed himself, along with his brothers, to be the object of this charity, saying: 'As you did it to one of the least of these my brethren, you did it to me' (Mt 25:40). In assuming human nature he has united to himself all humanity in a supernatural solidarity which makes of it one single family. He has made charity the distinguishing mark of his disciples, in the words: 'By this all men will know that you are my disciples, if you have love for one another'" (Vatican II, *Apostolicam actuositatem*, 8).

Even though Christ is purity itself, and temperance and humility, he does not, however, make any one of these virtues the distinguishing mark of his disciples: he makes charity that mark. "The Master's message and example are clear and precise. He confirmed his teaching with deeds. Yet I have often thought that, after twenty centuries, it is still a *new* commandment, for very few people have taken the trouble to practise it. The others, the majority of men, both in the past and still today, have chosen to ignore it. Their selfishness has led them to the conclusion: 'Why should I complicate my life? I have more than enough to do just looking after myself.'

"Such an attitude is not good enough for us Christians. If we profess the same faith and are really eager to follow in the clear footprints left by Christ when he walked on this earth, we cannot be content merely with avoiding doing unto others the evil that we would not have them do unto us. That is a lot, but it is still very little when we consider that our love is to be measured in terms of Jesus' own conduct. Besides, he does not give us this standard as a distant target, as a crowning point of a whole lifetime of struggle. It is — it ought to be, I repeat, so that you may turn it into specific resolutions — our starting point, for our Lord presents it as a sign of Christianity: 'By this shall all men know that you are my disciples'" (St Josemaría Escrivá, *Friends of God*, 223).

And this is what in fact happened among Christians in the early centuries in the midst of pagan society, so much so that Tertuallian, writing around the end of the second century, reported that people could indeed say, looking at the way these Christians lived: "See how they love one another" (*Apologeticum*, 39).

Jesus reveals the Father

14 [1]"Let not your hearts be troubled; believe[e] in God, believe also in me. [2]In my Father's house are many rooms; if it were not so, would I have told you that I go to prepare a place for you? [3]And when I go and prepare a place for you, I will come again and will take you to myself, that where I am you may be also. [4]And you know the way where I am going."[f] [5]Thomas said

Jn 14:27
Mk 11:22

Jn 12:26; 17:24
Heb 6:19f

13:36–38. Once again Peter in his simplicity and sincerity tells his Master that he is ready to follow him even to the point of dying for him. But he is not yet ready for that. Our Lord, St Augustine comments, "establishes here a delay; he does not destroy the hope, indeed he confirms it by saying, 'You shall follow afterwards! Why are you in haste, Peter? As yet the rock has not made you strong inwardly: do not be brought down by your presumption. Now you cannot follow me, but do not despair: later, you will'" (*In Ioann. Evang.*, 66, 1). Peter had certainly meant what he said, but his resolution was not very solid. Later on he would develop a fortitude based on humility; then, not considering himself worthy to die in the way his master did, he will die on a cross, head downwards, rooting in the soil of Rome that solid stone which endures in those who succeed him and forming the basis on which the Church, which is indefectible, is built.

Peter's denials, which are signs of his weakness, were amply compensated for by his profound repentance. "Let everyone draw from this example of contrition, and if he has fallen let him not despair, but always remember that he can become worthy of forgiveness" (St Bede, *In Ioann. Evang. expositio*, in loc.).

14:1–3. Apparently this prediction of Peter's denial has saddened the disciples.

Jesus cheers them up by telling them that he is going away to prepare a place for them in heaven, for heaven they will eventually attain, despite their shortcomings and dragging their feet. The return which Jesus refers to includes his second coming (Parousia) at the end of the world (cf. 1 Cor 4:5; 11:36; 1 Thess 4:16–17; 1 Jn 2:28) and his meeting with each soul after death: Christ has prepared a heavenly dwelling place through his work of redemption. Therefore, his words can be regarded as being addressed not only to the Twelve but also to everyone who believes in him over the course of the centuries. The Lord will bring with him into his glory all those who have believed in him and have stayed faithful to him.

14:4–7. The Apostles did not really understand what Jesus was telling them: hence Thomas' question. The Lord explains that he is the way to the Father. "It was necessary for him to say 'I am the Way' to show them that they really knew what they thought they were ignorant of, because they knew him" (St Augustine, *In Ioann. Evang.*, 66, 2).

Jesus is the way to the Father— through what he teaches, for by keeping to his teaching we will reach heaven; through faith, which he inspires, because he came to this world so "that whoever believes in him may have eternal life" (Jn 3:15); through his example, since no one

---

e. Or *you believe* **f.** Other ancient authorities read *where I am going you know, and the way you know*

Jn 11:25
Mt 11:27

Rom 5:1ff
Heb 10:20

to him, "Lord, we do not know where you are going; how can we know the way?" ⁶Jesus said to him, "I am the way, and the truth, and the life; no one comes to the Father, but by me. ⁷If you had known me, you would have known my Father also; henceforth you know him and have seen him."

Jn 12:45
Mt 17:17
Heb 1:3

Jn 12:49

⁸Philip said to him, "Lord, show us the Father, and we shall be satisfied." ⁹Jesus said to him, "Have I been with you so long, and yet you do not know me, Philip? He who has seen me has seen the Father; how can you say, 'Show us the Father'? ¹⁰Do you not believe that I am in the Father and the Father in me? The words

---

can go to the Father without imitating the Son; through his merits, which make it possible for us to enter our heavenly home; and above all he is the way because he reveals the Father, with whom he is one because of his divine nature.

"Just as children by listening to their mothers, and prattling with them, learn to speak their language, so we, by keeping close to the Saviour in mediation, and observing his words, his actions, and his affections, shall learn, with the help of his grace, to speak, to act, and to will like him.

"We must pause here ... ; we can reach God the Father by no other route ...; the Divinity could not well be contemplated by us in this world below if it were not united to the sacred humanity of the Saviour, whose life and death are the most appropriate, sweet, delicious and profitable subject which we can choose for our ordinary meditations" (St Francis de Sales, *Introduction to the Devout Life*, part 2, chaps. 1, 2).

"I am the way": he is the only path linking heaven and earth. "He is speaking to all men, but in a special way he is thinking of people who, like you and me, are determined to take our Christian vocation seriously: he wants God to be forever in our thoughts, on our lips and in everything we do, including our most ordinary and routine actions.

"Jesus is the way. Behind him on this earth of ours he has left the clear outlines of his footprints. They are indelible signs which neither the erosion of time nor the treachery of the evil one have been able to erase" (St J. Escrivá, *Friends of God*, 127). Jesus' words do much more than provide an answer to Thomas' question; he tells us, "I am the way, and the truth, and the life". Being the Truth and the Life is something proper to the Son of God become man, who St John says in the prologue of his Gospel is "full of truth and grace" (1:14). He is the Truth because by coming to this world he shows that God is faithful to his promises, and because he teaches the truth about who God is and tells us that true worship must be "in spirit and truth" (Jn 4:23). He is the Life because from all eternity he has divine life with his Father (cf. Jn 1:4), and because he makes us, through grace, sharers in that divine life. This is why the Gospel says: "This is eternal life, that they know thee, the only true God, and Jesus Christ whom thou has sent" (Jn 17:3).

By his reply Jesus is, "as it were, saying, By which route do you want to go? I am the Way. To where do you want to go? I am the Truth. Where do you want to remain? I am the Life. Every man can attain an understanding of the Truth and the Life; but not all find the Way. The wise of this world realize that

that I say to you I do not speak on my own authority; but the Father who dwells in me does his works. [11]Believe me that I am in the Father and the Father in me; or else believe me for the sake of the works themselves.

[12]Truly, truly, I say to you, he who believes in me will also do the works that I do; and greater works than these will he do; because I go to the Father. [13]Whatever you ask in my name, I will do it, that the Father may be glorified in the Son; [14]if you ask[g] anything in my name, I will do it.

Jn 10:25, 38;
14:20

Mk 16:19f

Jn 15:7–16
Mk 11:24
1 Jn 5:14

Jn 15:10;
16:23f

God is eternal life and knowable truth; but the Word of God, who is Truth and Life joined to the Father, has become the Way by taking a human nature. Make your way contemplating his humility and you will reach God" (St Augustine, *De verbis Domini sermones*, 54).

14:8–11. The apostles still find our Lord's words very mysterious, because they cannot understand the oneness of Father and Son. Hence Philip's persistence. Then Jesus "upbraids the apostle for not yet knowing him, even though his works are proper to God—walking on the water, controlling the wind, forgiving sins, raising the dead. This is why he reproves him: for not recognizing his divine condition through his human nature" (St Augustine, *De Trinitate*, book 7).

Obviously the sight of the Father which Jesus refers to in this passage is a vision through faith, for no one has ever seen God as he is (cf. Jn 1:18; 6:46). All manifestations of God, or "theophanies", have been through some medium; they are only a reflexion of God's greatness. The highest expression which we have of God our Father is in Christ Jesus, the Son of God sent among men. "He did this by the total fact of his presence and self-manifestation—by words and works, signs and miracles, but above all by his death and glorious resurrection from the

dead, and finally by sending the Spirit of truth. He revealed that God was with us, to deliver us from the darkness of sin and death, and to raise us up to eternal life" (Vatican II, *Dei Verbum*, 4).

14:12–14. Before leaving this world, the Lord promises his apostles to make them sharers in his power so that God's salvation may be manifested through them. These "works" are the miracles they will work in the name of Jesus Christ (cf. Acts 3:1–10; 5:15–16, etc.), and especially the conversion of people to the Christian faith and their sanctification by preaching and the ministry of the sacraments. They can be considered greater works than Jesus' own insofar as, by the apostles' ministry, the Gospel was not only preached in Palestine but was spread to the ends of the earth; but this extraordinary power of apostolic preaching proceeds from Christ, who has ascended to the Father: after undergoing the humiliation of the cross Jesus has been glorified and from heaven he manifests his power by acting through the apostles.

The apostles' power, therefore, derives from Christ glorified. Christ our Lord says as much: "Whatever you ask in my name, I will do it". "It is not that he who believes in me will be greater than me, but only that I shall then do greater works than

g. Other ancient authorities add *me*

Promise of the Holy Spirit

1 Jn 5:3
Deut 6:4–9
Jn 14:26;
15:26; 16:7
1 Jn 2:1
Jn 7:35; 16:13
Mt 10:20
Rom 8:26
Jn 6:57; 16:16

[15]"If you love me, you will keep my commandments. [16]And I will pray the Father, and he will give you another Counsellor, to be with you for ever, [17]even the Spirit of truth, whom the world cannot receive, because it neither sees him nor knows him; you know him, for he dwells with you, and will be in you.

[18]"I will not leave you desolate; I will come to you. [19]Yet a little while, and the world will see me no more, but you will see

---

now; greater, by him who believes in me, than I now do by myself without him" (St Augustine, *In Ioann. Evang.*, 72, 1).

Jesus Christ is our intercessor in heaven; therefore, he promises us that everything we ask for in his name, he will do. Asking in his name (cf. 15:7, 16; 16:23–24) means appealing to the power of the risen Christ, believing that he is all-powerful and merciful because he is true God; and it also means asking for what is conducive to our salvation, for Jesus is our Saviour. Thus, by "whatever you ask" we must understand what is for the good of the asker. When our Lord does not give what we ask for, the reason is that it would not make for our salvation. In this way we can see that he is our Saviour both when he refuses us what we ask and when he grants it.

14:15. Genuine love must express itself in deeds. "This indeed is love: obeying and believing in the loved one" (St John Chrysostom, *Hom. on St John*, 74). Therefore, Jesus wants us to understand that love of God, if it is to be authentic, must be reflected in a life of generous and faithful self-giving, obedient to the will of God: he who accepts God's commandments and obeys them, he it is who loves him (cf. Jn 14:21). St John himself exhorts us in another passage not to "love in word or speech but in deed and in truth" (1 Jn 3:18), and he teaches us that "this is the love of God, that we keep his commandments" (1 Jn 5:3).

14:16–17. On a number of occasions the Lord promises the apostles that he will send them the Holy Spirit (cf. 14:26; 15:26; 16:7–14; Mt 10:20). Here he tells them that one result of his mediation with the Father will be the coming of the Paraclete. The Holy Spirit in fact does come down on the disciples after our Lord's ascension (cf. Acts 2:1–13), sent by the Father and by the Son. In promising here that through him the Father will send them the Holy Spirit, Jesus is revealing the mystery of the Blessed Trinity.

"Counsellor": the Greek word sometimes anglicized as "paraclete" means, etymologically, "called to be beside one" to accompany, console, protect, defend. Hence the word is translated as Counsellor, Advocate, etc. Jesus speaks of the Holy Spirit as "another Counsellor", because he will be given them in Christ's place as Advocate or Defender to help them, since Jesus is going to ascend to heaven. In 1 John 2:1 Jesus Christ is described as a Paraclete: "We have an advocate with the Father, Jesus Christ, the righteous". Jesus Christ, then, also is our Advocate and Mediator in heaven where he is with the Father (cf. Heb 7:25). It is now the role of the Holy Spirit to guide, protect and vivify the Church, "for there are, as we know, two factors which Christ has promised and arranged in different ways to continue his mission [...]: the apostolate and the Spirit. The apostolate is the external and objective

me; because I live, you will live also. ²⁰In that day you will know that I am in my Father, and you in me, and I in you. ²¹He who has my commandments and keeps them, he it is who loves me; and he who loves me will be loved by my Father, and I will love him and manifest myself to him. ²²Judas (not Iscariot) said to him, "Lord, how is it that you will manifest yourself to us, and not to the world?" ²³Jesus answered him, "If a man loves me, he will keep my word, and my Father will love him, and we will come to him

Jn 17:21–23
2 Cor 3:18
1 Jn 5:3

Acts 10:41
Jn 14:21; 13:34
Prov 8:17
Mt 10:20; 28:20
Eph 3:17
2 Cor 6:16

---

factor, it forms the material body, so to speak, of the Church and is the source of her visible and social structures. The Holy Spirit acts internally within each person, as well as on the whole community, animating, vivifying, sanctifying" (Paul VI, Opening Address at the third session of Vatican II, 14 September 1964).

The Holy Spirit is Counsellor as we make our way in this world amid difficulties and the temptation to feel depressed. "In spite of our great limitations, we can look up to heaven with confidence and joy: God loves us and frees us from our sins. The presence and the action of the Holy Spirit in the Church are a foretaste of eternal happiness, of the joy and peace for which we are destined by God" (St Josemaría Escrivá, *Christ Is Passing By*, 128).

14:18–20. At various points in the Supper, we can see the apostles growing sad when the Lord bids them farewell (cf. Jn 15:16; 16:22). Jesus speaks to them with great tenderness, calling them "little children" (Jn 13:33) and "friends" (Jn 15:15), and he promises that he will not leave them alone, for he will send the Holy Spirit, and he himself will return to be with them again. And in fact he will see them again after the Resurrection when he appears to them over a period of forty days to tell them about the Kingdom of God (cf. Acts 1:3). When he ascends into heaven they will see him no

longer; yet Jesus still continues to be in the midst of his disciples as he promised he would (cf. Mt 28:20), and we will see him face to face in heaven. "Then it shall be that we will be able to see that which we believe. For even now he is with us, and we in him [...]; but now we know by believing, whereas then we shall know by beholding. As long as we are in the body, such as it is now, that is, corruptible, which weighs down the soul, we are making our way towards the Lord: for we walk by faith, not by sight. But then we shall see him directly, we shall see him as he is" (St Augustine, *In Ioann. Evang.*, 75, 4).

14:22–23. It was commonly held by the Jews that when the Messiah came he would be revealed to the whole world as King and Saviour. The apostles take Jesus' words as a revelation for themselves alone, and they are puzzled. Hence the question from Judas Thaddeus. It is interesting to note how easy the Apostles' relations with our Lord are: they simply ask him about things they do not know and get him to clear up any doubts they have. This is a good example of how we should approach Jesus, who is also our Teacher and Friend.

Jesus' reply may seem evasive but in fact, by referring to the form his manifestation takes, he explains why he does not reveal himself to the world: he makes himself known to him who loves him and keeps his commandments. God repeat-

Jn 7:16
1 Jn 2:5

and make our home with him. ²⁴He who does not love me does not keep my words; and the word which you hear is not mine but the Father's who sent me.

---

edly revealed himself in the Old Testament and promised to dwell in the midst of the people (cf. Ex 29:45; Ezek 37:26–27; etc.); but here Jesus speaks of a presence of God in each person. St Paul refers to this presence when he asserts that each of us is a temple of the Holy Spirit (cf. 2 Cor 6:16–17). St Augustine, in reflecting on God's ineffable nearness in the soul, exclaims: "Late have I loved you, O beauty so ancient and so new, late have I loved you! You were within me, and I was in the world outside myself. I searched for you in the world outside myself... . You were with me, but I was not with you. The beautiful things of this world kept me far from you and yet, if they had not been in you, they would have had no being at all. You called me; you cried aloud to me; you broke my barrier of deafness; you shone upon me; your radiance enveloped me; you cured my blindness" (*Confessions*, 10, 27, 38).

Jesus is referring to the indwelling of the Holy Spirit in the soul renewed by grace: "Our heart now needs to distinguish and adore each one of the divine Persons. The soul is, as it were, making a discovery in the supernatural life, like a little child opening his eyes to the world about him. The soul spends time lovingly with the Father and the Son and the Holy Spirit, and readily submits to the work of the lifegiving Paraclete, who gives himself to us with no merit on our part, bestowing his gifts and the supernatural virtues!" (St Josemaría Escrivá, *Friends of God*, 306).

14:25–26. Jesus has expounded his teaching very clearly, but the Apostles do not yet fully understand it; they will do

so later on, when they receive the Holy Spirit who will guide them unto all truth (cf. Jn 16:13). "And so the Holy Spirit did teach them and remind them: he taught them what Christ had not said because they could not take it in, and he reminded them of what the Lord has taught and which, either because of the obscurity of the things or because of the dullness of their minds, they had not been able to retain" (Theophylact, *Enarratio in Evangelium Ioannis*, ad loc.).

The word translated here as "bring to your remembrance" also includes the idea of "suggesting": the Holy Spirit will recall to the apostles' memory what they have already heard Jesus say and he will give them light to enable them to discover the depth and richness of everything they have seen and heard. Thus, "the Apostles handed on to their hearers what he had said and done, but with that fuller understanding which they, instructed by the glorious events of Christ (cf. Jn 2:33) and enlightened by the Spirit of truth, now enjoyed" (Vatican II, *Dei Verbum*, 19).

"Christ has not left his followers without guidance in the task of understanding and living the Gospel. Before returning to his Father, he promised to send his Holy Spirit to the Church: 'But the Counsellor, the Holy Spirit, whom the Father will send in my name, he will teach you all things, and bring to your remembrance all I have said to you'" (Jn 14:26).

"This same Spirit guides the successors of the Apostles, your bishops, united with the Bishop of Rome, to whom it was entrusted to preserve the faith and to 'preach the gospel to the whole creation'

25"These things I have spoken to you, while I am still with you. 26But the Counsellor, the Holy Spirit, whom the Father will send in my name, he will teach you all things,* and bring to your remembrance all that I have said to you. 27Peace I leave with you;

Jn 14:16
Mt 10:19ff
1 Jn 2:27

Jn 14:1; 16:33
Eph 2:14, 18

(Mk 16:15). Listen to their voices, for they bring you the word of the Lord" (John Paul II, Homily at Knock Shrine, 30 September 1979).

In the Gospels is consigned to writing, under the charism of divine inspiration, the apostles' version of everything they had witnessed—and the understanding of it, which they obtained after Pentecost. So it is that these sacred writers "faithfully hand on what Jesus, the Son of God, while he lived among men, really did and taught for their eternal salvation, until the day when he was taken up (cf. Acts 1:1–2)" (Vatican II, *Dei Verbum*, 19). This is why the Church so earnestly recommends the reading of Holy Scripture, particularly the Gospels. "How I wish your bearing and conversation were such that, on seeing or hearing you, people would say: This man reads the life of Jesus Christ" (St Josemaría Escrivá, *The Way*, 2).

14:27. Wishing a person peace was, and still is, the usual form of greeting among Jews and Arabs. It is the greeting Jesus used, and which the apostles continued to use, as we can see from their letters (cf. 1 Pet 1–2; 3 Jn 15; Rom 1:7; etc.). The Church still uses it in the liturgy: for example, before Communion the celebrant wishes those present peace, a condition for worthily sharing in the holy sacrifice (cf. Mt 5:23–25) and also a fruit of that sacrifice. On our Lord's lips this common greeting acquires its deepest meaning; peace is one of the great messianic gifts (cf. Is 9:7; 48:18; Mic 5:5; Mt 10:22; Lk 2:14; 19:38). The peace which Jesus gives us completely transcends the

peace of the world (cf. the note on Mt 10:34–37), which can be superficial and misleading and compatible with injustice. The peace of Christ is, above all, reconciliation with God and reconciliation of men with one another; it is one of the fruits of the Holy Spirit (cf. Gal 5:22–23); it is "serenity of mind, tranquillity of soul, simplicity of heart, a bond of love, a union of charity: no one can inherit God if he does not keep his testament of peace, or live in unity with Christ if he is separated from Christianity" (St Augustine, *De verbis Domini serm*, 58).

"'Christ is our peace' (Eph 2:14). And today and forever he repeats to us: 'My peace I give to you, my peace I leave with you'. [...] Never before in the history of mankind has peace been so much talked about and so ardently desired as in our day. [...] And yet again and again, one can see how peace is undermined and destroyed. [...] Peace is the result of many converging attitudes and realities; it is the product of moral concerns, of ethical principles based on the Gospel message and fortified by it. [...] In his message for the 1971 Day of Peace, my reverend predecessor, that pilgrim for peace, Paul VI, said: 'True peace must be founded upon justice, upon a sense of the untouchable dignity of man, upon the recognition of an indelible and happy equality between men, upon the basic principle of human brotherhood, that is, of the respect and true love due to each man, because he is man'. [...] Every human being has inalienable rights that must be respected. Each human community—ethnic, historical, cultural or

Phil 4:7

Jn 14:3, 6, 18
Lk 24:52

Jn 13:19; 16:14

Jn 12:31
Eph 2:2

Jn 10:18

my peace I give to you; not as the world gives do I give to you. Let not your hearts be troubled, neither let them be afraid. ²⁸You heard me say to you, 'I go away, and I will come to you.' If you loved me, you would have rejoiced, because I go to the Father; for the Father is greater than I. ²⁹And now I have told you before it takes place, so that when it does take place, you may believe. ³⁰I will no longer talk much with you, for the ruler of this world is coming. He has no power over me; ³¹but I do as the Father has

---

religious—has rights which must be respected. Peace is threatened every time one of these rights is violated. The moral law, guardian of human rights, protector of the dignity of man, cannot be set aside by any person or group, or by the State itself, for any cause, not even for security or in the interests of law and order. The law of God stands in judgment over all reasons of State. As long as injustices exist in any of the areas that touch upon the dignity of the human person, be it in the political, social or economic field, be it in the cultural or religious sphere, true peace will not exist. [...] Peace cannot be established by violence, peace can never flourish in a climate of terror, intimidation and death. It is Jesus himself who said: 'All who take the sword will perish by the sword' (Mt 26:52). This is the word of God, and it commands this generation of violent men to desist from hatred and violence and to repent" (John Paul II, Homily at Drogheda, 29 September 1979). The peace and joy which Christ brings us should be typical of believers: "Get rid of those scruples that deprive you of peace. What takes away your peace of soul cannot come from God. When God comes to you, you will realize the truth of those greetings: My peace I give to you ... , my peace I leave you ... , my peace be with you ... , and you will feel it even in the midst of troubles" (St Josemaría Escrivá, *The Way*, 258).

14:28. Jesus Christ, as Only-begotten Son of God, possesses divine glory for all eternity; but while he is on earth this glory is veiled and hidden behind his holy human nature (cf. 17:5; Phil 2:7). It only shows itself on a few occasions, such as when he performs miracles (cf. 2:11) or at the Transfiguration (cf. Mt 17:1–8 and par.). Now, through his death, resurrection and ascension into heaven Jesus will be glorified—in his body also—as he returns to the Father and enters into his glory. Therefore, his departure from this world should be a source of joy for his disciples; but they do not properly understand what he is saying, and they are saddened because they are more aware of the Master being physically separated from them than the glory which awaits him.

When Jesus says that the Father is greater than he, he is thinking about his human nature; as man Jesus is going to be glorified, ascending as he does to the right hand of the Father. Jesus Christ "is equal to the Father in his divinity, less than the Father in his humanity" (*Athanasian Creed*). St Augustine exhorts us to "acknowledge the twofold nature of Christ—the divine, by which he is equal to the Father; the human, by which he is less than the Father. But the one and the other are together not two, but one Christ" (*In Ioann. Evang.*, 78, 3). However, although the Father and the Son are equal in nature, eternity and dignity, our Lord's words can also be under-

commanded me, so that the world may know that I love the Father. Rise, let us go hence.

Mt 26:46
Mk 14:42

The vine and the branches

15 ¹"I am the true vine, and my Father is the vinedresser. ²Every branch of mine that bears no fruit, he takes away, and every branch that does bear fruit he prunes that it may bear

Is 5:1
Jer 2:21
Ps 80:8–15
Sir 24:23

---

stood by taking "greater" to refer to his origin: only the Father is "beginning without beginning", whereas the Son proceeds eternally from the Father by way of a generation which is also eternal. Jesus Christ is God from God, Light from Light, True God from True God (cf. *Nicene Creed*).

14:30. Clearly the world is good, for it has been created by God, and God loved it so much that he sent his Only-begotten Son (Cf. Jn 3:16). However, in this passage "world" means all those who reject Christ; and "the ruler of this world" is the devil (cf. Jn 1:10; 7:7; 15:18–19). The devil opposed the work of Jesus right from the start of his public life when he tempted him in the desert (cf. Mt 4:1–11 and par.). Now, in the passion, he will apparently overcome Christ. This is the hour of the power of darkness when, availing of Judas' treachery (cf. Lk 22:53; Jn 13:27), the devil manages to have our Lord arrested and crucified.

15:1. The comparison of the chosen people with a vine was used in the Old Testament: Psalm 80 speaks of the uprooting of the vine in Egypt and its re-planting in another land; and in Isaiah's Song of the Vineyard (5:1–7) God complains that despite the care and love he has lavished on it, his vineyard has yielded only wild grapes. Jesus previously used this imagery in his parable about the murderous tenants (Mt 21:33–

43) to signify the Jews' rejection of the Son and the calling of the Gentiles. But here the comparison has a different, more personal meaning: Christ explains that he himself is the true vine, because the old vine, the original chosen people, has been succeeded by the new vine, the Church, whose head is Christ (cf. 1 Cor 3:9). To be fruitful one must be joined to the new, true vine, Christ: it is no longer a matter of simply belonging to a community but of living the life of Christ, the life of grace, which is the nourishment which passes life on to the believer and enables him to yield fruits of eternal life. This image of the vine also helps us understand the unity of the Church, Christ's mystical body, in which all the members are intimately united with the head and thereby are also united to one another (1 Cor 12:12–26; Rom 12:4–5; Eph 4:15–16).

15:2. Our Lord is describing two situations: that of those who, although they are still joined to the vine externally, yield no fruit; and that of those who do yield fruit but could yield still more. The Letter of St James carries the same message when it says that faith alone is not enough (cf. Jas 2:17). Although it is true that faith is the beginning of salvation and that without faith we cannot please God, it is also true that a living faith must yield fruit in the form of deeds. "For in Christ Jesus neither circumcision nor uncircumcision is of any avail, but faith working through love" (Gal 5:6). So, one can say

Mt 15:13;
21:33

1 Cor 12:12–27
2 Cor 3:5

Mt 3:10; 13:6,
40
Ezek 15:1–8
Mt 11:24

Mt 5:16
Rom 7:4

more fruit. ³You are already made clean by the word which I have spoken to you. ⁴Abide in me, and I in you. As the branch cannot bear fruit by itself, unless it abides in the vine, neither can you, unless you abide in me. ⁵I am the vine, you are the branches. He who abides in me, and I in him, he it is that bears much fruit, for apart from me you can do nothing. ⁶If a man does not abide in me, he is cast forth as a branch and withers; and the branches are gathered, thrown into the fire and burned. ⁷If you abide in me, and my words abide in you, ask whatever you will, and it shall be done for you. ⁸By this my Father is glorified, that you bear much fruit, and so prove to be my disciples.

that in order to produce fruit pleasing to God, it is not enough to have received Baptism and to profess the faith externally: a person has to share in Christ's life through grace and has to cooperate with him in his work of redemption.

Jesus uses the same verb to refer to the pruning of the branches as he uses to refer to the cleanness of the disciples in the next verse: literally the translation should run: "He cleanses him who bears fruit so that he bear more fruit". In other words, he is making it quite clear that God is not content with a half-hearted commitment, and therefore he purifies his own by means of contradictions and difficulties, which are a form of pruning, to produce more fruit. In this we can see an explanation of the purpose of suffering: "Have you not heard the Master himself tell the parable of the vine and the branches? Here we can find consolation. He demands much of you, for you are the branch that bears fruit. And he must prune you *'ut fructum plus afferas* —to make you bear more fruit'. Of course that cutting, that pruning, hurts. But, afterwards, what richness in your fruits, what maturity in your actions" (St Josemaría Escrivá, *The Way*, 701).

15:3. After washing Peter's feet Jesus had already said that his apostles were clean, though not all of them (cf. Jn

13:10). Here, once more, he refers to that inner cleansing which results from accepting his teachings. "For Christ's word in the first place cleanses us from errors, by instructing us (cf. Tit 1:9) [...]; secondly, it purifies our hearts of earthly affections, filling them with desire for heavenly things [...]; finally, his word purifies us with the strength of faith, for 'he cleansed their hearts by faith' (Acts 15:9)" (St Thomas Aquinas, *Comm. on St John*, in loc.).

15:4–5. Our Lord draws more conclusions from the image of the vine and the branches. Now he emphasizes that anyone who is separated from him is good for nothing, like a branch separated from the vine. "You see, the branches are full of fruit, because they share in the sap that come from the stem. Otherwise, from the tiny buds we knew just a few months back, they could not have produced the sweet ripe fruit that gladdens the eye and makes the heart rejoice (cf. Ps 103:15). Here and there on the ground we may find some dry twigs, lying half-buried in the soil. Once they too were branches of the vine; now they lie there withered and dead, a perfect image of barrenness: 'apart from me, you can do nothing'" (St Josemaría Escrivá, *Friends of God*, 245).

The life of union with Christ is necessarily something which goes far beyond

The law of love

⁹As the Father has loved me, so have I loved you; abide in my love. ¹⁰If you keep my commandments, you will abide in my love, just as I have kept my Father's commandments and abide in his love. ¹¹These things I have spoken to you, that my joy may be in you, and that your joy may be full.

¹²"This is my commandment, that you love one another as I have loved you. ¹³Greater love has no man than this, that a man

Jn 10:14, 15

Jn 14:15; 8:29
1 Jn 2:4, 8

Jn 16:24; 17:13
1 Jn 1:4

Jn 13:34
1 Jn 3:11
Mk 12:31

---

one's private life: it has to be focused on the good of others; and if this happens, a fruitful apostolate is the result, for "apostolate, of whatever kind it be, must be an overflow of the interior life" (St Josemaría Escrivá, *Friends of God*, 239). The Second Vatican Council, quoting this page from St John, teaches what a Christian apostolate should be: "Christ, sent by the Father, is the source of the Church's whole apostolate. Clearly then, the fruitfulness of the apostolate of lay people depends on their living union with Christ; as the Lord himself said: 'He who abides in me, and I in him, he it is that bears much fruit, for apart from me you can do nothing'. This life of intimate union with Christ in the Church is maintained by the spiritual helps common to all the faithful, chiefly by active participation in the liturgy. Laymen should make such a use of these helps that, while meeting their human obligations in the ordinary conditions of life, they do not separate their union with Christ from their ordinary life; but through the very performance of their tasks, which are God's will for them, actually promote the growth of their union with him" (*Apostolicam actuositatem*, 4).

15:6. If a person is not united to Christ by means of grace he will ultimately meet the same fate as the dead branches—fire. There is a clear parallelism with other images our Lord uses—the parables of the

sound tree and the bad tree (Mt 7:15–20), the dragnet (Mt 13:47–50), and the invitation to the wedding (Mt 22:11–14), etc. Here is how St Augustine comments on this passage: "The wood of the vine is the more contemptible if it does not abide in the vine, and the more glorious if it does abide ... . For, being cut off it is profitable neither for the vinedresser nor for the carpenter. For one of these only is it useful— the vine or the fire. If it is not in the vine, it goes to the fire; to avoid going to the fire it must be joined to the vine" (*In Ioann. Evang.*, 81, 3).

15:9–11. Christ's love for Christians is a reflection of the love the three divine Persons have for one another and for all men: "We love, because he first loved us" (1 Jn 4:19).

The certainty that God loves us is the source of Christian joy (v. 11), but it is also something which calls for a fruitful response on our part, which should take the form of a fervent desire to do God's will in everything, that is, to keep his commandments, in imitation of Jesus Christ, who did the will of his Father (cf. Jn 4:34).

15:12–15. Jesus insists on the "new commandment", which he himself keeps by giving his life for us. See the note on Jn 13:34–35.

Christ's friendship with the Christian, which our Lord expresses in a very spe-

Jn 10:11
1 Jn 3:16
Jn 8:31
Mt 12:50; 28:10
Jn 13:18
Rom 6:20–23
lay down his life for his friends. [14]You are my friends if you do what I command you. [15]No longer do I call you servants,[h] for the servant[i] does not know what his master is doing; but I have called you friends, for all that I have heard from my Father I have made known to you. [16]You did not choose me, but I chose you and appointed you that you should go and bear fruit and that your fruit should abide; so that whatever you ask the Father in my name, he may give it to you. [17]This I command you, to love one another.

Jn 7:7
1 Jn 3:13
Jn 17:14–16
1 Jn 4:5
A hostile world

[18]"If the world hates you, know that it has hated me before it hated you.* [19]If you were of the world, the world would love its own;

---

cial way in this passage, is something very evident in St Josemaría Escrivá's preaching: "The life of the Christian who decides to behave in accordance with the greatness of his vocation is so to speak a prolonged echo of those words of our Lord, 'No longer do I call you my servants; a servant is one who does not understand what his master is about, whereas I have made known to you all that my Father has told me; and so I have called you my friends' (Jn 15:15). When we decide to be docile and follow the will of God, hitherto unimagined horizons open up before us [...]. There is nothing better than, recognizing that Love has made us slaves of God. From the moment we recognize this we cease being slaves and become friends, sons" (St Josemaría Escrivá, *Friends of God*, 35].

"Sons of God, *Friends of God*. [...] Jesus Christ is truly God and truly Man, he is our Brother and our Friend. If we make an effort to get to know him well, 'we will share in the joy of being God's friends' [ibid., 300]. If we do all we can to keep him company, from Bethlehem to Calvary, sharing his joys and sufferings, we will become worthy of entering into

loving conversation with him. As the Liturgy of the Hours sings, *calicem Domini biberunt, et amici Dei facti sunt*, they drank the chalice of the Lord and so became friends of God.

"Being his children and being his friends are two inseparable realities for those who love God. We go to him as children, carrying on a trusting dialogue that should fill the whole of our lives; and we go to him as friends. [...] In the same way our divine sonship urges us to translate the overflow of our interior life into apostolic activity, just as our friendship with God leads us to place ourselves at 'the service of all men. We are called to use the gifts God has given us as instruments to help others discover Christ' [ibid., 258]" (Monsignor A. del Portillo in the foreword to Escrivá, *Friends of God*).

15:16. There are three ideas contained in these words of our Lord. One, that the calling which the apostles received and which every Christian also receives does not originate in the individual's good desires but in Christ's free choice. It was not the apostles who chose the Lord as Master, in the way someone would go

h. Or *slaves* **i.** Or *slave*

160

but because you are not of the world, but I chose you out of the world, therefore the world hates you. ²⁰Remember the word that I said to you, 'A servantⁱ is not greater than his master.' If they persecuted me, they will persecute you; if they kept my word, they will keep yours also. ²¹But all this they will do to you on my account, because they do not know him who sent me. ²²If I had not come and spoken to them, they would not have sin; but now they have no excuse for their sin. ²³He who hates me hates my Father also. ²⁴If I had not done among them the works which no one else did, they would not have sin; but now they have seen and hated both me and my Father. ²⁵It is to fulfil the word that is writ-

Jn 13:16
Mt 10:24

Jn 10:22
Mt 5:11
Mk 13:13
Acts 5:41

Jn 5:23
1 Jn 2:23

Jn 9:41; 14:11

Ps 35:19; 69:4

---

about choosing a rabbi: it was Christ who chose them. The second idea is that the apostles' mission and the mission of every Christian is to follow Christ, to seek holiness and contribute to the spread of the Gospel. The third teaching refers to the effectiveness of prayer done in the name of Christ; which is why the Church usually ends the prayers of the liturgy with the invocation "Through Jesus Christ our Lord ...".

The three ideas are all interconnected: prayer is necessary if the Christian life is to prove fruitful, for it is "God who gives the growth" (1 Cor 3:7); and the obligation to seek holiness and to be apostolic derives from the fact that it is Christ himself who has given us this mission. "Bear in mind, son, that you are not just a soul who has joined other souls in order to do a good thing. That is a lot, but it's still little. You are the apostle who is carrying out an imperative command from Christ" (St Josemaría Escrivá, *The Way*, 941–942).

15:18–19. Jesus states that there can be no compromise between him and the world, the kingdom of sin: anyone who lives in sin abhors the light (cf. Jn 3:19–20). This is why Christ is persecuted, and why the apostles will be in their turn. "The

hostility of the perverse sounds like praise for our life", St Gregory says, "because it shows that we have at least some rectitude if we are an annoyance to those who do not love God; no one can be pleasing to God and to God's enemies at the same time. He who seeks to please those who oppose God is no friend of God; and he who submits himself to the truth will fight against those who strive against the truth" (*In Ezechielem homiliae*, 9).

15:22–25. Our Lord points out that those who deny him would not have sin had he not revealed himself, had the Light not shone; but it has shone and they have no excuse now (cf. Jn 9:41; Mt 12:31ff). "This is the sin", St Augustine comments, "that they did not believe in what Christ said and did. We are not to suppose that they had no sin before he spoke to them and worked miracles among them; but this sin, their not believing in him, is mentioned in this way, because in this sin of unbelief are all other sins rooted. For if they had believed in him, the rest would be forgiven" (*In Ioann. Evang.*, 91, 1).

Hatred of Christ, who "went about doing good" (Acts 10:38), cannot be explained except by men being deeply affected by the devil's hatred of God. The

i. Or *slave*

Jn 14:26
Lk 24:49

ten in their law, 'They hated me without a cause.' ²⁶But when the Counsellor comes, whom I shall send to you from the Father, even the Spirit of truth, who proceeds from the Father, he will bear witness to me; ²⁷and you also are witnesses, because you have been with me from the beginning.

Lk 1:2
Acts 1:8; 5:32

The action of the Holy Spirit

Jn 14:29
Jn 9:22
Mt 5:11; 24:9
Lk 6:22
Acts 26:9–11
Jn 15:21
Jn 17:12
Lk 22:53
Jn 7:33; 13:36;
14:5

16 ¹"I have said all this to you to keep you from falling away. ²They will put you out of the synagogues; indeed, the hour is coming when whoever kills you will think he is offering service to God. ³And they will do this because they have not known the Father, nor me. ⁴But I have said these things to you, that when their hour comes you may remember that I told you of them.

"I did not say these things to you from the beginning, because I was with you. ⁵But now I am going to him who sent me; yet

---

Old Testament foretold that he would be hated so viciously: "Let not those rejoice over me who are wrongfully my foes, and let not those wink the eye who hate me without cause" (Ps 35:19; cf. also Ps 2:1–2; 22:16–18).

15:26–27. Just before the ascension our Lord will again charge the apostles with the mission to bear witness to him (cf. Acts 1:8). They have been witnesses to the public ministry, death and resurrection of Christ, which is a condition for belonging to the apostolic college, as we see when Matthias is elected to take the place of Judas (cf. Acts 1:21–22). But the public preaching of the Twelve and the life of the Church will not start until the Holy Spirit comes. Every Christian should be a living witness to Jesus, and the Church as a whole is a permanent testimony to him: "The mission of the Church is carried out by means of that activity through which, in obedience to Christ's command and moved by the grace and love of the Holy Spirit, the Church makes itself fully present to all men and peoples in order to lead them to the faith, freedom and peace of Christ by the

example of its life and teaching, by the sacraments and other means of grace" (Vatican II, *Ad gentes*, 5).

16:2–3. Fanaticism can even bring a person to think that it is permissible to commit a crime in order to serve the cause of religion—as happened with those Jews who persecuted Jesus to the point of bringing about his death, and who later persecuted the Church. Paul of Tarsus was a typical example of misguided zeal (cf. Acts 22:3–16); but once Paul realized he was wrong he changed and became one of Christ's most fervent apostles. As Jesus predicted, the Church has often experienced this sort of fanatical, diabolical hatred. At other times this false zeal, though not so obvious, takes the form of systematic and unjust opposition to the things of God. "In the moments of struggle and opposition, when perhaps 'the good' fill your way with obstacles, lift up your apostolic heart: listen to Jesus as he speaks of the grain of mustard-seed and of the leaven. And say to him '*Edissere nobis parabolam*: Explain the parable to me.'

"And you will feel the joy of contem-

none of you asks me, 'Where are you going?' ⁶But because I have said these things to you, sorrow has filled your hearts. ⁷Nevertheless I tell you the truth: it is to your advantage that I go away, for if I do not go away, the Counsellor will not come to you; but if I go, I will send him to you. ⁸And when he comes, he will convince the world of sin and of righteousness and of judgment: ⁹of sin, because they do not believe in me; ¹⁰of righteousness, because I go to the Father, and you will see me no more;* ¹¹of judgment, because the ruler of this world is judged.

¹²"I have yet many things to say to you, but you cannot bear them now. ¹³When the Spirit of truth comes, he will guide you into all the truth; for he will not speak of his own authority, but whatever he hears he will speak, and he will declare to you the things

Jn 14:16; 26:28

1 Cor 14:24
Heb 14:12
Acts 24:25
Jn 3:18
Rom 1:18
Acts 5:31
Rom 4:25
Jn 12:31; 14:30

1 Cor 3:1
Heb 5:11ff

Jn 14:26
Jm 2:27
Acts 8:31

---

plating the victory to come: the birds of the air lodging in the branches of your apostolate, now only in its beginnings, and the whole of the meal leavened" (St Josemaría Escrivá, *The Way*, 695).

In these cases, as our Lord also pointed out, those who persecute God's true servants think they are serving him: they confuse God's interest with a deformed idea of religion.

16:4. Here Jesus prophesies not only his own death (cf. Mt 16:21–23) but also the persecution his disciples will suffer. He warns them of the contradictions they will experience so that they will not be scandalized or depressed when they do arise; in fact, difficulties will give them an opportunity to demonstrate their faith.

16:6–7. The thought that he is going to leave them saddens the apostles, and our Lord consoles them with the promise of the Paraclete, the Consoler. Later (vv. 20ff), he assures them that their sadness will turn into a joy which no one can take away from them.

Jesus speaks about the Holy Spirit three times during the discourse of the Last Supper. The first time (14:15ff), he says that another Paraclete (advocate, consoler) will come, sent by the Father, to be with them forever; secondly, he says (14:26) that he himself will send them, on behalf of the Father, the Spirit of truth who will teach them everything; and now he unfolds for them the complete plan of salvation and announces that the Holy Spirit will be sent once he ascends into heaven.

16:8–12. The word "world" here means all those who have not believed in Christ and have rejected him. These the Holy Spirit will accuse of sin because of their unbelief. He will accuse them of unrighteousness because he will show that Jesus was the Just One who was never guilty of sin (cf. Jn 8:46; Heb 4:15) and therefore is in glory beside his Father. And, finally, he will indict them by demonstrating that the devil, the prince of this world, has been overthrown through the death of Christ, which rescues man from the power of the Evil One and gives him grace to avoid the snares he lays.

16:13. It is the Holy Spirit who makes fully understood the truth revealed by Christ. As Vatican II teaches, our Lord "completed and perfected Revelation and confirmed it ... finally by sending the

Jn 17:10

that are to come. [14]He will glorify me, for he will take what is mine and declare it to you. [15]All that the Father has is mine; therefore I said that he will take what is mine and declare it to you.

Fullness of joy

Jn 14:19

[16]"A little while, and you will see me no more; again a little while, and you will see me." [17]Some of his disciples said to one another, "What is this that he says to us, 'A little while, and you will not see me, and again a little while, and you will see me'; and, 'because I go to the Father'?" [18]They said, "What does he mean by 'a little while'? We do not know what he means." [19]Jesus knew

Lk 9:45

that they wanted to ask him; so he said to them, "Is this what you are asking yourselves, what I meant by saying, 'A little while, and you will not see me, and again a little while, and you will see

Rev 11:10

me'? [20]Truly, truly, I say to you, you will weep and lament, but the world will rejoice; you will be sorrowful, but your sorrow will

Is 26:17–18;
66:14

turn into joy. [21]When a woman is in travail she has sorrow, because her hour has come; but when she is delivered of the child,

---

Spirit of truth" (Vatican II, *Dei Verbum*, 4). Cf. the note on Jn 14:25–26.

16:14–15. Jesus Christ here reveals some aspects of the mystery of the Blessed Trinity. He teaches that the three divine Persons have the same nature when he says that everything that the Father has belongs to the Son, and everything the Son has belongs to the Father (cf. Jn 17:10) and that the Spirit also has what is common to the Father and the Son, that is, the divine essence. The activity specific to the Holy Spirit is that of glorifying Christ, reminding and clarifying for the disciples everything the Master taught them (cf. Jn 16:13). On being inspired by the Holy Spirit to recognize the Father through the Son, men render glory to Christ; and glorifying Christ is the same as giving glory to God (cf. Jn 17:1, 3–5, 10).

16:16–22. Earlier our Lord consoled the disciples by assuring them that he would send them the Holy Spirit after he went

away (v. 7). Now he gives them further consolation: he is not leaving them permanently, he will come back to stay with them. However, the apostles fail to grasp what he means, and they ask each other what they make of it. Our Lord does not give them a direct explanation, perhaps because they would not understand what he meant (as happened before: cf. Mt 16:21–23 and par.). But he does emphasize that though they are sad now they will soon be rejoicing: after suffering tribulation they will be filled with a joy they will never lose (cf. Jn 17:13). This is a reference primarily to the Resurrection (cf. Lk 24:41), but also to their definitive encounter with Christ in heaven. This image of the woman giving birth (frequently used in the Old Testament to express intense pain) is also often used, particularly by the prophets, to mean the birth of the new messianic people (cf. Is 21:3; 26:17; 66:7; Jer 30:6; Hos 13:13; Mic 4:9–10). The words of Jesus reported here seem to be the fulfilment of those prophecies. The birth of the messianic

she no longer remembers the anguish, for joy that a child[j] is born into the world. 22So you have sorrow now, but I will see you again and your hearts will rejoice, and no one will take your joy from you. 23In that day you will ask nothing of me. Truly, truly, I say to you, if you ask anything of the Father, he will give it to you in my name. 24Hitherto you have asked nothing in my name; ask, and you will receive, that your joy may be full.

25"I have said this to you in figures; the hour is coming when I shall no longer speak to you in figures but tell you plainly of the Father. 26In that day you will ask in my name; and I do not say to you that I shall pray the Father for you; 27for the Father himself loves you, because you have loved me and have believed that I came from the Father. 28I came from the Father and have come into the world; again, I am leaving the world and going to the Father."

29His disciples said, "Ah, now you are speaking plainly, not in any figure! 30Now we know that you know all things, and need none to question you; by this we believe that you came from God." 31Jesus answered them, "Do you now believe? 32The hour is

Jn 20:20

Jn 14:13, 14, 20
1 Jn 5:14
Mt 7:7
Mk 11:24

Jn 15:11; 17:3
1 Jn 1:4

Jn 10:6
Mt 13:34f

Jn 14:21–23

Jn 16:25

Jn 2:25

Zech 13:7
Mt 26:31, 45, 56

---

people—the Church of Christ—involves intense pain, not only for Jesus but also, to some degree, for the apostles. But this pain, like birthpains, will be made up for by the joy of the final coming of the Kingdom of Christ: "I consider," says St Paul, "that the sufferings of this present time are not worth comparing with the glory that is to be revealed to us" (Rom 8:18).

16:23–24. See the note on Jn 14:12–14.

16:25–30. As can be seen also from other passages in the Gospels, Jesus spent time explaining his doctrine in more detail to his apostles than to the crowd (cf. Mk 4:10–12 and par.)—to train them for their mission of preaching the Gospel to the whole world (cf. Mt 28:18–20). However, our Lord also used metaphors or parables when imparting instruction to the apostles, and he does so in this discourse of the Last Supper—the

vine, the woman giving birth, etc.: he stimulates their curiosity and they, because they do not understand, ask him questions (cf. vv. 17–18). Jesus now tells them that the time is coming when he will speak to them in a completely clear way so that they will know exactly what he means. This he will do after the Resurrection (cf. Acts 1:3). But even now, since he knows their thoughts, he is making it even plainer to them that he is God, for only God can know what is happening inside someone (cf. Jn 2:25). Verse 28, "I came from the Father and have come into the world; again, I am leaving the world and going to the Father" summarizes the mystery of Christ's Person (cf. Jn 1:14; 20:31).

16:31–32. Jesus moderates the apostles' enthusiasm, which expresses itself in a spontaneous confession of faith; he does this by asking them a question which has two dimensions. On the one hand, it is a

j. Greek *a human being*

Mk 14:27, 50
Jn 8:29; 19:27

coming, indeed it has come, when you will be scattered, every man to his home, and will leave me alone; yet I am not alone, for

Jn 14:27
Rom 5:1
1 Jn 5:4

the Father is with me. ³³I have said this to you, that in me you may have peace. In the world you have tribulation; but be of good cheer, I have overcome the world."

The priestly prayer of Jesus

Jn 11:41;
13:31

17 ¹When Jesus had spoken these words, he lifted his eyes to heaven and said,* "Father, the hour has come, glorify thy

Mt 11:27
Wis 15:3
Jer 13:31–34
1 Jn 5:20

Son that the Son may glorify thee, ²since thou hast given him power over all flesh, to give eternal life to all whom thou hast given him. ³And this is eternal life, that they know thee the only

---

kind of reproach for their having taken too long to believe in him: it is true that there were other occasions when they expressed faith in the Master (cf. Jn 6:68–69; etc.), but until now they have not fully realized that he is the One sent by the Father. The question also refers to the fragility of their faith: they believe, and yet very soon they will abandon him into the hands of his enemies. Jesus requires us to have a firm faith: it is not enough to show it in moments of enthusiasm, it has to stand the test of difficulties and opposition.

16:33. The Second Vatican Council teaches in connexion with this passage: "The Lord Jesus who said 'Be of good cheer, I have overcome the world' (Jn 16:33), did not by these words promise complete victory to his Church in this world. This sacred Council rejoices that the earth which has been sown with the seed of the Gospel is now bringing forth fruit in many places under the guidance of the Spirit of the Lord, who is filling the world" (*Presbyterorum ordinis*, 22).

17:1–26. At the end of the discourse of the Last Supper (chaps. 13–16) begins what is called the Priestly Prayer of Jesus, which takes up all of chapter 17. It is

given that name because Jesus addresses his Father in a very moving dialogue in which, as Priest, he offers him the imminent sacrifice of his passion and death. It shows us the essential elements of his redemptive mission and provides us with teaching and a model for our own prayer. "The Lord, the Only-begotten and co-eternal with the Father, could have prayed in silence if necessary, but he desired to show himself to the Father in the attitude of a supplicant because he is our Teacher [...] Accordingly this prayer for his disciples was useful not only to those who heard it, but to all who would read it" (St Augustine, *In Ioann. Evang.*, 104, 2).

The Priestly Prayer consists of three parts: in the first (vv 1–5) Jesus asks for the glorification of his holy human nature and the acceptance, by the Father of his sacrifice on the cross. In the second part (vv. 6–19) he prays for his disciples, whom he is going to send out into the world to proclaim the redemption which he is now about to accomplish. And then (vv. 20–26) he prays for unity among all those who will believe in him over the course of the centuries, until they achieve full union with him in heaven.

17:1–5. The word "glory" here refers to the splendour, power and honour which

166

true God, and Jesus Christ whom thou hast sent. ⁴I glorified thee on earth, having accomplished the work which thou gavest me to do; ⁵and now, Father, glorify thou me in thy own presence with the glory which I had with thee before the world was made.*

1 Thess 1:9
Jn 4:34

Jn 17:24; 1:1
Phil 2:6–11

⁶"I have manifested thy name to the men whom thou gavest me out of the world; thine they were, and thou gavest them to me, and they have kept thy word. ⁷Now they know that everything that thou hast given me is from thee; ⁸for I have given them the words which thou gavest me, and they have received them and know in truth that I came from thee; and they have believed that thou didst send me. ⁹I am praying for them; I am not praying for the world but for those whom thou hast given me, for they are thine; ¹⁰all

Jn 17:9
Mt 6:9

Jn 16:30

Jn 6:37, 44, 65

---

belong to God. The Son is God equal to the Father, and from the time of his incarnation and birth and especially through his death and resurrection his divinity has been made manifest. "We have beheld his glory, glory as of the only Son from the Father" (Jn 1:14). The glorification of Jesus has three dimensions to it. 1) It promotes the glory of the Father, because Christ, in obedience to God's redemptive decree (cf. Phil 2:6), makes the Father known and so brings God's saving work to completion. 2) Christ is glorified because his divinity, which he has voluntarily disguised, will eventually be manifested through his human nature which will be seen after the Resurrection invested with the very authority of God himself over all creation (vv. 2, 5). 3) Christ, through his glorification, gives man the opportunity to attain eternal life, to know God the Father and Jesus Christ, his only Son: this in turn redounds to the glorification of the Father and of Jesus while also involving man's participation in divine glory (v. 3).

"The Son glorifies you, making you known to all those you have given him. Furthermore, if the knowledge of God is life eternal, we the more tend to life, the more we advance in this knowledge. [...] There shall the praise of God be without end, where there shall be full knowledge of God; and because in heaven this knowledge shall be full, there shall glorifying be of the highest" (St Augustine, *In Ioann. Evang.*, 105, 3).

17:6–8. Our Lord has prayed for himself; now he prays for his apostles, who will continue his redemptive work in the world. In praying for them, Jesus describes some of the prerogatives of those who will form part of the apostolic college.

First, there is the prerogative of being chosen by God: "thine they were ...". God the Father chose them from all eternity (cf. Eph 1:3–4) and in due course Jesus revealed this to them: "The Lord Jesus, having prayed at length to the Father, called to himself those whom he willed and appointed twelve to be with him, whom he might send to preach the kingdom of God (cf. Mk 3:13–19; Mt 10:1–42). These apostles (cf. Lk 6:13) he constituted in the form of a college or permanent assembly, at the head of which he placed Peter, chosen from among them (cf. Jn 21:15–17)" (Vatican II, *Lumen gentium*, 19). Also, the Apostles enjoy the privilege of hearing God's teaching direct from Jesus. From this teaching, which they accept with docility,

Jn 16:15
Lk 15:31
Jn 10:30
Mt 6:13

Jn 6:39
2 Thess 2:3

mine are thine, and thine are mine, and I am glorified in them. [11]And now I am no more in the world, but they are in the world, and I am coming to thee. Holy Father, keep them in thy name, which thou hast given me, that they may be one, even as we are one. [12]While I was with them, I kept them in my name, which thou hast given me; I have guarded them, and none of them is lost but the son of perdition, that the scripture might be fulfilled. [13]But

---

they learn that Jesus came from the Father and that therefore he is God's envoy (v. 8): that is, they are given to know the relationships that exist between the Father and the Son.

The Christian, who also is a disciple of Jesus, gradually acquires knowledge of God and of divine things through living a life of faith and maintaining a personal relationship with Jesus Christ.

"Recalling this human refinement of Christ, who spent his life in the service of others, we are doing much more than describing a pattern of human behaviour; we are discovering God. Everything Christ did has a transcendental value. It shows us the nature of God and beckons us to believe in the love of God who created us and wants us to share his intimate life" (St Josemaría Escrivá, *Christ Is Passing By*, 109).

17:11–19. Jesus now asks the Father to give his disciples four things—unity, perseverance, joy and holiness. By praying to him to keep them in his name (v. 11) he is asking for their perseverance in the teaching he has given them (cf. v. 6) and in communion with him. An immediate consequence of this perseverance is unity: "that they may be one, even as we are one"; this unity which he asks for his disciples is a reflection of the unity of the three divine Persons.

He also prays that none of them should be lost, that the Father should guard and protect them, just as he himself protected them while he was with

them. Thirdly, as a result of their union with God and perseverance they will share in the joy of Christ (v. 13): in this life, the more we know God the more closely we are joined to him, the happier will we be; in eternal life our joy will be complete, because our knowledge and love of God will have reached its climax.

Finally, he prays for those who, though living in the world, are not of the world, that they may be truly holy and carry out the mission he has entrusted to them, just as he did the work his Father gave him to do.

17:12. "That the scripture might be fulfilled": this is an allusion to what he said to the apostles a little earlier (Jn 13:18) by directly quoting Holy Scripture: "He who ate my bread has lifted his heel against me" (Ps 41:9). Jesus makes these references to Judas' treachery in order to strengthen the apostles' faith by showing that he knew everything in advance and that the Scriptures had already foretold what would happen.

However, Judas went astray through his own fault and not because God arranged things that way; his treachery had been taking shape little by little, through his petty infidelities, and despite our Lord helping him to repent and get back on the right road (cf. the note on Jn 13:31–32); Judas did not respond to this grace and was responsible for his own downfall. God, who sees the future, predicted the treachery of Judas in the Scripture; Christ, being true God, knew

now I am coming to thee; and these things I speak in the world, that they may have my joy fulfilled in themselves. [14]I have given them thy word; and the world has hated them because they are not of the world, even as I am not of the world. [15]I do not pray that thou shouldst take them out of the world, but that thou shouldst keep them from the evil one.[k] [16]They are not of the world, even as I am not of the world. [17]Sanctify them in the truth; thy word is

Jn 15:11
Acts 1:16, 20
1 Jn 1:4
Jn 15:19
2 Thess 3:3
1 Jn 5:18
Mt 6:13
Lk 22:32
Jn 16:13

---

that Judas would betray him and it is with immense sorrow that he now tells the apostles.

17:14–16. In Scripture, "world" has a number of meanings. First, it means the whole of creation (Gen 1:1ff) and, within creation, mankind, which God loves most tenderly (Prov 8:31). This is the meaning intended here when our Lord says, "I do not pray that thou shouldst take them out of the world, but that thou shouldst keep them from the evil one" (v. 15). "I have taught this constantly using words from Holy Scripture. The world is not evil, because it has come from God's hands, because it is his creation, because Yahweh looked upon it and saw that it was good (cf. Gen 1:7ff). We ourselves, mankind, make it evil and ugly with our sins and infidelities. Have no doubt: any kind of evasion from the honest realities of daily life is for you, men and women of the world, something opposed to the will of God" (St J. Escrivá, *Conversations*, 114).

In the second place, "world" refers to the things of this world, which do not last and which can be at odds with the things of the spirit (cf. Mt 16:26).

Finally, because evil men have been enslaved by sin and by the devil, "the ruler of this world" (Jn 12:31; 16:11), the "world" sometimes means God's enemy, something opposed to Christ and his followers (cf. Jn 1:10). In this sense the "world" is evil, and therefore Jesus is

not of the world, nor are his disciples (v. 16). It is also this pejorative meaning which is used by traditional teaching which describes the world, the flesh and the devil as enemies of the soul against which one has to be forever vigilant. "The world, the flesh and the devil are a band of adventurers who take advantage of the weakness of that savage you bear within you. In exchange for the glittering tinsel of a pleasure—which is worth nothing—they want you to hand over to them the pure gold and the pearls and the diamonds and rubies drenched in the living and redeeming blood of your God, which are the price and the treasure of your eternity" (St Josemaría Escrivá, *The Way*, 708).

17:17–19. Jesus prays for the holiness of his disciples. God alone is the Holy One; in his holiness people and things share. "Sanctifying" has to do with consecrating and dedicating something to God, excluding it from being used for profane purposes; thus God says to Jeremiah: "Before I formed you in the womb I knew you, and before you were born I consecrated you; I appointed you a prophet to the nations" (Jer 1:5). If something is to be consecrated to God it must be perfect, that is, holy. Hence, a consecrated person needs to have moral sanctity, needs to be practising the moral virtues. Our Lord here asks for both things for his disciples, because they

k. Or *from evil*

169

Jn 20:21 truth. ¹⁸As thou didst send me into the world, so I have sent them Heb 2:11; 10:20 into the world. ¹⁹And for their sake I consecrate myself, that they also may be consecrated in truth.

---

need them if they are to fulfil their supernatural mission in the world.

"For their sake I consecrate myself": these words mean that Jesus Christ, who has been burdened with the sins of men, consecrates himself to the Father through his sacrifice on the cross. By this are all Christians sanctified: "So Jesus also suffered outside the gate in order to sanctify the people through his own blood" (Heb 13:12). So, after Christ's death, men have been made sons of God by Baptism, sharers in the divine nature and enabled to attain the holiness to which they have been called (cf. Vatican II, *Lumen gentium*, 40).

17:20–23. Since it is Christ who is praying for the Church his prayer is infallibly effective, and therefore there will always be only one true Church of Jesus Christ. Unity is therefore an essential property of the Church. "We believe that the Church founded by Jesus Christ and for which he prayed is indefectibly one in faith, in worship and in the bond of hierarchical communion" (Paul VI, *Creed of the People of God*, 21). Moreover, Christ's prayer also indicates what the basis of the Church's unity will be and what effects will follow from it.

The source from which the unity of the Church flows is the intimate unity of the three divine Persons among whom there is mutual love and self-giving. "The Lord Jesus, when praying to the Father 'that they may all be one ... even as we are one' (Jn 17:21–22), has opened up new horizons closed to human reason by implying that there is a certain parallel between the union existing among the divine persons and the union of the sons

of God in truth and love. It follows, then, that if man is the only creature on earth that God has wanted for its own sake, man can fully discover his true self only in the sincere giving of himself" (Vatican II, *Gaudium et spes*, 24). The unity of the church is also grounded on the union of the faithful with Jesus Christ and through him with the Father (v. 23). Thus, the fullness of unity—*consummati in unum*—is attained through the supernatural grace which comes to us from Christ (cf. Jn 15:5).

The fruits of the unity of the Church are, on the one hand, the world believing in Christ and in his divine mission (vv. 21, 23); and, on the other, Christians themselves and all men recognizing God's special love for his faithful, a love which is a reflection of the love of the three divine Persons for each other. And so, Jesus' prayer embraces all mankind, for all are invited to be friends of God (cf. 1 Tim 2:4). "Thou hast loved them even as thou hast loved me": this, according to St Thomas Aquinas, "does not mean strict equality of love but similarity and like motivation. It is as if he were saying: the love with which you have loved me is the reason and the cause of your loving them, for, precisely because you love men do you love those who love me" (*Comm. on St John*, in loc.) Besides noting this theological explanation, we should also ponder on how expressively Christ describes his ardent love for men. The entire discourse of the Last Supper gives us a glimpse of the depth of Jesus' feelings—which infinitely exceeds anything we are capable of experiencing. Once again all we can do is bow down before the mystery of God made man.

²⁰"I do not pray for these only, but also for those who believe   Jn 17:9
in me through their word, ²¹that they may all be one; even as thou,
Father, art in me, and I in thee, that they also may be in us, so that   Gal 3:28

17:20. Christ prays for the Church, for all those who, over the course of centuries, will believe in him through the preaching of the apostles. "That divine mission, which was committed by Christ to the Apostles, is destined to last until the end of the world (cf. Mt 28:20), since the Gospel, which they were charged to hand on, is, for the Church, the principle of all its life for all time. For that very reason the Apostles were careful to appoint successors in this hierarchically constituted society" (*Lumen gentium*, 20).

The apostolic origin and basis of the Church is what is termed its "apostolicity", a special characteristic of the Church which we confess in the Creed. Apostolicity consists in the Pope and the bishops being successors of Peter and the apostles, holding the authority of the apostles and proclaiming the same teaching as they did. "The sacred synod teaches that the bishops have by divine institution taken the place of the apostles as pastors of the Church, in such wise that whoever listens to them is listening to Christ and whoever despises them despises Christ and him who sent Christ (cf. Lk 10:16)" (Vatican II, *Lumen gentium*, 20).

17:21. Union of Christians with Christ begets unity among themselves. This unity of the Church ultimately redounds to the benefit of all mankind, because since the Church is one and unique, she is seen as a sign raised up for the nations to see, inviting all to believe in Christ as sent by God come to save all men. The Church carries on this mission of salvation through its union with Christ, calling all mankind to join the Church and by so

doing to share in union with Christ and the Father.

The Second Vatican Council, speaking of the principles of ecumenism, links the Church's unity with her universality: "Almost everyone, though in different ways, longs for the one visible Church of God, a Church truly universal and sent forth to the whole world that the world may be converted to the Gospel and so be saved, to the glory of God" (*Unitatis redintegratio*, 1). This universality is another characteristic of the Church, technically described as "catholicity". "For many centuries now the Church has been spread throughout the world, and it numbers persons of all races and walks of life. But the universality of the Church does not depend on its geographical distribution, even though this is a visible sign and a motive of credibility. The Church was catholic already at Pentecost: it was born catholic from the wounded heart of Jesus, as a fire which the Holy Spirit enkindled.

"In the second century the Christians called the Church catholic in order to distinguish it from sects which, using the name of Christ, were betraying its doctrine in one way or another. 'We call it catholic', writes St Cyril, 'not only because it is spread throughout the world, from one extreme to the other, but because in a universal way and without defect it teaches all the dogmas which men ought to know, of both the visible and the invisible, the celestial and the earthly. Likewise because it draws to true worship all types of men, governors and citizens, the learned and the ignorant. And finally, because it cures and heals all kinds of sins, whether of the soul or of

Acts 4:32

1 Cor 6:17
Gal 2:20

Jn 10:29;
12:26, 32
Eph 1:4

the world may believe that thou hast sent me. ²²The glory which thou hast given me I have given to them, that they may be one even as we are one, ²³I in them and thou in me, that they may become perfectly one, so that the world may know that thou hast sent me and hast loved them even as thou has loved me. ²⁴Father, I desire that they also, whom thou hast given me, may be with me where I am, to behold my glory which thou has given me in thy love for me before the foundation of the world. ²⁵O righteous

the body, possessing in addition—by whatever name it may be called—all the forms of virtue, in deeds and in words and in every kind of spiritual life' (*Cathechesis*, 18, 23)" (St Josemaría Escrivá, *In Love with the Church*, 9).

Every Christian should have the same desire for unity as Jesus Christ expresses in his prayer to the Father. "A privileged instrument for participation in pursuit of the unity of all Christians is prayer. Jesus Christ himself left us his final wish for unity through prayer to the Father: 'that they may all be one; even as thou, Father, art in me, and I in thee, that they also may be in us, so that the world may believe that thou hast sent me' (Jn 17:21).

"Also the Second Vatican Council strongly recommended to us prayer for the unity of Christians, defining it 'the soul of the whole ecumenical movement' (*Unitatis redintegratio*, 8). As the soul to the body, so prayer gives life, consistency, spirit, and finality to the ecumenical movement.

"Prayer puts us, first and foremost, before the Lord, purifies us in intentions, in sentiments, in our heart, and produces that 'interior conversion', without which there is no real ecumenism (cf. *Unitatis redintegratio*, 7).

"Prayer, furthermore, reminds us that unity, ultimately, is a gift from God, a gift for which we must ask and for which we must prepare in order that we may be granted it" (John Paul II, General Audience, 17 January 1979).

17:22–23. Jesus possesses glory, a manifestation of divinity, because he is God, equal to the Father (cf. the note on Jn 17:1–5). When he says that he is giving this glory to his disciples, he is indicating that through grace he makes us "partakers of the divine nature" (2 Pet 1:4). Glory and justification by grace are very closely united, as we can see from Sacred Scripture: "Those whom he predestines he also called, and those whom he called he also justified, and those whom he justified he also glorified" (Rom 8:30). The change grace works in Christians makes us ever more like Christ, who is the likeness of the Father (cf. 2 Cor 4:4; Heb 1:2–3): by communicating his glory Christ joins the faithful to God by giving them a share in supernatural life, which is the source of the holiness of Christians and of the Church: "Now we can understand better how [...] one of the principal aspects of her holiness is that unity centred on the mystery of the one and triune God. 'There is one body and one Spirit, just as you were called to the one hope that belongs to your call, one Lord, one faith, one baptism; one God and Father of us all, who is above all and through all and in all' (Eph 4:4–6)" (St Josemaría Escrivá, *In Love with the Church*, 5).

17:24. Jesus concludes his prayer by asking that all Christians attain the blessedness of heaven. The word he uses, "I desire", not "I pray", indicates that he is asking for the most important thing of

Father, the world has not known thee, but I have known thee; and
these know that thou hast sent me. ²⁶I made known to them thy
name, and I will make it known, that the love with which thou has
loved me may be in them, and I in them."

Ex 3:13
Jn 17:6

10. THE PASSION AND DEATH OF JESUS

Arrest of Jesus

18 ¹When Jesus had spoken these words, he went forth with
his disciples across the Kidron valley, where there was a

Mt 26:30, 36
Mk 14:26, 32
Lk 23:39
2 Sam 15:23

all, for what his Father wants—that all
may be saved and come to a knowledge
of the truth (cf. 1 Tim 2:4): which is
essentially the mission of the Church—
the salvation of souls.

As long as we are on earth we share
in God's life through knowledge (faith)
and love (charity); but only in heaven
will we attain the fulness of this supernatural life, the Church has her sights
fixed on eternity, she is eschatological:
that is, by having in this world all the
resources necessary for teaching God's
truth, for rendering him true worship and
communicating the life of grace, she
keeps alive people's hope of attaining the
fulness of eternal life: "The Church, to
which we are all called in Jesus Christ,
and in which by the grace of God we
acquire holiness, will receive its perfection only in the glory of heaven, when
will come the time of the renewal of all
things (Acts 3:21). At that time, together
with the human race, the universe itself,
which is so closely related to man and
which attains its destiny through him,
will be perfectly reestablished in Christ
(cf. Eph 1:10; Col 1:20; 2 Pet 3:10–13)"
(Vatican II, *Lumen gentium*, 48).

17:25–26. God's revelation of himself
through Christ causes us to begin to share
in the divine life, a sharing which will
reach its climax in heaven: "God alone

can give us the right and full knowledge
of this reality by revealing himself as
Father, Son and Holy Spirit, in whose
eternal life we are by grace called to
share, here below in the obscurity of faith
and after death in eternal light" (Paul VI,
Creed of the People of God).

Christ has revealed to us all we need
to know in order to participate in the
mutual love of the divine Persons—primarily, the mystery of who he is and
what his mission is and, with that, the
mystery of God himself ("I made known
to them thy name"), thus fulfilling what
he had announced: "No one knows the
father except the Son and any one to
whom the Son chooses to reveal him"
(Mt 11:27). Christ continues to make
known his Father's love, by means of the
Church, in which he is always present: "I
am with you always, to the close of the
age" (Mt 28:20).

18:1. The previous chapter, dealing as it
did with the glory of the Son of God (cf.
Jn 17:1, 4, 10, 22, 24), is a magnificent
prologue to our Lord's passion and death,
which St John presents as part of Christ's
glorification: he emphasizes that Jesus
freely accepted his death (14:31) and
freely allowed himself to be arrested
(18:4, 11). The Gospel shows our Lord's
superiority over his judges (18:20–21)
and accusers (19:8, 12); and his majestic

Lk 21:37 garden, which he and his disciples entered. ²Now Judas, who betrayed him, also knew the place; for Jesus often met there with

---

serenity in the face of physical pain, which makes one more aware of the Redemption, the triumph of the cross, than of Jesus' actual sufferings.

Chapters 18 and 19 cover the passion and death of our Lord—events so important and decisive that all the books of the New Testament deal with them, in some way or other. Thus, the Synoptic Gospels give us extensive accounts of what happened; in the Acts of the Apostles these events, together with the resurrection, form the core of the apostles' preachings. St Paul explains the redemptive value of Jesus Christ's sacrifice, and the catholic epistles speak of his salvific death, as does the book of Revelation, where the Victor, enthroned in heaven, is the sacrificed Lamb, Jesus Christ. It should also be noted that whenever these sacred writings mention our Lord's death they go on to refer to his glorious resurrection.

St John's Gospel locates these events in five places. The first (18:1–12) is Gethsemane, where Jesus is arrested; after this (18:13–27) he is taken to the house of Annas, where the religious trial begins and Peter denies Jesus before the high priest's servants. The third scene is the praetorium (18:28—19:16), where Jesus is tried by the Roman procurator: St John gives an extensive account of his trial, highlighting the true character of Christ's kingship and his rejection by the Jews, who call for his crucifixion. He then goes on (19:17–37) to describe the events which occur after the procurator's unjust sentence; this scene centres on Calvary. St John then reports the burial of our Lord in the unused tomb near Calvary belonging to Joseph of Arimathea.

The climax of all these events is the glorification of Jesus, of which he him-

self has spoken (cf. Jn 17:1–5)—his resurrection and exaltation to his Father's side.

Here is Fray Luis de Granada's advice on how to meditate on the passion of our Lord: "There are five things we can reflect on when we think about the sacred passion. [...] First, we can incline our hearts to sorrow and repentance for our sins; the passion of our Lord helps us do this because it is evident that everything he suffered he suffered on account of sins, so that if there were no sins in the world, there would have been no need for such painful reparation. Therefore, sins —yours and mine, like everyone else's— were the executioners who bound him and lashed him and crowned him with thorns and put him on the cross. So you can see how right it is for you to feel the enormity and malice of your sins, for it was these which really caused so much suffering, not because these sins required the Son of God to suffer but because divine justice chose to ask for such great atonement.

"We have here excellent motives, not only to abhor sin but also to love virtues: we have the example of this Lord's virtues, which so clearly shine out during his sacred passion: we can follow these virtues and learn to imitate them, especially his great humility, gentleness and silence, as well as the other virtues, for this is one of the best and most effective ways of meditating on the sacred passion—the way of imitation.

"At other times we should fix our attention on the great good the Lord does us here, reflecting on how much he loved us and how much he gave us and how much it cost him to do so. [...] At other times it is good to focus our attention on knowledge of God, that is, to consider his

his disciples. ³So Judas, procuring a band of soldiers and some officers from the chief priests and the Pharisees, went there with lanterns and torches and weapons. ⁴Then Jesus, knowing all that

Mt 26:47–56
Mk 14:43–52
Lk 22:47–53

Jn 19:28

---

great goodness, his mercy, his justice, his kindness, and particularly his ardent charity, which shines forth in the sacred passion as nowhere else. For just as it is a greater proof of love to suffer evils on behalf of one's friend than to do good things for him, and God could do both […], it pleased his divine nature to assume a nature which could suffer evils, very great evils, so that man could be quite convinced of God's love and thereby be moved to love him who so loved man.

"Finally, at other times one can reflect […] on the wisdom of God in choosing this manner of atoning for mankind: that is, making satisfaction for our sins, inflaming our charity, curing our pride, our greed and our love of comfort, and inclining our souls to the virtue of humanity […], abhorrence of sin and love for the Cross" (*Life of Jesus Christ*, 15).

18:1–2. "When Jesus had spoken these words": this is a formula often used in the Fourth Gospel to indicate a new episode linked with what has just been recounted (cf. Jn 2:12; 3:22; 5:1; 6:1; 13:21; etc.).

The Kidron (etymologically "turbid") was a brook which carried water only during rainy weather; it divided Jerusalem from the Mount of Olives, on the slopes of which lay the garden of Gethsemane (cf. Mt 26:30; Lk 21:37; 22:39). The distance from the Cenacle, where the Last Supper took place, to the garden of Gethsemane was little more than a kilometre.

18:3. Because Judea was occupied by Romans, there was a garrison stationed at Jerusalem—a cohort (600 men) quartered in the Antonia tower, under the authority of a tribune. In the Greek what is translated here as "a band of soldiers" is "the cohort", the name for the whole unit being used though only part is meant: it does not mean that 600 soldiers came out to arrest Jesus. Presumably the Jewish authorities, who had their own temple guard—referred to here as "officers from the chief priests and the Pharisees"— must have sought some assistance from the military. Judas' part consisted in leading the way to where Jesus was and identifying the man to be arrested.

18:4–9. Only the Fourth Gospel reports this episode prior to Jesus' arrest, recalling the words of the Psalm: "Then my enemies will be turned back in the day when I call" (Ps 56:9). Our Lord's majesty is apparent: he surrenders himself freely and voluntarily. This does not, however, mean that the Jews involved are free from blame. St Augustine comments on this passage: "The persecutors, who came with the traitor to lay hold of Jesus, found him whom they sought and heard him say, 'I am he'. Why did they not lay hold of him but fell back to the ground? Because that was what he wished, who could do whatever he wished. Had he not allowed himself to be taken by them, they would have been unable to effect their plan, but neither would he have done what he came to do. They in their rage sought him to put him to death; but he also sought us by dying for us. Therefore, after he displayed his power to those who had no power to hold him, they did lay hands on him and by means of them, all unwitting, he did what he wanted to do" (*In Ioann. Evang.*, 112, 3).

It is also moving to see how Jesus

was to befall him, came forward and said to them, "Whom do you seek?" ⁵They answered him, "Jesus of Nazareth." Jesus said to them, "I am he." Judas, who betrayed him, was standing with them. ⁶When he said to them, "I am he," they drew back and fell to the ground. ⁷Again he asked them, "Whom do you seek?" And they said, "Jesus of Nazareth," ⁸Jesus answered, "I told you that I am he; so, if you seek me, let these men go." ⁹This was to fulfil the word which he had spoken, "Of those whom you gavest me I lost not one." ¹⁰Then Simon Peter, having a sword, drew it and struck the high priest's slave and cut off his right ear. The slave's name was Malchus. ¹¹Jesus said to Peter, "Put your sword into its sheath; shall I not drink the cup which the Father has given me?"

¹²So the band of soldiers and their captain and the officers of the Jews seized Jesus and bound him.

Jesus before the chief priests. Peter's denials

¹³First they led him to Annas; for he was the father-in-law of Caiaphas, who was high priest that year.* ¹⁴It was Caiaphas who had given counsel to the Jews that it was expedient that one man should die for the people.

¹⁵Simon Peter followed Jesus, and so did another disciple. As this disciple was known to the high priest, he entered the court of

Margin references:
Jn 8:24
Jn 17:12; 6:39
Mt 26:29
Mt 26:57–68
Mk 14:53–72
Lk 22:54–71
Jn 11:49f
Jn 20:3
Acts 3:1

---

takes care of his disciples, even though he himself is in danger. He had promised that none of his own should perish, except Judas Iscariot (cf. Jn 6:39; 17:12); although his promise referred to protecting them from eternal punishment, our Lord is also concerned about their immediate safety, for as yet they are not ready for martyrdom.

18:10–11. Once again we see Peter's impetuosity and loyalty; he comes to our Lord's defence, risking his own life, but he still does not understand God's plan of salvation: he still cannot come to terms with the idea of Christ dying—just as he could not when Christ first foretold his passion (cf. Mt 16:21–22). Our Lord does not accept Peter's violent defence: he refers back to what he said in his prayer in Gethsemane (cf. Mt 26:39), where he freely accepted his Father's will, giving himself up to his captors in order to accomplish the Redemption.

We should show reverence to God's will with the same docility and meekness as Jesus accepting his passion. "Stages: to be resigned to the will of God; to conform to the will of God; to want the will of God; to love the will of God" (St Josemaría Escrivá, *The Way*, 774).

18:13–18. Jesus is brought to the house of Annas, who, although he was no longer high priest, still exercised great religious and political influence (cf. the note on Lk 3:2). These two disciples, St Peter and the other disciple, probably John himself, are disconcerted; they do not know what to do, so they follow Jesus at a distance. Their attachment to him was not yet sufficiently supernatural; discouragement has displaced bravery and loyalty—and will soon lead to Peter's triple denial. However noble his feelings, a Christian will be unable to live up to the demands

the high priest along with Jesus, [16]while Peter stood outside at the door. So the other disciple, who was known to the high priest, went out and spoke to the maid who kept the door, and brought Peter in. [17]The maid who kept the door said to Peter, "Are not you also one of this man's disciples?" He said, "I am not." [18]Now the servants[1] and officers had made a charcoal fire, because it was cold, and they were standing and warming themselves; Peter also was with them, standing and warming himself.

[19]The high priest then questioned Jesus about his disciples and his teaching. [20]Jesus answered him, "I have spoken openly to the world; I have always taught in synagogues and in the temple, where all Jews come together; I have said nothing secretly. [21]Why do you ask me? Ask those who have heard me, what I said to them; they know what I said." [22]When he had said this, one of the officers standing by struck Jesus with his hand, saying, "Is that how you answer the high priest?" [23]Jesus answered him, "If I have spoken wrongly, bear witness to the wrong; but if I have spoken rightly, why do you strike me?" [24]Annas then sent him bound to Caiaphas the high priest.

[25]Now Simon Peter was standing and warming himself. They said to him, "Are not you also one of his disciples?" He denied it

Jn 7:14, 26
Mt 10:27
Is 45:19

Jn 19:3
Acts 23:2

Jn 18:18

---

of his faith unless his life has a basis of deep piety.

18:19–21. During his first interrogation—preliminary to his later examination by the Sanhedrin (Lk 22:66–71)—Jesus lays stress on the fact that he has always acted openly: everyone has had an opportunity to listen to him and to witness his miracles—so much so that at times he has been acclaimed as the Messiah (cf. Jn 12:12–19 and par.). The chief priests themselves have seen him in the temple and in the synagogues; but not wishing to see (cf. Jn 9:39–41), or believe (cf. Jn 10:37–38), they make out that his objectives are hidden and sinister.

18:22–23. Again, we see Jesus' serenity; he is master of the situation, as he is throughout his passion. To the unjust

accusation made by this servant, our Lord replies meekly, but he does defend his conduct and points to the injustice with which he is being treated. This is how we should behave if people mistreat us in any way. Well-argued defence of one's rights is compatible with meekness and humility (cf. Acts 22:25).

18:25–27. Peter's denials are treated in less detail here than in the Synoptic Gospels, but here, as there, we can see the apostles' humility and sincerity, which lead them to tell about their own weaknesses. Peter's repentance is not referred to here, but is implied by the mention of the cock crowing: the very brevity of St John's account points to the fact that this episode is well known to the early Christians. After the Resurrection the full scope of Jesus' forgiveness will

1. Or *slaves*

177

and said, "I am not." [26]One of the servants[1] of the high priest, a kinsman of the man whose ear Peter had cut off, asked, "Did I not see you in the garden with him?" [27]Peter again denied it; and at once the cock crowed.

Mt 27:1f
Mk 15:1
Lk 23:1

Mt 23:11, 14
Mk 15:2, 5

The trial before Pilate: Jesus is King

[28]Then they led Jesus from the house of Caiaphas to the praetorium. It was early. They themselves did not enter the praetorium, so that they might not be defiled, but might eat the passover.* [29]So

---

be evidenced when he confirms Peter in his mission as leader of the apostles (cf. Jn 21:15–17). "In this adventure of love we should not be depressed by our falls, not even by serious falls, if we go to God in the sacrament of Penance contrite and resolved to improve. A Christian is not a neurotic collector of good behaviour reports. Jesus Christ our Lord was moved as much by Peter's repentance after his fall as by John's innocence and faithfulness. Jesus understands our weakness and draws us to himself on an inclined plane. He wants us to make an effort to climb a little each day" (St Josemaría Escrivá, *Christ Is Passing By*, 75).

18:28. The Synoptics also report the trial before Pilate, but St John gives a longer and more detailed account: John 18:28— 19:16 is the centre of the five parts of his account of the Passion (cf. the note on 18:1). He describes the events that take place in the praetorium, highlighting the majesty of Christ as the messianic King, and also his rejection by the Jews.

There are seven stages here, marked by Pilate's entrances and exits. First (vv. 29–32) the Jews indict Jesus in a general way as an "evildoer". Then follows the dialogue between Pilate and Jesus (vv. 36–37) which culminates in Christ stating that he is a King, after which Pilate tries to save our Lord (vv. 38–40) by asking the people if they want him to release "the King of the Jews".

The centrepoint of the account (19:1– 3) is the crowning with thorns, with the soldiers mockingly doing obeisance to Christ as "King of the Jews". After this our Lord is led out wearing the crown of thorns and draped in the purple robe (vv. 4–7)—the shameful scene of the *Ecce Homo*. The Jews' accusation now turns on Jesus' making himself the Son of God. Once again, Pilate, in the praetorium again, speaks with Jesus (vv. 8–12) and tries to probe further into his divine origin. The Jews then concentrate their hatred in a directly political accusation: "Everyone who makes himself a king sets himself against Caesar" (Jn 19:12). Finally (vv. 13–16), in a very formal way, stating time and place, St John narrates how Pilate points to Jesus and says: "Here is your King!" And the leaders of the Jews openly reject him who was and is the genuine King spoken of by the prophets.

"Praetorium": this was the Roman name for the official residence of the praetor or of other senior officials in the provinces of the Empire, such as the procurator or prefect in Palestine. Pilate's usual residence was on the coast, in Caesarea, but he normally moved to Jerusalem for the major festival periods, bringing additional troops to be used in the event of civil disorder. In Jerusalem, at this time and later, the procurator resided in Herod's palace (in the western part of the upper city) or else in the

Pilate went out to them and said, "What accusation do you bring against this man?"* ³⁰They answered him, "If this man were not an evildoer, we would not have handed him over." ³¹Pilate said to them, "Take him yourselves and judge him by your own law." The Jews said to him, "It is not lawful for us to put any man to death."* ³²This was to fulfil the word which Jesus had spoken to show by what death he was to die.

Lk 23:2, 5

Jn 19:6f
Acts 18:15

Jn 3:14; 12:32f
Mt 20:19

³³Pilate entered the praetorium again and called Jesus, and said to him, "Are you the King of the Jews?" ³⁴Jesus answered, "Do

Mt 16:13

Antonia tower, a fortress backing onto the northeastern corner of the temple esplanade. It is not known for certain which of these two buildings was the praetorium mentioned in the Gospel; it was more likely the latter.

"So that they might not be defiled": Jewish tradition at the time (*Mishnah*; *Ohalot* treatise 7, 7) laid down that anyone who entered a Gentile or pagan house incurred seven days' legal defilement (cf. Acts 10:28); such defilement would have prevented them from celebrating the Passover. It is surprising that the chief priests had a scruple of this sort given their criminal inclinations against Jesus. Once more our Lord's accusation of them is seen to be well founded: "You blind guides, straining out a gnat and swallowing a camel" (Mt 23:24).

18:29–32. St John has omitted part of the interrogation which took place in the house of Caiaphas and which is reported in the Synoptics (Mt 26:57–66 and par.), which tell us that the meeting at Caiaphas' terminated with Jesus being declared deserving of death for the blasphemy of proclaiming himself the Son of God (cf. Mt 26:65–66). Under the Law of Moses blasphemy was punishable by stoning (cf. Lev 24:16); but they do not proceed to stone him—which they certainly could have done, even though the Romans were in control: they were ready to stone the adulterous woman (cf. Jn 8:1–11) and a short time later they did stone St Stephen (cf. Acts: 54–60)— because they wanted to bring the people along with them, and they knew that many of them regarded Jesus as Prophet and Messiah (cf. Mt 24:45–46; Mk 12:12; Lk 20:19). Not daring to stone him, they will shrewdly manage to turn a religious charge into a political question and have the authority of the Empire brought to bear on their side; they preferred to denounce Jesus to the procurator as a revolutionary who plotted against Caesar by declaring himself to be the Messiah and King of the Jews; by acting in this way they avoided risking the people's wrath and ensured that Jesus would be condemned by the Roman authorities to death by crucifixion.

Our Lord had foretold a number of times that he would die in this way (cf. Jn 3:14; 8:28; 12:32–33); as St Peter later put it, "Christ redeemed us from the curse of the law, having become a curse for us—for it is written, 'Cursed be every one who hangs on a tree'" (Gal 3:13; cf. Deut 21:23).

18:33–34. There is no onus on Pilate to interfere in religious questions, but because the accusation levelled against Jesus had to do with politics and public order, he begins his interrogation naturally by examining him on the main charge: "Are you the King of the Jews?"

By replying with another question,

179

Mt 20:19
Mk 10:33
Lk 18:32

Jn 8:47; 10:27
1 Tim 6:13

you say this of your own accord, or did others say it to you about me?" ³⁵Pilate answered, "Am I a Jew? Your own nation and the chief priests have handed you over to me; what have you done?" ³⁶Jesus answered, "My kingship is not of this world; if my kingship were of this world, my servants would fight, that I might not be handed over to the Jews; but my kingship is not from the world." ³⁷Pilate said to him, "So you are a king?" Jesus answered, "You say that I am a king. For this I was born, and for this I have

---

Jesus is not refusing to answer: he wishes to make quite clear, as he has always done, that his mission is a spiritual one. And really Pilate's was not an easy question to answer, because, to a Gentile, a king of the Jews meant simply a subverter of the Empire; whereas, to a Jewish nationalist, the King-Messiah was a politico-religious liberator who would obtain their freedom from Rome. The true character of Christ's messiahship completely transcends both these concepts—as Jesus explains to the procurator, although he realizes how enormously difficult it is for Pilate to understand what Christ's kingship really involves.

18:35-36. After the miracle of the multiplication of the loaves and the fish, Jesus refused to be proclaimed king because the people were thinking in terms of an earthly kingdom (cf. Jn 6:15). However, Jesus did enter Jerusalem in triumph, and he did accept acclamation as King-Messiah. Now, in the passion, he acknowledges before Pilate that he is truly a king, making it clear that his kingship is not an earthly one. Thus, "those who expected the Messiah to have visible temporal power were mistaken. 'The kingdom of God does not mean food and drink but righteousness and peace and joy in the Holy Spirit' (Rom 14:17). Truth and justice, peace and joy in the Holy Spirit. That is the kingdom of Christ: the divine activity which saves men and which will

reach its culmination when history ends and the Lord comes from the heights of paradise finally to judge men" (St J. Escrivá, *Christ Is Passing By*, 180).

18:37. This is what his kingship really is: his kingdom is "the kingdom of Truth and Life, the kingdom of Holiness and Grace, the kingdom of Justice, Love and Peace" (*Roman Missal*, Preface of the Mass of Christ the King). Christ reigns over those who accept and practise the truth revealed by him—his Father's love for the world (Jn 3:16; 1 Jn 4:9). He became man to make this truth known and to enable men to accept it. And so, those who recognize Christ's kingship and sovereignty accept his authority, and he thus reigns over them in an eternal and universal kingdom.

For its part, "the Church, looking to Christ who bears witness to the truth, must always and everywhere ask herself, and in a certain sense also the contemporary 'world', how to make good emerge from man, how to liberate the dynamism of the good that is in man, in order that it may be stronger than evil, than any moral, social or other evil" (John Paul II, General Audience, 21 February 1979).

"If we [Christians] are trying to have Christ as our king we must be consistent. We must start by giving him our heart. Not to do that and still talk about the kingdom of Christ would be completely hollow. There would be no real Christian

come into the world, to bear witness to the truth. Every one who is of the truth hears my voice." [38]Pilate said to him, "What is truth?"

After he had said this, he went out to the Jews again, and told them, "I find no crime in him. [39]But you have a custom that I should release one man for you at the Passover; will you have me release for you the King of the Jews?" [40]They cried out again, "Not this man, but Barabbas!" Now Barabbas was a robber.

Mt 27:15–23
Mk 15:6–14
Lk 23:17–23

---

substance in our behaviour. We would be making an outward show of a faith which simply did not exist. We would be misusing God's name to human advantage. [...] If we let Christ reign in our souls, we will not become authoritarian. Rather we will serve everyone. How I like that word: service! To serve my king, and through him, all those who have been redeemed by his blood. I really wish we Christians knew how to serve, for only by serving can we know and love Christ and make him known and loved" (St J. Escrivá, *Christ Is Passing By*, 181–182).

By his death and resurrection, Jesus shows that the accusations laid against him were based on lies: it was he who was telling the truth, not his judges and accusers, and God confirms the truth of Jesus—the truth of his words, of his deeds, of his revelation—by the singular miracle of his resurrection. To men Christ's kingship may seem paradoxical: he dies, yet he lives for ever; he is defeated and crucified, yet he is victorious. "When Jesus Christ himself appeared as a prisoner before Pilate's tribunal and was interrogated by him ... did he not answer: 'For this I was born, and for this I have come into the world, to bear witness to the truth'? It was as if with these words [...] he was once more confirming what he had said earlier: 'You will know the truth, and the truth will make you free'. In the course of so many centuries, of so many generations, from the time of the Apostles on, is it not

often Jesus Christ himself that has made an appearance at the side of people judged for the sake of the truth? And has he not gone to death with people condemned for the sake of truth? Does he ever cease to be the continuous spokesman and advocate for the person who lives 'in spirit and truth' (cf. Jn 4:23)? Just as he does not cease to be it before the Father, he is it also with regard to the history of man" (John Paul II, *Redemptor hominis*, 12).

18:38–40. The outcome of the interrogation is that Pilate becomes convinced of Jesus' innocence (cf. Jn 19:4, 12). He probably realizes that the accusations made against Jesus were really an internal matter in which the Jews were trying to involve him; but the Jewish authorities are very irate. It is not easy for him to find a way out. He tries to do so by making concessions: first, he has recourse to a passover privilege, offering them the choice between a criminal and Jesus, but this does not work; so he looks for other ways to save him, and here also he fails. His cowardice and indecision cause him to yield to pressure and commit the injustice of condemning to death a man he knows to be innocent.

"The mystery of innocent suffering is one of the most obscure points on the entire horizon of human wisdom; and here it is affirmed in the most flagrant way. But before we uncover something of this problem, there already grows up

Mt 27:26;
28:31
Mk 15:15, 17–
20

Is 50:6

Jn 5:18; 10:33
Lev 24:16

The scourging at the pillar and the crowning with thorns

19 ¹Then Pilate took Jesus and scourged him. ²And the soldiers plaited a crown of thorns, and put it on his head, and arrayed him in a purple robe; ³they came up to him, saying, "Hail, King of the Jews!" and struck him with their hands. ⁴Pilate went out again, and said to them, "Behold, I am bringing him out to you, that you may know that I find no crime in him." ⁵So Jesus came out, wearing the crown of thorns and the purple robe. Pilate said to them, "Here is the man!" ⁶When the chief priests and the officers saw him, they cried out, "Crucify him, crucify him!" Pilate said to them, "Take him yourselves and crucify him, for I find no crime in him." ⁷The Jews answered him, "We have a law, and by that law he ought to die, because he has made himself the

---

in us an unrestrained affection for the innocent one who suffers, for Jesus, [...] and for all innocent people—whether they be young or old—who are also suffering, and whose pain we cannot explain. The way of the cross leads us to meet the first person in a sorrowful procession of innocent people who suffer. And this first blameless and suffering person uncovers for us in the end the secret of his passion. It is a sacrifice" (Paul VI, Address on Good Friday, 12 April 1974).

19:1–3. Christ's prophecy is fulfilled to the letter: the Son of man "will be delivered to the Gentiles, and will be mocked and shamefully treated and spit upon; they will scourge him and kill him, and on the third day he will rise" (Lk 18:32f; cf. Mt 20:18f).

Scourging was one of the most severe punishments permitted under Roman law. The criminal was draped over a pillar or other form of support, his naked back exposed to the lash or *flagellum*.

Scourging was generally used as a preliminary to crucifixion to weaken the criminal and thereby hasten his death.

Crowning with thorns was not an official part of the punishment; it was an initiative of the soldiers themselves, a product of their cruelty and desire to mock Jesus. On the stone pavement in the Antonia tower some drawings have been found which must have been used in what was called the "king game": dice were thrown to pick out a mock king among those condemned, who was subjected to taunting before being led off for crucifixion.

St John locates this episode at the centre of his narrative of the events in the praetorium. He thereby highlights the crowning with thorns as the point at which Christ's kingship is at its most patent: the soldiers proclaim him as King of the Jews only in a sarcastic way (cf. Mk 15:15, 16–19), but the Evangelist gives us to understand that he is indeed the King.

19:5. Wearing the insignia of royalty, Christ, despite this tragic parody, still projects the majesty of the King of Kings. In Revelation 5:12 St John will say: "Worthy is the Lamb who was slain, to receive power and wealth and wisdom and might and honour and glory and blessing!"

"Imagine that divine face: swollen by blows, covered in spittle, torn by thorns, furrowed with blood, here fresh blood, there ugly dried blood. And, since the

Son of God."* [8]When Pilate heard these words, he was the more afraid; [9]he entered the praetorium again and said to Jesus, "Where are you from?"* But Jesus gave no answer. [10]Pilate therefore said to him, "You will not speak to me? Do you not know that I have the power to release you, and the power to crucify you?" [11]Jesus answered him, "You would have no power over me unless it had been given you from above; therefore he who delivered me to you has the greater sin."

Jn 10:18
Acts 2:23

Pilate hands Jesus over

[12]Upon this Pilate sought to release him, but the Jews cried out, "If you release this man, you are not Caesar's friend; every one who makes himself a king sets himself against Caesar." [13]When

Acts 17:7

---

sacred Lamb had his hands tied, he could not use them to wipe away the blood running into his eyes, and so those two luminaries of heaven were eclipsed and almost blinded and made mere pieces of flesh. Finally, so disfigured was he that one could not make out who he was; he scarcely seemed human; he had become an altarpiece depicting suffering, painted by those cruel artists and their evil president, producing this pitiful figure to plead his case before his enemies" (Fray Luis de Granada, *Life of Jesus Christ*, 24).

19:6–7. When Pilate hears the Jews accuse Jesus of claiming to be the Son of God, he grows still more alarmed: his wife has already unnerved him by sending him a message, after a dream, not to have anything to do with this "righteous man". But the shouting (v. 12) orchestrated by the Jewish authorities pressures him into agreeing to condemn Jesus.

Although technically Jesus is crucified for supposedly committing a political crime (cf. the note on Jn 18:29–32), in fact it is on clearly religious ground that he is sent to death.

19:8–11. Pilate is impressed by Jesus' silence, by his not defending himself, and

when the procurator says that he has power to release him or to condemn him, our Lord then says something quite unexpected—that all power on earth comes from God. This means that in the last analysis even if people talk about the sovereignty of the king or of the people, such authority is never absolute; it is only relative, being subject to the absolute sovereignty of God: hence no human law can be just, and therefore binding in conscience, if it does not accord with divine law.

"He who delivered me"—a reference to all those who have contrived our Lord's death, that is, Judas, Caiaphas, the Jewish leaders, etc. (cf. 18:30–35). They are the ones who really sent Christ to the cross; but this does not exonerate Pontius Pilate from blame.

19:13. "The Pavement", in Greek *lithostrotos*, literally a "pavement", a "flagged expanse", therefore a yard or plaza paved with flags. The Hebrew word "Gabbatha" is not the equivalent of the Greek *lithostrotos*; it means a "height" or "eminence". But both words refer to the same place; however, its precise location is uncertain due to doubts about where the praetorium was located: cf. the note on Jn 18:28.

Pilate heard these words, he brought Jesus out and sat down on the judgment seat at a place called The Pavement, and in Hebrew, Gabbatha. [14]Now it was the day of Preparation for the Passover; it was about the sixth hour. He said to the Jews, "Here is your King!" [15]They cried out, "Away with him, away with him, crucify him!" Pilate said to them, "Shall I crucify your King?" The chief priests answered, "We have no king but Caesar." [16]Then he handed him over to them to be crucified.

Jn 18:22–37

Jn 19:6

Mt 27:31; 33:37f
Mk 15:20, 22,
25–27
Lk 23:33, 38

Grammatically the Greek could be translated as follows: "Pilate ... brought Jesus out and sat him down on the judgment seat": in which case the Evangelist implies that Pilate was ridiculing the Jewish leaders by a mock enthronement of the "King of the Jews". This would fit in with Pilate's attitude towards the Jewish leaders from this point onwards (vv. 14–22) and with the purpose of the inspired writer, who would see in this the enthronement of Christ as King.

19:14. "The day of Preparation", the *Parasceve*. The sixth hour began at midday. Around this time all leavened bread was removed from the houses and replaced by unleavened bread for the paschal meal (cf. Ex 12:15ff), and the lamb was officially sacrificed in the temple. St John notes that this was the time at which Jesus was condemned, thereby underlining the coincidence between the time of the death sentence and the time the lamb was sacrificed: Christ is the new Paschal Lamb; as St Paul says (1 Cor 5:7), "Christ, our paschal lamb, has been sacrificed."

There is some difficulty in reconciling what St John says about the sixth hour with the information given in Mark 15:25 about Jesus being crucified at the third hour. Various explanations are offered, the best being that Mark is referring to the end of the third hour and John to the beginning of the sixth hour: both would then be talking of around midday.

19:15. The history of the Jewish people helps us understand the tragic paradox of the attitude of the Jewish authorities at this point. The Jews were very conscious all along of being the people of God. For example, they proudly asserted that they had no Father but God (cf. Jn 8:4). In the Old Testament Yahweh is the true King of Israel (cf. Deut 33:5; Num 23:21; 1 Kings 22:19; Is 6:5); when they wanted to copy the neighbouring peoples and asked Samuel for a king (cf. 1 Sam 8:5, 20), Samuel resisted, because Israel had only one absolute sovereign, Yahweh (1 Sam 8:6–9). But eventually God gave in to their request and himself designated who should be king over his people. His first choice, Saul, was given a sacred anointing, as were David and his successors. This rite of anointing showed that the Israelite king was God's vicar. When the kings failed to meet the people's expectations, they increasingly yearned for the messianic king, the descendant or "Son" of David, the Anointed *par excellence* or Messiah, who would rule his people, liberate them from their enemies and lead them to rule the world (cf. 2 Sam 7:16; Ps 24:7; 44:4–5, etc.). For centuries they strove heroically for this ideal, rejecting foreign domination.

During Christ's time they also opposed Rome and Herod, whom, not being a Jew, they regarded as an illegitimate king. However, at this point in the Passion, they hypocritically accept the Roman emperor as their true and only

The crucifixion and death of Jesus

¹⁷So they took Jesus, and he went out, bearing his own cross, to the place called the place of a skull, which is called in Hebrew Golgotha. ¹⁸There they crucified him, and with him two others, Gen 22:6

king. They also reject the "easy yoke" of Christ (cf. Mt 11:30) and bring the full weight of Rome down upon him.

"They themselves submitted to the punishment; therefore, the Lord handed them over. Thus, because they unanimously rejected God's government, the Lord let them be brought down through their own condemnation: for, rejecting the domination of Christ, they brought upon themselves that of Caesar" (St John Chrysostom, *Hom. on St John*, 83).

A similar kind of tragedy occurs when people who have been baptized and therefore have become part of the new people of God, throw off the "easy yoke" of Christ's sovereignty by their obstinacy in sin and submit to the terrible tyranny of the devil (cf. 2 Pet 2:21).

19:17. "The place of a skull" or Calvary seems to have got its name from the fact that it was shaped like a skull or head.

St Paul points to the parallelism that exists between Adam's disobedience and Christ's obedience (cf. Rom 5:12). On the feast of the Triumph of the Cross the Church sings "where life was lost, there life has been restored", to show how, just as the devil won victory by the tree of Paradise, so he was overpowered by Christ on the tree of the cross.

St John is the only Evangelist who clearly states that Jesus carried his own cross; the other three mention that Simon of Cyrene helped to carry it. See the notes on Mt 27:32 and Lk 23:26.

Christ's decisiveness in accepting the cross is an example which we should follow in our daily life: "You yourself must decide of your own free will to take

up the cross; otherwise, your tongue may say that you are imitating Christ, but your actions will belie your words. That way, you will never get to know the Master intimately, or love him truly. It is really important that we Christians convince ourselves of this. We are not walking with our Lord unless we are spontaneously depriving ourselves of many things that our whims, vanity, pleasure or self-interest clamour for" (St Josemaría Escrivá, *Friends of God*, 129).

As Simeon had prophesied, Jesus would be a "sign that is spoken against" (Lk 2:34)—a standard raised on high which leaves no room for indifference, demanding that every man decide for or against him and his cross: "he was going therefore to the place where he was to be crucified, bearing his own Cross. An extraordinary spectacle: to impiety, something to jeer at; to piety, a great mystery. [...] Impiety looks on and laughs at a king bearing, instead of a sceptre, the wood of his punishment; piety looks on and sees the King bearing that cross for himself to be fixed on, a cross which would thereafter shine on the brows of kings; an object of contempt in the eyes of the impious, but something in which hereafter the hearts of the saints should glorify, as St Paul would later say, But God forbid that I should glory; save in the cross of our Lord Jesus Christ" (St Augustine, *In Ioann. Evang.*, 117, 3).

19:18. Knowing what crucifixion in ancient times entailed will help us understand better the extent of the humiliation and suffering Jesus bore for love of us. Crucifixion was a penalty reserved for

Heb 13:12

one on either side, and Jesus between them. [19]Pilate also wrote a title and put it on the cross; it read, "Jesus of Nazareth, the King of the Jews." [20]Many of the Jews read this title, for the place where Jesus was crucified was near the city; and it was written in Hebrew, in Latin, and in Greek. [21]The chief priests of the Jews then said to Pilate, "Do not write, 'The King of the Jews,' but 'This man said, I am King of the Jews.'" [22]Pilate answered, "What I have written I have written."

slaves, and applied to the most serious crimes; it was the most horrific and painful form of death possible; it was also an exemplary public punishment and therefore was carried out in a public place, with the body of the criminal being left exposed for days afterwards. These words of Cicero show how infamous a punishment it was: "That a Roman citizen should be bound is an abuse; that he be lashed is a crime; that he be put to death is virtually parricide; what, then, shall I say, if he be hung on a cross? There is no word fit to describe a deed so horrible" (*In Verrem*, 2, 5, 66).

A person undergoing crucifixion died after a painful agony involving loss of blood, fever caused by his wounds, thirst, and asphyxiation, etc. Sometimes the executioners hastened death by breaking the person's legs or piercing him with a lance, as in our Lord's case. This helps us understand better what St Paul says to the Philippians about Christ's humiliation on the cross: "[he] emptied himself, taking the form of a servant [or slave], being born in the likeness of men ...; he humbled himself and became obedient unto death, even death on a cross" (Phil 2:7–8).

St John says little about the other two people being crucified, perhaps because the Synoptic Gospels had already spoken about them (see the notes on Lk 23:39–43).

19:19–22. The "title" was the technical term then used in Roman law to indicate

the grounds on which the person was being punished. It was usually written on a board prominently displayed, summarizing the official document which was forwarded to the legal archives in Rome. This explains why, when the chief priests ask Pilate to change the wording of the inscription, the procurator firmly refuses to do so: the sentence, once dictated, was irrevocable; that is what he means when he says, "What I have written I have written." In the case of Christ, this title written in different languages proclaims his universal kingship, for it could be read by people from all over the world who had come to celebrate the Passover—thus confirming our Lord's words: "You say that I am a king. For this I was born, and for this I have come into the world" (Jn 18:37).

In establishing the feast of Christ the King, Pope Pius XI explained: "He is said to reign 'in the minds of men', both by reason of the keenness of his intellect and the extent of his knowledge, and also because he is Truth itself and it is from him that truth must be obediently received by all mankind. He reigns, too, in the wills of men, for in him the human will was perfectly and entirely obedient to the holy will of God, and further by his grace and inspiration he so subjects our free will as to incite us to the most noble endeavours. He is King of our hearts, too, by reason of his 'charity which surpasseth all knowledge', and his mercy and kindness which draw all men

²³When the soldiers had crucified Jesus they took his garments and made four parts, one for each soldier; also his tunic. But the tunic was without seam, woven from top to bottom; ²⁴so they said to one another, "Let us not tear it, but cast lots for it to see whose it shall be." This was to fulfil the scripture,

> "They parted my garments among them,
> and for my clothing they cast lots."

²⁵So the soldiers did this. But standing by the cross of Jesus were his mother, and his mother's sister, Mary the wife of Clopas, and Mary Magdalene. ²⁶When Jesus saw his mother, and the disciple

Mt 27:35
Mk 15:24
Lk 23:24

Ps 22:18

Mt 27:55f
Mk 15:40f
Lk 23:49

Jn 2:4; 13:23

---

to him; for there never was, nor ever will be a man loved so much and so universally as Jesus Christ" (*Quas primas*).

19:23–24. And so the prophecy of Psalm 22 is fulfilled which describes so accurately the sufferings of the Messiah: "They divide my garments among them, and for my raiment they cast lots" (v. 18). The Fathers have seen in this seamless tunic a symbol of the unity of the Church (cf. St Augustine, *In Ioann. Evang.*, 118, 4).

19:25. Whereas the Apostles, with the exception of St John, abandon Jesus in the hour of his humiliation, these pious women, who had followed him during his public life (cf. Lk 8:2–3) now stay with their Master as he dies on the cross (cf. the note on Mt 27:55–56).

Pope John Paul II explains that our Lady's faithfulness was shown in four ways: first, in her generous desire to do all that God wanted of her (cf. Lk 1:34); second, in her total acceptance of God's will (cf. Lk 1:46f); third, in the consistency between her life and the commitment of faith which she made; and, finally, in her withstanding this test. "And only a consistency that lasts throughout the whole of life can be called faithfulness. Mary's 'fiat' in the Annunciation finds its fullness in the silent 'fiat' that she repeats at the foot of the Cross" (Homily in Mexico Cathedral, 26 January 1979).

The Church has always recognized the dignity of women and their important role in salvation history. It is enough to recall the veneration which from the earliest times the Christian people have had for the Mother of Christ, the Woman *par excellence* and the most sublime and most privileged creature ever to come from the hands of God. Addressing a special message to women, the Second Vatican Council said, among other things: "Women in trial, who stand upright at the foot of the cross like Mary, you who so often in history have given to men the strength to battle unto the very end and to give witness to the point of martyrdom, aid them now still once more to retain courage in their great undertakings, while at the same time maintaining patience and an esteem for humble beginnings" (Vatican II, *Message to women*, 8 December 1965).

19:26–27. "The spotless purity of John's whole life makes him strong before the cross. The other apostles fly from Golgotha; he, with the Mother of Christ, remains. Don't forget that purity strengthens and invigorates character" (St Josemaría Escrivá, *The Way*, 144).

Our Lord's gesture in entrusting his Blessed Mother to the disciple's care, has a dual meaning (see pp. 34ff). For one thing it expresses his filial love for the Virgin Mary. St Augustine sees it as

whom he loved standing near, he said to his mother, "Woman, behold, your son!" [27]Then he said to the disciple, "Behold, your mother!" And from that hour the disciple took her to his own home.*

Mt 27:48–50
Mk 15:36f
Lk 23:46
Ps 69:21

[28]After this Jesus, knowing that all was now finished, said (to fulfil the scripture), "I thirst." [29]A bowl full of vinegar stood there; so they put a sponge full of vinegar on hyssop and held it to his

---

a lesson Jesus gives us on how to keep the fourth commandment: "Here is a lesson in morals. He is doing what he tells us to do and, like a good Teacher, he instructs his own by example, that it is the duty of good children to take care of their parents; as though the wood on which his dying members were fixed were also the chair of the teaching Master" (St Augustine, *In Ioann. Evang.*, 119, 2).

Our Lord's words also declare that Mary is our Mother: "The Blessed Virgin also advanced in her pilgrimage of faith, and faithfully persevered in her union with her Son unto the cross, where she stood, in keeping with the divine plan, enduring with her only begotten Son the intensity of his suffering, associating herself with his sacrifice in her mother's heart, and lovingly consenting to the immolation of this victim who was born of her. Finally, she was given by the same Christ Jesus dying on the cross as a mother to his disciple" (Vatican II, *Lumen Gentium*, 58).

All Christians, who are represented in the person of John, are children of Mary. By giving us his Mother to be our Mother, Christ demonstrates his love for his own to the end (cf. Jn 13:1). Our Lady's acceptance of John as her son shows her motherly care for us: "the son of God, and your Son, from the Cross indicated a man to you, Mary, and said: 'Behold, your son' (Jn 19:26). And in that man he entrusted to you every person, he entrusted everyone to you. And you, who at the moment of the Ann-

unciation, concentrated the whole programme of your life in those simple words: 'Behold I am the handmaid of the Lord; let it be to me according to your word' (Lk 1:38): embrace everyone, draw close to everyone, seek everyone out with motherly care. Thus is accomplished what the last Council said about your presence in the mystery of Christ and the Church. In a wonderful way you are wherever men and women, his brother and sisters, are present, wherever the Church is present" (John Paul II, Homily in the Basilica of Guadalupe, 27 January 1979).

"John, the disciple whom Jesus loved, brought Mary into his home, into his life. Spiritual writers have seen these words of the Gospel as an invitation to all Christians to bring Mary into their lives. Mary certainly wants us to invoke her, to approach her confidently, to appeal to her as our mother, asking her to 'show that you are our mother'" (St Josemaría Escrivá, *Christ Is Passing By*, 140).

John Paul II constantly treats our Lady as his Mother. In bidding farewell to the Virgin of Czestochowa he prayed in this way: "Our Lady of the Bright Mountain, Mother of the Church! Once more I consecrate myself to you 'in your maternal slavery of love'. *Totus tuus!* I am all yours! I consecrate to you the whole Church—everywhere and to the ends of the earth! I consecrate to you humanity; I consecrate to you all men and women, my brothers and sisters. All peoples and all nations. I consecrate to you Europe and all the continents. I con-

mouth. [30]When Jesus had received the vinegar, he said, "It is finished"; and he bowed his head and gave up his spirit.

Jesus' side is pierced. The burial

[31]Since it was the day of Preparation, in order to prevent the bodies from remaining on the cross on the sabbath (for that sab-

Deut 21:23

---

secrate to you Rome and Poland, united, through your servant, by a fresh bond of love. Mother, accept us! Mother, do not abandon us! Mother, be our guide!" (Farewell Address at Jasna Gora Shrine, 6 June 1979).

19:28–29. This was foretold in the Old Testament: "They gave me poison for food, and for my thirst they gave me vinegar to drink" (Ps 69:21). This does not mean that they gave Jesus vinegar to increase his suffering; it was customary to offer victims of crucifixion water mixed with vinegar to relieve their thirst. In addition to the natural dehydration Jesus was suffering, we can see in his thirst an expression of his burning desire to do his Father's will and to save all souls: "On the cross he cried out *Sitio!*, 'I thirst'. He thirsts for us, for our love, for our souls and for all the souls we ought to be bringing to him along the way of the Cross, which is the way to immortality and heavenly glory" (St Josemaría Escrivá, *Friends of God*, 202).

19:30. Jesus, nailed on the cross, dies to atone for all the sins and vileness of man. Despite his sufferings he dies serenely, majestically, bowing his head now that he has accomplished the mission entrusted to him. "Who can sleep when he wishes to, as Jesus died when he wished to? Who can lay aside his clothing when he wishes to, as he put off the flesh when he chose to? ... What must we hope or fear to find his power when he comes in judgment, if it can be seen to be so great

at the moment of his death!" (St Augustine, *In Ioann. Evang.*, 119, 6).

"Let us meditate on our Lord, wounded from head to foot out of love for us. Using a phrase which approaches the truth, although it does not express its full reality, we can repeat the words of an ancient writer: 'The body of Christ is a portrait in pain'. At the first sight of Christ bruised and broken—just a lifeless body taken down from the cross and given to his Mother—at the sight of Jesus destroyed in this way, we might have thought he had failed utterly. Where are the crowds that once followed him, where is the kingdom he foretold? But this is victory, not defeat. We are nearer the resurrection than ever before; we are going to see the glory which he has won with his obedience" (St Josemaría Escrivá, *Christ Is Passing By*, 95).

19:31–33. Jesus dies on the Preparation day of the Passover—the *Parasceve*—that is, the eve, when the paschal lambs were officially sacrificed in the temple. By stressing this, the Evangelist implies that Christ's sacrifice took the place of the sacrifices of the Old Law and inaugurated the New Alliance in his blood (cf. Heb 9:12).

The Law of Moses required that the bodies should be taken down before nightfall (cf. Deut 21:22–23); this is why Pilate is asked to have their legs broken, to bring on death and allow them to be buried before it gets dark, particularly since the next day is the feast of the Passover.

bath was a high day), the Jews asked Pilate that their legs might be broken, and that they might be taken away. [32]So the soldiers came and broke the legs of the first, and of the other who had been crucified with him; [33]but when they came to Jesus and saw that he was already dead, they did not break his legs. [34]But one of the soldiers pierced his side with a spear, and at once there came out blood and water. [35]He who saw it has borne witness—his testimony is true, and he knows that he tells the truth—that you also may believe. [36]For these things took place that the scripture might be fulfilled, "Not a bone of him shall be broken." [37]And again another scripture says, "They shall look on him whom they have pierced."

Ex 12:46
Num 9:12
Ps 34:20
Zech 12:10
Rev 1:7

19:34. The outflow of blood and water has a natural explanation. Probably the water was an accumulation of liquid in the lungs due to Jesus' intense sufferings. As on other occasions, the historical events narrated in the Fourth Gospel are laden with meaning. St Augustine and Christian tradition see the sacraments and the Church itself flowing from Jesus' open side: "Here was opened wide the door of life, from which the sacraments of the Church have flowed out, without which there is no entering in unto life which is true life. [...] Here the second Adam with bowed head slept upon the cross, that thence a wife might be formed of him, flowing from his side while he slept. O death, by which the dead come back to life!! Is there anything purer than this blood, any wound more healing!" (St Augustine, *In Ioann. Evang.*, 120, 2).

The Second Vatican Council, for its part, teaches: "The Church—that is, the kingdom of Christ—already present in mystery, grows visibly through the power of God in the world. The origin and growth of the Church are symbolized by the blood and water which flowed from the open side of the crucified Jesus" (Vatican II, *Lumen gentium*, 3).

"Jesus on the cross, with his heart overflowing with love for man, is such an eloquent commentary on the value of people and things that words only get in the way. People, their happiness and their life, are so important that the very Son of God gave himself to redeem and cleanse and raise them up" (St Josemaría Escrivá, *Christ Is Passing By*, 165).

19:35. St John's Gospel presents itself as a truthful witness of the events of our Lord's life and of their spiritual and doctrinal significance. From the words of John the Baptist at the outset of Jesus' public ministry (1:19) to the final paragraph of the Gospel (21:24–25), everything forms part of a testimony to the sublime phenomenon of the Word of Life made Man. Here the evangelist explicitly states that he was an eyewitness (cf. also Jn 20:30–31; 1 Jn 1:1–3).

19:36. This quotation refers to the precept of the Law that no bone of the paschal lamb should be broken (cf. Ex 12:46): again John's Gospel is telling us that Jesus is the true paschal Lamb who takes away the sins of the world (cf. Jn 1:29).

19:37. The account of the Passion concludes with a quotation from Zechariah (12:10) foretelling the salvation resulting from the mysterious suffering and death of a redeemer. The evangelist thereby evokes the salvation wrought by Christ,

³⁸After this Joseph of Arimathea, who was a disciple of Jesus, but secretly, for fear of the Jews, asked Pilate that he might take away the body of Jesus, and Pilate gave him leave. So he came and took away his body. ³⁹Nicodemus also, who had at first come to him by night, came bringing a mixture of myrrh and aloes, about a hundred pounds' weight. ⁴⁰They took the body of Jesus, and bound it in linen cloths with the spices, as is the burial custom of the Jews. ⁴¹Now in the place where he was crucified there was a garden, and in the garden a new tomb where no one had ever been laid. ⁴²So because of the Jewish day of Preparation, as the tomb was close at hand, they laid Jesus there.

Mt 27:57–60
Mk 15:42–46
Lk 23:50–54

Jn 3:1
Mt 2:1

Jn 11:44

---

who, nailed to the cross, has fulfilled God's promise of redemption (cf. Jn 12:32). Everyone who looks upon him with faith receives the effects of his passion. Thus, the good thief, looking at Christ on the cross, recognized his kingship, placed his trust in him and received the promise of heaven (cf. Lk 23:42–43).

In the liturgy of Good Friday the Church invites us to contemplate and adore the cross: "Behold the wood of the Cross, on which was nailed the salvation of the world", and from the earliest time of the Church the crucifix has been the sign reminding Christians of the supreme point of Christ's love, when he died on the cross and freed us from eternal death. "Your crucifix.—As a Christian, you should always carry your crucifix with you. And place it on your desk. And kiss it before going to bed and when you wake up: and when our poor body rebels against your soul, kiss it again" (St Josemaría Escrivá, *The Way*, 302).

19:38–39. Our Lord's sacrifice produces its firstfruits: people who were previously afraid now boldly confess themselves disciples of Christ and attend to his dead body with exquisite refinement and generosity. The evangelist mentions that Joseph of Arimathea and Nicodemus used a mixture of myrrh and aloes in lavish amount. Myrrh is a very expensive aromatic resin, and aloes a juice extracted from the leaves of certain plants. They were used as an expression of veneration for the dead.

19:40. The Fourth Gospel adds to the information on the burial given by the Synoptics. Sacred Scripture did not specify what form burial should take, with the result that the Jews followed the custom of the time. After piously taking our Lord's body down from the cross, they probably washed it carefully (cf. Acts 9:37), perfumed it and wrapped it in a linen cloth, covering the head with a sudarium or napkin (cf. Jn 20:5–6). But because of the imminence of the sabbath rest, they were unable to anoint the body with balsam, which the women planned to do once the sabbath was past (cf. Mk 16:1; Lk 24:1). Jesus himself, when he praised Mary for anointing him at Bethany, had foretold in a veiled way that his body would not be embalmed (cf. the note on Jn 12:7–8).

19:41. Many of the Fathers have probed the mystic meaning of the garden—usually to point out that Christ, who was arrested in the Garden of Olives and buried in another garden, has redeemed us superabundantly from that first sin which was committed also in a garden, the Garden of Paradise. They comment

11. APPEARANCES OF THE RISEN CHRIST

Mt 28:1–8
Mk 16:1–8
Lk 24:1–11

Jn 13:23

The empty tomb

20 ¹Now on the first day of the week Mary Magdalene came to the tomb early, while it was still dark, and saw that the stone had been taken away from the tomb. ²So she ran, and went to Simon Peter and the other disciple, the one whom Jesus loved, and said to them, "They have taken the Lord out of the tomb, and we do not know where they have laid him." ³Peter then came out with the other disciple, and they went toward the tomb. ⁴They

---

that because Jesus was the only one to be buried in this new tomb there would be no doubt that it was he and not someone else that rose from the dead. St Augustine also observes that "just as in the womb of the Virgin Mary none was conceived before him, none after him, so in this tomb none before him, none after was buried" (*In Ioann. Evang.*, 120, 5).

Among the truths of Christian doctrine to do with Christ's death and burial are these: "one, that the body of Christ was in no degree corrupted in the sepulchre, according to the prediction of the Prophet, 'Thou wilt not give thy holy one to see corruption' (Ps 16:10; Acts 2:31); the other ... that burial, passion and death apply to Christ Jesus not as God but as man, yet they are also attributed to God, since, as is clear, they are predicted with propriety of that Person who is at once perfect God and perfect man" (St Pius V, *Catechism*, 1, 5, 9).

20:1–2. All four Gospels report the first testimonies of the holy women and the disciples regarding Christ's glorious resurrection, beginning with the fact of the empty tomb (cf. Mt 28:1–15; Mk 16:1ff; Lk 24:1–12) and then telling of the various appearances of the risen Jesus.

Mary Magdalene was one of the women who provided for our Lord during his journeys (Lk 8:1–3); along with the Virgin Mary she bravely stayed with him right up to his final moments (Jn 19:25), and she saw where his body was laid (Lk 23:55). Now, after the obligatory sabbath rest, she goes to visit the tomb. The Gospel points out that she went "early, while it was still dark": her love and veneration led her to go without delay, to be with our Lord's body.

20:4. The Fourth Gospel makes it clear that, although the women, and specifically Mary Magdalene, were the first to reach the tomb, the Apostles were the first to enter it and see the evidence that Christ had risen (the empty tomb, the linen clothes "lying" and the napkin in a place by itself). Bearing witness to this will be an essential factor in the mission which Christ will entrust to them: "You shall be my witnesses in Jerusalem ... and to the end of the earth" (Acts 1:8; cf. Acts 2:32). John, who reached the tomb first (perhaps because he was the younger), did not go in, out of deference to Peter. This is an indication that Peter was already regarded as leader of the apostles.

20:5–7. The words the evangelist uses to describe what Peter and he saw in the empty tomb convey with vivid realism the impression it made on them, etching on their memory details which at first sight seem irrelevant.

both ran, but the other disciple outran Peter and reached the tomb first; ⁵and stooping to look in, he saw the linen cloths lying there, but he did not go in. ⁶Then Simon Peter came, following him, and went into the tomb; he saw the linen cloths lying, ⁷and the napkin, which had been on his head, not lying with the linen cloths but rolled up in a place by itself. ⁸Then the other disciple, who reached the tomb first, also went in, and he saw and believed; ⁹for as yet they did not know the scripture, that he must rise from the dead. ¹⁰Then the disciples went back to their homes.

Lk 24:12

Jn 19:40

Jn 2:22
1 Cor 15:4
Acts 2:24–32

The whole scene inside the tomb in some way caused them to intuit that the Lord had risen. Some of the words contained in the account need further explanation, so terse is the translation.

"The linen clothes lying there": the Greek participle translated as "lying there" seems to indicate that the clothes were flattened, deflated, as if they were emptied when the body of Jesus rose and disappeared—as if it had come out of the clothes and bandages without their being unrolled, passing right through them (just as later he entered the Cenacle when the doors were shut). This would explain the clothes being "fallen", "flat", "lying", which is how the Greek literally translates, after Jesus' body—which had filled them—left them. One can readily understand how this would amaze a witness, how unforgettable the scene would be.

"The napkin ... rolled up in a place by itself": the first point to note is that the napkin, which had been wrapped round the head, was not on top of the clothes, but placed to one side. The second, even more surprising thing is that, like the clothes, it was still rolled up but, unlike the clothes, it still had a certain volume, like a container, possibly due to the stiffness given it by the ointments: this is what the Greek participle, here translated as "rolled", seems to indicate.

From these details concerning the empty tomb one deduces that Jesus' body must have risen in a heavenly manner, that is, in a way which transcended the laws of nature. It was not only a matter of the body being reanimated, as happened, for example, in the case of Lazarus, who had to be unbound before he could walk (cf. Jn 11:44).

20:8–10. As Mary Magdalene had told them, the Lord was not in the tomb; but the two apostles realized that there was no question of any robbery, which was what she thought had happened, because they saw the special way the clothes and napkin were; they now began to understand what the Master had so often told them about his death and resurrection (cf. Mt 16:21; Mk 8:31; Lk 9:22; etc.; cf. also the notes on Mt 12:39–40 and Lk 18:31–40).

The empty tomb and the other facts were perceptible to the senses; but the resurrection, even though it had effects that could be tested by experience, requires faith if it is to be accepted. Christ's resurrection is a real, historic fact: his body and soul were reunited. But since his was a glorious resurrection unlike Lazarus', far beyond our capacity in this life to understand what happened, and outside the scope of sense experience, a special gift of God is required—the gift of faith—to know and accept as a certainty this fact which, while it is historical, is also supernatural. Therefore, St Thomas Aquinas can say that "the indi-

The appearance to Mary Magdalene

Mt 28:9–10
Mk 16:9–11
Jn 1:51
Heb 1:14

[11]But Mary stood weeping outside the tomb, and as she wept she stooped to look into the tomb; [12]and she saw two angels in white, sitting where the body of Jesus had lain, one at the head and one at the feet. [13]They said to her, "Woman, why are you weeping?" She said to them, "Because they have taken away my Lord, and I do not know where they have laid him." [14]Saying this, she turned round and saw Jesus standing, but she did not know that it was Jesus. [15]Jesus said to her, "Woman, why are you weeping? Whom do you seek?" Supposing him to be the gardener, she said to him, "Sir, if you have carried him away, tell me where you have laid him, and I will take him away." [16]Jesus said to her, "Mary." She turned and said to him in Hebrew, "Rabboni!" (which means Teacher).

Jn 21:4

Mk 10:51

vidual arguments taken alone are not sufficient proof of Christ's resurrection, but taken together, in a cumulative way, they manifest it perfectly. Particularly important in this regard are the spiritual proofs (cf. specially Lk 24:25–27), the angelic testimony (cf. Lk 24:4–7) and Christ's own post-resurrection word confirmed by miracles (cf. Jn 3:13; Mt 16:21; 17:22; 20:18)" (St Thomas Aquinas, *Summa theologiae*, 3, 55, 6 ad 1).

In addition to Christ's predictions about his passion, death and resurrection (cf. Jn 2:19; Mt 16:21; Mk 9:31; Lk 9:22), the Old Testament also foretells the glorious victory of the Messiah and, in some way, his resurrection (cf. Ps 16:9; Is 52:13; Hos 6:2). The apostles begin to grasp the true meaning of Scripture after the resurrection, particularly once they receive the Holy Spirit, who fully enlightens their minds to understand the content of the Word of God. It is easy to imagine the surprise and elation they all feel when Peter and John tell them what they have seen in the tomb.

20:11–18. Mary's affection and sensitivity lead her to be concerned about what has become of the dead body of Jesus. This woman out of whom seven demons

were cast (cf. Lk 8:2) stayed faithful during his passion and even now her love is still ardent: our Lord has freed her from the Evil One and she responded to that grace humbly and generously.

After consoling Mary Magdalene, Jesus gives her a message for the Apostles, whom he tenderly calls his "brethren". This message implies that he and they have the same Father, though each in an essentially different way: "I am ascending to my Father"—my own father by nature—"and to your Father"—for he is your father through the adoption I have won for you by my death. Jesus, the Good Shepherd, shows his great mercy and understanding by gathering together all his disciples who had abandoned him during his passion and were now in hiding for fear of the Jews (v. 19).

Mary Magdalene's perseverance teaches us that anyone who sincerely keeps searching for Jesus Christ will eventually find him. Jesus' gesture in calling his disciples his "brethren" despite their having run away should fill us with love in the midst of our own infidelities.

20:15. From Jesus' dialogue with Mary Magdalene, we can see the frame of mind all his disciples must have been in: they were not expecting the resurrection.

[17]Jesus said to her, "Do not hold me, for I have not yet ascended to the Father; but go to my brethren and say to them, I am ascending to my Father and your Father, to my God and your God."* [18]Mary Magdalene went and said to the disciples, "I have seen the Lord"; and she told them that he had said these things to her.

Heb 2:11
Rom 8:29
Ps 22:22

Jesus' first appearance to the disciples

[19]On the evening of that day, the first day of the week, the doors being shut where the disciples were, for fear of the Jews, Jesus came and stood among them and said to them, "Peace be with you." [20]When he had said this, he showed them his hands and his side. Then the disciples were glad when they saw the Lord. [21]Jesus said to them again, "Peace be with you. As the Father has

Mk 16:14–18
Lk 24:36–49
Jn 14:27

Jn 16:22
1 Jn 1:1
Jn 17:18
Mt 28:18ff

20:17. "Do not hold me": the use of the negative imperative in the Greek, reflected in the New Vulgate ("noli me tenere") indicates that our Lord is telling Mary to release her hold on him, to let him go, since she will have another chance to see him before his ascension into heaven.

20:19–20. Jesus appears to the apostles on the evening of the day on which he rose. He presents himself without any need for the doors to be opened, by using the qualities of his glorified body; but in order to dispel any impression that he is only a spirit he shows them his hands and his side: there is no longer any doubt of its being Jesus himself, about his being truly risen from the dead. He greets them twice using the words of greeting customary among the Jews, with the same tenderness as he previously used put into this salutation. These friendly words dispel the fear and shame the apostles must have been feeling at behaving so disloyally during his passion: he has recreated the normal atmosphere of intimacy, and now he will endow them with transcendental powers.

20:21. Pope Leo XIII explained how Christ transferred his own mission to the apostles: "What did he wish in regard to the Church founded, or about to be founded? This: to transmit to it the same mission and the same mandate which he had received from the Father, that they should be perpetuated. This he clearly resolved to do: this he actually did. [Here the Pope cites John 20:21 and John 17:18.]. [...] When about to ascend into heaven he sends his Apostles in virtue of the same power by which he had been sent from the Father; and he charges them to spread abroad and propagate his teachings (cf. Mt 21:19), so that those obeying the Apostles might be saved, and those disobeying should perish (cf. Mk 16:16). [...] Hence he commands that the teaching of the Apostles should be religiously accepted and piously kept as if it were his own: 'He who hears you hears me, and he who rejects you rejects me' (Lk 10:16). Wherefore the Apostles are ambassadors of Christ as he is the ambassador of the Father" (*Satis cognitum*). In this mission the bishops are the successors of the apostles: "Christ sent the Apostles, as he himself had been sent by the Father, and then through the apostles made their successors, the bishops, sharers in his consecration and mission. The function of the bishops' ministry was handed over in a subordinate degree to priests so that they might be appointed in

195

Jn 7:39
Gen 2:7
1 Cor 15:45
Mt 16:19; 18:18

sent me, even so I send you." ²²And when he had said this, he breathed on them, and said to them, "Receive the Holy Spirit. ²³If you forgive the sins of any, they are forgiven; if you retain the sins of any, they are retained."

A second appearance with Thomas present

Jn 11:16; 14:5

²⁴Now Thomas, one of the twelve, called the Twin, was not with them when Jesus came. ²⁵So the other disciples told him, "We have seen the Lord." But he said to them, "Unless I see in his hand the print of the nails, and place my finger in the mark of the nails, and place my hand in his side, I will not believe."

Jn 19:34
1 Jn 1:1

Jn 20:19

²⁶Eight days later, his disciples were again in the house, and Thomas was with them. The doors were shut, but Jesus came and

---

the order of the priesthood and be co-workers of the episcopal order for the proper fulfilment of the apostolic mission that had been entrusted to it by Christ" (Vatican II, *Presbyterorum ordinis*, 2).

20:22–23. The Church has always understood—and has in fact defined—that Jesus Christ here conferred on the Apostles authority to forgive sins, a power which is exercised in the sacrament of Penance. "The Lord then especially instituted the sacrament of Penance when, after being risen from the dead, he breathed upon his disciples and said: 'Receive the Holy Spirit ...'. The consensus of all the Fathers has always acknowledged that by this action so sublime and words so clear the power of forgiving and retaining sins was given to the Apostles and their lawful successors for reconciling the faithful who have fallen after Baptism" (Council of Trent, *De Paenitentia*, chap. 1).

The sacrament of Penance is the most sublime expression of God's mercy, described so vividly in Jesus' parable of the prodigal son (cf. Lk 15:11–32). The Lord always awaits us, with his arms wide open, waiting for us to repent—and then he will forgive us and restore us to the dignity of being his sons.

The popes have consistently recommended Christians to have regular recourse to this sacrament: "For a constant and speedy advancement in the path of virtue we highly recommend the pious practice of frequent confession, introduced by the Church under the guidance of the Holy Spirit; for by this means we grow in a true knowledge of ourselves and in Christian humility, bad habits are uprooted, spiritual negligence and apathy are prevented, the conscience is purified and the will strengthened, salutary spiritual direction is obtained, and grace is increased by the efficacy of the sacrament itself" (Pius XII, *Mystici Corporis*).

20:24–28. Thomas' doubting moves our Lord to give him special proof that his risen body is quite real. By so doing he bolsters the faith of those who would later on find faith in him. "Surely you do not think", St Gregory the Great comments, "that it was a pure accident that that chosen disciple was missing; who on his return was told about the appearance and on hearing about it doubted; doubting, so that he might touch and believe by touching? It was not an accident; God arranged that it should happen. His clemency acted in this wonderful way so

stood among them, and said, "Peace be with you." ²⁷Then he said to Thomas, "Put your finger here, and see my hands; and put out your hand, and place it in my side; do not be faithless, but believing." ²⁸Thomas answered him, "My Lord and my God!" ²⁹Jesus said to him, "Have you believed because you have seen me? Blessed are those who have not seen and yet believe."

³⁰Now Jesus did many other signs in the presence of the disciples, which are not written in this book; ³¹but these are written that you may believe that Jesus is the Christ, the Son of God, and that believing you may have life in his name.

Mk 16:44
Lk 24:25

Jn 1:1
Jn 1:50
1 Pet 1:8

Jn 2:11; 21:25

Jn 1:12
1 Jn 5:13
Rom 1:17
Acts 3:16

---

that through the doubting disciple touching the wounds in his Master's body, our own wounds of incredulity might be healed. [...] And so the disciple, doubting and touching, was changed into a witness of the truth and of the resurrection" (*In Evangelia homiliae*, 26, 7).

Thomas' reply is not simply an exclamation: it is an assertion, an admirable act of faith in the divinity of Christ: "My Lord and my God!" These words are an ejaculatory prayer often used by Christians, especially as an act of faith in the real presence of Christ in the Blessed Eucharist.

20:29. St Gregory the Great explains these words of our Lord as follows: "By St Paul saying 'faith is the assurance of things hoped for, the conviction of things unseen' (Heb 11:1), it becomes clear that faith has to do with things which are not seen, for those which are seen are no longer the object of faith, but rather of experience. Well then, why is Thomas told, when he saw and touched, 'Because you have seen, you have believed'? Because he saw one thing, and believed another. It is certain that mortal man cannot see divinity; therefore, he saw the man and recognized him as God, saying, 'My Lord and my God.' In conclusion: seeing, he believed, because contemplating that real man he exclaimed that he was God, whom he could not see" (*In*

Evangelia homiliae, 27, 8).

Like everyone else Thomas needed the grace of God to believe, but in addition to this grace he was given an exceptional proof; his faith would have more merit had he accepted the testimony of the other apostles. Revealed truths are normally transmitted by word, by the testimony of other people who, sent by Christ and aided by the Holy Spirit, preach the deposit of faith (cf. Mk 16:15–16). "So faith comes from what is heard, and what is heard comes from the preaching of Christ" (Rom 10:17). The preaching of the Gospel, therefore, carries with it sufficient guarantees of credibility, and by accepting that preaching man "offers the full submission of his intellect and will to God who reveals, willingly assenting to the revelation given" (Vatican II, *Dei Verbum*, 5).

"What follows pleases us greatly: 'Blessed are those who have not seen and yet believe.' For undoubtedly it is we who are meant, who confess with our soul him whom we have not seen in the flesh. It refers to us, provided we live in accordance with the faith, for only he truly believes who practises what he believes" (*In Evangelia homiliae*, 26, 9).

20:30–31. This is a kind of first epilogue or conclusion to the Gospel of St John. The most common opinion is that he added chapter 21 later, which covers

The miraculous catch of fish

21 *[1]After this Jesus revealed himself again to the disciples by the Sea of Tiberias; and he revealed himself in this way. [2]Simon Peter, Thomas called the Twin, Nathanael of Cana in Galilee, the sons of Zebedee, and two others of his disciples were together. [3]Simon Peter said to them, "I am going fishing." They said to him, "We will go with you." They went out and got into the boat; but that night they caught nothing.

[4]Just as day was breaking, Jesus stood on the beach; yet the disciples did not know that it was Jesus. [5]Jesus said to them, "Children, have you any fish?" They answered him, "No." [6]He said to them, "Cast the net on the right side of the boat, and you will find some." So they cast it and now they were not able to haul it in, for the quantity of fish. [7]That disciple whom Jesus loved* said to Peter, "It is the Lord!" When Simon Peter heard that it was the Lord, he put on his clothes, for he was stripped for work, and sprang into the sea. [8]But the other disciples came in the

Margin references:
Jn 1:45–49; 11:16; 20:26–29
Lk 5:5

Jn 20:14
Lk 24:16

Lk 24:41

Lk 5:4–7

Jn 13:23

---

such important events as the triple confession of St Peter, confirmation of his primacy and our Lord's prophecy about the death of the beloved disciple. These verses sum up the inspired writer's whole purpose in writing his Gospel—to have men believe that Jesus was the Messiah, the Christ announced by the prophets in the Old Testament, the Son of God, so that by believing this saving truth, which is the core of Revelation, they might already begin to partake of eternal life (cf. Jn 1:12; 2:23; 3:18; 14:13; 15:16; 16:23–26).

21:1–3. There are some very significant things in this account: we find the disciples "by the sea of Tiberias", which means they have done what the risen Christ had told them to do (cf. Mt 28:7); they are together, which shows that there is a close fraternity among them; Peter takes the initiative, which in a way shows his authority; and they have gone back to their old jobs as fishermen, probably waiting for our Lord to give them new instructions.

This episode is reminiscent of the first miraculous draught of fish (cf. Lk 5:1–11), where our Lord promised Peter he would make him a fisher of men; now he is going to confirm him in his mission as visible head of the Church.

21:4–8. The risen Jesus goes in search of his disciples, to encourage them and tell them more about the great mission he had entrusted to them. This account describes a very moving scene, our Lord together with his own: "He passes by, close to the Apostles, close to those souls who have given themselves to him, and they do not realize he is there. How often Christ is not only near us, but in us; yet we still live in such a human way! [...] They, the disciples, recall what they have heard so often from their Master's lips: fishers of men, apostles. And they realize that all things are possible, because it is he who is directing their fishing.

"'Whereupon the disciple whom Jesus loved said to Peter, "It is the Lord!"'' Love, love is farsighted. Love is the first to appreciate kindness. The adolescent

boat, dragging the net full of fish, for they were not far from the land, but about a hundred yards[m] off.

[9]When they got out on land, they saw a charcoal fire there, with fish lying on it, and bread. [10]Jesus said to them, "Bring some of the fish that you have just caught." [11]So Simon Peter went aboard and hauled the net ashore, full of large fish, a hundred and fifty-three of them; and although there were so many, the net was not torn. [12]Jesus said to them, "Come and have breakfast." Now none of the disciples dared ask him, "Who are you?" They knew it was the Lord. [13]Jesus came and took the bread and gave it to them, and so with the fish. [14]This was now the third time that Jesus was revealed to the disciples after he was raised from the dead.

Jn 6:11
Jn 20:19, 26

Peter's primacy

[15]When they had finished breakfast, Jesus said to Simon Peter, "Simon, son of John, do you love me more than these?" He said to him, "Yes, Lord; you know that I love you." He said to him,

Jn 1:42
Mt 16:17

---

apostle, who felt a deep and firm affection for Jesus, because he loved Christ with all the purity and tenderness of a heart that had never been corrupted, exclaimed: 'It is the Lord!'

"'When Simon Peter heard that it was the Lord, he put on his clothes and sprang into the sea.' Peter personifies faith. Full of marvellous daring, he leaps into the sea. With a love like John's and a faith like Peter's, what is there that can stop us?" (St J. Escrivá, *Friends of God*, 265–266).

21:9–14. We can sense here the deep impression this appearance of the risen Jesus must have made on the apostles, and how sweet a memory St John kept of it. After the resurrection Jesus showed the same tenderness as characterized his public ministry. He makes use of natural things—the fire, the fish, etc.—to show that he really is there, and he maintains the familiar tone typical of when he lived with the disciples.

The Fathers and Doctors of the Church have often dwelt on the mystical meaning of this episode: the boat is the Church, whose unity is symbolized by the net which is not torn; the sea is the world, Peter in the boat stands for supreme authority in the Church, and the number of fish signifies the number of the elect (cf. St Thomas Aquinas, *Comm. on St John*, in loc.).

21:15–17. Jesus Christ had promised Peter that he would be the primate of the Church (cf. Mt 16:16–19 and the note on same). Despite his three denials during our Lord's passion, Christ now confers on him the primacy he promised.

"Jesus questions Peter, three times, as if to give him a triple chance to atone for his triple denial. Peter has learned his lesson from the bitter experience of his wretchedness. Aware of his weakness, he is deeply convinced that rash claims are pointless. Instead he puts everything in Christ's hands. 'Lord, you know well that I love you'" (St J. Escrivá, *Friends of God*, 267). The primacy was given to Peter directly and immediately. So the

m. Greek *two hundred cubits*

199

1 Pet 5:2, 4   "Feed my lambs." [16]A second time he said to him, "Simon, son of John, do you love me?" He said to him, "Yes, Lord; you know I
Jn 13:38; 16:30   love you." He said to him, "Tend my sheep." [17]He said to him the third time, "Simon, son of John, do you love me?" Peter was grieved because he said to him the third time, "Do you love me?" And he said to him, "Lord, you know everything; you know that I love you." Jesus said to him, "Feed my sheep.* [18]Truly, truly, I
Mt 16:22   say to you, when you were young, you girded yourself and walked where you would; but when you are old, you will stretch out your hands, and another will gird you and carry you where
Jn 13:36   you do not wish to go." [19](This he said to show by what death he was to glorify God.) And after this he said to him, "Follow me."
Jn 13:23; 18:15   [20]Peter turned and saw following them the disciple whom Jesus loved, who had lain close to his breast at the supper and had said, "Lord, who is it that is going to betray you?" [21]When Peter

Church has always understood—and so Vatican I defined: "We therefore teach and declare that, according to the testimony of the Gospel, the primacy of jurisdiction over the universal Church of God was immediately and directly promised and given to Blessed Peter the Apostle by Christ our Lord. [...] And it was upon Simon Peter alone that Jesus after his resurrection bestowed the jurisdiction of chief pastor and ruler over all his fold in the words: 'Feed my lambs; feed my sheep'" (*Pastor aeternus*, chap. 1).

The primacy is a grace conferred on Peter and his successors, the popes; it is one of the basic elements in the Church, designed to guard and protect its unity: "In order that the episcopate also might be one and undivided, and that [...] the multitude of the faithful might be kept secure in the oneness of faith and communion, he set Blessed Peter over the rest of the Apostles, and fixed in him the abiding principle of this twofold unity, and its visible foundation" (*Pastor aeternus, Dz-Sch* 3051; cf. Vatican II, *Lumen gentium*, 18). Therefore, the primacy of Peter is perpetuated in each of his successors: this is something which Christ dis-

posed; it is not based on human legislation or custom.

By virtue of the primacy, Peter, and each of his successors, is the shepherd of the whole Church and vicar of Christ on earth, because he exercises vicariously Christ's own authority. Love for the Pope, whom St Catherine of Siena used to call "the sweet Christ on earth", should express itself in prayer, sacrifice and obedience.

21:18–19. According to Tradition, St Peter followed his Master to the point of dying by crucifixion, head downwards, "Peter and Paul suffered martyrdom in Rome during Nero's persecution of Christians, which took place between the years 64 and 68. St Clement, the successor of the same Peter in the see of the Church of Rome, recalls this when, writing to the Corinthians, he puts before them 'the generous example of these two athletes': 'due to jealousy and envy, those who were the principal and holiest columns suffered persecution and fought the fight unto death'" (Paul VI, *Petrum et Paulum*).

"Follow me!": these words would have reminded the apostle of the first call

saw him, he said to Jesus, "Lord, what about this man?" [22]Jesus said to him, "If it is my will that he remain until I come, what is that to you? Follow me!" [23]The saying spread abroad among the brethren that this disciple was not to die; yet Jesus did not say to him that he was not to die, but, "If it is my will that he remain until I come, what is that to you?"

Conclusion

[24]This is the disciple who is bearing witness to these things, and who has written these things; and we know that his testimony is true.

Jn 15:27; 19:35
3 Jn 12

[25]But there are also many other things which Jesus did; were every one of them to be written, I suppose that the world itself could not contain the books that would be written.

Jn 20:30

---

he received (cf. Mt 4:19) and of the fact that Christ requires of his disciples complete self-surrender: "If any man would come after me, let him deny himself and take up the cross daily and follow me" (Lk 9:23). St Peter himself, in one of his letters, also testifies to the cross being something all Christians must carry: "For to this you have been called, because Christ also suffered for you, leaving you an example, that you should follow in his steps" (1 Pet 2:21).

21:20–23. According to St Irenaeus (*Against Heresies*, 2, 22, 5; 3, 3, 4), St John outlived all the other apostles, into the reign of Trajan AD 89–117). Possibly the evangelist wrote these verses to dispel the idea that he would not die. The important thing is not to be curious about what the future will bring but to serve the Lord faithfully, keeping to the way he has marked out for one.

21:24. This is an appeal to the testimony of the disciple "whom Jesus loved" as a guarantee of the veracity of everything contained in the book: everything which this Gospel says should be accepted by its readers as being absolutely true.

Many modern commentators think that vv. 24 and 25 were added by disci-

ples of the apostle, as a conclusion to the Gospel, when it began to be circulated, a short time after St John completed it. Be that as it may, the fact is that both verses are to be found in all extant manuscripts of the Fouth Gospel.

21:25. St John's account, written under the inspiration of the Holy Spirit, has as its purpose the strengthening of our faith in Jesus Christ through reflecting on what our Lord said and did. Like the Fourth Gospel, we shall never be able to capture the full richness and depth of our Lord's personality. "Once we begin to be interested in Christ, one's interest can never cease. There is always something more to be known, to be said—infinitely more. St John the evangelist ends his Gospel making this very point (Jn 21:25). Everything to do with Christ is so rich, there are such depths for us to explore; such light, strength, joy, desire have their source in him. [...] His coming to the world, his presence in history and culture and [...] his vital relationship with our conscience: everything suggests that it is unseemly, unscientific and irreverent ever to think that we need not and cannot advance further in contemplation of Jesus Christ" (Paul VI, General Audience, 20 February 1974).

New Vulgate Text

EVANGELIUM SECUNDUM IOANNEM

[1] [1]In principio erat Verbum, et Verbum erat apud Deum, et Deus erat Verbum. [2]Hoc erat in principio apud Deum. [3]Omnia per ipsum facta sunt, et sine ipso factum est nihil, quod factum est; [4]in ipso vita erat, et vita erat lux hominum, [5]et lux in tenebris lucet, et tenebrae eam non comprehenderunt. [6]Fuit homo missus a Deo, cui nomen erat Ioannes; [7]hic venit in testimonium, ut testimonium perhiberet de lumine, ut omnes crederent per illum. [8]Non erat ille lux, sed ut testimonium perhiberet de lumine. [9]Erat lux vera, quae illuminat omnem hominem, veniens in mundum. [10]In mundo erat, et mundus per ipsum factus est, et mundus eum non cognovit. [11]In propria venit, et sui eum non receperunt. [12]Quotquot autem acceperunt eum, dedit eis potestatem filios Dei fieri, his, qui credunt in nomine eius, [13]qui non ex sanguinibus neque ex voluntate carnis neque ex voluntate viri, sed ex Deo nati sunt. [14]Et Verbum caro factum est et habitavit in nobis; et vidimus gloriam eius, gloriam quasi Unigeniti a Patre, plenum gratiae et veritatis. [15]Ioannes testimonium perhibet de ipso, et clamat dicens: «Hic erat, quem dixi: Qui post me venturus est, ante me factus est, quia prior me erat». [16]Et de plenitudine eius nos omnes accepimus, et gratiam pro gratia; [17]quia lex per Moysen data est, gratia et veritas per Iesum Christum facta est. [18]Deum nemo vidit umquam; Unigenitus Deus, qui est in sinum Patris, ipse enarravit. [19]Et hoc est testimonium Ioannis, quando miserunt ad eum Iudaei ab Hierosolymis sacerdotes et Levitas, ut interrogarent eum: «Tu quis es?». [20]Et confessus est et non negavit; et confessus est: «Non sum ego Christus». [21]Et interrogaverunt eum: «Quid ergo? Elias es tu?». Et dicit: «Non sum». «Propheta es tu?». Et respondit: «Non». [22]Dixerunt ergo ei: «Quis es? Ut responsum demus his, qui miserunt nos. Quid dicis de teipso?». [23]Ait: *«Ego vox clamantis in deserto: / "Dirigite viam Domini"*, sicut dixit Isaias propheta». [24]Et qui missi fuerant, erant ex pharisaeis; [25]et interrogaverunt eum et dixerunt ei: «Quid ergo baptizas, si tu non es Christus neque Elias neque propheta?». [26]Respondit eis Ioannes dicens: «Ego baptizo in aqua; medius vestrum stat, quem vos non scitis, [27]qui post me venturus est, cuius ego non sum dignus, ut solvam eius corrigiam calceamenti». [28]Haec in Bethania facta sunt trans Iordanem, ubi erat Ioannes baptizans. [29]Altera die videt Iesum venientem ad se et ait: «Ecce agnus Dei, qui tollit peccatum mundi. [30]Hic est, de quo dixi: Post me venit vir, qui ante me factus est, quia prior me erat. [31]Et ego nesciebam eum, sed ut manifestetur Israel, propterea veni ego in aqua baptizans». [32]Et testimonium perhibuit Ioannes dicens: «Vidi Spiritum descendentem quasi columbam de caelo, et mansit super eum; [33]et ego nesciebam eum, sed, qui misit me baptizare in aqua, ille mihi dixit: 'Super quem videris Spiritum descendentem et manentem super eum, hic est qui baptizat in Spiritu Sancto'. [34]Et ego vidi et testimonium perhibui quia hic est Filius Dei». [35]Altera die iterum stabat Ioannes et ex discipulis eius duo, [36]et respiciens Iesum ambulantem dicit: «Ecce agnus Dei». [37]Et audierunt eum duo discipuli loquentem et secuti sunt Iesum. [38]Conversus autem Iesus et videns eos sequentes se dicit eis: «Quid quaeritis?». Qui dixerunt ei: «Rabbi —quod dicitur interpretatum Magister— ubi manes?». [39]Dicit eis: «Venite et videbitis». Venerunt ergo et viderunt, ubi maneret, et apud eum manserunt die illo; hora erat quasi decima. [40]Erat Andreas, frater Simonis Petri, unus ex duobus, qui audierant ab Ioanne et secuti fuerant eum. [41]Invenit hic primum fratrem suum Simonem et dicit ei: «Invenimus Messiam» —quod est interpretatum Christus—; [42]adduxit eum ad Iesum. Intuitus eum Iesus dixit: «Tu es Simon filius Ioannis; tu vocaberis Cephas» —quod interpretatur Petrus—. [43]In crastinum voluit exire in Galilaeam et invenit Philippum. Et dicit ei Iesus: «Sequere me». [44]Erat autem Philippus a Bethsaida, civitate Andreae et Petri. [45]Invenit Philippus Nathanael et dicit ei: «Quem scripsit Moyses in Lege et Prophetae invenimus, Iesum filium Ioseph a Nazareth». [46]Et dixit ei Nathanael: «A Nazareth potest aliquid boni esse?». Dicit ei Philippus: «Veni et vide». [47]Vidit Iesus Nathanael venientem ad se et dicit de eo: «Ecce vere Israelita, in quo dolus non est». [48]Dicit ei Nathanael: «Unde me nosti?». Respondit Iesus et dixit ei: «Priusquam te Philippus vocaret, cum esses sub ficu, vidi te». [49]Respondit ei Nathanael: «Rabbi, tu es Filius Dei, tu rex es Israel!». [50]Respondit Iesus et dixit ei: «Quia dixi tibi: Vidi te sub ficu, credis? Maiora his videbis». [51]Et dicit ei: «Amen, amen dico vobis: Videbitis *caelum apertum* et *angelos Dei ascendentes et descendentes* supra Filium hominis».   [2] [1]Et die tertio nuptiae factae sunt in Cana Galilaeae, et erat mater Iesu ibi; [2]vocatus est autem et Iesus et discipuli eius ad nuptias. [3]Et deficiente vino, dicit mater Iesu ad eum: «Vinum non habent». [4]Et dicit ei Iesus: «Quid mihi et tibi, mulier? Nondum venit hora mea». [5]Dicit mater eius ministris: «Quodcumque dixerit vobis, facite». [6]Erant autem ibi lapideae hydriae sex positae secundum purificationem Iudaeorum, capientes singulae metretas binas vel ternas. [7]Dicit eis Iesus: «Implete hydrias aqua». Et impleverunt eas usque ad summum. [8]Et dicit eis: «Haurite nunc et ferte architriclino». Illi autem tulerunt. [9]Ut autem gustavit architriclinus aquam vinum factam et non sciebat unde esset, ministri autem sciebant, qui hauserant aquam, vocat sponsum architriclinus [10]et dicit ei: «Omnis homo primum bonum vinum ponit et, cum inebriati fuerint, id quod deterius est; tu servasti bonum vinum usque adhuc». [11]Hoc fecit initium signorum Iesus in Cana Galilaeae et manifestavit gloriam suam, et crediderunt in eum discipuli eius. [12]Post hoc descendit Capharnaum ipse et mater eius et fratres eius et discipuli eius, et ibi manserunt non multis diebus. [13]Et prope erat Pascha Iudaeorum, et ascendit Hierosolymam Iesus. [14]Et invenit in templo vendentes boves et oves et columbas, et nummularios sedentes; [15]et, cum fecisset flagellum de funiculis, omnes eiecit de templo, oves quoque et boves, et nummulariorum effudit aes et mensas subvertit; [16]et his, qui columbas vendebant, dixit: «Auferte ista hinc! Nolite facere domum Patris mei domum negotiationis». [17]Recordati sunt discipuli eius quia scriptum est: *Zelus domus tuae comedit me*. [18]Responderunt ergo Iudaei et dixerunt ei: «Quod signum ostendis nobis, quia haec facis?». [19]Respondit Iesus et dixit eis: «Solvite templum hoc et in tribus diebus excitabo illud». [20]Dixerunt ergo Iudaei: «Quadraginta et sex annis aedificatum est templum hoc, et tu tribus diebus excitabis illud?». [21]Ille autem dicebat de templo corporis sui. [22]Cum ergo resurrexisset a mortuis, recordati sunt discipuli eius quia hoc dicebat, et crediderunt Scripturae et sermoni, quem dixit Iesus. [23]Cum autem esset Hierosolymis in Pascha, in die festo, multi crediderunt in nomine eius, videntes signa eius, quae faciebat. [24]Ipse autem Iesus non credebat semetipsum eis, eo quod ipse nosset omnes, [25]et quia opus ei non erat, ut quis testimonium perhiberet de homine: ipse enim sciebat quid esset in homine.   [3] [1]Erat autem homo ex pharisaeis, Nicodemus nomine, princeps Iudaeorum; [2]hic venit ad eum nocte et dixit ei: «Rabbi, scimus quia a Deo venisti magister: nemo enim potest haec signa facere, quae tu facis, nisi fuerit Deus cum eo». [3]Respondit Iesus et dixit ei: «Amen, amen dico tibi: Nisi quis natus fuerit desuper, non potest videre regnum Dei». [4]Dicit ad eum Nicodemus: «Quomodo potest homo nasci, cum senex sit? Numquid potest in ventrem matris suae iterato introire et nasci?». [5]Respondit Iesus: «Amen, amen dico tibi: Nisi quis natus fuerit ex aqua et Spiritu, non potest introire in regnum Dei. [6]Quod natum est ex carne, caro est; et, quod natum est ex Spiritu, spiritus est. [7]Non mireris quia dixi tibi: Oportet vos nasci denuo. [8]Spiritus, ubi vult, spirat, et vocem eius audis, sed non scis unde veniat et quo vadat; sic est omnis, qui natus est ex Spiritu». [9]Respondit Nicodemus et dixit ei: «Quomodo possunt haec fieri?». [10]Respondit Iesus et dixit ei: «Tu es magister Israel et haec ignoras? [11]Amen, amen dico tibi: Quod scimus, loquimur et, quod vidimus, testamur, et testimonium nostrum non accipitis. [12]Si terrena dixi vobis, et non creditis, quomodo, si dixero vobis caelestia, credetis? [13]Et nemo ascendit in caelum, nisi qui descendit de caelo, Filius hominis. [14]Et sicut Moyses exaltavit serpentem in deserto, ita exaltari oportet Filium hominis, [15]ut omnis, qui credit, in ipso habeat vitam aeternam». [16]Sic enim dilexit Deus mundum, ut Filium suum unigenitum daret, ut omnis, qui credit in eum, non pereat, sed habeat vitam aeternam. [17]Non enim misit Deus Filium in mundum, ut iudicet mundum, sed ut salvetur mundus per ipsum. [18]Qui credit in eum, non iudicatur; qui autem non credit, iam iudicatus est, quia non credidit in nomen Unigeniti Filii Dei. [19]Hoc est autem iudicium: Lux venit in mundum, et dilexerunt homines magis tenebras quam lucem; erant enim eorum mala opera. [20]Omnis enim, qui mala agit, odit lucem et non venit ad lucem, ut non arguantur opera eius; [21]qui autem facit veritatem, venit ad lucem, ut manifestentur eius opera, quia in Deo sunt facta. [22]Post haec venit Iesus et discipuli eius in Iudaeam terram, et illic demorabatur cum eis et baptizabat. [23]Erat autem et Ioannes baptizans in Enon iuxta Salim, quia aquae multae erant illic, et adveniebant et baptizabantur; [24]nondum enim missus fuerat in carcerem Ioannes. [25]Facta est ergo quaestio ex discipulis Ioannis cum Iudaeo de purificatione. [26]Et venerunt ad Ioannem et dixerunt ei: «Rabbi, qui erat tecum trans Iordanem, cui tu testimonium perhibuisti, ecce hic baptizat et omnes veniunt ad eum!». [27]Respondit Ioannes et dixit: «Non potest homo accipere quidquam, nisi fuerit ei datum de caelo. [28]Ipsi vos mihi testimonium perhibetis quod dixerim: Non sum ego Christus, sed: Missus sum ante illum. [29]Qui habet sponsam, sponsus est; amicus autem sponsi, qui stat et audit eum, gaudio gaudet propter vocem sponsi. Hoc ergo gaudium meum impletum est. [30]Illum oportet crescere, me autem minui». [31]Qui de sursum venit, supra omnes est; qui est de terra, de terra est et de terra loquitur. Qui de caelo venit, supra omnes est; [32]et quod vidit et audivit, hoc testatur, et testimonium eius nemo accipit. [33]Qui accipit eius testimonium, signavit quia Deus verax est. [34]Quem enim misit Deus, verba Dei loquitur, non enim ad mensuram dat Spiritum. [35]Pater diligit Filium et omnia dedit in manu eius. [36]Qui credit in Filium, habet vitam aeternam; qui autem incredulus est Filio, non videbit vitam, sed ira Dei manet super eum.   [4] [1]Ut ergo cognovit Iesus quia audierunt pharisaei quia Iesus plures discipulos facit et baptizat quam Ioannes, [2]—quamquam Iesus ipse non baptizaret sed discipuli eius— [3]reliquit Iudaeam et abiit iterum in Galilaeam. [4]Oportebat autem eum transire per Samariam. [5]Venit ergo in civitatem Samariae, quae dicitur Sichar, iuxta praedium, quod dedit Iacob Ioseph filio suo; [6]erat autem ibi fons Iacob. Iesus ergo fatigatus ex itinere sedebat sic super fontem; hora erat quasi sexta. [7]Venit mulier de Samaria haurire aquam. Dicit ei Iesus: «Da mihi bibere»; [8]discipuli enim eius abierant in civitatem, ut cibos emerent. [9]Dicit ergo ei mulier illa Samaritana: «Quomodo tu Iudaeus cum sis, bibere a me poscis, quae sum mulier Samaritana?». Non enim coutuntur Iudaei Samaritanis. [10]Respondit Iesus et dixit ei: «Si scires donum Dei et quis est, qui dicit tibi: "Da mihi bibere", tu forsitan petisses ab eo et dedisset tibi aquam vivam». [11]Dicit ei mulier: «Domine, neque in quo haurias habes, et puteus altus est; unde ergo habes aquam vivam? [12]Numquid tu maior es patre nostro Iacob, qui dedit nobis puteum, et ipse ex eo bibit et filii eius et pecora eius?». [13]Respondit Iesus et dixit ei: «Omnis, qui bibit ex aqua hac, sitiet iterum; [14]qui autem biberit ex aqua, quam ego dabo ei, non sitiet in aeternum, sed aqua, quam dabo ei, fiet in eo fons aquae salientis in vitam aeternam». [15]Dicit ad eum mulier: «Domine, da mihi hanc aquam, ut non sitiam, neque veniam huc haurire». [16]Dicit ei: «Vade, voca virum tuum et veni huc». [17]Respondit mulier et dixit ei: «Non habeo virum». Dicit ei Iesus: «Bene dixisti: "Non habeo virum"; [18]quinque enim viros habuisti, et nunc, quem habes, non est tuus vir. Hoc vere dixisti». [19]Dicit ei mulier: «Domine, video quia propheta es tu. [20]Patres nostri in monte hoc adoraverunt, et vos dicitis quia in Hierosolymis est locus, ubi adorare oportet». [21]Dicit ei Iesus: «Crede mihi, mulier, quia venit hora quando neque in monte hoc neque in Hierosolymis adorabitis Patrem. [22]Vos adoratis, quod nescitis; nos adoramus, quod scimus, quia salus ex Iudaeis est. [23]Sed venit hora et nunc est, quando veri adoratores adorabunt Patrem in Spiritu et veritate; nam et Pater tales quaerit, qui adorent eum. [24]Spiritus est Deus, et eos, qui adorant eum, in Spiritu et veritate oportet adorare». [25]Dicit ei mulier: «Scio quia Messias venit —qui dicitur Christus—; cum venerit ille, nobis annuntiabit omnia». [26]Dicit ei Iesus: «Ego sum, qui loquor tecum». [27]Et continuo venerunt discipuli eius et mirabantur quia cum muliere loquebatur; nemo tamen dixit: «Quid quaeris aut quid loqueris cum ea?». [28]Reliquit ergo hydriam suam mulier et abiit in civitatem et dicit illis hominibus: [29]«Venite, videte hominem, qui dixit mihi omnia, quaecumque feci; numquid ipse est Christus?». [30]Exierunt de civitate et veniebant ad eum. [31]Interea rogabant eum discipuli dicentes: «Rabbi, manduca». [32]Ille autem dixit eis: «Ego cibum habeo manducare, quem vos nescitis». [33]Dicebant ergo discipuli ad invicem: «Numquid aliquis attulit ei manducare?». [34]Dicit eis Iesus: «Meus cibus est, ut faciam voluntatem eius, qui misit me, et ut perficiam opus eius. [35]Nonne vos dicitis: "Adhuc quattuor menses sunt, et messis venit"? Ecce dico vobis: Levate oculos vestros et videte regiones quia albae sunt ad messem! Iam [36]qui metit, mercedem accipit et congregat fructum in vitam aeternam, ut et qui seminat, simul gaudeat et qui metit. [37]In hoc enim est verbum verum: Alius est qui seminat, et alius est qui metit. [38]Ego misi vos metere, quod vos non laborastis; alii laboraverunt, et vos in laborem eorum introistis». [39]Ex civitate autem illa multi crediderunt in eum Samaritanorum propter verbum mulieris testimonium perhibentis: «Dixit mihi omnia, quaecumque feci!». [40]Cum venissent ergo ad illum Samaritani, rogaverunt eum, ut apud ipsos maneret; et mansit ibi duos dies. [41]Et multo plures crediderunt propter sermonem eius; [42]et mulieri dicebant: «Iam non propter tuam loquelam credimus; ipsi enim audivimus et scimus quia hic est vere Salvator mundi!». [43]Post duos autem dies exiit inde in Galilaeam; [44]ipse enim Iesus testimonium perhibuit quia propheta in sua patria honorem non habet. [45]Cum ergo venisset in Galilaeam, exceperunt eum Galilaei, cum omnia vidissent, quae fecerat Hierosolymis in die festo; et ipsi enim venerant in diem festum. [46]Venit ergo iterum in Cana Galilaeae, ubi fecit aquam vinum. Et erat quidam regius, cuius filius infirmabatur Capharnaum; [47]hic cum audisset quia Iesus advenerit a Iudaea in Galilaeam, abiit ad eum et rogabat ut descenderet et sanaret filium eius; incipiebat enim mori. [48]Dixit ergo Iesus ad eum: «Nisi signa et prodigia videritis, non credetis». [49]Dicit ad eum regius: «Domine, descende priusquam moriatur puer meus». [50]Dicit ei Iesus: «Vade. Filius tuus vivit». Credidit homo sermoni, quem dixit ei Iesus, et ibat. [51]Iam autem eo descendente, servi eius occurrerunt ei dicentes quia puer eius vivit. [52]Interrogabat ergo horam ab eis, in qua melius habuerit. Dixerunt ergo ei: «Heri hora septima reliquit eum febris». [53]Cognovit ergo pater quia illa hora erat, in qua dixit ei Iesus: «Filius tuus vivit», et credidit ipse et domus eius tota. [54]Hoc iterum secundum signum fecit Iesus, cum venisset a Iudaea in Galilaeam.

[5] [1]Post haec erat dies festus Iudaeorum, et ascendit Iesus Hierosolymam. [2]Est autem Hierosolymis, super Probatica, piscina, quae cognominatur Hebraice Bethsatha, quinque porticus habens. [3]In his

iacebat multitudo languentium, caecorum, claudorum, aridorum. [5]Erat autem quidam homo ibi triginta et octo annos habens in infirmitate sua. [6]Hunc cum vidisset Iesus iacentem, et cognovisset quia multum iam tempus habet, dicit ei: «Vis sanus fieri?». [7]Respondit ei languidus: «Domine, hominem non habeo, ut, cum turbata fuerit aqua, mittat me in piscinam; dum autem venio ego, alius ante me descendit». [8]Dicit ei Iesus: «Surge, tolle grabatum tuum et ambula». [9]Et statim sanus factus est homo, et sustulit grabatum suum et ambulabat. Erat autem sabbatum in illo die. [10]Dicebant ergo Iudaei illi, qui sanatus fuerat: «Sabbatum est, et non licet tibi tollere grabatum tuum». [11]Ille autem respondit eis: «Qui me fecit sanum, ille mihi dixit: "Tolle grabatum tuum et ambula"». [12]Interrogaverunt eum: «Quis est ille homo, qui dixit tibi: "Tolle et ambula"?». [13]Is autem, qui sanus fuerat effectus, nesciebat quis esset; Iesus enim declinavit a turba constituta in loco. [14]Postea invenit eum Iesus in templo, et dixit illi: «Ecce sanus factus es; iam noli peccare, ne deterius tibi aliquid contingat». [15]Abiit ille homo et nuntiavit Iudaeis quia Iesus esset, qui fecit eum sanum. [16]Et propterea persequebantur Iudaei Iesum, quia haec faciebat in sabbato. [17]Iesus autem respondit eis: «Pater meus usque modo operatur, et ego operor». [18]Propterea ergo magis quaerebant eum Iudaei interficere, quia non solum solvebat sabbatum, sed et Patrem suum dicebat Deum, aequalem se faciens Deo. [19]Respondit itaque Iesus et dixit eis: «Amen, amen dico vobis: Non potest Filius a se facere quidquam, nisi quod viderit Patrem facientem; quaecumque enim ille faciat, haec et Filius similiter facit. [20]Pater enim diligit Filium et omnia demonstrat ei, quae ipse facit, et maiora his demonstrabit ei opera, ut vos miremini. [21]Sicut enim Pater suscitat mortuos et vivificat, sic et Filius, quos vult, vivificat. [22]Neque enim Pater iudicat quemquam, sed iudicium omne dedit Filio, [23]ut omnes honorificent Filium, sicut honorificant Patrem. Qui non honorificat Filium, non honorificat Patrem, qui misit illum. [24]Amen, amen dico vobis: Qui verbum meum audit et credit ei, qui misit me, habet vitam aeternam et in iudicium non venit, sed transiit a morte in vitam. [25]Amen, amen dico vobis: Venit hora, et nunc est, quando mortui audient vocem Filii Dei et, qui audierint, vivent. [26]Sicut enim Pater habet vitam in semetipso, sic dedit et Filio vitam habere in semetipso; [27]et potestatem dedit ei iudicium facere, quia Filius hominis est. [28]Nolite mirari hoc, quia venit hora, in qua omnes, qui in monumentis sunt, audient vocem eius [29]et procedent, qui bona fecerunt, in resurrectionem vitae, qui vero mala egerunt, in resurrectionem iudicii. [30]Non possum ego a meipso facere quidquam; sicut audio, iudico, et iudicium meum iustum est, quia non quaero voluntatem meam, sed voluntatem eius, qui misit me. [31]Si ego testimonium perhibeo de meipso, testimonium meum non est verum; [32]alius est, qui testimonium perhibet de me, et scio quia verum est testimonium, quod perhibet de me. [33]Vos misistis ad Ioannem, et testimonium perhibuit veritati; [34]ego autem non ab homine testimonium accipio, sed haec dico, ut vos salvi sitis. [35]Ille erat lucerna ardens et lucens, vos autem voluistis exsultare ad horam in luce eius. [36]Ego autem habeo testimonium maius Ioanne; opera enim, quae dedit mihi Pater, ut perficiam ea, ipsa opera, quae ego facio, testimonium perhibent de me quia Pater me misit; [37]et, qui misit me, Pater, ipse testimonium perhibuit de me. Neque vocem eius umquam audistis, neque speciem eius vidistis, [38]et verbum eius non habetis in vobis manens, quia, quem misit ille, huic vos non creditis. [39]Scrutamini Scripturas, quia vos putatis in ipsis vitam aeternam habere; et illae sunt, quae testimonium perhibent de me. [40]Et non vultis venire ad me, ut vitam habeatis. [41]Gloriam ab hominibus non accipio, [42]sed cognovi vos, quia dilectionem Dei non habetis in vobis. [43]Ego veni in nomine Patris mei, et non accipitis me; si alius venerit in nomine suo, illum accipietis. [44]Quomodo potestis vos credere, qui gloriam ab invicem accipitis, et gloriam, quae a solo est Deo, non quaeritis? [45]Nolite putare quia ego accusaturus sim vos apud Patrem; est qui accuset vos: Moyses, in quo vos speratis. [46]Si enim crederetis Moysi, crederetis forsitan et mihi; de me enim ille scripsit. [47]Si autem illius litteris non creditis, quomodo meis verbis credetis?». [6] [1]Post haec abiit Iesus trans mare Galilaeae, quod est Tiberiadis. [2]Et sequebatur eum multitudo magna, quia videbant signa, quae faciebat super his, qui infirmabantur. [3]Subiit autem in montem Iesus et ibi sedebat cum discipulis suis. [4]Erat autem proximum Pascha, dies festus Iudaeorum. [5]Cum sublevasset ergo oculos Iesus et vidisset quia multitudo magna venit ad eum, dicit ad Philippum: «Unde ememus panes, ut manducent hi?». [6]Hoc autem dicebat tentans eum; ipse enim sciebat quid esset facturus. [7]Respondit ei Philippus: «Ducentorum denariorum panes non sufficiunt eis, ut unusquisque modicum quid accipiat!». [8]Dicit ei unus ex discipulis eius, Andreas frater Simonis Petri: [9]«Est puer hic, qui habet quinque panes hordeaceos et duos pisces; sed haec quid sunt propter tantos?». [10]Dixit Iesus: «Facite homines discumbere». Erat autem fenum multum in loco. Discubuerunt ergo viri numero quasi quinque milia. [11]Accepit ergo panes Iesus et, cum gratias egisset, distribuit discumbentibus, similiter et ex piscibus, quantum volebant. [12]Ut autem impleti sunt, dicit discipulis suis: «Colligite, quae superaverunt, fragmenta, ne quid pereat». [13]Collegerunt ergo et impleverunt duodecim cophinos fragmentorum ex quinque panibus hordeaceis, quae superfuerunt his, qui manducaverunt. [14]Illi ergo homines, cum vidissent quod fecerat signum, dicebant: «Hic est vere propheta, qui venit in mundum!». [15]Iesus ergo, cum cognovisset quia venturi essent, ut raperent eum et facerent eum regem, secessit iterum in montem ipse solus. [16]Ut autem sero factum est, descenderunt discipuli eius ad mare [17]et, cum ascendissent navem, veniebant trans mare in Capharnaum. Et tenebrae iam factae erant, et nondum venerat ad eos Iesus. [18]Mare autem, vento magno flante, exsurgebat. [19]Cum remigassent ergo quasi stadia viginti quinque aut triginta, vident Iesum ambulantem super mare et proximum navi fieri, et timuerunt. [20]Ille autem dicit eis: «Ego sum, nolite timere!». [21]Volebant ergo accipere eum in navem, et statim fuit navis ad terram, in quam ibant. [22]Altera die turba, quae stabat trans mare, vidit quia navicula alia non erat ibi nisi una et quia non introisset cum discipulis suis Iesus in navem, sed soli discipuli eius abiissent; [23]aliae supervenerunt naves a Tiberiade iuxta locum, ubi manducaverant panem, gratias agente Domino. [24]Cum ergo vidisset turba quia Iesus non esset ibi neque discipuli eius, ascenderunt ipsi naviculas et venerunt Capharnaum quaerentes Iesum. [25]Et cum invenissent eum trans mare, dixerunt ei: «Rabbi, quando huc venisti?». [26]Respondit eis Iesus et dixit: «Amen, amen dico vobis: Quaeritis me non quia vidistis signa, sed quia manducastis ex panibus et saturati estis. [27]Operamini non cibum, qui perit, sed cibum, qui permanet in vitam aeternam, quem Filius hominis vobis dabit; hunc enim Pater signavit Deus!». [28]Dixerunt ergo ad eum: «Quid faciemus, ut operemur opera Dei?». [29]Respondit Iesus et dixit eis: «Hoc est opus Dei, ut credatis in eum, quem misit ille». [30]Dixerunt ergo ei: «Quod ergo tu facis signum, ut videamus et credamus tibi? Quid operaris? [31]Patres nostri manna manducaverunt in deserto, sicut scriptum est: *"Panem de caelo dedit eis manducare"*». [32]Dixit ergo eis Iesus: «Amen, amen dico vobis: Non Moyses dedit vobis panem de caelo, sed Pater meus dat vobis panem de caelo verum: [33]panis enim Dei est, qui descendit de caelo et dat vitam mundo». [34]Dixerunt ergo ad eum: «Domine, semper da nobis panem hunc».[35]Dixit eis Iesus: «Ego sum panis vitae. Qui venit ad me, non esuriet; et, qui credit in me, non sitiet umquam. [36]Sed dixi vobis quia et vidistis me, et non creditis. [37]Omne, quod dat mihi Pater, ad me veniet, et eum, qui venit ad me, non eiciam foras, [38]quia descendi de caelo, non ut faciam voluntatem meam sed voluntatem eius, qui misit me. [39]Haec est autem voluntas eius, qui misit me, ut omne, quod dedit mihi, non perdam ex eo, sed resuscitem illud in novissimo die. [40]Haec est enim voluntas Patris mei, ut omnis, qui videt Filium et credit in eum, habeat vitam aeternam; et resuscitabo eum ego in novissimo die». [41]Murmurabant ergo Iudaei de illo quia dixisset: «Ego sum panis, qui de caelo descendi», [42]et dicebant: «Nonne hic est Iesus filius Ioseph, cuius nos novimus patrem et matrem? Quomodo dicit nunc: "De caelo descendi"?». [43]Respondit Iesus et dixit eis: «Nolite murmurare in invicem. [44]Nemo potest venire ad me, nisi Pater, qui misit me, traxerit eum; et ego resuscitabo eum in novissimo die. [45]Est scriptum in Prophetis: *"Et erunt omnes docibiles Dei"*. Omnis, qui audivit a Patre et didicit, venit ad me. [46]Non quia Patrem vidit quisquam, nisi is qui est a Deo, hic vidit Patrem. [47]Amen, amen dico vobis: Qui credit, habet vitam aeternam. [48]Ego sum panis vitae. [49]Patres vestri manducaverunt in deserto manna et mortui sunt. [50]Hic est panis de caelo descendens, ut, si quis ex ipso manducaverit, non moriatur. [51]Ego sum panis vivus, qui de caelo descendi. Si quis manducaverit ex hoc pane, vivet in aeternum; panis autem, quem ego dabo, caro mea est pro mundi vita». [52]Litigabant ergo Iudaei ad invicem dicentes: «Quomodo potest hic nobis carnem suam dare ad manducandum?». [53]Dixit ergo eis Iesus: «Amen, amen dico vobis: Nisi manducaveritis carnem Filii hominis et biberitis eius sanguinem, non habetis vitam in vobismetipsis. [54]Qui manducat meam carnem et bibit meum sanguinem, habet vitam aeternam; et ego resuscitabo eum in novissimo die. [55]Caro enim mea verus est cibus, et sanguis meus verus est potus. [56]Qui manducat meam carnem et bibit meum sanguinem, in me manet, et ego in illo. [57]Sicut misit me vivens Pater, et ego vivo propter Patrem; et, qui manducat me, et ipse vivet propter me. [58]Hic est panis, qui de caelo descendit, non sicut manducaverunt patres et mortui sunt; qui manducat hunc panem, vivet in aeternum». [59]Haec dixit in synagoga docens in Capharnaum. [60]Multi ergo audientes ex discipulis eius dixerunt: «Durus est hic sermo! Quis potest eum audire?». [61]Sciens autem Iesus apud semetipsum quia murmurarent de hoc discipuli eius, dixit eis: «Hoc vos scandalizat? [62]Si ergo videritis Filium hominis ascendentem, ubi erat prius? [63]Spiritus est, qui vivificat, caro non prodest quidquam; verba, quae ego locutus sum vobis, Spiritus sunt et vita sunt. [64]Sed sunt quidam ex vobis, qui non credunt». Sciebat enim ab initio Iesus, qui essent non credentes, et quis traditurus esset eum. [65]Et dicebat: «Propterea dixi vobis: Nemo potest venire ad me, nisi fuerit ei datum a Patre». [66]Ex hoc multi discipulorum eius abierunt retro et iam non cum illo ambulabant. [67]Dixit ergo Iesus ad Duodecim: «Numquid et vos vultis abire?». [68]Respondit ei Simon Petrus: «Domine, ad quem ibimus? Verba vitae aeternae habes; [69]et nos credidimus et cognovimus quia tu es Sanctus Dei». [70]Respondit eis Iesus: «Nonne ego vos Duodecim elegi? Et ex vobis unus Diabolus est?». [71]Dicebat autem Iudam Simonis Iscariotis: hic enim erat traditurus eum, cum esset unus ex Duodecim.   [7] [1]Et post haec ambulabat Iesus in Galilaeam; non enim volebat in Iudaeam ambulare, quia quaerebant eum Iudaei interficere. [2]Erat autem in proximo dies festus Iudaeorum, Scenopegia. [3]Dixerunt ergo ad eum fratres eius: «Transi hinc et vade in Iudaeam, ut et discipuli tui videant opera tua, quae facis. [4]Nemo quippe in occulto quid facit et quaerit ipse in palam esse. Si haec facis, manifesta teipsum mundo». [5]Neque enim fratres eius credebant in eum. [6]Dicit ergo eis Iesus: «Tempus meum nondum adest, tempus autem vestrum semper est paratum. [7]Non potest mundus odisse vos, me autem odit, quia ego testimonium perhibeo de illo quia opera eius mala sunt. [8]Vos ascendite ad diem festum, ego non ascendo ad diem festum istum, quia meum tempus nondum impletum est». [9]Haec autem cum dixisset, ipse mansit in Galilaea. [10]Ut autem ascenderunt fratres eius ad diem festum, tunc et ipse ascendit, non manifeste sed quasi in occulto. [11]Iudaei ergo quaerebant eum in die festo et dicebant: «Ubi est ille?». [12]Et murmur multus de eo erat in turba. Alii quidem dicebant: «Bonus est!»; alii autem dicebant: «Non, sed seducit turbam!». [13]Nemo tamen palam loquebatur de illo propter metum Iudaeorum. [14]Iam autem die festo mediante, ascendit Iesus in templum et docebat. [15]Mirabantur ergo Iudaei dicentes: «Quomodo hic litteras scit, cum non didicerit?». [16]Respondit ergo eis Iesus et dixit: «Mea doctrina non est mea sed eius, qui misit me. [17]Si quis voluerit voluntatem eius facere, cognoscet de doctrina utrum ex Deo sit, an ego a meipso loquar. [18]Qui a semetipso loquitur, gloriam propriam quaerit; qui autem quaerit gloriam eius, qui misit illum, hic verax est, et iniustitia in illo non est. [19]Nonne Moyses dedit vobis legem? Et nemo ex vobis facit legem. Quid me quaeritis interficere?». [20]Respondit turba: «Daemonium habes! Quis te quaerit interficere?». [21]Respondit Iesus et dixit eis: «Unum opus feci, et omnes miramini. [22]Propterea Moyses dedit vobis circumcisionem — non quia ex Moyse est sed ex patribus— et in sabbato circumciditis hominem. [23]Si circumcisionem accipit homo in sabbato, ut non solvatur lex Moysis, mihi indignamini quia totum hominem sanum feci in sabbato? [24]Nolite iudicare secundum faciem, sed iustum iudicium iudicate». [25]Dicebant ergo quidam ex Hierosolymitis: «Nonne hic est, quem quaerunt interficere? [26]Et ecce palam loquitur, et nihil ei dicunt. Numquid vere cognoverunt principes quia hic est Christus? [27]Sed hunc scimus unde sit, Christus autem cum venerit, nemo scit unde sit». [28]Clamavit ergo docens in templo Iesus et dicens: «Et me scitis et unde sim scitis. Et a meipso non veni, sed est verus, qui misit me, quem vos non scitis. [29]Ego scio eum, quia ab ipso sum, et ipse me misit». [30]Quaerebant ergo eum apprehendere, et nemo misit in illum manus, quia nondum venerat hora eius. [31]De turba autem multi crediderunt in eum et dicebant: «Christus cum venerit, numquid plura signa faciet quam quae hic fecit?». [32]Audierunt pharisaei turbam murmurantem de illo haec et miserunt pontifices et pharisaei ministros, ut apprehenderent eum. [33]Dixit ergo Iesus: «Adhuc modicum tempus vobiscum sum et vado ad eum, qui misit me. [34]Quaeretis me et non invenietis; et ubi sum ego, vos non potestis venire». [35]Dixerunt ergo Iudaei ad seipsos: «Quo hic iturus est, quia nos non inveniemus eum? Numquid in dispersionem Graecorum iturus est et docturus Graecos? [36]Quis est hic sermo, quem dixit: "Quaeretis me et non invenietis" et: "Ubi sum ego, vos non potestis venire"?». [37]In novissimo autem die magno festivitatis stabat Iesus et clamavit dicens: «Si quis sitit, veniat ad me et bibat, [38]qui credit in me. Sicut dixit Scriptura, flumina de ventre eius fluent aquae vivae». [39]Hoc autem dixit de Spiritu, quem accepturi erant qui crediderant in eum. Nondum enim erat Spiritus, quia Iesus nondum fuerat glorificatus. [40]Ex illa ergo turba, cum audissent hos sermones, dicebant: «Hic est vere propheta!»; [41]alii dicebant: «Hic est Christus!»; quidam autem dicebant: «Numquid a Galilaea Christus venit? [42]Nonne Scriptura dixit: *Ex semine David*, et *de Bethlehem* castello, ubi erat David, *venit* Christus"?». [43]Dissensio itaque facta est in turba propter eum. [44]Quidam autem ex ipsis volebant apprehendere eum, sed nemo misit super illum manus. [45]Venerunt ergo ministri ad pontifices et pharisaeos, et dixerunt eis illi: «Quare non adduxistis eum?». [46]Responderunt ministri: «Numquam sic locutus est homo». [47]Responderunt ergo eis pharisaei: «Numquid et vos seducti estis? [48]Numquid aliquis ex principibus credidit in eum aut ex pharisaeis? [49]Sed turba haec, quae non novit legem, maledicti sunt!». [50]Dicit Nicodemus ad eos, ille qui venit ad eum antea, qui unus erat ex ipsis: [51]«Numquid lex nostra iudicat hominem, nisi audierit ab ipso prius et cognoverit quid faciat?». [52]Responderunt et dixerunt ei: «Numquid et tu ex Galilaea es? Scrutare et vide quia propheta a Galilaea non surgit!». [53]Et reversi sunt unusquisque in domum suam. **[8]** [1]Iesus autem perrexit in montem Oliveti. [2]Diluculo autem iterum venit in templum, et omnis populus veniebat ad eum, et sedens docebat eos. [3]Adducunt autem scribae et pharisaei mulierem in adulterio deprehensam et statuerunt eam in medio [4]et dicunt ei: «Magister, haec mulier manifesto deprehensa est in adulterio. [5]In lege autem Moyses mandavit nobis huiusmodi lapidare; tu ergo quid dicis?». [6]Hoc autem dicebant tentantes eum, ut possent accusare eum. Iesus autem inclinans se deorsum digito scribebat in terra. [7]Cum autem perseverarent interrogantes eum, erexit se et dixit eis: «Qui sine peccato est vestrum, primus in illam lapidem mittat»; [8]et iterum se inclinans scribebat in terra. [9]Audientes autem unus post unum exibant, incipientes a senioribus, et remansit solus, et mulier in medio stans. [10]Erigens autem se Iesus dixit ei: «Mulier, ubi sunt? Nemo te condemnavit?». [11]Quae dixit: «Nemo, Domine». Dixit autem Iesus: «Nec ego te condemno; vade et amplius iam noli peccare». [12]Iterum ergo locutus est eis Iesus dicens: «Ego sum lux mundi; qui sequitur me, non ambulabit in tenebris, sed habebit lucem vitae». [13]Dixerunt ergo ei pharisaei: «Tu de teipso testimonium perhibes; testimonium tuum non est verum». [14]Respondit Iesus et dixit eis: «Et si ego testimonium perhibeo de meipso, verum est testimonium meum, quia scio unde veni et quo vado; vos autem nescitis unde venio aut quo vado. [15]Vos secundum carnem iudicatis, ego non iudico quemquam. [16]Et si iudico ego, iudicium meum verum est, quia solus non sum, sed ego et, qui me misit, Pater. [17]Sed et in lege vestra scriptum est quia duorum hominum testimonium verum est. [18]Ego sum, qui testimonium perhibeo de meipso, et testimonium perhibet de me, qui misit me, Pater». [19]Dicebant ergo ei: «Ubi est Pater tuus?». Respondit Iesus: «Neque me scitis neque Patrem meum; si me sciretis, forsitan et Patrem meum sciretis». [20]Haec verba locutus est in gazophylacio docens in templo; et nemo apprehendit eum, quia necdum venerat hora eius. [21]Dixit ergo iterum eis: «Ego vado, et quaeretis me et in peccato vestro moriemini! Quo ego vado, vos non potestis venire». [22]Dicebant ergo Iudaei: «Numquid interficiet semetipsum, quia dicit: "Quo ego vado, vos non potestis venire"?». [23]Et dicebat eis: «Vos de deorsum estis, ego de supernis sum; vos de mundo hoc estis, ego non sum de hoc mundo. [24]Dixi ergo vobis quia moriemini in peccatis vestris; si enim non credideritis quia ego sum, moriemini in peccatis vestris». [25]Dicebant ergo ei: «Tu quis es?». Dixit eis Iesus: «In principio: id quod et loquor vobis! [26]Multa habeo de vobis loqui et iudicare; sed, qui misit me, verax est, et ego, quae audivi ab eo, haec loquor ad mundum». [27]Non cognoverunt quia Patrem eis dicebat. [28]Dixit ergo eis Iesus: «Cum exaltaveritis Filium hominis, tunc cognoscetis quia ego sum, et a meipso facio nihil, sed, sicut docuit me Pater, haec loquor. [29]Et qui me misit, mecum est; non reliquit me solum, quia ego, quae placita sunt ei, facio semper». [30]Haec illo loquente, multi crediderunt in eum. [31]Dicebat ergo Iesus ad eos, qui crediderunt ei, Iudaeos: «Si vos manseritis in sermone meo, vere discipuli mei estis [32]et cognoscetis veritatem, et veritas liberabit vos». [33]Responderunt ei: «Semen Abrahae sumus et nemine servivimus umquam? Quomodo tu dicis: "Liberi fietis"?». [34]Respondit eis Iesus: «Amen, amen dico vobis: Omnis, qui facit peccatum, servus est. [35]Servus autem non manet in domo in aeternum; filius manet in aeternum. [36]Si ergo Filius vos liberaverit, vere liberi eritis. [37]Scio quia semen Abrahae estis; sed quaeritis me interficere, quia sermo meus non capit in vobis. [38]Ego, quae vidi apud Patrem, loquor; et vos ergo, quae audivistis a patre, facitis». [39]Responderunt et dixerunt ei: «Pater noster Abraham est». Dicit eis Iesus: «Si filii Abrahae essetis, opera Abrahae faceretis. [40]Nunc autem quaeritis me interficere, hominem, qui veritatem vobis locutus sum, quam audivi a Deo; hoc Abraham non fecit. [41]Vos facitis opera patris vestri». Dixerunt itaque ei: «Nos ex fornicatione non sumus nati; unum patrem habemus Deum!». [42]Dixit eis Iesus: «Si Deus pater vester esset, diligeretis me; ego enim ex Deo processi et veni, neque enim a meipso veni, sed ille me misit. [43]Quare loquelam meam non cognoscitis? Quia non potestis audire sermonem meum. [44]Vos ex patre Diabolo estis et desideria patris vestri vultis facere. Ille homicida erat ab initio et in veritate non stabat, quia non est veritas in eo. Cum loquitur mendacium, ex propriis loquitur, quia mendax est et pater eius. [45]Ego autem quia veritatem dico non creditis mihi. [46]Quis ex vobis arguit me de peccato? Si veritatem dico, quare vos non creditis mihi? [47]Qui est ex Deo, verba Dei audit; propterea vos non auditis, quia ex Deo non estis». [48]Responderunt Iudaei et dixerunt ei: «Nonne bene dicimus nos quia Samaritanus es tu et daemonium habes?». [49]Respondit Iesus: «Ego daemonium non habeo, sed honorifico Patrem meum, et vos inhonoratis me. [50]Ego autem non quaero gloriam meam; est qui quaerit et iudicat. [51]Amen, amen dico vobis: Si quis sermonem meum servaverit, mortem non videbit in aeternum». [52]Dixerunt ergo ei Iudaei: «Nunc cognovimus quia daemonium habes. Abraham mortuus est et prophetae, et tu dicis: "Si quis sermonem meum servaverit, non gustabit mortem in aeternum". [53]Numquid tu maior es patre nostro Abraham, qui mortuus est? Et prophetae mortui sunt! Quem teipsum facis?». [54]Respondit Iesus: «Si ego glorifico meipsum, gloria mea nihil est; est Pater meus, qui glorificat me, quem vos dicitis: "Deus noster est!", [55]et non cognovistis eum. Ego autem novi eum. Et si dixero: Non scio eum, ero similis vobis, mendax; sed scio eum et sermonem eius servo. [56]Abraham pater vester exsultavit, ut videret diem meum, et vidit et gavisus est». [57]Dixerunt ergo Iudaei ad eum: «Quinquaginta annos nondum habes et Abraham vidisti?». [58]Dixit eis Iesus: «Amen, amen dico vobis: Antequam Abraham fieret, ego sum». [59]Tulerunt ergo lapides, ut iacerent in eum; Iesus autem abscondit se et exivit de templo. [9] [1]Et praeteriens vidit hominem caecum a nativitate. [2]Et interrogaverunt eum discipuli sui dicentes: «Rabbi, quis peccavit, hic aut parentes eius, ut caecus nasceretur?». [3]Respondit Iesus: «Neque hic peccavit neque parentes eius, sed ut manifestentur opera Dei in illo. [4]Nos oportet operari opera eius, qui misit me, donec dies est; venit nox, quando nemo potest operari. [5]Quamdiu in mundo sum, lux sum mundi». [6]Haec cum dixisset, exspuit in terram et fecit lutum ex sputo et linivit lutum super oculos eius [7]et dixit ei: «Vade, lava in natatoria Siloae!»—quod interpretatur Missus—. Abiit ergo et lavit et venit videns. [8]Itaque vicini et, qui videbant eum prius quia mendicus erat, dicebant: «Nonne hic est, qui sedebat et mendicabat?»; ⁹alii dicebant: «Hic est!»; alii dicebant: «Nequaquam, sed similis est eius!». Ille dicebat: «Ego sum!». ¹⁰Dicebant ergo ei: «Quomodo igitur aperti sunt oculi tibi?». ¹¹Respondit ille: «Homo, qui dicitur Iesus, lutum fecit et unxit oculos meos et dixit mihi: 'Vade ad Siloam et lava!'. Abii ergo et lavi et vidi». ¹²Et dixerunt ei: «Ubi est ille?». Ait: «Nescio». ¹³Adducunt eum ad pharisaeos, qui caecus fuerat. ¹⁴Erat autem sabbatum, in qua die lutum fecit Iesus et aperuit oculos eius. ¹⁵Iterum ergo interrogabant et eum pharisaei quomodo vidisset. Ille autem dixit eis: «Lutum posuit super oculos meos, et lavi et video». ¹⁶Dicebant ergo ex pharisaeis quidam: «Non est hic homo a Deo, quia sabbatum non custodit!»; alii autem dicebant: «Quomodo potest homo peccator haec signa facere?». Et schisma erat in eis. ¹⁷Dicunt ergo caeco iterum: «Tu quid dicis de eo quia aperuit oculos tuos?». Ille autem dixit: «Propheta est!». ¹⁸Non crediderunt ergo Iudaei de illo quia caecus fuisset et vidisset, donec vocaverunt parentes eius, qui viderat. ¹⁹Et interrogaverunt eos dicentes: «Hic est filius vester, quem vos dicitis quia caecus natus est? Quomodo ergo nunc videt?». ²⁰Responderunt ergo parentes eius et dixerunt: «Scimus quia hic est filius noster et quia caecus natus est. ²¹Quomodo autem nunc videat nescimus, aut quis eius aperuit oculos nos nescimus; ipsum interrogate. Aetatem habet; ipse de se loquetur!». ²²Haec dixerunt parentes eius, quia timebant Iudaeos; iam enim conspiraverant Iudaei, ut, si quis eum confiteretur Christum, extra synagogam fieret. ²³Propterea parentes eius dixerunt: «Aetatem habet; ipsum interrogate!». ²⁴Vocaverunt ergo rursum hominem, qui fuerat caecus, et dixerunt ei: «Da gloriam Deo! Nos scimus quia hic homo peccator est». ²⁵Respondit ergo ille: «Si peccator est nescio; unum scio quia caecus cum essem, modo video». ²⁶Dixerunt ergo illi: «Quid fecit tibi? Quomodo aperuit oculos tuos?». ²⁷Respondit eis: «Dixi vobis iam, et non audistis; quid iterum vultis audire? Numquid et vos vultis discipuli eius fieri?». ²⁸Et maledixerunt ei et dixerunt: «Tu discipulus illius es, nos autem Moysis discipuli sumus. ²⁹Nos scimus quia Moysi locutus est Deus, hunc autem nescimus unde sit». ³⁰Respondit homo et dixit eis: «In hoc enim mirabile est quia vos nescitis unde sit, et aperuit meos oculos! ³¹Scimus quia peccatores Deus non audit, sed si quis Dei cultor est et voluntatem eius facit, hunc exaudit. ³²A saeculo non est auditum quia aperuit quis oculos caeci nati; ³³nisi esset hic a Deo, non poterat facere quidquam». ³⁴Responderunt et dixerunt ei: «In peccatis tu natus es totus et tu doces nos?». Et eiecerunt eum foras. ³⁵Audivit Iesus quia eiecerunt eum foras et, cum invenisset eum, dixit ei: «Tu credis in Filium hominis?». ³⁶Respondit ille et dixit: «Et quis est, Domine, ut credam in eum?». ³⁷Dixit ei Iesus: «Et vidisti eum et, qui loquitur tecum, ipse est». ³⁸At ille ait: «Credo, Domine!»; et adoravit eum. ³⁹Et dixit Iesus: «In iudicium ego in hunc mundum veni, ut, qui non vident, videant, et, qui vident, caeci fiant». ⁴⁰Audierunt haec ex pharisaeis, qui cum ipso erant, et dixerunt ei: «Numquid et nos caeci sumus?». ⁴¹Dixit eis Iesus: «Si caeci essetis, non haberetis peccatum. Nunc vero dicitis: "Videmus!"; peccatum vestrum manet». **[10]** ¹«Amen, amen dico vobis: Qui non intrat per ostium in ovile ovium, sed ascendit aliunde, ille fur est et latro; ²qui autem intrat per ostium, pastor est ovium. ³Huic ostiarius aperit, et oves vocem eius audiunt, et proprias oves vocat nominatim et educit eas. ⁴Cum proprias omnes emiserit, ante eas vadit, et oves illum sequuntur, quia sciunt vocem eius; ⁵alienum autem non sequentur, sed fugient ab eo, quia non noverunt vocem alienorum». ⁶Hoc proverbium dixit eis Iesus; illi autem non cognoverunt quid esset, quod loquebatur eis. ⁷Dixit ergo iterum Iesus: «Amen, amen dico vobis: Ego sum ostium ovium. ⁸Omnes, quotquot venerunt ante me, fures sunt et latrones, sed non audierunt eos oves. ⁹Ego sum ostium: per me si quis introierit, salvabitur et ingredietur et egredietur et pascua inveniet. ¹⁰Fur non venit, nisi ut furetur et mactet et perdat; ego veni, ut vitam habeant et abundantius habeant. ¹¹Ego sum pastor bonus: bonus pastor animam suam ponit pro ovibus; ¹²mercennarius et, qui non est pastor, cuius non sunt oves propriae, videt lupum venientem et dimittit oves et fugit —et lupus rapit eas et dispergit— ¹³quia mercennarius est, et non pertinet ad eum de ovibus. ¹⁴Ego sum pastor bonus: et cognosco meas, et cognoscunt me meae, ¹⁵sicut cognoscit me Pater, et ego cognosco Patrem; et animam meam pono pro ovibus. ¹⁶Et alias oves habeo, quae non sunt ex hoc ovili, et illas oportet me adducere, et vocem meam audient et fient unus grex, unus pastor. ¹⁷Propterea me Pater diligit, quia ego pono animam meam, ut iterum sumam eam. ¹⁸Nemo tollit eam a me, sed ego pono eam a meipso. Potestatem habeo ponendi eam et potestatem habeo iterum sumendi eam. Hoc mandatum accepi a Patre meo». ¹⁹Dissensio iterum facta est inter Iudaeos propter sermones hos. ²⁰Dicebant autem multi ex ipsis: «Daemonium habet et insanit! Quid eum auditis?». ²¹Alii dicebant: «Haec verba non sunt daemonium habentis! Numquid daemonium potest caecorum oculos aperire?». ²²Facta sunt tunc Encaenia in Hierosolymis. Hiems erat; ²³et ambulabat Iesus in templo in porticu Salomonis. ²⁴Circumdederunt ergo eum Iudaei et dicebant ei: «Quousque animam nostram tollis? Si tu es Christus, dic nobis palam!». ²⁵Respondit eis Iesus: «Dixi vobis, et non creditis; opera, quae ego facio in nomine Patris mei, haec testimonium perhibent de me. ²⁶Sed vos non creditis, quia non estis ex ovibus meis. ²⁷Oves meae vocem meam audiunt, et ego cognosco eas, et sequuntur me, [28]et ego vitam aeternam do eis, et non peribunt in aeternum, et non rapiet eas quisquam de manu mea. [29]Pater meus quod dedit mihi, maius omnibus est, et nemo potest rapere de manu Patris. [30]Ego et Pater unum sumus». [31]Sustulerunt iterum lapides Iudaei, ut lapidarent eum. [32]Respondit eis Iesus: «Multa opera bona ostendi vobis ex Patre; propter quod eorum opus me lapidatis?». [33]Responderunt ei Iudaei: «De bono opere non lapidamus te sed de blasphemia, et quia tu, homo cum sis, facis teipsum Deum». [34]Respondit eis Iesus: «Nonne scriptum est in lege vestra: *"Ego dixi: Dii estis?"* [35]Si illos dixit deos ad quos sermo Dei factus est, et non potest solvi Scriptura, [36]quem Pater sanctificavit et misit in mundum, vos dicitis: "Blasphemas!", quia dixi: Filius Dei sum? [37]Si non facio opera Patris mei, nolite credere mihi; [38]si autem facio, et si mihi non vultis credere, operibus credite, ut cognoscatis et sciatis quia in me est Pater, et ego in Patre». [39]Quaerebant ergo iterum eum prehendere; et exivit de manibus eorum. [40]Et abiit iterum trans Iordanem, in eum locum, ubi erat Ioannes baptizans primum, et mansit illic. [41]Et multi venerunt ad eum et dicebant: «Ioannes quidem signum fecit nullum; omnia autem, quaecumque dixit Ioannes de hoc, vera erant». [42]Et multi crediderunt in eum illic.   **[11]** [1]Erat autem quidam languens Lazarus a Bethania, de castello Mariae et Marthae sororis eius. [2]Maria autem erat, quae unxit Dominum unguento et extersit pedes eius capillis suis, cuius frater Lazarus infirmabatur. [3]Miserunt ergo sorores ad eum dicentes: «Domine, ecce, quem amas, infirmatur». [4]Audiens autem Iesus dixit: «Infirmitas haec non est ad mortem sed pro gloria Dei, ut glorificetur Filius Dei per eam».[5]Diligebat autem Iesus Martham et sororem eius et Lazarum. [6]Ut ergo audivit quia infirmabatur, tunc quidem mansit in loco, in quo erat, duobus diebus; [7]deinde post hoc dicit discipulis: «Eamus in Iudaeam iterum». [8]Dicunt ei discipuli: «Rabbi, nunc quaerebant te Iudaei lapidare, et iterum vadis illuc?». [9]Respondit Iesus: «Nonne duodecim horae sunt diei? Si quis ambulaverit in die, non offendit, quia lucem huius mundi videt; [10]si quis autem ambulaverit in nocte, offendit, quia lux non est in eo». [11]Haec ait et post hoc dicit eis: «Lazarus amicus noster dormit, sed vado, ut a somno exsuscitem eum». [12]Dixerunt ergo ei discipuli: «Domine, si dormit, salvus erit». [13]Dixerat autem Iesus de morte eius, illi autem putaverunt quia de dormitione somni diceret. [14]Tunc ergo dixit eis Iesus manifeste: «Lazarus mortuus est, [15]et gaudeo propter vos, ut credatis, quoniam non eram ibi; sed eamus ad eum». [16]Dixit ergo Thomas, qui dicitur Didymus, ad condiscipulos: «Eamus et nos, ut moriamur cum eo!». [17]Venit itaque Iesus et invenit eum quattuor dies iam in monumento habentem. [18]Erat autem Bethania iuxta Hierosolymam quasi stadiis quindecim. [19]Multi autem ex Iudaeis venerant ad Martham et Mariam, ut consolarentur eas de fratre. [20]Martha ergo ut audivit quia Iesus venit, occurrit illi; Maria autem domi sedebat. [21]Dixit ergo Martha ad Iesum: «Domine, si fuisses hic, frater meus non esset mortuus! [22]Sed et nunc scio quia, quaecumque poposceris a Deo, dabit tibi Deus». [23]Dicit illi Iesus: «Resurget frater tuus». [24]Dicit ei Martha: «Scio quia resurget in resurrectione in novissimo die». [25]Dixit ei Iesus: «Ego sum resurrectio et vita. Qui credit in me, et si mortuus fuerit, vivet; [26]et omnis, qui vivit et credit in me, non morietur in aeternum. Credis hoc?». [27]Ait illi: «Utique, Domine; ego credidi quia tu es Christus Filius Dei, qui in mundum venisti». [28]Et cum haec dixisset, abiit et vocavit Mariam sororem suam silentio dicens: «Magister adest et vocat te». [29]Illa autem ut audivit, surrexit cito et venit ad eum; [30]nondum enim venerat Iesus in castellum, sed erat adhuc in illo loco, ubi occurrerat ei Martha. [31]Iudaei igitur, qui erant cum ea in domo et consolabantur eam, cum vidissent Mariam quia cito surrexit et exiit, secuti sunt eam putantes: «Vadit ad monumentum, ut ploret ibi». [32]Maria ergo, cum venisset, ubi erat Iesus, videns eum cecidit ad pedes eius dicens ei: «Domine, si fuisses hic, non esset mortuus frater meus!». [33]Iesus ergo, ut vidit eam plorantem et Iudaeos, qui venerant cum ea, plorantes, fremuit spiritu et turbavit seipsum [34]et dixit: «Ubi posuistis eum?». Dicunt ei: «Domine, veni et vide». [35]Lacrimatus est Iesus. [36]Dicebant ergo Iudaei: «Ecce quomodo amabat eum!». [37]Quidam autem dixerunt ex ipsis: «Non poterat hic, qui aperuit oculos caeci, facere, ut et hic non moreretur?». [38]Iesus ergo rursum fremens in semetipso, venit ad monumentum; erat autem spelunca, et lapis superpositus erat ei. [39]Ait Iesus: «Tollite lapidem!». Dicit ei Martha, soror eius, qui mortuus fuerat: «Domine, iam foetet; quatriduanus enim est!». [40]Dicit ei Iesus: «Nonne dixi tibi quoniam si credideris, videbis gloriam Dei?». [41]Tulerunt ergo lapidem. Iesus autem, elevatis sursum oculis, dixit: «Pater, gratias ago tibi quoniam audisti me. [42]Ego autem sciebam quia semper me audis, sed propter populum, qui circumstat dixi, ut credant quia tu me misisti». [43]Et haec cum dixisset, voce magna clamavit: «Lazare, veni foras!». [44]Prodiit, qui fuerat mortuus, ligatus pedes et manus institis; et facies illius sudario erat ligata. Dicit Iesus eis: «Solvite eum et sinite eum abire». [45]Multi ergo ex Iudaeis, qui venerant ad Mariam et viderant, quae fecit, crediderunt in eum; [46]quidam autem ex ipsis abierunt ad pharisaeos et dixerunt eis, quae fecit Iesus. [47]Collegerunt ergo pontifices et pharisaei concilium et dicebant: «Quid facimus, quia hic homo multa signa facit? [48]Si dimittimus eum sic, omnes credent in eum, et venient Romani et tollent nostrum et locum et gentem!». [49]Unus autem ex ipsis, Caiphas, cum esset pontifex anni illius, dixit eis:

«Vos nescitis quidquam, ⁵⁰nec cogitatis quia expedit vobis, ut unus moriatur homo pro populo, et non tota gens pereat!». ⁵¹Hoc autem a semetipso non dixit, sed cum esset pontifex anni illius, prophetavit quia Iesus moriturus erat pro gente ⁵²et non tantum pro gente sed et ut filios Dei, qui erant dispersi, congregaret in unum. ⁵³Ab illo ergo die cogitaverunt, ut interficerent eum. ⁵⁴Iesus ergo iam non in palam ambulabat apud Iudaeos, sed abiit inde in regionem iuxta desertum, in civitatem, quae dicitur Ephraim, et ibi morabatur cum discipulis. ⁵⁵Proximum autem erat Pascha Iudaeorum, et ascenderunt multi Hierosolymam de regione ante Pascha, ut sanctificarent seipsos. ⁵⁶Quaerebant ergo Iesum et colloquebantur ad invicem in templo stantes: «Quid videtur vobis? Numquid veniet ad diem festum?». ⁵⁷Dederant autem pontifices et pharisaei mandatum, ut si quis cognoverit, ubi sit, indicet, ut apprehendant eum.   **[12]** ¹Iesus ergo ante sex dies Paschae venit Bethaniam, ubi erat Lazarus, quem suscitavit a mortuis Iesus. ²Fecerunt ergo ei cenam ibi, et Martha ministrabat, Lazarus vero unus erat ex discumbentibus cum eo. ³Maria ergo accepit libram unguenti nardi puri, pretiosi et unxit pedes Iesu et extersit capillis suis pedes eius; domus autem impleta est ex odore unguenti. ⁴Dicit autem Iudas Iscariotes, unus ex discipulis eius, qui erat eum traditurus: ⁵«Quare hoc unguentum non veniit trecentis denariis et datum est egenis?». ⁶Dixit autem hoc, non quia de egenis pertinebat ad eum, sed quia fur erat et, loculos habens, ea, quae mittebantur, portabat. ⁷Dixit ergo Iesus: «Sine illam, ut in diem sepulturae meae servet illud. ⁸Pauperes enim semper habetis vobiscum, me autem non semper habetis». ⁹Cognovit ergo turba multa ex Iudaeis quia illic est, et venerunt non propter Iesum tantum, sed ut et Lazarum viderent, quem suscitavit a mortuis. ¹⁰Cogitaverunt autem principes sacerdotum, ut et Lazarum interficerent, ¹¹quia multi propter illum abibant ex Iudaeis et credebant in Iesum. ¹²In crastinum turba multa, quae venerat ad diem festum, cum audissent quia venit Iesus Hierosolymam, ¹³acceperunt ramos palmarum et processerunt obviam ei et clamabant: «*Hosanna! / Benedictus, qui venit in nomine Domini, / et rex Israel!*». ¹⁴Invenit autem Iesus asellum et sedit super eum, sicut scriptum est: ¹⁵«*Noli timere, filia Sion. / Ecce rex tuus venit / sedens super pullum asinae*». ¹⁶Haec non cognoverunt discipuli eius primum, sed quando glorificatus est Iesus, tunc recordati sunt quia haec erant scripta de eo, et haec fecerunt ei. ¹⁷Testimonium ergo perhibebat turba, quae erat cum eo, quando Lazarum vocavit de monumento et suscitavit eum a mortuis. ¹⁸Propterea et obviam venit ei turba, quia audierunt eum fecisse hoc signum. ¹⁹Pharisaei ergo dixerunt ad semetipsos: «Videtis quia nihil proficitis? Ecce mundus post eum abiit!». ²⁰Erant autem Graeci quidam ex his, qui ascenderant, ut adorarent in die festo; ²¹hi ergo accesserunt ad Philippum, qui erat a Bethsaida Galilaeae, et rogabant eum dicentes: «Domine, volumus Iesum videre». ²²Venit Philippus et dicit Andreae; venit Andreas et Philippus et dicunt Iesu. ²³Iesus autem respondet eis dicens: «Venit hora, ut glorificetur Filius hominis. ²⁴Amen, amen dico vobis: Nisi granum frumenti cadens in terram mortuum fuerit, ipsum solum manet; si autem mortuum fuerit, multum fructum affert. ²⁵Qui amat animam suam, perdit eam; et, qui odit animam suam in hoc mundo, in vitam aeternam custodiet eam. ²⁶Si quis mihi ministrat, me sequatur, et ubi sum ego, illic et minister meus erit; si quis mihi ministraverit, honorificabit eum Pater. ²⁷Nunc anima mea turbata est. Et quid dicam? Pater, salvifica me ex hora hac? Sed propterea veni in horam hanc. ²⁸Pater, glorifica tuum nomen!». Venit ergo vox de caelo: «Et glorificavi et iterum glorificabo». ²⁹Turba ergo, quae stabat et audierat, dicebat tonitruum factum esse; alii dicebant: «Angelus ei locutus est». ³⁰Respondit Iesus et dixit: «Non propter me vox haec facta est sed propter vos. ³¹Nunc iudicium est huius mundi, nunc princeps huius mundi eicietur foras; ³²et ego, si exaltatus fuero a terra, omnes traham ad meipsum». ³³Hoc autem dicebat significans, qua morte esset moriturus. ³⁴Respondit ergo ei turba: «Nos audivimus ex lege quia Christus manet in aeternum; et quomodo tu dicis: "Oportet exaltari Filium hominis"? Quis est iste Filius hominis?». ³⁵Dixit ergo eis Iesus: «Adhuc modicum tempus lumen in vobis est. Ambulate, dum lucem habetis, ut non tenebrae vos comprehendant; et qui ambulat in tenebris, nescit quo vadat. ³⁶Dum lucem habetis, credite in lucem, ut filii lucis fiatis». Haec locutus est Iesus et abiit et abscondit se ab eis. ³⁷Cum autem tanta signa fecisset coram eis, non credebant in eum, ³⁸ut sermo Isaiae prophetae impleretur, quem dixit: «*Domine, quis credidit auditui nostro, / et brachium Domini cui revelatum est?*». ³⁹Propterea non poterant credere, quia iterum dixit Isaias: ⁴⁰«*Excaecavit oculos eorum / et induravit eorum cor, / ut non videant oculis / et intellegant corde et convertantur, / et sanem eos*». ⁴¹Haec dixit Isaias, quia vidit gloriam eius et locutus est de eo. ⁴²Verumtamen et ex principibus multi crediderunt in eum, sed propter pharisaeos non confitebantur, ut de synagoga non eicerentur; ⁴³dilexerunt enim gloriam hominum magis quam gloriam Dei. ⁴⁴Iesus autem clamavit et dixit: «Qui credit in me, non credit in me sed in eum, qui misit me; ⁴⁵et, qui videt me, videt eum, qui misit me. ⁴⁶Ego lux in mundum veni, ut omnis, qui credit in me, in tenebris non maneat. ⁴⁷Et si quis audierit verba mea et non custodierit, ego non iudico eum; non enim veni, ut iudicem mundum, sed ut salvificem mundum. ⁴⁸Qui spernit me et non accipit verba mea, habet, qui iudicet eum: sermo, quem locutus sum, ille iudicabit eum in novissimo die, [49]quia ego ex meipso non sum locutus, sed, qui misit me, Pater, ipse mihi mandatum dedit quid dicam et quid loquar. [50]Et scio quia mandatum eius vita aeterna est. Quae ergo ego loquor, sicut dixit mihi Pater, sic loquor». [13] [1]Ante diem autem festum Paschae, sciens Iesus quia venit eius hora, ut transeat ex hoc mundo ad Patrem, cum dilexisset suos, qui erant in mundo, in finem dilexit eos. [2]Et in cena, cum Diabolus iam misisset in corde, ut traderet eum Iudas Simonis Iscariotis, [3]sciens quia omnia dedit ei Pater in manus et quia a Deo exivit et ad Deum vadit, [4]surgit a cena et ponit vestimenta sua et, cum accepisset linteum, praecinxit se. [5]Deinde mittit aquam in pelvem et coepit lavare pedes discipulorum et extergere linteo, quo erat praecinctus. [6]Venit ergo ad Simonem Petrum. Dicit ei: «Domine, tu mihi lavas pedes?». [7]Respondit Iesus et dixit ei: «Quod ego facio, tu nescis modo, scies autem postea». [8]Dicit ei Petrus: «Non lavabis mihi pedes in aeternum!». Respondit Iesus ei: «Si non lavero te, non habes partem mecum». [9]Dicit ei Simon Petrus: «Domine, non tantum pedes meos, sed et manus et caput!». [10]Dicit ei Iesus: «Qui lotus est non indiget nisi ut pedes lavet, sed est mundus totus; et vos mundi estis, sed non omnes». [11]Sciebat enim quisnam esset, qui traderet eum; propterea dixit: «Non estis mundi omnes». [12]Postquam ergo lavit pedes eorum et accepit vestimenta sua, cum recubuisset iterum, dixit eis: «Scitis quid fecerim vobis? [13]Vos vocatis me: "Magister" et: "Domine", et bene dicitis; sum etenim. [14]Si ergo ego lavi vestros pedes, Dominus et Magister, et vos debetis alter alterius lavare pedes. [15]Exemplum enim dedi vobis, ut, quemadmodum ego feci vobis, et vos faciatis. [16]Amen, amen dico vobis: Non est servus maior domino suo, neque apostolus maior eo, qui misit illum. [17]Si haec scitis, beati estis, si facitis ea. [18]Non de omnibus vobis dico, ego scio, quos elegerim, sed ut impleatur Scriptura: *"Qui manducat meum panem, levavit contra me calcaneum suum"*. [19]Amodo dico vobis priusquam fiat, ut credatis cum factum fuerit, quia ego sum. [20]Amen, amen dico vobis: Qui accipit, si quem misero, me accipit; qui autem me accipit, accipit eum, qui me misit». [21]Cum haec dixisset Iesus, turbatus est spiritu et protestatus est et dixit: «Amen, amen dico vobis: Unus ex vobis tradet me». [22]Aspiciebant ad invicem discipuli, haesitantes de quo diceret. [23]Erat recumbens unus ex discipulis eius in sinu Iesu, quem diligebat Iesus. [24]Innuit ergo huic Simon Petrus, ut interrogaret: «Quis est, de quo dicit?». [25]Cum ergo recumberet ille ita supra pectus Iesu, dicit ei: «Domine, quis est?». [26]Respondet Iesus: «Ille est, cui ego intinctam buccellam porrexero». Cum ergo intinxisset buccellam dat Iudae Simonis Iscariotis. [27]Et post buccellam tunc introivit in illum Satanas. Dicit ergo ei Iesus: «Quod facis, fac citius». [28]Hoc autem nemo scivit discumbentium ad quid dixerit ei; [29]quidam enim putabant quia loculos habebat Iudas, quia dicit ei Iesus: «Eme ea, quae opus sunt nobis ad diem festum», aut egenis ut aliquid daret. [30]Cum ergo accepisset ille buccellam, exivit continuo; erat autem nox. [31]Cum ergo exisset, dicit Iesus: «Nunc clarificatus est Filius hominis, et Deus clarificatus est in eo; [32]si Deus clarificatus est in eo, et Deus clarificabit eum in semetipso, et continuo clarificabit eum. [33]Filioli, adhuc modicum vobiscum sum; quaeretis me, et sicut dixi Iudaeis: Quo ego vado, vos non potestis venire, et vobis dico modo. [34]Mandatum novum do vobis, ut diligatis invicem; sicut dilexi vos, ut et vos diligatis invicem. [35]In hoc cognoscent omnes quia mei discipuli estis: si dilectionem habueritis ad invicem». [36]Dicit ei Simon Petrus: «Domine, quo vadis?». Respondit Iesus: «Quo vado, non potes me modo sequi, sequeris autem postea». [37]Dicit ei Petrus: «Domine, quare non possum te sequi modo? Animam meam pro te ponam». [38]Respondet Iesus: «Animam tuam pro me pones? Amen, amen dico tibi: Non cantabit gallus, donec me ter neges. [14] [1]Non turbetur cor vestrum. Creditis in Deum et in me credite. [2]In domo Patris mei mansiones multae sunt; si quo minus, dixissem vobis quia vado parare vobis locum? [3]Et si abiero et praeparavero vobis locum, iterum venio et accipiam vos ad meipsum, ut, ubi sum ego, et vos sitis. [4]Et quo ego vado, scitis viam». [5]Dicit ei Thomas: «Domine, nescimus quo vadis; quomodo possumus viam scire?». [6]Dicit ei Iesus: «Ego sum via et veritas et vita; nemo venit ad Patrem nisi per me. [7]Si cognovistis me, et Patrem meum utique cognoscetis; et amodo cognoscitis eum et vidistis eum». [8]Dicit ei Philippus: «Domine, ostende nobis Patrem, et sufficit nobis». [9]Dicit ei Iesus: «Tanto tempore vobiscum sum, et non cognovisti me, Philippe? Qui vidit me, vidit Patrem. Quomodo tu dicis: "Ostende nobis Patrem"? [10]Non credis quia ego in Patre, et Pater in me est? Verba, quae ego loquor vobis, a meipso non loquor; Pater autem in me manens facit opera sua. [11]Credite mihi quia ego in Patre, et Pater in me est; alioquin propter opera ipsa credite. [12]Amen, amen dico vobis: Qui credit in me, opera, quae ego facio, et ipse faciet et maiora horum faciet, quia ego ad Patrem vado. [13]Et quodcumque petieritis in nomine meo, hoc faciam, ut glorificetur Pater in Filio; [14]si quid petieritis me in nomine meo, ego faciam. [15]Si diligitis me, mandata mea servabitis; [16]et ego rogabo Patrem, et alium Paraclitum dabit vobis, ut maneat vobiscum in aeternum, [17]Spiritum veritatis, quem mundus non potest accipere, quia non videt eum nec cognoscit. Vos cognoscitis eum, quia apud vos manet; et in vobis erit. [18]Non relinquam vos orphanos, venio ad vos. [19]Adhuc modicum, et mundus me iam non videt; vos autem videtis me, quia ego vivo et vos vivetis. [20]In illo die vos cognoscetis quia ego sum in Patre meo, et vos in me et ego in vobis. [21]Qui habet mandata mea et servat ea, ille est qui diligit me; qui autem diligit me, diligetur a Patre meo, et ego diligam eum et manifestabo ei meipsum». [22]Dicit ei Iudas, non ille Iscariotes: «Domine, et quid factum est, quia nobis manifestaturus es teipsum et non mundo?». [23]Respondit Iesus et dixit ei: «Si quis diligit me, sermonem meum servabit, et Pater meus diliget eum, et ad eum veniemus et mansionem apud eum faciemus; [24]qui non diligit me, sermones meos non servat. Et sermo quem auditis, non est meus, sed eius qui misit me, Patris. [25]Haec locutus sum vobis apud vos manens. [26]Paraclitus autem, Spiritus Sanctus, quem mittet Pater in nomine meo, ille vos docebit omnia et suggeret vobis omnia, quae dixi vobis. [27]Pacem relinquo vobis, pacem meam do vobis; non quomodo mundus dat, ego do vobis. Non turbetur cor vestrum neque formidet. [28]Audistis quia ego dixi vobis: Vado et venio ad vos. Si diligeretis me, gauderetis quia vado ad Patrem, quia Pater maior me est. [29]Et nunc dixi vobis, priusquam fiat, ut, cum factum fuerit, credatis. [30]Iam non multa loquar vobiscum, venit enim princeps mundi et in me non habet quidquam, [31]sed, ut cognoscat mundus quia diligo Patrem, et sicut mandatum dedit mihi Pater, sic facio. Surgite, eamus hinc.   **[15]** [1]Ego sum vitis vera, et Pater meus agricola est. [2]Omnem palmitem in me non ferentem fructum, tollit eum; et omnem, qui fert fructum, purgat eum, ut fructum plus afferat. [3]Iam vos mundi estis propter sermonem, quem locutus sum vobis. [4]Manete in me, et ego in vobis. Sicut palmes non potest ferre fructum a semetipso, nisi manserit in vite, sic nec vos, nisi in me manseritis. [5]Ego sum vitis, vos palmites. Qui manet in me, et ego in eo, hic fert fructum multum, quia sine me nihil potestis facere. [6]Si quis in me non manserit, missus est foras sicut palmes et aruit, et colligunt eos et in ignem mittunt, et ardent. [7]Si manseritis in me, et verba mea in vobis manserint, quodcumque volueritis, petite, et fiet vobis. [8]In hoc clarificatus est Pater meus, ut fructum multum afferatis et efficiamini mei discipuli. [9]Sicut dilexit me Pater, et ego dilexi vos; manete in dilectione mea. [10]Si praecepta mea servaveritis, manebitis in dilectione mea, sicut ego Patris mei praecepta servavi et maneo in eius dilectione. [11]Haec locutus sum vobis, ut gaudium meum in vobis sit, et gaudium vestrum impleatur. [12]Hoc est praeceptum meum, ut diligatis invicem, sicut dilexi vos; [13]maiorem hac dilectionem nemo habet, ut animam suam quis ponat pro amicis suis. [14]Vos amici mei estis, si feceritis, quae ego praecipio vobis. [15]Iam non dico vos servos, quia servus nescit quid facit dominus eius; vos autem dixi amicos, quia omnia, quae audivi a Patre meo, nota feci vobis. [16]Non vos me elegistis, sed ego elegi vos et posui vos, ut vos eatis et fructum afferatis, et fructus vester maneat, ut quodcumque petieritis Patrem in nomine meo, det vobis. [17]Haec mando vobis, ut diligatis invicem. [18]Si mundus vos odit, scitote quia me priorem vobis odio habuit. [19]Si de mundo essetis, mundus, quod suum est, diligeret; quia vero de mundo non estis, sed ego elegi vos de mundo, propterea odit vos mundus. [20]Mementote sermonis, quem ego dixi vobis: Non est servus maior domino suo. Si me persecuti sunt, et vos persequentur; si sermonem meum servaverunt, et vestrum servabunt. [21]Sed haec omnia facient vobis propter nomen meum, quia nesciunt eum, qui misit me. [22]Si non venissem et locutus fuissem eis, peccatum non haberent; nunc autem excusationem non habent de peccato suo. [23]Qui me odit, et Patrem meum odit. [24]Si opera non fecissem in eis, quae nemo alius fecit, peccatum non haberent; nunc autem et viderunt et oderunt et me et Patrem meum. [25]Sed ut impleatur sermo, qui in lege eorum scriptus est: *"Odio me habuerunt gratis"*. [26]Cum autem venerit Paraclitus, quem ego mittam vobis a Patre, Spiritum veritatis, qui a Patre procedit, ille testimonium perhibebit de me; [27]sed et vos testimonium perhibetis, quia ab initio mecum estis.   **[16]** [1]Haec locutus sum vobis, ut non scandalizemini. [2]Absque synagogis facient vos; sed venit hora, ut omnis, qui interficit vos, arbitretur obsequium se praestare Deo. [3]Et haec facient, quia non noverunt Patrem neque me. [4]Sed haec locutus sum vobis, ut, cum venerit hora eorum, reminiscamini eorum, quia ego dixi vobis. Haec autem vobis ab initio non dixi, quia vobiscum eram. [5]At nunc vado ad eum, qui me misit, et nemo ex vobis interrogat me: "Quo vadis?". [6]Sed quia haec locutus sum vobis, tristitia implevit cor vestrum. [7]Sed ego veritatem dico vobis: Expedit vobis, ut ego vadam. Si enim non abiero, Paraclitus non veniet ad vos; si autem abiero, mittam eum ad vos. [8]Et cum venerit ille, arguet mundum de peccato et de iustitia et de iudicio: [9]de peccato quidem, quia non credunt in me; [10]de iustitia vero, quia ad Patrem vado, et iam non videtis me; [11]de iudicio autem, quia princeps mundi huius iudicatus est. [12]Adhuc multa habeo vobis dicere, sed non potestis portare modo. [13]Cum autem venerit ille, Spiritus veritatis, deducet vos in omnem veritatem; non enim loquetur a semetipso, sed quaecumque audiet, loquetur et, quae ventura sunt, annuntiabit vobis. [14]Ille me clarificabit, quia de meo accipiet et annuntiabit vobis. [15]Omnia, quaecumque habet Pater, mea sunt; propterea dixi quia de meo accipit et annuntiabit vobis. [16]Modicum, et iam non videtis me, et iterum modicum, et videbitis me». [17]Dixerunt ergo ex discipulis eius ad invicem: «Quid est hoc, quod dicit nobis: "Modicum, et non videtis me, et iterum modicum et videbitis me" et: "Vado ad Patrem"?». [18]Dicebant ergo: «Quid est hoc, quod dicit: "Modicum"? Nescimus quid loquitur». [19]Cognovit Iesus quia volebant eum interrogare et dixit eis: «De hoc quaeritis inter vos quia dixi: "Modicum, et non videtis me, et iterum modicum, et videbitis me"? [20]Amen, amen dico vobis quia plorabitis et flebitis vos, mundus autem gaudebit; vos contristabimini, sed tristitia vestra vertetur in gaudium. [21]Mulier, cum parit, tristitiam habet, quia venit hora eius; cum autem pepererit puerum, iam non meminit pressurae propter gaudium quia natus est homo in mundum. [22]Et vos igitur nunc quidem tristitiam habetis; iterum autem videbo vos, et gaudebit cor vestrum, et gaudium vestrum nemo tollit a vobis. [23]Et in illo die me non rogabitis quidquam. Amen, amen dico vobis: Si quid petieritis Patrem in nomine meo, dabit vobis. [24]Usque modo non petistis quidquam in nomine meo. Petite et accipietis, ut gaudium vestrum sit plenum. [25]Haec in proverbiis locutus sum vobis; venit hora, cum iam non in proverbiis loquar vobis, sed palam de Patre annuntiabo vobis. [26]Illo die in nomine meo petetis, et non dico vobis quia ego rogabo Patrem de vobis; [27]ipse enim Pater amat vos, quia vos me amastis et credidistis quia ego a Deo exivi. [28]Exivi a Patre et veni in mundum; iterum relinquo mundum et vado ad Patrem». [29]Dicunt discipuli eius: «Ecce nunc palam loqueris, et proverbium nullum dicis. [30]Nunc scimus quia scis omnia et non opus est tibi, ut quis te interroget; in hoc credimus quia a Deo existi». [31]Respondit eis Iesus: «Modo creditis? [32]Ecce venit hora et iam venit, ut dispergamini unusquisque in propria et me solum relinquatis; et non sum solus, quia Pater mecum est. [33]Haec locutus sum vobis, ut in me pacem habeatis; in mundo pressuram habetis, sed confidite, ego vici mundum». **[17]** [1]Haec locutus est Iesus; et sublevatis oculis suis in caelum dixit: «Pater, venit hora: clarifica Filium tuum, ut Filius clarificet te, [2]sicut dedisti ei potestatem omnis carnis, ut omne, quod dedisti ei, det eis vitam aeternam. [3]Haec est autem vita aeterna, ut cognoscant te solum verum Deum et, quem misisti, Iesum Christum. [4]Ego te clarificavi super terram: opus consummavi, quod dedisti mihi, ut faciam; [5]et nunc clarifica me tu, Pater, apud temetipsum claritate, quam habebam, priusquam mundus esset, apud te. [6]Manifestavi nomen tuum hominibus, quos dedisti mihi de mundo. Tui erant, et mihi eos dedisti, et sermonem tuum servaverunt. [7]Nunc cognoverunt quia omnia, quae dedisti mihi, abs te sunt, [8]quia verba, quae dedisti mihi, dedi eis, et ipsi acceperunt et cognoverunt vere quia a te exivi, et crediderunt quia tu me misisti. [9]Ego pro eis rogo; non pro mundo rogo, sed pro his, quos dedisti mihi, quia tui sunt, [10]et mea omnia tua sunt et tua mea; et clarificatus sum in eis. [11]Et iam non sum in mundo, et hi in mundo sunt, et ego ad te venio. Pater sancte, serva eos in nomine tuo, quod dedisti mihi, ut sint unum sicut nos. [12]Cum essem cum eis, ego servabam eos in nomine tuo, quod dedisti mihi et custodivi, et nemo ex his periit nisi filius perditionis, ut Scriptura impleatur. [13]Nunc autem ad te venio et haec loquor in mundo, ut habeant gaudium meum impletum in semetipsis. [14]Ego dedi eis sermonem tuum, et mundus odio eos habuit, quia non sunt de mundo, sicut ego non sum de mundo. [15]Non rogo, ut tollas eos de mundo, sed ut serves eos ex Malo. [16]De mundo non sunt, sicut ego non sum de mundo. [17]Sanctifica eos in veritate; sermo tuus veritas est. [18]Sicut me misisti in mundum, et ego misi eos in mundum; [19]et pro eis ego sanctifico meipsum, ut sint et ipsi sanctificati in veritate. [20]Non pro his autem rogo tantum, sed et pro eis, qui credituri sunt per verbum eorum in me, [21]ut omnes unum sint, sicut tu, Pater, in me et ego in te, ut et ipsi in nobis unum sint: ut mundus credat quia tu me misisti. [22]Et ego claritatem, quam dedisti mihi, dedi illis, ut sint unum, sicut nos unum sumus; [23]ego in eis, et tu in me, ut sint consummati in unum: ut cognoscat mundus quia tu me misisti et dilexisti eos, sicut me dilexisti. [24]Pater, quod dedisti mihi, volo, ut ubi ego sum, et illi sint mecum, ut videant claritatem meam, quam dedisti mihi, quia dilexisti me ante constitutionem mundi. [25]Pater iuste, et mundus te non cognovit; ego autem te cognovi et hi cognoverunt quia tu me misisti, [26]et notum feci eis nomen tuum et notum faciam, ut dilectio, qua dilexisti me, in ipsis sit, et ego in ipsis». **[18]** [1]Haec cum dixisset Iesus, egressus est cum discipulis suis trans torrentem Cedron, ubi erat hortus, in quem introivit ipse et discipuli eius. [2]Sciebat autem et Iudas, qui tradebat eum, locum, quia frequenter Iesus convenerat illuc cum discipulis suis. [3]Iudas ergo, cum accepisset cohortem et a pontificibus et pharisaeis ministros, venit illuc cum lanternis et facibus et armis. [4]Iesus itaque, sciens omnia, quae ventura erant super eum, processit et dicit eis: «Quem quaeritis?». [5]Responderunt ei: «Iesum Nazarenum». Dicit eis: «Ego sum!». Stabat autem et Iudas, qui tradebat eum, cum ipsis. [6]Ut ergo dixit eis: «Ego sum!», abierunt retrorsum et ceciderunt in terram. [7]Iterum ergo eos interrogavit: «Quem quaeritis?». Illi autem dixerunt: «Iesum Nazarenum». [8]Respondit Iesus: «Dixi vobis: Ego sum! Si ergo me quaeritis, sinite hos abire», [9]ut impleretur sermo quem dixit: «Quos dedisti mihi, non perdidi ex ipsis quemquam». [10]Simon ergo Petrus, habens gladium, eduxit eum et percussit pontificis servum et abscidit eius auriculam dextram. Erat autem nomen servo Malchus. [11]Dixit ergo Iesus Petro: «Mitte gladium in vaginam; calicem, quem dedit mihi Pater, non bibam illum?». [12]Cohors ergo et tribunus et ministri Iudaeorum comprehenderunt Iesum et ligaverunt eum [13]et adduxerunt ad Annam primum; erat enim socer Caiphae, qui erat pontifex anni illius. [14]Erat autem Caiphas, qui consilium dederat Iudaeis: «Expedit unum hominem mori pro populo». [15]Sequebatur autem Iesum Simon Petrus et alius discipulus. Discipulus autem ille erat notus pontifici et introivit cum Iesu in atrium pontificis; [16]Petrus autem stabat ad ostium foris. Exivit ergo discipulus alius, qui erat notus pontifici, et dixit ostiariae et introduxit Petrum. [17]Dicit ergo Petro ancilla ostiaria: «Numquid et tu ex discipulis es hominis istius?». Dicit ille: «Non sum!». [18]Stabant autem servi et ministri, qui prunas fecerant, quia frigus erat, et calefaciebant se; erat autem cum eis et Petrus stans et calefaciens se. [19]Pontifex ergo interrogavit Iesum de discipulis suis et de doctrina eius. [20]Respondit ei Iesus: «Ego palam locutus sum mundo; ego semper docui in synagoga et in templo, quo omnes Iudaei conveniunt, et in occulto locutus sum nihil. [21]Quid me interrogas? Interroga eos, qui audierunt quid locutus sum ipsis; ecce hi sciunt, quae dixerim ego». [22]Haec autem cum dixisset, unus assistens ministrorum dedit alapam Iesu dicens: «Sic respondes pontifici?». [23]Respondit ei Iesus: «Si male locutus sum, testimonium perhibe de malo; si autem bene, quid me caedis?». [24]Misit ergo eum Annas ligatum ad Caipham pontificem. [25]Erat autem Simon Petrus stans et calefaciens se. Dixerunt ergo ei: «Numquid et tu ex discipulis eius es?». Negavit ille et dixit: «Non sum!». [26]Dicit unus ex servis pontificis, cognatus eius, cuius abscidit Petrus auriculam: «Nonne ego te vidi in horto cum illo?». [27]Iterum ergo negavit Petrus; et statim gallus cantavit. [28]Adducunt ergo Iesum a Caipha in praetorium. Erat autem mane. Et ipsi non introierunt in praetorium, ut non contaminarentur, sed manducarent Pascha. [29]Exivit ergo Pilatus ad eos foras et dicit: «Quam accusationem affertis adversus hominem hunc?». [30]Responderunt et dixerunt ei: «Si non esset hic malefactor, non tibi tradidissemus eum». [31]Dixit ergo eis Pilatus: «Accipite eum vos et secundum legem vestram iudicate eum!». Dixerunt ei Iudaei: «Nobis non licet interficere quemquam», [32]ut sermo Iesu impleretur, quem dixit, significans qua esset morte moriturus. [33]Introivit ergo iterum in praetorium Pilatus et vocavit Iesum et dixit ei: «Tu es rex Iudaeorum?». [34]Respondit Iesus: «A temetipso tu hoc dicis, an alii tibi dixerunt de me?». [35]Respondit Pilatus: «Numquid ego Iudaeus sum? Gens tua et pontifices tradiderunt te mihi; quid fecisti?». [36]Respondit Iesus: «Regnum meum non est de mundo hoc; si ex hoc mundo esset regnum meum, ministri mei decertarent, ut non traderer Iudaeis; nunc autem meum regnum non est hinc». [37]Dixit itaque ei Pilatus: «Ergo rex es tu?». Respondit Iesus: «Tu dicis quia rex sum. Ego in hoc natus sum et ad hoc veni in mundum, ut testimonium perhibeam veritati; omnis, qui est ex veritate, audit meam vocem». [38]Dicit ei Pilatus: «Quid est veritas?». Et cum hoc dixisset, iterum exivit ad Iudaeos et dicit eis: «Ego nullam invenio in eo causam. [39]Est autem consuetudo vobis, ut unum dimittam vobis in Pascha; vultis ergo dimittam vobis regem Iudaeorum?». [40]Clamaverunt ergo rursum dicentes: «Non hunc, sed Barabbam!». Erat autem Barabbas latro.   **[19]** [1]Tunc ergo apprehendit Pilatus Iesum et flagellavit. [2]Et milites, plectentes coronam de spinis, imposuerunt capiti eius et veste purpurea circumdederunt eum; [3]et veniebant ad eum et dicebant: «Ave, rex Iudaeorum!», et dabant ei alapas. [4]Et exiit iterum Pilatus foras et dicit eis: «Ecce adduco vobis eum foras, ut cognoscatis quia in eo invenio causam nullam». [5]Exiit ergo Iesus foras, portans spineam coronam et purpureum vestimentum. Et dicit eis: «Ecce homo!». [6]Cum ergo vidissent eum pontifices et ministri, clamaverunt dicentes: «Crucifige, crucifige!». Dicit eis Pilatus: «Accipite eum vos et crucifigite; ego enim non invenio in eo causam». [7]Responderunt ei Iudaei: «Nos legem habemus, et secundum legem debet mori, quia Filium Dei se fecit». [8]Cum ergo audisset Pilatus hunc sermonem, magis timuit [9]et ingressus est praetorium iterum et dicit ad Iesum: «Unde es tu?». Iesus autem responsum non dedit ei. [10]Dicit ergo ei Pilatus: «Mihi non loqueris? Nescis quia potestatem habeo dimittere te et potestatem habeo crucifigere te?». [11]Respondit Iesus: «Non haberes potestatem adversum me ullam, nisi tibi esset datum desuper; propterea qui tradidit me tibi, maius peccatum habet». [12]Exinde quaerebat Pilatus dimittere eum; Iudaei autem clamabant dicentes: «Si hunc dimittis, non es amicus Caesaris! Omnis, qui se regem facit, contradicit Caesari». [13]Pilatus ergo, cum audisset hos sermones, adduxit foras Iesum et sedit pro tribunali in locum, qui dicitur Lithostrotos, Hebraice autem Gabbatha. [14]Erat autem Parasceve Paschae, hora erat quasi sexta. Et dicit Iudaeis: «Ecce rex vester!». [15]Clamaverunt ergo illi: «Tolle, tolle, crucifige eum!». Dicit eis Pilatus: «Regem vestrum crucifigam?». Responderunt pontifices: «Non habemus regem nisi Caesarem». [16]Tunc ergo tradidit eis illum, ut crucifigeretur. Susceperunt ergo Iesum. [17]Et baiulans sibi crucem exivit in eum, qui dicitur Calvariae locum, quod Hebraice dicitur Golgotha, [18]ubi eum crucifixerunt et cum eo alios duos hinc et hinc, medium autem Iesum. [19]Scripsit autem et titulum Pilatus et posuit super crucem; erat autem scriptum: «Iesus Nazarenus Rex Iudaeorum». [20]Hunc ergo titulum multi legerunt Iudaeorum, quia prope civitatem erat locus, ubi crucifixus est Iesus; et erat scriptum Hebraice, Latine, Graece. [21]Dicebant ergo Pilato pontifices Iudaeorum: «Noli scribere: Rex Iudaeorum, sed: Ipse dixit: 'Rex sum Iudaeorum'». [22]Respondit Pilatus: «Quod scripsi, scripsi!». [23]Milites ergo cum crucifixissent Iesum, acceperunt vestimenta eius et fecerunt quattuor partes, unicuique militi partem, et tunicam. Erat autem tunica inconsutilis, desuper contexta per totum. [24]Dixerunt ergo ad invicem: «Non scindamus eam, sed sortiamur de illa, cuius sit», ut Scriptura impleatur dicens: *«Partiti sunt vestimenta mea sibi / et in vestem meam miserunt sortem»*. Et milites quidem haec fecerunt. [25]Stabant autem iuxta crucem Iesu mater eius et soror matris eius, Maria Cleopae, et Maria Magdalene. [26]Cum vidisset ergo Iesus matrem et discipulum stantem, quem diligebat, dicit matri: «Mulier, ecce filius tuus». [27]Deinde dicit discipulo: «Ecce mater tua». Et ex illa hora accepit eam discipulus in sua. [28]Post hoc sciens Iesus quia iam omnia consummata sunt, ut consummaretur Scriptura, dicit: «Sitio». [29]Vas positum erat aceto plenum; spongiam ergo plenam aceto hyssopo circumponentes, obtulerunt ori eius. [30]Cum ergo accepisset acetum, Iesus dixit: «Consummatum est!». Et inclinato capite tradidit spiritum. [31]Iudaei ergo, quoniam Parasceve erat, ut non remanerent in cruce corpora sabbato, erat enim magnus dies illius sabbati, rogaverunt Pilatum, ut frangerentur eorum crura, et tollerentur. [32]Venerunt ergo milites et primi quidem fregerunt crura et alterius, qui crucifixus est cum eo; [33]ad Iesum autem cum venissent, ut viderunt eum iam mortuum, non fregerunt eius crura, [34]sed unus militum lancea latus eius aperuit, et continuo exivit sanguis et aqua. [35]Et qui vidit, testimonium perhibuit, et verum est eius testimonium, et ille scit quia vera dicit, ut et vos credatis. [36]Facta sunt enim haec, ut Scriptura impleatur: «*Os non comminuetur eius*», [37]et iterum alia Scriptura dicit: «*Videbunt in quem transfixerunt*». [38]Post haec autem rogavit Pilatum Ioseph ab Arimathaea, qui erat discipulus Iesu, occultus autem propter metum Iudaeorum, ut tolleret corpus Iesu; et permisit Pilatus. Venit ergo et tulit corpus eius. [39]Venit autem et Nicodemus, qui venerat ad eum nocte primum, ferens mixturam myrrhae et aloes quasi libras centum. [40]Acceperunt ergo corpus Iesu et ligaverunt illud linteis cum aromatibus, sicut mos Iudaeis est sepelire. [41]Erat autem in loco, ubi crucifixus est, hortus, et in horto monumentum novum, in quo nondum quisquam positus erat. [42]Ibi ergo propter Parascevem Iudaeorum, quia iuxta erat monumentum, posuerunt Iesum. **[20]** [1]Prima autem sabbatorum Maria Magdalene venit mane, cum adhuc tenebrae essent, ad monumentum, et videt lapidem sublatum a monumento. [2]Currit ergo et venit ad Simonem Petrum et ad alium discipulum, quem amabat Iesus, et dicit eis: «Tulerunt Dominum de monumento, et nescimus, ubi posuerunt eum!». [3]Exiit ergo Petrus et ille alius discipulus, et veniebant ad monumentum. [4]Currebant autem duo simul, et ille alius discipulus praecucurrit citius Petro et venit primus ad monumentum; [5]et cum se inclinasset, videt posita linteamina, non tamen introivit. [6]Venit ergo et Simon Petrus sequens eum et introivit in monumentum; et videt linteamina posita [7]et sudarium, quod fuerat super caput eius, non cum linteaminibus positum, sed separatim involutum in unum locum. [8]Tunc ergo introivit et alter discipulus, qui venerat primus ad monumentum, et vidit et credidit. [9]Nondum enim sciebant Scripturam quia oportet eum a mortuis resurgere. [10]Abierunt ergo iterum ad semetipsos discipuli. [11]Maria autem stabat ad monumentum foris plorans. Dum ergo fleret, inclinavit se in monumentum [12]et videt duos angelos in albis sedentes, unum ad caput et unum ad pedes, ubi positum fuerat corpus Iesu. [13]Et dicunt ei illi: «Mulier, quid ploras?». Dicit eis: «Tulerunt Dominum meum, et nescio, ubi posuerunt eum». [14]Haec cum dixisset, conversa est retrorsum et videt Iesum stantem et non sciebat quia Iesus est. [15]Dicit ei Iesus: «Mulier, quid ploras? Quem quaeris?». Illa, existimans quia hortulanus esset, dicit ei: «Domine, si tu sustulisti eum, dicito mihi, ubi posuisti eum, et ego eum tollam». [16]Dicit ei Iesus: «Maria!». Conversa illa dicit ei Hebraice: «Rabbuni!»—quod dicitur Magister—. [17]Dicit ei Iesus: «Iam noli me tenere, nondum enim ascendi ad Patrem; vade autem ad fratres meos et dic eis: Ascendo ad Patrem meum et Patrem vestrum, et Deum meum et Deum vestrum». [18]Venit Maria Magdalene annuntians discipulis: «Vidi Dominum!», et quia haec dixit ei. [19]Cum esset ergo sero die illa prima sabbatorum, et fores essent clausae, ubi erant discipuli propter metum Iudaeorum, venit Iesus et stetit in medio et dicit eis: «Pax vobis!». [20]Et hoc cum dixisset, ostendit eis manus et latus. Gavisi sunt ergo discipuli, viso Domino. [21]Dixit ergo eis iterum: «Pax vobis! Sicut misit me Pater, et ego mitto vos». [22]Et cum hoc dixisset, insufflavit et dicit eis: «Accipite Spiritum Sanctum. [23]Quorum remiseritis peccata, remissa sunt eis; quorum retinueritis, retenta sunt». [24]Thomas autem, unus ex Duodecim, qui dicitur Didymus, non erat cum eis, quando venit Iesus. [25]Dicebant ergo ei alii discipuli: «Vidimus Dominum!». Ille autem dixit eis: «Nisi videro in manibus eius signum clavorum et mittam digitum meum in signum clavorum et mittam manum meam in latus eius, non credam». [26]Et post dies octo iterum erant discipuli eius intus, et Thomas cum eis. Venit Iesus ianuis clausis et stetit in medio et dixit: «Pax vobis!». [27]Deinde dicit Thomae: «Infer digitum tuum huc et vide manus meas et affer manum tuam et mitte in latus meum, et noli fieri incredulus sed fidelis!». [28]Respondit Thomas et dixit ei: «Dominus meus et Deus meus!». [29]Dicit ei Iesus: «Quia vidisti me, credidisti. Beati, qui non viderunt et crediderunt!». [30]Multa quidem et alia signa fecit Iesus in conspectu discipulorum suorum, quae non sunt scripta in libro hoc; [31]haec autem scripta sunt, ut credatis quia Iesus est Christus Filius Dei, et ut credentes vitam habeatis in nomine eius. **[21]** [1]Postea manifestavit se iterum Iesus discipulis ad mare Tiberiadis; manifestavit autem sic. [2]Erant simul Simon Petrus et Thomas, qui dicitur Didymus, et Nathanael, qui erat a Cana Galilaeae, et filii Zebedaei et alii ex discipulis eius duo. [3]Dicit eis Simon Petrus: «Vado piscari». Dicunt ei: «Venimus et nos tecum». Exierunt et ascenderunt in navem; et illa nocte nihil prendiderunt. [4]Mane autem iam facto, stetit Iesus in litore; non tamen sciebant discipuli quia Iesus est. [5]Dicit ergo eis Iesus: «Pueri, numquid pulmentarium habetis?». Responderunt ei: «Non». [6]Ille autem dixit eis: «Mittite in dexteram navigii rete et invenietis». Miserunt ergo et iam non valebant illud trahere a multitudine piscium. [7]Dicit ergo discipulus ille, quem diligebat Iesus, Petro: «Dominus est!». Simon ergo Petrus, cum audisset quia Dominus est, tunicam succinxit se, erat enim nudus, et misit se in mare; [8]alii autem discipuli navigio venerunt, non enim longe erant a terra, sed quasi cubitis ducentis, trahentes rete piscium. [9]Ut ergo descenderunt in terram, vident prunas positas et piscem superpositum et panem. [10]Dicit eis Iesus: «Afferte de piscibus, quos prendidistis nunc». [11]Ascendit ergo Simon Petrus et traxit rete in terram, plenum magnis piscibus centum quinquaginta tribus; et cum tanti essent, non est scissum rete. [12]Dicit eis Iesus: «Venite, prandete». Nemo autem audebat discipulorum interrogare eum: «Tu quis es?», scientes quia Dominus est. [13]Venit Iesus et accipit panem et dat eis et piscem similiter. [14]Hoc iam tertio manifestatus est Iesus discipulis, cum resurrexisset a mortuis. [15]Cum ergo prandissent, dicit Simoni Petro Iesus: «Simon Ioannis, diligis me plus his?». Dicit ei: «Etiam, Domine, tu scis quia amo te». Dicit ei: «Pasce agnos meos». [16]Dicit ei iterum secundo: «Simon Ioannis, diligis me?». Ait illi: «Etiam, Domine, tu scis quia amo te». Dicit ei: «Pasce oves meas». [17]Dicit ei tertio: «Simon Ioannis, amas me?». Contristatus est Petrus quia dixit ei tertio: «Amas me?», et dicit ei: «Domine, tu omnia scis, tu cognoscis quia amo te». Dicit ei: «Pasce oves meas. [18]Amen, amen dico tibi: Cum esses iunior, cingebas teipsum et ambulabas, ubi volebas; cum autem senueris, extendes manus tuas, et alius te cinget et ducet, quo non vis». [19]Hoc autem dixit significans qua morte clarificaturus esset Deum. Et hoc cum dixisset, dicit ei: «Sequere me». [20]Conversus Petrus videt illum discipulum, quem diligebat Iesus, sequentem, qui et recubuit in cena super pectus eius et dixit: «Domine, quis est qui tradit te?». [21]Hunc ergo cum vidisset Petrus, dicit Iesu: «Domine, hic autem quid?». [22]Dicit ei Iesus: «Si eum volo manere donec veniam, quid ad te? Tu me sequere». [23]Exivit ergo sermo iste in fratres quia discipulus ille non moritur. Non autem dixit ei Iesus: «Non moritur», sed: «Si eum volo manere donec veniam, quid ad te?». [24]Hic est discipulus, qui testimonium perhibet de his et scripsit haec, et scimus quia verum est testimonium eius. [25]Sunt autem et alia multa, quae fecit Iesus, quae si scribantur per singula, nec ipsum arbitror mundum capere eos, qui scribendi sunt, libros.

Explanatory Notes

Asterisks in the text of the New Testament refer to these "Explanatory Notes" in the RSVCE.

THE GOSPEL ACCORDING TO JOHN

1:1: John begins by giving his Gospel a theological background. By speaking at once of "the Word" he implies that his readers are familiar with the term. To Gentiles it indicated some form of divine revelation or self-expression. Jews would equate it with the divine Wisdom described in Proverbs, which already appears as something more than a divine quality and has some relation with the visible world. In Sirach and Wisdom the idea is further developed. In the last-named book, Wisdom appears as a pre-existing person, taking part in the creation of the world and having a mission to reveal God to his creatures; cf. Wisdom 7:22—8:1.

1:5, *light . . . darkness*: One of the familiar themes of the Gospel.

1:29: John applies to Jesus the Messianic prophecy of Is 53:6–7, perhaps worded more explicitly by the evangelist in later years.

2:4, *what have you to do with me?* While this expression always implies a divergence of view, the precise meaning is to be determined by the context, which here shows that it is not an unqualified refusal, still less a rebuke.

2:12, *brethren*: See note on Mt 12:46.

3:22, *baptized*: A baptism like that of John. The time for baptism "in the Spirit" had not yet come.

3:24: From the other Gospels we learn that, after John was arrested, Jesus withdrew from Judea.

4:20, *this mountain*: Gerizim, on which the Samaritans worshiped.

5:18, *broke the sabbath*: i.e., broke the sabbath as interpreted by them; see note on Mt 12:14.

6:51: Jesus is the "living bread," both as Word of God (verses 32ff) and as sacrificial victim for the salvation of man.

6:52: A natural question to ask. Jesus answers, not by explaining it away, but by re-emphasizing the reality, though not, of course, in the crude sense implied in their question.

6:62: When Jesus ascends into heaven they will know that he spoke the truth.

7:3, *brethren*: See note on Mt 12:46.

7:53—8:11: This passage, though absent from some of the most ancient manuscripts, is regarded as inspired and canonical by the Church. The style suggests that it is not by St John, and that it belongs to the Synoptic Tradition.

8:21, *die in your sin*: Theirs is that sin against the truth which is the sin against the Holy Spirit; cf. Mt 12:31.

8:41: They mean, "We are not idolaters," and protest their fidelity to God their Father: see notes on Rev 14:4 and 17:2.

8:56, *he saw it* either in prophetic vision while on earth or by some special privilege after death.

8:58: The present tense indicates Christ's eternal existence as God.

9:4: Jesus explains in advance the purpose of the miracle.

10:14, *the good shepherd*: The name has Messianic significance; cf. Ezek 34.

10:18: Throughout the Gospel, Jesus insists that he is master of his own life and no one takes it from him; cf. 18:6 (at his arrest); 19:11 (before Pilate); 19:30 (on the cross).

11:6, *stayed two days longer*: This is explained in verse 15.

11:50: Caiaphas agreed that, as Jesus was not (in their opinion) the Messiah, any popular insurrection now could only end in disaster; so it was better, he argued, to do away with him. He was unconscious of the deeper meaning of his words, namely that Jesus must die for the salvation of man.

12:1: Here begins the last week of Jesus' public life. This is described in great detail, as was the first week in chapter 1.

12:32, *lifted up*: i.e., on the cross; but the words also contain a reference to his going up into heaven. The two mysteries are inseparable.

219

Explanatory Notes

13:1: John begins here to unfold the mystery of the love of Jesus for "his own". Note the solemn introduction to the "hour" of his passion and death.

13:34, *new commandment*: Jesus gives a new depth to the familiar commandment of the Old Testament. The standard now is, "as I have loved you".

14:26, *all things*: After Jesus has gone to his Father, the Holy Spirit will complete his revelation to the world.

15:18: Jesus contrasts the love his disciples have with the hatred the world bears them.

16:10: Jesus is taken from them because they did not receive him.

17:1–26: The priestly prayer of Jesus, before his sacrifice.

17:5: Declares his pre-existence.

18:13: According to Jewish law the high-priesthood was for life. The Romans had deposed Annas, the legal holder, in AD 15, and appointed another in his place, but many Jews continued to recognize Annas.

18:28: They would have contracted a legal impurity by entering the house of a pagan.

18:29: See note on Lk 23:2.

18:31: Crucifixion was a Roman not a Jewish punishment.

19:7: At last, because of Pilate's reluctance, they produce the real charge.

19:8–9: Pilate is afraid and asks Jesus where he comes from—not his country but his mysterious origins, as implied in the charge.

19:27, *took her to his own home*: Joseph must now have been dead.

20:17: The death and resurrection of Jesus had put an end to the ordinary familiar relationships of human life, and the time of lasting companionship had not yet come.

21:1–25: This chapter was added later, either by the evangelist or by a disciple; cf. 20:30–31 and 21:24.

21:7: John remembered a similar miracle before; cf. Lk 5:6.

21:15–17: The threefold question addressed to Peter alone corresponds to the threefold denial. Jesus gives Peter charge over his flock.

Changes in the RSV for the Catholic Edition

| | TEXT | | FOOTNOTES | |
	RSV	RSVCE	RSV	RSVCE
Jn 2:12	brothers	brethren		
Jn 6:7			[l]Delete existing note and substitute:	[l]The denarius was a day's wage for a labourer
Jn 7:3,5,10	brothers	brethren		
Jn 7:52		[r](Insert into the text here) [53] They went each to his own house,[1] but Jesus went to the Mount of Olives. [2]Early in the morning he came again to the temple; and he sat down and taught them. [3]The scribes and the Pharisees brought a woman who had been caught in adultery, and placing her in the midst [4]they said to him, "Teacher, this woman has been caught in the act of adultery. [5]Now in the law Moses commanded us to stone such. What do you say about her?" [6] This they said to test him, that they		[r]Some ancient authorities insert 7:53–8:11 either at the end of this gospel or after Lk 21:38, with variations of the text. Others omit it altogether.

⟶

Explanatory Notes

TEXT		FOOTNOTES	
RSV	RSVCE	RSV	RSVCE

might have some charge to bring against him. Jesus bent down and wrote with his finger on the ground. [7]And as they continued to ask him, he stood up and said to them, "Let him who is without sin among you be the first to throw a stone at her." [8]And once more he bent down and wrote with his finger on the ground. [9]But when they heard it, they went away, one by one, beginning with the eldest, and Jesus was left alone with the woman standing before him. [10]Jesus looked up and said to her, "Woman, where are they? Has no one condemned you?" [11]She said, "No one, Lord." And Jesus said, "Neither do I condemn you: go, and do not sin again."

Jn 12:5

[b]Delete existing note and substitute:

[b]The denarius was a day's wage for a labourer

Headings added to the Biblical Text

PROLOGUE

Part One: Jesus is manifested as the Messiah by his signs and words

1. INTRODUCTION
The witness of John the Baptist 1:19
The calling of the first disciples 1:35

2. JESUS, THE AUTHOR OF THE NEW ECONOMY OF
SALVATION. FIRST SIGNS OF FAITH
The wedding at Cana—the first sign worked by Jesus
2:1
Cleansing of the temple—Christ, God's new temple 2:13
Nicodemus visits Jesus 3:1
The Baptist again bears witness 3:22
Jesus and the Samaritan woman 4:1
Curing of a royal official's son—the second sign worked
by Jesus 4:46

3. JESUS REVEALS HIS DIVINITY
Curing of a paralyzed man 5:1
The authority of the Son of God 5:19

4. JESUS IS THE BREAD OF LIFE
Miracle of the loaves and fish 6:1
Jesus walks on water 6:16
The people look for Jesus 6:22
The discourse on the Bread of Life 6:26
Jesus is the one who reveals the Father 6:35
Jesus is the Bread of Life in the Eucharist 6:48
The disciples' reaction 6:60

5. JESUS, SENT BY THE FATHER, IS THE LIGHT OF
THE WORLD AND THE GOOD SHEPHERD

Jesus goes up to Jerusalem during the feast of the
Tabernacles 7:1
Jesus' teaching comes from God 7:14
Jesus comes from God 7:25
Jesus must return to the Father 7:31
Different opinions about Jesus 7:40
The adulterous woman—Jesus as judge 8:2
Jesus, the light of the world 8:12
Jesus says that he has been sent by the Father 8:21
"The truth will set you free" 8:31
The true children of Abraham 8:39
"Before Abraham was, I am" 8:52
Curing of the man born blind 9:1
The blindness of the Jews 9:24
The Good Shepherd 10:1

6. JESUS AND THE FATHER
Jesus and the Father are one 10:22
An attempt to stone Jesus 10:31

7. JESUS IS THE RESURRECTION AND THE LIFE
Jesus' reaction to the death of Lazarus 11:1
The raising of Lazarus 11:38
The Sanhedrin decides on the death of Jesus 11:45

8. JESUS IS ACCLAIMED AS THE MESSIANIC KING
Mary anoints our Lord at Bethany 12:1
The Messiah's entry into Jerusalem 12:12
Jesus announces his glorification 12:20
Jesus appeals for faith in himself 12:37

Part Two: Jesus is manifested as the Messiah Son of God in his passion, death and resurrection

9. THE LAST SUPPER
Jesus washes his disciples' feet 13:1
The treachery of Judas foretold 13:21
The new commandment. The disciples' desertion
foretold 13:31
Jesus reveals the Father 14:1
Promise of the Holy Spirit 14:15
The vine and the branches 15:1
The law of love 15:9
A hostile world 15:18
The action of the Holy Spirit 16:1
Fullness of joy 16:16
The priestly prayer of Jesus 17:1

10. THE PASSION AND DEATH OF JESUS
Arrest of Jesus 18:1

Jesus before the chief priests. Peter's denials 18:13
The trial before Pilate: Jesus is King 18:28
The scourging at the pillar and the crowning with thorns
19:1
Pilate hands Jesus over 19:12
The crucifixion and death of Jesus 19:17
Jesus' side is pierced. The burial 19:31

11. APPEARANCES OF THE RISEN CHRIST
The empty tomb 20:1
The appearance to Mary Magdalene 20:11
Jesus' first appearance to the disciples 20:19
A second appearance with Thomas present 20:24
The miraculous catch of fish 21:1
Peter's primacy 21:15
Conclusion 21:24

Sources quoted in the Navarre Bible
New Testament Commentary

1. DOCUMENTS OF THE CHURCH AND OF POPES

Benedict XII
Const. *Benedictus Deus*, 29 January 1336
Benedict XV
Enc. *Humani generis redemptionem*, 15 June 1917
Enc. *Spiritus Paraclitus*, 1 September 1920
Clement of Rome, St
Letter to the Corinthians
Constantinople, First Council of
Nicene-Constantinopolitan Creed
Constantinople, Third Council of
Definitio de duabus
in Christo voluntatibus et operationibus
Florence, Council of
Decree *Pro Jacobitis*
Laetentur coeli
Decree *Pro Armeniis*
John Paul II
Addresses and homilies
Apos. Exhort. *Catechesi tradendae*, 16 October 1979
Apos. Exhort. *Familiaris consortio*, 22 November 1981
Apos. Exhort. *Reconciliatio et paenitentia*, 2 December 1984
Apos. Letter. *Salvifici doloris*, 11 February 1984
Bull, *Aperite portas*, 6 January 1983
Enc. *Redemptor hominis*, 4 March 1979
Enc. *Dives in misericordia*, 30 November 1980
Enc. *Dominum et Vivificantem*, 30 May 1986
Enc. *Laborem exercens*, 14 September 1981
Letter to all priests, 8 April 1979
Letter to all bishops, 24 February 1980
Gelasius I
Ne forte
Gregory the Great, St
Epistula ad Theodorum medicum contra Fabianum
Exposition on the Seven Penitential
Ne forte
In Evangelia homiliae
In Ezechielem homiliae
Moralia in Job

Regulae pastoralis liber
Innocent III
Letter *Eius exemplo*, 18 December 1208
John XXIII
Pacem in terris, 11 April 1963
Enc. *Ad Petri cathedram*, 29 June 1959
Lateran Council (649)
Canons
Leo the Great, St
Homilies and sermons
Licet per nostros
Promisisse mememeni
Leo IX
Creed
Leo XIII
Enc. *Aeterni Patris*, 4 August 1879
Enc. *Immortale Dei*, 1 November 1885
Enc. *Libertas praestantissimum*, 20 June 1888
Enc. *Sapientiae christianae*, 18 January 1890
Enc. *Rerum novarum*, 15 May 1891
Enc. *Providentissimus Deus*, 18 November 1893
Enc. *Divinum illud munus*, 9 May 1897
Lateran, Fourth Council of (1215)
De fide catholica
Lyons, Second Council of (1274)
Doctrina de gratia
Profession of faith of Michael Palaeologue
Orange, Second Council of (529)
De gratia
Paul IV
Const. *Cum quorumdam*, 7 August 1555
Paul VI
Enc. *Ecclesiam suam*, 6 August 1964
Enc. *Mysterium fidei*, 9 September 1965
Apos. Exhort. *Marialis cultus*, 2 February 1967
Apos. Letter *Petrum et Paulum*, 27 February 1967
Enc. *Populorum progressio*, 26 March 1967
Enc. *Sacerdotalis coelibatus*, 24 June 1967
Creed of the People of God: Solemn Profession of Faith, 30 June 1968
Apos. Letter *Octagesima adveniens*, 14 June 1971

225

Sources quoted in the Commentary

Apos. Exhort. *Gaudete in Domino*, 9 May 1975
Apos. Exhort. *Evangelii nuntiandi*, 8 Dec. 1975
Homilies and addresses
Pius V, St
*Catechism of the Council of Trent for Parish
    Priests* or *Pius V Catechism*
Pius IX, Bl.
Bull *Ineffabilis Deus*, 8 December 1854
Syllabus of Errors
Pius X, St
Enc. *E supreme apostolatus*, 4 October 1903
Enc. *Ad Diem illum*, 2 February 1904
Enc. *Acerbo nimis*, 15 April 1905
Catechism of Christian Doctrine, 15 July 1905
Decree *Lamentabili*, 3 July 1907
Enc. *Haerent animo*, 4 August 1908
Pius XI
Enc. *Quas primas*, 11 December 1925
Enc. *Divini illius magistri*, 31 December 1929
Enc. *Mens nostra*, 20 December 1929
Enc. *Casti connubii*, 31 December 1930
Enc. *Quadragesimo anno*, 15 May 1931
Enc. *Ad catholici sacerdotii*, 20 December 1935
Pius XII
Enc. *Mystici Corporis*, 29 June 1943
Enc. *Mediator Dei*, 20 November 1947
Enc. *Divino afflante Spiritu*, 30 September 1943
Enc. *Humani generis*, 12 August 1950
Apost. Const. *Menti nostrae*, 23 September 1950
Enc. *Sacra virginitas*, 25 March 1954
Enc. *Ad caeli Reginam*, 11 October 1954
Homilies and addresses
Quierzy, Council of (833)
*Doctrina de libero arbitrio hominis et de
    praedestinatione*
Trent, Council of (1545–1563)
De sacris imaginibus

De Purgatorio
De reformatione
De sacramento ordinis
De libris sacris
De peccato originale
De SS. Eucharistia
De iustificatione
De SS. Missae sacrificio
De sacramento matrimonio
Doctrina de peccato originali
Doctrina de sacramento extremae unctionis
Doctrina de sacramento paenitentiae
Toledo, Ninth Council of (655)
De Redemptione
Toledo, Eleventh Council of (675)
De Trinitate Creed
Valence, Third Council of (855)
De praedestinatione
Vatican, First Council of the (1869–1870)
Dogm. Const. *Dei Filius*
Dogm. Const. *Pastor aeternus*
Vatican, Second Council of the   (1963–
    1965)
Const. *Sacrosanctum Concilium*
Decree *Christus Dominus*
Decl. *Dignitatis humanae*
Decl. *Gravissimum educationis*
Decl. *Nostrae aetate*
Decree *Optatam totius*
Decree *Ad gentes*
Decree *Apostolicam actuositatem*
Decree *Perfectae caritatis*
Decree *Presbyterorum ordinis*
Decree *Unitatis redintegratio*
Dogm. Const. *Dei Verbum*
Dogm. Const. *Lumen gentium*
Past. Const. *Gaudium et spes*

Liturgical Texts

Roman Missal: Missale Romanum, editio typica altera (Vatican City, 1975)
The Divine Office (London, Sydney, Dublin, 1974)

Other Church Documents

Code of Canon Law
Codex Iuris Canonici (Vatican City, 1983)
Congregation for the Doctrine of the Faith
Declaration concerning Sexual Ethics,
    December 1975
Instruction on Infant Baptism, 20 October 1980
Inter insigniores, 15 October 1976
*Letter on certain questions concerning
    Eschatology*, 17 May 1979

Libertatis conscientia, 22 March 1986
Sacerdotium ministeriale, 6 August 1983
Libertatis nuntius, 6 August 1984
Mysterium Filii Dei, 21 February 1972
Pontifical Biblical Commission
Replies
New Vulgate
*Nova Vulgata Bibliorum Sacrorum editio typica
    altera* (Vatican City, 1986)

Sources quoted in the Commentary

2. THE FATHERS, ECCLESIASTICAL WRITERS AND OTHER AUTHORS

Alphonsus Mary Liguori, St
Christmas Novena
The Love of Our Lord Jesus Christ reduced to practice
Meditations for Advent
Thoughts on the Passion
Shorter Sermons
Sunday Sermons
Treasury of Teaching Material
Ambrose, St
De sacramentis
De mysteriis
De officiis ministrorum
Exameron
Expositio Evangelii secundum Lucam
Expositio in Ps 118
Treatise on the Mysteries
Anastasius of Sinai, St
Sermon on the Holy Synaxis
Anon.
Apostolic Constitutions
Didache, or *Teaching of the Twelve Apostles*
Letter to Diognetus
Shepherd of Hermas
Anselm, St
Prayers and Meditations
Aphraates
Demonstratio
Athanasius, St
Adversus Antigonum
De decretis nicaenae synodi
De Incarnatio contra arianos
Historia arianorum
Oratio I contra arianos
Oratio II contra arianos
Oratio contra gentes
Augustine, St
The City of God
Confessions
Contra Adimantum Manichaei discipulum
De Actis cum Felice Manicheo
De agone christiano
De bono matrimonii
De bono viduitatis
De catechizandis rudibus
De civitate Dei
De coniugiis adulterinis
De consensu Evangelistarum
De correptione et gratia
De doctrina christiana
De dono perseverantiae
De fide et operibus

De fide et symbolo
De Genesi ad litteram
De gratia et libero arbitrio
De natura et gratia
De praedestinatione sanctorum
De sermo Domini in monte
De spiritu et littera
De Trinitate
De verbis Domini sermones
Enarrationes in Psalmos
Enchiridion
Expositio epistulae ad Galatas
In I Epist. Ioann. ad Parthos
In Ioannis Evangelium tractatus
Letters
Quaestiones in Heptateuchum
Sermo ad Cassariensis Ecclesiae plebem
Sermo de Nativitate Domini
Sermons
Basil, St
De Spiritu Sancto
Homilia in Julittam martyrem
In Psalmos homiliae
Bede, St
Explanatio Apocalypsis
In Ioannis Evangelium expositio
In Lucae Evangelium expositio
In Marci Evangelium expositio
In primam Epistolam Petri
In primam Epistolam S. Ioanis
Sermo super Qui audientes gavisi sunt
Super Acta Apostolorum expositio
Super divi Iacobi Epistolam
Bernal, Salvador
Monsignor Josemaría Escrivá de Balaguer, Dublin, 1977
Bernard, St
Book of Consideration
De Beata Virgine
De fallacia et brevitate vitae
De laudibus novae militiae
Divine amoris
Meditationes piissimae de cognitionis humanae conditionis
Sermons on Psalm 90
Sermon on Song of Songs
Sermons
Bonaventure, St
In IV Libri sententiarum
Speculum Beatae Virgine
Borromeo, St Charles
Homilies

227

Sources quoted in the Commentary

Catherine of Siena, St
Dialogue
Cano, Melchor
De locis
Cassian, John
Collationes
De institutis coenobiorum
Clement of Alexandria
Catechesis III, De Baptismo
Commentary on Luke
Quis dives salvetur?
Stromata
Cyprian, St
De bono patientiae
De dominica oratione
De mortalitate
De opere et eleemosynis
De unitate Ecclesiae
De zelo et livore
Epist. ad Fortunatum
Quod idola dii non sint
Cyril of Alexandria, St
Commentarium in Lucam
Explanation of Hebrews
Homilia XXVIII in Mattheum
Cyril of Jerusalem, St
Catecheses
Mystagogical Catechesis
Diadochus of Photike
Chapters on Spiritual Perfection
Ephrem, St
Armenian Commentary on Acts
Commentarium in Epistolam ad Haebreos
Eusebius of Caesarea
Ecclesiastical History
Francis de Sales, St
Introduction to the Devout Life
Treatise on the Love of God
Francis of Assisi, St
Little Flowers
Reflections on Christ's Wounds
Fulgentius of Ruspe
Contra Fabianum libri decem
De fide ad Petrum
Gregory Nazianzen, St
Orationes theologicae
Sermons
Gregory of Nyssa, St
De instituto christiano
De perfecta christiana forma
On the Life of Moses
Oratio catechetica magna
Oratio I in beatitudinibus
Oratio I in Christi resurrectionem

Hippolytus, St
De consummatione saeculi
Ignatius of Antioch, St
Letter to Polycarp
Letters to various churches
Ignatius, Loyola, St
Spiritual Exercises
Irenaeus, St
Against Heresies
Proof of Apostolic Preaching
Jerome, St
Ad Nepotianum
Adversus Helvidium
Comm. in Ionam
Commentary on Galatians
Commentary on St Mark's Gospel
Contra Luciferianos
Dialogus contra pelagianos
Expositio in Evangelium secundum Lucam
Homilies to neophytes on Psalm 41
Letters
On Famous Men
John of Avila, St
Audi, filia
Lecciones sobre Gálatas
Sermons
John Chrysostom, St
Ante exilium homilia
Adversus Iudaeos
Baptismal Catechesis
De coemeterio et de cruce
De incomprehensibile Dei natura
De sacerdotio
De virginitate
Fifth homily on Anna
Hom. De Cruce et latrone
Homilies on St Matthew's Gospel, St John's
      Gospel, Acts of the Apostles, Romans,
      Ephesians, 1 and 2 Corinthians, Colossians,
      1 and 2 Timothy, 1 and 2 Thessalonians,
      Philippians, Philemon, Hebrews
II Hom. De proditione Iudae
Paraeneses ad Theodorum lapsum
Second homily in praise of St Paul
Sermon recorded by Metaphrastus
John of the Cross, St
A Prayer of the Soul enkindled by Love
Ascent of Mount Carmel
Dark Night of the Soul
Spiritual Canticle
John Damascene, St
De fide orthodoxa
John Mary Vianney, St
Sermons

Sources quoted in the Commentary

Josemaría Escrivá, St
Christ Is Passing By
Conversations
The Forge
Friends of God
Furrow
Holy Rosary
In Love with the Church
The Way
The Way of the Cross
Josephus, Flavius
Against Apion
Jewish Antiquities
The Jewish War
Justin Martyr, St
Dialogue with Tryphon
First and Second Apologies
à Kempis, Thomas
The Imitation of Christ
Luis de Granada, Fray
Book of Prayer and Meditation
Guide for Sinners
Introducción al símbolo de la fe
Life of Jesus Christ
Sermon on Public Sins
Suma de la vida cristiana
Luis de Léon, Fray
Exposición del Libro de Job
Minucius Felix
Octavius
Newman, J.H.
Biglietto Speech
Discourses to Mixed Congregations
Historical Sketches
Origen
Contra Celsum
Homilies on Genesis
Homilies on St John
In Exodum homiliae
Homiliae in Iesu nave
In Leviticum homiliae
In Matth. comm.
In Rom. comm.
Philo of Alexandria
De sacrificio Abel
Photius
Ad Amphilochium
Polycarp, St
Letter to the Philippians
del Portillo, A.
On Priesthood, Chicago, 1974
Primasius
Commentariorum super Apocalypsim B. Ioannis libri quinque
Prosper of Aquitaine, St
De vita contemplativa

Pseudo-Dionysius
De divinis nominibus
Pseudo-Macarius
Homilies
Severian of Gabala
Commentary on 1 Thessalonians
Teresa of Avila, St
Book of Foundations
Exclamations of the Soul to God
Interior Castle
Life
Poems
Way of Perfection
Tertullian
Against Marcion
Apologeticum
De baptismo
De oratione
Theodore the Studite, St
Oratio in adorationis crucis
Theodoret of Cyrrhus
Interpretatio Ep. ad Haebreos
Theophylact
Enarratio in Evangelium Marci
Thérèse de Lisieux, St
The Autobiography of a Saint
Thomas Aquinas, St
Adoro te devote
Commentary on St John = Super Evangelium S. Ioannis lectura
Commentaries on St Matthew's Gospel, Romans, 1 and 2 Corinthians, Galatians, Ephesians, Colossians, Philippians, 1 and 2 Timothy, 1 and 2 Thessalonians, Titus, Hebrews
De veritate
Expositio quorumdam propositionum ex Epistola ad Romanos
On the Lord's Prayer
On the two commandments of Love and the ten commandments of the Law
Summa contra gentiles
Summa theologiae
Super Symbolum Apostolorum
Thomas More, St
De tristitia Christi
Victorinus of Pettau
Commentary on the Apocalypse
Vincent Ferrer, St
Treatise on the Spiritual Life
Vincent of Lerins, St
Commonitorium
Zosimus, St
Epist. Enc. "Tractoria" ad Ecclesias Orientales